State and Local Government

Fourteenth Edition

EDITOR

Bruce Stinebrickner
DePauw University

Bruce Stinebrickner is Professor of Political Science and University Professor at DePauw University in Greencastle, Indiana, and has taught American politics at DePauw since 1987. He has also taught at Lehman College of the City University of New York (1974–1976), at the University of Queensland in Brisbane, Australia (1976–1987), and in DePauw programs in Argentina (1990) and Germany (1993). He served fourteen years as chair of his department at DePauw after heading his department at the University of Queensland for two years. He earned his BA *magna cum laude* from Georgetown University in 1968, his MPhil from Yale University in 1972, and his PhD from Yale in 1974.

Professor Stinebrickner is the co-author (with Robert A. Dahl) of *Modern Political Analysis*, sixth edition (Prentice Hall, 2003) and has published articles on the American presidential selection process, American local governments, the career patterns of Australian politicians, and freedom of the press. He has served as editor of the thirteen earlier editions of this book as well as thirty-one editions of its American Government counterpart in the McGraw-Hill/Contemporary Learning Series Annual Editions series. His current research interests focus on government policies involving children (e.g., schooling, child custody, and foster care). In both his teaching and his writing, Professor Stinebrickner applies insights on politics gained from living, teaching, and lecturing abroad.

Higher Education

Boston   Burr Ridge, IL   Dubuque, IA   New York   San Francisco   St. Louis
Bangkok   Bogotá   Caracas   Kuala Lumpur   Lisbon   London   Madrid   Mexico City
Milan   Montreal   New Delhi   Santiago   Seoul   Singapore   Sydney   Taipei   Toronto

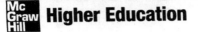

Higher Education

ANNUAL EDITIONS: STATE AND LOCAL GOVERNMENT, FOURTEENTH EDITION

Published by McGraw-Hill, a business unit of The McGraw-Hill Companies, Inc., 1221 Avenue of the Americas, New York, NY 10020. Copyright © 2009 by The McGraw-Hill Companies, Inc. All rights reserved. Previous edition(s) 1984–2008. No part of this publication may be reproduced or distributed in any form or by any means, or stored in a database or retrieval system, without the prior written consent of The McGraw-Hill Companies, Inc., including, but not limited to, in any network or other electronic storage or transmission, or broadcast for distance learning.

Some ancillaries, including electronic and print components, may not be available to customers outside the United States.

Annual Editions® is a registered trademark of The McGraw-Hill Companies, Inc.
Annual Editions is published by the **Contemporary Learning Series** group within the McGraw-Hill Higher Education division.

1 2 3 4 5 6 7 8 9 0 QPD/QPD 0 9 8

ISBN 978–0–07–351631–8
MHID 0–07–351631–7
ISSN 1093–7021

Managing Editor: *Larry Loeppke*
Senior Managing Editor: *Faye Schilling*
Developmental Editor: *Debra Henricks*
Editorial Coordinator: *Mary Foust*
Editorial Assistant: *Nancy Meissner*
Production Service Assistant: *Rita Hingtgen*
Permissions Coordinator: *Lenny J. Behnke*
Senior Marketing Manager: *Julie Keck*
Marketing Communications Specialist: *Mary Klein*
Marketing Coordinator: *Alice Link*
Project Manager: *Sandy Wille*
Design Specialist: *Tara McDermott*
Senior Production Supervisor: *Laura Fuller*
Cover Graphics: *Kristine Jubeck*

Compositor: Laserwords Private Limited
Cover Images: © Debra Henricks (both)

Library in Congress Cataloging-in-Publication Data
Main entry under title: Annual Editions: State and Local Government, 14/e.
1. State and Local Government—Periodicals. I. Stinebrickner, Bruce, *comp*. II. Title: State and Local Government
658'.05

www.mhhe.com

Editors/Advisory Board

Members of the Advisory Board are instrumental in the final selection of articles for each edition of ANNUAL EDITIONS. Their review of articles for content, level, currentness, and appropriateness provides critical direction to the editor and staff. We think that you will find their careful consideration well reflected in this volume.

Preface

In publishing ANNUAL EDITIONS we recognize the enormous role played by the magazines, newspapers, and journals of the public press in providing current, first-rate educational information in a broad spectrum of interest areas. Many of these articles are appropriate for students, researchers, and professionals seeking accurate, current material to help bridge the gap between principles and theories and the real world. These articles, however, become more useful for study when those of lasting value are carefully collected, organized, indexed, and reproduced in a low-cost format, which provides easy and permanent access when the material is needed. That is the role played by ANNUAL EDITIONS.

This book is the fourteenth edition of an anthology on the state and local government. Beginning in 1984 with the first edition, the book has been designed for use in college courses on state and local government, and in state and local government segments of courses on American government. The educational goal is to provide a collection of up-to-date articles that are informative and interesting to students who are learning about subnational governments in the United States.

The 50 state governments and more than 80,000 local governments in the United States have a great deal in common. They also exhibit remarkable diversity. Inevitably, the content of the book as a whole reflects this commonality and diversity. Some of the selections treat individual states or localities in considerable detail. Other articles focus on particular dimensions of more than one state or local government. Still other articles explicitly compare and contrast regions, states, or localities. Taken together, the selections provide an overview of similarities and differences among the state and the local governments in the United States.

When Republican Newt Gingrich became Speaker of the House of Representatives in 1995, he and his fellow Republican members of Congress said that they would shift significant government responsibilities from the national government in Washington to the 50 states. Two prominent bills signed into law by President Clinton, one restricting unfunded mandates and the other reforming the welfare system, were aimed at making the states more important and more autonomous actors in the American federal system. Taking their turn in this process of devolution, some state governments shifted certain responsibilities to their local governments. The events of September 11, 2001, however, partly reversed these trends, as national, state, and local responsibilities for public safety and what came to be known as "homeland security" were reconsidered and modified. Every selection in this book can be read against this general background of continuing—indeed, probably never-ending—attempts to arrive at an appropriate division of powers and responsibilities among the national, state, and local governments.

The book is divided into seven units. Unit 1 is devoted to several eighteenth- and nineteenth-century commentaries on American federalism and the state and local governments. Unit 2 discusses the relations among the national, state, and local governments, and provides a mixed assessment of how much shifting of power and responsibility has actually occurred, and how well the changes that have occurred are working. Unit 3 covers elections, political parties, interest groups, referenda, and related matters, and pays considerable attention to unusual features of state and local "linkages." Unit 4 turns to government institutions. Local politics and policy issues—in cities and suburbs, as well as in counties and small towns—provide the subject matter for Unit 5, while Unit 6 is devoted to revenues, expenditures, and economic development. Unit 7 concludes the book with an examination of service delivery and policy issues facing the state and local governments.

The book generally groups together articles that treat particular aspects of the governing processes of the state and local governments in the same units and sections. For example, Unit 4 covers government institutions at both the state and local levels, with individual sections devoted to the state *and* local legislatures, executives, and courts, respectively. Unit 5, which discusses metropolitan areas, is an exception to this general rule in that it focuses primarily on issues involving local governments.

Deciding what articles to include when preparing this fourteenth edition of *Annual Editions: State and Local Government* was not easy. I assessed articles according to significance and relevance of the subject matter, readability for students, and usefulness for stimulating students' interest in state and local government. Potential selections were evaluated not only as they stood alone, but also as complements to other likely selections.

I solicit responses to this edition, as well as suggestions of articles for use in the next edition. In other words, readers are cordially invited to become advisers and collaborators in future editions by completing and mailing the postpaid article rating form at the end of this book.

Bruce Stinebrickner
Editor

Contents

UNIT 1
Early Commentaries

UNIT 2
Intergovernmental Relations

The concepts in bold italics are developed in the article. For further expansion, please refer to the Topic Guide.

UNIT 3
Linkages Between Citizens and Governments

The concepts in bold italics are developed in the article. For further expansion, please refer to the Topic Guide.

UNIT 4
Government Institutions and Officeholders

The concepts in bold italics are developed in the article. For further expansion, please refer to the Topic Guide.

The concepts in bold italics are developed in the article. For further expansion, please refer to the Topic Guide.

UNIT 5
Cities and Suburbs, Counties, Towns, and Homeowners Associations

UNIT 6
Revenues and Economic Development

The concepts in bold italics are developed in the article. For further expansion, please refer to the Topic Guide.

This facility is smoke free.

No Smoking

UNIT 7
Service Delivery and Policy Issues

The concepts in bold italics are developed in the article. For further expansion, please refer to the Topic Guide.

Correlation Guide

The *Annual Editions* series provides students with convenient, inexpensive access to current, carefully selected articles from the public press. **Annual Editions: State and Local Government, 14/e** is an easy-to-use reader that presents articles on important topics such as *economic development, elections, policymaking,* and many more. For more information on *Annual Editions* and other *McGraw-Hill Contemporary Learning Series* titles, visit www.mhcls.com.

This convenient guide matches the units in **State and Local Government, 14/e** with the corresponding chapters in one of our best-selling McGraw-Hill Government textbooks by Saffell/Basehart.

Annual Editions: State and Local Government, 14/e	State and Local Government, 9/e by Saffell/Basehart
Unit 1: Early Commentaries	**Chapter 1:** The Setting of State and Local Government
Unit 2: Intergovernmental Relations	**Chapter 2:** Intergovernmental Relations
Unit 3: Linkages Between Citizens and Governments	**Chapter 3:** Political Parties and Interest Groups **Chapter 4:** Political Participation and Elections
Unit 4: Government Institutions and Officeholders	**Chapter 5:** State and Local Legislatures **Chapter 6:** Governors, Bureaucrats, and Mayors **Chapter 7:** Courts, Police, and Corrections
Unit 5: Cities and Suburbs, Counties, Towns, and Homeowners Associations	**Chapter 8:** Suburbs, Metropolitan Areas, and Rural Communities
Unit 6: Revenues and Economic Development	**Chapter 9:** Financing State and Local Government
Unit 7: Service Delivery and Policy Issues	**Chapter 10:** State and Local Policymaking: Conflict and Accommodation

Topic Guide

This topic guide suggests how the selections in this book relate to the subjects covered in your course. You may want to use the topics listed on these pages to search the Web more easily.

On the following pages a number of Web sites have been gathered specifically for this book. They are arranged to reflect the units of this *Annual Edition*. You can link to these sites by going to the student online support site at *http://www.mhcls.com/online/*.

All the articles that relate to each topic are listed below the bold-faced term.

Internet References

The following Internet sites have been selected to support the articles found in this reader. These sites were available at the time of publication. However, because Web sites often change their structure and content, the information listed may no longer be available. We invite you to visit *http://www.mhcls.com* for easy access to these sites.

AE: State and Local Government, 14/e

General Sources

Library of Congress
http://www.loc.gov/rr/news/stategov/stategov.html

The Library of Congress provides this page of meta-indexes of state and local government information. Links are available to numerous national, state, and local sites.

State and Local Government on the Net
http://www.yahoo.com

Click on Regional, then U.S. States to search individual states for elected officials, state government jobs, state groups, and for other links to local government sites.

U.S. State & Local Gateway
http://www.statelocal.gov/

Developed to provide easy access to federal information that applies to state and local governments, this Web site contains information on various topics, current issues, hot links, and relevant organizations.

UNIT 1: Early Commentaries

Anti-Federalist Papers
http://www.constitution.org/afp/afp.htm

The Anti-Federalist Papers offered on this home page of the Constitution Society have been collated by Morton Borden in response to growing concern that noncompliance with the U.S. Constitution and state constitutions is creating a crisis of legitimacy that is threatening freedom and civil rights.

The Federalist Papers Online
http://memory.loc.gov/const/fed/fedpapers.html

This site contains the full text of all 85 essays as well as The Declaration of Independence and the Constitution, complete with the Bill of Rights and all the Amendments.

UNIT 2: Intergovernmental Relations

Congress
http://congress.org

User-friendly, this site is a very effective starting point for Web users in search of Capitol Hill political information. The site allows access to a complete and reliable directory of information about the members of the U.S. House of Representatives and Senate, and it includes a congressional directory, House and Senate committee assignments, as well as the ability to communicate with specific members.

Council of State Governments
http://www.csg.org

This resource is dedicated to promoting state solutions regionally and nationally. From it you can access the federalism plan of states' leaders, court victories in federalism, other proposals, and Web resources.

National Center for State Courts
http://www.ncsconline.org/

Click here to find the latest news about the courts, information about state courts, and the best court-related Web sites.

Supreme Court/Legal Information Institute (LII)
http://supct.law.cornell.edu/supct/index.html

Open this site for current and historical information about the Supreme Court. The LII archive contains many opinions issued since May 1990 as well as a collection of nearly 600 of the most historical decisions of the Court.

UNIT 3: Linkages Between Citizens and Governments

Direct Democracy Center
http://www.realdemocracy.com/

In response to voter apathy, this organization has organized a site on the Web for free and open discussion of direct democracy as an alternative to our present form of government.

PEJ Local TV News Project
http://www.journalism.org/resources/research/reports/localTV/default.asp

The Project for Excellence in Journalism has created this news project in order to clarify the definition of quality in local television news. Explore this site to find out how the project will work and its goals, and to contribute your own thoughts.

U.S. Federalism Web Site
http://www.usconstitution.net/consttop_fedr.html

This site concerns federalism and electronic democracy and contains many links to direct democracy and other citizen-power sites.

UNIT 4: Government Institutions and Officeholders

Center for the American Women in Politics (CAWP)
http://www.rci.rutgers.edu/~cawp/

At this site of CAWP you can find full-text fact sheets on everything from women in elective office to statewide elective executive women. It includes a gender gap fact sheet and facts on sex differences in voter turnout.

Council on Licensure, Enforcement and Regulation (CLEAR)
http://www.clearhq.org

CLEAR is an association of individuals, groups, and agencies that is a forum for improving the quality and understanding of regulation in order to enhance public protection.

Internet References

EMILY's List of Women in State Legislatures

http://www.emilyslist.org/

This state-by-state site list of women in state legislatures also contains a search feature, What's New, Survey, and Feedback.

National Conference of State Legislatures

http://www.ncsl.org/index.htm

Legislative Policy Issues, Internet Links, About State Legislatures, State-Federal Relations, and more may be accessed at this site.

NGA (National Governors Association) Online

http://www.nga.org

The National Governor's Association and the NGA Center for Best Practices are joined at this site. Navigate through The Organization, The Governors, News and Information, Key State Issues, and a Site Index. What's New and Noteworthy appear on the first page.

UNIT 5: Cities and Suburbs, Counties, Towns, and Homeowner Associations

ICMA: International City/County Management Association

http://www.icma.org/othersites/

The list of Web sites offered here by ICMA include: Communications, Economic Development, Housing Resources, Human Resources, Public Safety, Public Works, and Technology.

Innovation Groups (IG)

http://www.ig.org

IG is a network of top cities and local government leaders that provides support to pioneer new approaches to managing cities. The group provides networking, research, and training opportunities to local governments.

National Association of Counties (NACo)

http://www.naco.org/

The National Association of Counties offers this entry into county government sites by individual states.

National League of Cities (NLC)

http://www.nlc.org

The NLC Web site leads to Legislative Priorities, Local Government Access, Policy Process, News and Events, Other Resources, and a search capability, all useful aids to people in municipal government.

UNIT 6: Revenues and Economic Development

Assessor.com

http://www.assessor.com

This is a primary site for understanding the property tax and what it means to householders. There are useful links to local assessment sites in every state, independent resources, and professional and educational organizations, including the Lincoln Institute of Land & Policy.

Economic Development Administration

http://www.doc.gov/eda

Here, the Department of Commerce site links to current fact sheets, the year 2000, regulations and notices, contacts and resources, all helpful to understanding state and local economic development issues.

National Association of Development Organizations (NADO)

http://www.nado.org/links/index.html

Called "the economic development community's tool box on the World Wide Web," this site leads to every national, state, and local government resource, to a host of independent agencies, and to other community development resources, including grant-giving foundations, rural development groups, and public interest groups.

UNIT 7: Service Delivery and Policy Issues

American Bar Association Juvenile Justice Center

http://www.abanet.org/crimjust/juvjus/links.html

From this site it is easy to access information about juvenile justice and other youth-related information. Crime statistics, advocacy tips, and legal resources are available here.

American Public Transit Association

http://www.apta.com

Information about every aspect of transportation is provided here. In addition, excellent links to federal and state agencies and organizations that deal with transportation issues, including links to all state departments of transportation are possible.

CECP Juvenile Justice Links

http://www.air-dc.org/cecp/links/jj.html

At this site, fact sheets and articles on juvenile justice issues, such as violent juvenile offenders, delinquency programs, and youth-oriented anti-crime programs are available, along with links to many juvenile justice organizations.

COPS (Office of Community Oriented Policing Services)

http://www.cops.usdoj.gov/

This home page of the Office of Community Oriented Policing Services is dedicated to helping communities fight crime by putting 100,000 additional officers on America's streets and by promoting community policing strategies nationwide. Their Web presence leads to success stories and links.

National Highway Traffic Safety Administration

http://www.nhtsa.dot.gov/

This section of the State Legislative Fact Sheet provides information on blood alcohol concentrations (BAC) and driving a motor vehicle. It contains Key Facts, Why 0.08?, Point/Counterpoint, Impact on the Criminal Justice System, and a map of States with BAC Per Se Laws.

U.S. Charter Schools

http://www.uscharterschools.org/

All you might need to know about charter schools is available at this page, including Starting & Running a Charter School, Resource Directory and Links, State Information & Contacts, Charter School Profiles, and Search for Information.

UNIT 1
Early Commentaries

Unit Selections

1. **The Federalist, No. 17,** Alexander Hamilton
2. **The Federalist, No. 45,** James Madison
3. **Nature of the American State,** James Bryce

Key Points to Consider

- How does the picture of the local governments provided by James Bryce in the late-nineteenth century compare with the American local governments of today?

- Do you think that the observations of Alexander Hamilton, James Madison, and James Bryce are out of date in the twenty-first century? Why or why not?

- Students of politics frequently refer to the historic writings of Plato, Aristotle, Machiavelli, Hobbes, Locke, Rousseau, and others. Selections in this section are examples of early or historic writings on American politics. Why do you think that those who study politics so often look to the classics, even centuries after they were written?

- Do you find the arguments and logic of *Federalist No. 17* and *No. 45* persuasive? Can you detect any flaws or mistakes?

- Which author do you find most interesting and helpful—Alexander Hamilton, James Madison, or James Bryce? Why?

Student Web Site
www.mhcls.com/online

Internet References
Anti-Federalist Papers
http://www.constitution.org/afp/afp.htm
The Federalist Papers Online
http://memory.loc.gov/const/fed/fedpapers.html

The American political system includes three levels of government—national, state, and local. Although not unique among nations today, this arrangement was unusual in the late-eighteenth century when the United States became independent. Early commentaries on the American political system paid considerable attention to each of these levels of government, as well as to the interaction between the three levels. These writings suggest the important role that the state and local governments have always played in the United States.

Debate about the desirability of the proposed new Constitution of 1787—the Constitution that remains in force to this day— often focused on the relationship between the national government and the states. Some people thought that the states were going to be too strong in the proposed new union, and others argued that the national government had more power. Three prominent supporters of the new Constitution—Alexander Hamilton, James Madison, and John Jay—wrote a series of articles in 1787–1788 explaining and defending it. Many of these articles, which came to be known as *The Federalist Papers,* discussed the federal relationship between the national government and the states. So did many of the writings of other early observers. This shows the importance that was attached to the new federal relationship right from the start.

Local government was also the subject of considerable attention in the early commentaries on the American political system. Alexis de Tocqueville, a French nobleman visiting the United States early in the nineteenth century, recorded his observations in a book entitled *Democracy in America* (1835). Tocqueville remarked on the extraordinary vitality of American local government institutions, comparing what he saw in the United States with European institutions of those times. Today American local government still plays a prominent role in the overall governing process, probably more so than in any other nation in the world.

Later in the nineteenth century, another foreign observer, James Bryce, published another influential commentary on the United States, *The American Commonwealth* (1888). Bryce, an Englishman, discussed American federalism and the American state and local governments. He described the similarities and differences among local government structures in different regions of the country, the nature of the states, and the lamentable

Library of Congress

performance of city governments. Like Tocqueville, Bryce was able to identify and analyze distinctive elements of the American system of government and make a lasting contribution to the study of the American political system.

Selections in this first section of the book come from *The Federalist Papers* and Bryce's *American Commonwealth.* These historic observations on American federalism, and the state and local governments provide a baseline against which the scenario of the current state and local government can be assessed.

The Federalist No. 17 (Hamilton)

To the People of the State of New York:

An objection, of a nature different from that which has been stated and answered, in my last address, may perhaps be likewise urged against the principle of legislation for the individual citizens of America. It may be said that it would tend to render the government of the Union too powerful, and to enable it to absorb those residuary authorities, which it might be judged proper to leave with the States for local purposes. Allowing the utmost latitude to the love of power which any reasonable man can require, I confess I am at a loss to discover what temptation the persons intrusted with the administration of the general government could ever feel to divest the States of the authorities of that description. The regulation of the mere domestic police of a State appears to me to hold out slender allurements to ambition. Commerce, finance, negotiation, and war seem to comprehend all the objects which have charms for minds governed by that passion; and all the powers necessary to those objects ought, in the first instance, to be lodged in the national depository. The administration of private justice between the citizens of the same State, the supervision of agriculture and of other concerns of a similar nature, all those things, in short, which are proper to be provided for by local legislation, can never be desirable cares of a general jurisdiction. It is therefore improbable that there should exist a disposition in the federal councils to usurp the powers with which they are connected; because the attempt to exercise those powers would be as troublesome as it would be nugatory; and the possession of them, for that reason, would contribute nothing to the dignity, to the importance, or to the splendor of the national government.

But let it be admitted, for argument's sake, that mere wantonness and lust of domination would be sufficient to beget that disposition; still it may be safely affirmed, that the sense of the constituent body of the national representatives, or, in other words, the people of the several States, would control the indulgence of so extravagant an appetite. It will always be far more easy for the State governments to encroach upon the national authorities, than for the national government to encroach upon the State authorities. The proof of this proposition turns upon the greater degree of influence which the State governments, if they administer their affairs with uprightness and prudence, will generally possess over the people; a circumstance which at the same time teaches us that there is an inherent and intrinsic weakness in all federal constitutions; and that too much pains cannot be taken in their organization, to give them all the force which is compatible with the principles of liberty.

The superiority of influence in favor of the particular governments would result partly from the diffusive construction of the national government, but chiefly from the nature of the objects to which the attention of the State administrations would be directed.

It is a known fact in human nature, that its affections are commonly weak in proportion to the distance or diffusiveness of the object. Upon the same principle that a man is more attached to his family than to his neighborhood, to his neighborhood than to the community at large, the people of each State would be apt to feel a stronger bias towards their local governments than towards the government of the Union; unless the force of that principle should be destroyed by a much better administration of the latter.

This strong propensity of the human heart would find powerful auxiliaries in the objects of State regulation.

The variety of more minute interests, which will necessarily fall under the superintendence of the local administrations, and which will form so many rivulets of influence, running through every part of the society, cannot be particularized, without involving a detail too tedious and uninteresting to compensate for the instruction it might afford.

There is one transcendent advantage belonging to the province of the State governments, which alone suffices to place the matter in a clear and satisfactory light,—I mean the ordinary administration of criminal and civil justice. This, of all others, is the most powerful, most universal, and most attractive source of popular obedience and attachment. It is that which, being the immediate and visible guardian of life and property, having its benefits and its terrors in constant activity before the public eye, regulating all those personal interests and familiar concerns in which the sensibility of individuals is more immediately awake, contributes, more than any other circumstance, to impressing upon the minds of the people, affection, esteem, and reverence towards the government. This great cement of society, which will diffuse itself almost wholly through the channels of the particular governments, independent of all other causes of influence, would insure them so decided an empire over their respective citizens as to render them at all times a complete counterpoise, and, not unfrequently, dangerous rivals to the power of the Union.

The operations of the national government, on the other hand, falling less immediately under the observation of the mass of the citizens, the benefits derived from it will chiefly be perceived and attended to by speculative men. Relating to more general interests, they will be less apt to come home to the feelings of the people; and, in proportion, less likely to inspire an habitual sense of obligation, and an active sentiment of attachment.

The reasoning on this head has been abundantly exemplified by the experience of all federal constitutions with which we are acquainted, and of all others which have borne the least analogy to them.

Though the ancient feudal systems were not, strictly speaking, confederacies, yet they partook of the nature of that species of association. There was a common head, chieftain, or sovereign, whose authority extended over the whole nation; and a number of subordinate vassals, or feudatories, who had large portions of land allotted to them, and numerous trains of inferior vassals or retainers, who occupied and cultivated that land upon the tenure of fealty or obedience to the persons of whom they held it. Each principal vassal was a kind of sovereign within his particular demesnes. The consequences of this situation were a continual opposition to authority of the sovereign, and frequent wars between the great barons or chief feudatories themselves. The power of the head of the nation was commonly too weak, either to preserve the public peace, or to protect the people against the oppressions of their immediate lords. This period of European affairs is emphatically styled by historians, the times of feudal anarchy.

When the sovereign happened to be a man of vigorous and warlike temper and of superior abilities, he would acquire a personal weight and influence, which answered, for the time, the purposes of a more regular authority. But in general, the power of the barons triumphed over that of the prince; and in many instances his dominion was entirely thrown off, and the great fiefs were erected into independent principalities of States. In those instances in which the monarch finally prevailed over his vassals, his success was chiefly owing to the tyranny of those vassals over their dependents. The barons, or nobles, equally the enemies of the sovereign and the oppressors of the common people, were dreaded and detested by both; till mutual danger and mutual interest effected a union between them fatal to the power of the aristocracy. Had the nobles, by a conduct of clemency and justice, preserved the fidelity and devotion of their retainers and followers, the contests between them and the prince must almost always have ended in their favor, and in the abridgment or subversion of the royal authority.

This is not an assertion founded merely in speculation or conjecture. Among other illustrations of its truth which might be cited, Scotland will furnish a cogent example. The spirit of clanship which was, at an early day, introduced into that kingdom, uniting the nobles and their dependents by ties equivalent to those of kindred, rendered the aristocracy a constant overmatch for the power of the monarch, till the incorporation with England subdued its fierce and ungovernable spirit, and reduced it within those rules of subordination which a more rational and more energetic system of civil polity had previously established in the latter kingdom.

The separate governments in a confederacy may aptly be compared with the feudal baronies; with this advantage in their favor, that from the reasons already explained, they will generally possess the confidence and good-will of the people, and with so important a support, will be able effectually to oppose all encroachments of the national government. It will be well if they are not able to counteract its legitimate and necessary authority. The points of similitude consist in the rivalship of power, applicable to both, and in the concentration of large portions of the strength of the community into particular deposits, in one case at the disposal of individuals, in the other case at the disposal of political bodies.

A concise review of the events that have attended confederate governments will further illustrate this important doctrine; an inattention to which has been the great source of our political mistakes, and has given our jealousy a direction to the wrong side. This review shall form the subject of some ensuing papers.

PUBLIUS

3

The Federalist No. 45 (Madison)

To the People of the State of New York:

Having shown that no one of the powers transferred to the federal government is unnecessary or improper, the next question to be considered is, whether the whole mass of them will be dangerous to the portion of authority left in the several States.

The adversaries to the plan of the convention, instead of considering in the first place what degree of power was absolutely necessary for the purposes of the federal government, have exhausted themselves in a secondary inquiry into the possible consequences of the proposed degree of power to the governments of the particular States. But if the Union, as has been shown, be essential to the security of the people of America against foreign danger; if it be essential to their security against contentions and wars among the different States; if it be essential to guard them against those violent and oppressive factions which embitter the blessings of liberty, and against those military establishments which must gradually poison its very fountain; if, in a word, the Union be essential to the happiness of the people of America, is it not preposterous, to urge as an objection to a government, without which the objects of the Union cannot be attained, that such a government may derogate from the importance of the governments of the individual States? Was, then, the American Revolution effected, was the American Confederacy formed, was the precious blood of thousands spilt, and the hard-earned substance of millions lavished, not that the people of America should enjoy peace, liberty, and safety, but that the government of the individual States, that particular municipal establishments, might enjoy a certain extent of power, and be arrayed with certain dignities and attributes of sovereignty? We have heard of the impious doctrine in the Old World, that the people were made for kings, not kings for the people. Is the same doctrine to be revived in the New, in another shape—that the solid happiness of the people is to be sacrificed to the views of political institutions of a different form? It is too early for politicians to presume on our forgetting that the public good, the real welfare of the great body of the people, is the supreme object to be pursued; and that no form of government whatever has any other value than as it may be fitted for the attainment of this object. Were the plan of the convention adverse to the public happiness, my voice would be, Reject the plan. Were the Union itself inconsistent with the public happiness, it would be, Abolish the Union. In like manner, as far as the sovereignty of the States cannot be reconciled to the happiness of the people, the voice of every good citizen must be, Let the former be sacrificed to the latter. How far the sacrifice is necessary, has been shown. How far the unsacrificed residue will be endangered, is the question before us.

Several important considerations have been touched in the course of these papers, which discountenance the supposition that the operation of the federal government will by degrees prove fatal to the State governments. The more I revolve the subject, the more fully I am persuaded that the balance is much more likely to be disturbed by the preponderacy of the last than of the first scale.

We have seen, in all the examples of ancient and modern confederacies, the strongest tendency continually betraying itself in the members, to despoil the general government of its authorities, with a very ineffectual capacity in the latter to defend itself against the encroachments. Although, in most of these examples, the system has been so dissimilar from that under consideration as greatly to weaken any inference concerning the latter from the fate of the former, yet, as the States will retain, under the proposed Constitution, a very extensive portion of active sovereignty, the inference ought not to be wholly disregarded. In the Achæan league it is probable that the federal head had a degree and species of power, which gave it a considerable likeness to the government framed by the convention. The Lycian Confederacy, as far as its principles and form and transmitted, must have borne a still greater analogy to it. Yet history does not inform us that either of them ever degenerated, or tended to degenerate, into one consolidated government. On the contrary, we know that the ruin of one of them proceeded from the incapacity of the federal authority to prevent the dissensions, and finally the disunion, of the subordinate authorities. These cases are the more worthy of our attention, as the external causes by which the component parts were pressed together were much more numerous and powerful than in our case; and consequently less powerful ligaments within would be sufficient to bind the members to the head, and to each other.

In the feudal system, we have seen a similar propensity exemplified. Notwithstanding the want of proper sympathy in every instance between the local sovereigns and the people, and the sympathy in some instances between the general sovereign and the latter, it usually happened that the local sovereigns prevailed in the rivalship for encroachments. Had no external dangers enforced internal harmony and subordination, and particularly, had the local sovereigns possessed the affections of the people, the great kingdoms in Europe would at this time consist of as many independent princes as there were formerly feudatory barons.

The State governments will have the advantage of the Federal government, whether we compare them in respect to the immediate dependence of the one on the other; to the weight of personal influence which each side will possess; to the powers respectively vested in them; to the predilection and probable support of the people; to the disposition and faculty of resisting and frustrating the measures of each other.

The State governments may be regarded as constituent and essential parts of the federal government; whilst the latter is nowise essential to the operation or organization of the former. Without the intervention of the State legislatures, the President of the United States cannot be elected at all. They must in all cases have a great share in his appointment, and will, perhaps, in most cases, of themselves determine it. The Senate will be elected absolutely and exclusively by the State legislatures. Even the House of Representatives, though drawn immediately from the people, will be chosen very much under the influence of that class of men, whose influence over the people obtains for themselves an election into the State legislatures. Thus, each of the principal branches of the federal government will owe its existence more or less to the favor of the State governments, and must consequently feel a dependence, which is much more likely to beget a disposition too obsequious than too overbearing towards them. On the other side, the component parts of the State governments will in no instance be indebted for their appointment to the direct agency of the federal government, and very little, if at all, to the local influence of its members.

The number of individuals employed under the Constitution of the United States will be much smaller than the number employed under the particular States. There will consequently be less of personal influence on the side of the former than of the latter. The members of the legislative, executive, and judiciary departments of thirteen and more States, the justices of peace, officers of militia, ministerial officers of justice, with all the country, corporation, and town officers, for three millions and more of people, intermixed, and having particular acquaintance with every class and circle of people, must exceed, beyond all proportion, both in number and influence, those of every description who will be employed in the administration of the federal system. Compare the members of the three great departments of the thirteen States, excluding from the judiciary department the justices of peace, with the members of the corresponding departments of the single government of the Union; compare the militia officers of three millions of people with the military and marine officers of any establishment which is within the compass of probability, or, I may add, of possibility, and in this view alone, we may pronounce the advantage of the States to be decisive. If the federal government is to have collectors of revenue, the State governments will have theirs also. And as those of the former will be principally on the sea-coast, and not very numerous, whilst those of the latter will be spread over the face of the country, and will be very numerous, the advantage in this view also lies on the same side. It is true, that the Confederacy is to possess, and may exercise, the power of collecting internal as well as external taxes throughout the States; but it is probable that this power will not be resorted to, except for supplemental purposes of revenue; that an option will then be given to the States to supply their quotas by previous collections of their own; and that the eventual collection, under the immediate authority of the Union, will generally be made by the officers, and according to the rules, appointed by the several States. Indeed it is extremely probable, that in other instances, particularly in the organization of the judicial power, the officers of the States will be clothed with the correspondent authority of the Union. Should it happen, however, that separate collectors of internal revenue should be appointed under the federal government, the influence of the whole number would not bear a comparison with that of the multitude of State officers in the opposite scale. Within every district to which a federal collector would be allotted, there would not be less than thirty or forty, or even more, officers of different descriptions, and many of them persons of character and weight, whose influence would lie on the side of the State.

The powers delegated by the proposed Constitution to the federal government are few and defined. Those which are to remain in the State governments are numerous and indefinite. The former will be exercised principally on external objects, as war, peace, negotiation, and foreign commerce; with which last the power of taxation will, for the most part, be connected. The powers reserved to the several States will extend to all the objects which, in the ordinary course of affairs, concern the lives, liberties, and properties of the people, and the internal order, improvement, and prosperity of the State.

The operations of the federal government will be most extensive and important in times of war and danger; those of the State governments in times of peace and security. As the former periods will probably bear a small proportion to the latter, the State governments will here enjoy another advantage over the federal government. The more adequate, indeed, the federal powers may be rendered to the national defence, the less frequent will be those scenes of danger which might favor their ascendancy over the governments of the particular States.

If the new Constitution be examined with accuracy and candor, it will be found that the change which it proposes consists much less in the addition of new powers to the Union, than in the invigoration of its original powers. The regulation of commerce, it is true, is a new power; but that seems to be an addition which few oppose, and from which no apprehensions are entertained. The powers relating to war and peace, armies and fleets, treaties and finance, with the other more considerable powers, are all vested in the existing Congress by the articles of Confederation. The proposed change does not enlarge these powers; it only substitutes a more effectual mode of administering them. The change relating to taxation may be regarded as the most important; and yet the present Congress have as complete authority to require of the States indefinite supplies of money for the common defense and general welfare, as the future Congress will have to require them of individual citizens; and the latter will be no more bound than the States themselves have been, to pay the quotas respectively taxed on them. Had the States complied punctually with the articles of Confederation, or could their compliance have been enforced by as peaceable means as may be used with success towards single persons, our past experience is very far from countenancing an opinion, that the State governments would have lost their constitutional powers, and have gradually undergone an entire consolidation. To maintain that such an event would have ensued, would be to say at once, that the existence of the State governments is incompatible with any system whatever that accomplishes the essential purposes of the Union.

PUBLIUS

Nature of the American State

JAMES BRYCE

As the dissimilarity of population and of external conditions seems to make for a diversity of constitutional and political arrangements between the States, so also does the large measure of legal independence which each of them enjoys under the Federal Constitution. No State can, as a commonwealth, politically deal with or act upon any other State. No diplomatic relations can exist nor treaties be made between States, no coercion can be exercised by one upon another. And although the government of the Union can act on a State, it rarely does act, and then only in certain strictly limited directions, which do not touch the inner political life of the commonwealth.

Let us pass on to consider the circumstances which work for uniformity among the States, and work more powerfully as time goes on.

He who looks at a map of the Union will be struck by the fact that so many of the boundary lines of the States are straight lines. Those lines tell the same tale as the geometrical plans of cities like St. Petersburg or Washington, where every street runs at the same angle to every other. The States are not natural growths. Their boundaries are for the most part not natural boundaries fixed by mountain ranges, nor even historical boundaries due to a series of events, but purely artificial boundaries, determined by an authority which carved the national territory into strips of convenient size, as a building company lays out its suburban lots. Of the States subsequent to the original thirteen, California is the only one with a genuine natural boundary, finding it in the chain of the Sierra Nevada on the east and the Pacific ocean on the west. No one of these later States can be regarded as a naturally developed political organism. They are trees planted by the forester, not self-sown with the help of the seed-scattering wind. This absence of physical lines of demarcation has tended and must tend to prevent the growth of local distinctions. Nature herself seems to have designed the Mississippi basin, as she has designed the unbroken levels of Russia, to be the dwelling-place of one people.

Each State makes its own Constitution; that is, the people agree on their form of government for themselves, with no interference from the other States or from the Union. This form is subject to one condition only: it must be republican.[1] But in each State the people who make the constitution have lately come from other States, where they have lived and worked under constitutions which are to their eyes the natural and almost necessary model for their new State to follow; and in the absence of an inventive spirit among the citizens, it was the obvious course for the newer States to copy the organizations of the older States, especially as these agreed with certain familiar features of the Federal Constitution. Hence the outlines, and even the phrases of the elder constitutions reappear in those of the more recently formed States. The precedents set by Virginia, for instance, had much influence on Tennessee, Alabama, Mississippi, and Florida, when they were engaged in making or amending their constitutions during the early part of this century.

Nowhere is population in such constant movement as in America. In some of the newer States only one-fourth or one-fifth of the inhabitants are natives of the United States. Many of the townsfolk, not a few even of the farmers, have been till lately citizens of some other State, and will, perhaps, soon move on farther west. These Western States are like a chain of lakes through which there flows a stream which mingles the waters of the higher with those of the lower. In such a constant flux of population local peculiarities are not readily developed, or if they have grown up when the district was still isolated, they disappear as the country becomes filled. Each State takes from its neighbours and gives to its neighbours, so that the process of assimilation is always going on over the whole wide area.

Still more important is the influence of railway communication, of newspapers, of the telegraph. A Greek city like Samos or Mitylene, holding her own island, preserved a distinctive character in spite of commercial intercourse and the sway of Athens. A Swiss canton like Uri or Appenzell, entrenched behind its mountain ramparts, remains, even now under the strengthened central government of the Swiss nation, unlike its neighbours of the lower country. But an American State traversed by great trunk lines of railway, and depending on the markets of the Atlantic cities and of Europe for the sale of its grain, cattle, bacon, and minerals, is attached by a hundred always tightening ties to other States, and touched by their weal or woe as nearly as by what befalls within its own limits. The leading newspapers are read over a vast area. The inhabitants of each State know every morning the events of yesterday over the whole Union.

Finally the political parties are the same in all the States. The tenets (if any) of each party are the same everywhere, their methods the same, their leaders the same, although of course a prominent man enjoys especial influence in his own State. Hence, State politics are largely swayed by forces and motives external to the particular State, and common to the whole country, or to great sections of it; and the growth of local parties, the emergence of local issues and development of local political schemes, are correspondingly restrained.

These considerations explain why the States, notwithstanding the original diversities between some of them, and the wide scope for political divergence which they all enjoy under the Federal Constitution, are so much less dissimilar and less peculiar than might have been expected. European statesmen have of late years been accustomed to think of federalism and local autonomy as convenient methods either for recognizing and giving free scope to the sentiment of nationality which may exist in any part of an empire, or for meeting the need for local institutions and distinct legislation which may arise from differences between such a part and the rest of the empire. It is one or other or both of these reasons that have moved statesmen in such cases as those of Finland in her relations to Russia, Hungary in her relations to German Austria, Iceland in her relations to Denmark, Bulgaria in her relations to the Turkish Sultan, Ireland in her relations to the United Kingdom. But the final causes, so to speak, of the recognition of the States of the American Union as autonomous commonwealths, have been different. Their self-government is not the consequence of differences which can be made harmless to the whole body politic only by being allowed free course. It has been due primarily to the historical fact that they existed as commonwealths before the Union came into being; secondarily, to the belief that localized government is the best guarantee for civic freedom, and to a sense of the difficulty of administering a vast territory and population from one centre and by one government.

I return to indicate the points in which the legal independence and right of self-government of the several States appears. Each of the forty-two has its own—

Constitution (whereof more anon).

Executive, consisting of a governor, and various other officials.

Legislature of two Houses.

System of local government in counties, cities, townships, and school districts.

System of State and local taxation.

Debts, which it may (and sometimes does) repudiate at its own pleasure.

Body of private law, including the whole law of real and personal property, of contracts, of torts, and of family relations.

Courts, from which no appeal lies (except in cases touching Federal legislation or the Federal constitution) to any Federal court.

System of procedure, civil and criminal.

Citizenship, which may admit persons (e.g. recent immigrants) to be citizens at times, or on conditions, wholly different from those prescribed by other States.

Three points deserve to be noted as illustrating what these attributes include.

I. A man gains active citizenship of the United States (*i.e.* a share in the government of the Union) only by becoming a citizen of some particular State. Being such citizen, he is forthwith entitled to the national franchise. That is to say, voting power in the State carries voting power in Federal elections, and however lax a State may be in its grant of such power, *e.g.* to foreigners just landed or to persons convicted of crime, these State voters will have the right of voting in congressional and presidential elections.[2] The only restriction on the States in this matter is that of the fourteenth and fifteenth Constitutional amendments,... They were intended to secure equal treatment to the negroes, and incidentally they declare the protection given to all citizens of the United States.[3] Whether they really enlarge it, that is to say, whether it did not exist by implication before, is a legal question, which I need not discuss.

II. The power of a State over all communities within its limits is absolute. It may grant or refuse local government as it pleases. The population of the city of Providence is more than one-third of that of the State of Rhode Island, the population of New York city more than one-fifth that of the State of New York. But the State might in either case extinguish the municipality, and govern the city by a single State commissioner appointed for the purpose, or leave it without any government whatever. The city would have no right of complaint to the Federal President or Congress against such a measure. Massachusetts has lately remodelled the city government of Boston just as the British Parliament might remodel that of Birmingham. Let an Englishman imagine a county council for Warwickshire suppressing the muncipality of Birmingham, or a Frenchman imagine the department of the Rhone extinguishing the municipality of Lyons, with no possibility of intervention by the central authority, and he will measure the difference between the American States and the local governments of Western Europe.

III. A State commands the allegiance of its citizens, and may punish them for treason against it. The power has rarely been exercised, but its undoubted legal existence had much to do with inducing the citizens of the Southern States to follow their governments into secession in 1861. They conceived themselves to owe allegiance to the State as well as to the Union, and when it became impossible to preserve both, because the State had declared its secession from the Union, they might hold the earlier and nearer authority to be paramount. Allegiance to the State must now, since the war, be taken to be subordinate to the Union. But allegiance to the State still exists; treason against the State is still possible. One cannot think of treason against Warwickshire or the department of the Rhone.

These are illustrations of the doctrine which Europeans often fail to grasp, that the American States were originally in a certain sense, and still for certain purposes remain, sovereign States. Each of the original thirteen became sovereign when it revolted from the mother country in 1776. By entering the Confederation of 1781–88 it parted with one or two of the attributes of sovereignty, by accepting the Federal Constitution in 1788 it subjected itself for certain specified purposes to a central government, but claimed to retain its sovereignty for all other purposes. That is to say, the authority of a State is an inherent, not a delegated, authority. It has all the powers which any independent government can have, except such as it can be affirmatively shown to have stripped itself of, while the Federal Government has only such powers as it can be affirmatively shown to have received. To use the legal expression, the presumption is always for a State, and the burden of proof lies upon any one who denies its authority in a particular matter.[4]

What State sovereignty means and includes is a question which incessantly engaged the most active legal and political minds of the nation, from 1789 down to 1870. Some thought it paramount to the rights of the Union. Some considered it as held in suspense by the Constitution, but capable of reviving as soon as a State should desire to separate from the Union. Some maintained that each State had in accepting the Constitution finally renounced its sovereignty, which thereafter existed only in the sense of such an undefined domestic legislative and administrative authority as had not been conferred upon Congress. The conflict of these views, which became acute in 1830 when South Carolina claimed the right of nullification, produced Secession and the war of 1861–65. Since the defeat of the Secessionists, the last of these views may be deemed to have been established, and the term "State sovereignty" is now but seldom heard. Even "States rights" have a different meaning from that which they had thirty years ago.[5] . . .

The Constitution, which had rendered many services to the American people, did them an inevitable disservice when it fixed their minds on the legal aspects of the question. Law was meant to be the servant of politics, and must not be suffered to become the master. A case had arisen which its formulae were unfit to deal with, a case which had to be settled on large moral and historical grounds. It was not merely the superior physical force of the North that prevailed; it was the moral forces which rule the world, forces which had long worked against slavery, and were ordained to save North America from the curse of hostile nations established side by side.

The word "sovereignty," which has in many ways clouded the domain of public law and jurisprudence, confused men's minds by making them assume that there must in every country exist, and be discoverable by legal inquiry, either one body invested legally with supreme power over all minor bodies, or several bodies which, though they had consented to form part of a larger body, were each in the last resort independent of it, and responsible to none but themselves.[6] They forgot that a Constitution may not have determined where legal supremacy shall dwell. Where the Constitution of the United States placed it was at any rate doubtful, so doubtful that it would have been better to drop technicalities, and recognize the broad fact that the legal claims of the States had become incompatible with the historical as well as legal claims of the nation. In the uncertainty as to where legal right resided, it would have been prudent to consider where physical force resided. The South however thought herself able to resist any physical force which the rest of the nation might bring against her. Thus encouraged, she took her stand on the doctrine of States Rights: and then followed a pouring out of blood and treasure such as was never spent on determining a point of law before, not even when Edward III and his successors waged war for a hundred years to establish the claim of females to inherit the crown of France.

What, then, do the rights of a State now include? Every right or power of a Government except:—

The right of secession (not abrogated in terms, but admitted since the war to be no longer claimable. It is expressly negatived in the recent Constitutions of several Southern States).

Powers which the Constitution withholds from the States (including that of intercourse with foreign governments).

Powers which the Constitution expressly confers on the Federal Government.

As respects some powers of the last class, however, the States may act concurrently with, or in default of action by, the Federal Government. It is only from contravention of its action that they must abstain. And where contravention is alleged to exist, whether legislative or executive, it is by a court of law, and, in case the decision is in the first instance favourable to the pretensions of the State, ultimately by a Federal court, that the question falls to be decided.[7]

A reference to the preceding list of what each State may create in the way of distinct institutions will show that these rights practically cover nearly all the ordinary relations of citizens to one another and to their Government.[8] An American may, through a long life, never be reminded of the Federal Government, except when he votes at presidential and congressional elections, lodges a complaint against the post-office, and opens his trunks for a custom-house officer on the pier at New York when he returns from a tour in Europe. His direct taxes are paid to officials acting under State laws. The State, or a local authority constituted by State statutes, registers his birth, appoints his guardian, pays for his schooling, gives him a share in the estate of his father deceased, licenses him when he enters a trade (if it be one needing a licence), marries him, divorces him, entertains civil actions against him, declares him a bankrupt, hangs him for murder. The police that guard his house, the local boards which look after the poor, control highways, impose water rates, manage schools—all these derive their legal powers from his State alone. Looking at this immense compass of State functions, Jefferson would seem to have been not far wrong when he said that the Federal government was nothing more than the American department of foreign affairs. But although the National government touches the direct interests of the citizen less than does the State government, it touches his sentiment more. Hence the strength of his attachment to the former and his interest in it must not be measured by the frequency of his dealings with it. In the partitionment of governmental functions between nation and State, the State gets the most but the nation the highest, so the balance between the two is preserved.

Thus every American citizen lives in a duality of which Europeans, always excepting the Swiss, and to some extent the Germans, have no experience. He lives under two governments and two sets of laws; he is animated by two patriotisms and owes two allegiances. That these should both be strong and rarely be in conflict is most fortunate. It is the result of skilful adjustment and long habit, of the fact that those whose votes control the two sets of governments are the same persons, but above all of that harmony of each set of institutions with the other set, a harmony due to the identity of the principles whereon both are founded, which makes each appear necessary to the stability of the other, the States to the nation as its basis, the National Government to the States as their protector.

Notes

1. The case of Kansas immediately before the War of Secession, and the cases of the rebel States, which were not readmitted after the war till they had accepted the constitutional amendments forbidding slavery and protecting the freedmen, are quite exceptional cases.

2. Congress has power to pass a uniform rule of naturalization (Const. Art. §. 8).

   Under the present naturalization laws a foreigner must have resided in the United States for five years, and for one year in the State or Territory where he seeks admission to United States citizenship, and must declare two years before he is admitted that he renounces allegiance to any foreign prince or state. Naturalization makes him a citizen not only of the United States, but of the State or Territory where he is admitted, but does not necessarily confer the electoral franchise, for that depends on State laws.

   In more than a third of the States the electoral franchise is now enjoyed by persons not naturalized as United States citizens.

3. "The line of distinction between the privileges and immunities of citizens of the United States, and those of citizens of the several States, must be traced along the boundary of their respective spheres of action, and the two classes must be as different in their nature as are the functions of their respective governments. A citizen of the United States as such has a right to participate in foreign and interstate commerce, to have the benefit of the postal laws, to make use in common with others of the navigable waters of the United States, and to pass from State to State, and into foreign countries, because over all these subjects the jurisdiction of the United States extends, and they are covered by its laws. The privileges suggest the immunities. Wherever it is the duty of the United States to give protection to a citizen against any harm, inconvenience, or deprivation, the citizen is entitled to an immunity which pertains to Federal citizenship. One very plain immunity is exemption from any tax, burden, or imposition under State laws as a condition to the enjoyment of any right or privilege under the laws of the United States.... Whatever one may claim as of right under the Constitution and laws of the United States by virtue of his citizenship, is a privilege of a citizen of the United States.

   Whatever the Constitution and laws of the United States entitle him to exemption from, he may claim an exemption in respect to. And such a right or privilege is abridged whenever the State law interferes with any legitimate operation of Federal authority which concerns his interest, whether it be an authority actively exerted, or resting only in the express or implied command or assurance of the Federal Constitution or law. But the United States can neither grant nor secure to its citizens rights or privileges which are not expressly or by reasonable implication placed under its jurisdiction, and all not so placed are left to the exclusive protection of the States."—Cooley, *Principles*, pp. 245–247.

4. It may of course be said that as the colonies associated themselves into a league, at the very time at which they revolted from the British Crown, and as their foreign relations were always managed by the authority and organs of this league, no one of them ever was for international purposes a free and independent sovereign State. This is true, and Abraham Lincoln was in this sense justified in saying that the Union was older than the States. But what are we to say of North Carolina and Rhode Island, after the acceptance of the Constitution of 1787–89 by the other eleven States? They were out of the old Confederation, for it had expired. They were not in the new Union, for they refused during many months to enter it. What else can they have been during these months except sovereign commonwealths?

5. States rights was a watchword in the South for many years. In 1851 there was a student at Harvard College from South Carolina who bore the name of States Rights Gist, baptized, so to speak, into Calhounism. He rose to be a brigadier-general in the Confederate army, and fell in the Civil War.

6. A further confusion arises from the fact that men are apt in talking of sovereignty to mix up legal supremacy with practical predominance. They ought to go together, and law seeks to make them go together. But it may happen that the person or body in whom law vests supreme authority is unable to enforce that authority: so the legal sovereign and the actual sovereign—that is to say, the force which will prevail in physical conflict—are different. There is always a strongest force; but the force recognized by law may not be really the strongest; and of several forces it may be impossible to tell, till they have come into actual physical conflict, which is the strongest.

7. See Chapter XXII. *ante.*

8. A recent American writer well observes that nearly all the great questions which have agitated England during the last sixty years would, had they arisen in America, have fallen within the sphere of State legislation.—Jameson, "Introduction to the Constitutional and Political History of the States," in *Johns Hopkins University Studies*.

UNIT 2

Intergovernmental Relations

Unit Selections

Key Points to Consider

- Do you think that the current state of intergovernmental relations in the United States is satisfactory or unsatisfactory?

- Which level of government do you think is contributing the most to the well-being of Americans? Why?

- Under what circumstances do you think the national government should try to impose national standards on the state and local governments? Under what circumstances do you think the state governments should impose state standards on the local governments?

- Should states and localities have the responsibility of performing more tasks and raising money to pay for them? Why or why not?

- In the aftermath of September 11, 2001, are you satisfied with the quality and degree of cooperation among the national, state, and local governments in the area of homeland security? Why or why not?

Student Web Site

www.mhcls.com/online

Internet References

Congress
http://congress.org

Council of State Governments
http://www.csg.org

National Center for State Courts
http://www.ncsconline.org/

Supreme Court/Legal Information Institute (LII)
http://supct.law.cornell.edu/supct/index.html

Three levels of government—national, state, and local—coexist in the American political system. They not only operate alongside one another, but they also cooperate and conflict with each other in carrying out their functions. The legal base for relationships among governments in the American political system include the United States Constitution, 50 State Constitutions, decisions by both the state and federal courts, and the state and national legislation. But legal guidelines do not prevent complications from arising in a three-tier system of government. These three levels of American government have often been likened to a layer cake: three layers in one overarching system of government. Still using the cake analogy, political scientist Morton Grodzins argued that a marble cake better represents the interactions of the local, state, and national governments.

According to Grodzins, these interactions are far less tidy than what the model of a layer cake suggests. Governments closest to the scene seem best able to handle certain kinds of problems, but at the same time, higher, more "distant" levels of government often have access to better sources of revenue to finance government activities. Citizens give different degrees of loyalty and support to different levels of government, and the competing ambitions of politicians at different levels of government can obstruct the much needed cooperation.

The formal relationship between the national government and the states is quite different from that between the states and their local governments. The national-state relationship is formally "federal" in character, which means that, in theory, the states and the national government each have autonomous spheres of responsibility. In contrast, the state-local relationship is not a federal one. Local governments are mere "creatures" of the states and are not on equal footing with their creators. In practical terms, however, the national government has generally gained the upper hand in dealings with the states, and in some circumstances, localities are on almost equal footing with state governments.

Public school governance illustrates some of the complexities of the intergovernmental relations in the American political system. Public schooling is usually viewed as primarily a local government function. But, as Grodzins pointed out, state governments play powerful roles by providing financial aid, certifying teachers, prescribing curriculum requirements, and regulating the measures concerning school safety and students' health. The national government is also involved in public schooling. In the last 50 years, the United States Supreme Court and lower federal courts have made numerous decisions aimed at ending racial segregation in public schools. In addition, for several decades national government grants have helped finance various activities such as school breakfasts and lunches, and special education programs. In 2001, the "No Child Left Behind" Act was enacted with President Bush's strong support, which introduced what some observers see as a historic new level of national government involvement in public schooling. Even this brief review of local, state, and national involvement in one area, schooling, should show why Grodzins believed that a marble cake better reflects the reality of the American three-tier system of government than a layer cake does. Intergovernmental transfers

© McGraw-Hill Companies, Inc./John Flournoy, photographer

of money are an important form of interaction among local, state, and national governments. "Strings" are almost always attached to money that one level of government transfers to another level. For example, when the national government provides grants to states and localities, requirements concerning the use of the money accompany the funds, although the extensiveness and specificity of the requirements vary greatly according to different grant programs. Similarly, the aid of the state governments to the local governments also involve strings of one kind or another.

Presidents and other government leaders often set forth proposals about how to structure the relations and divide the responsibilities among the national, state, and local governments. President Reagan's "new federalism" was aimed at shifting greater responsibility back to the states and localities. The change in direction that began under Reagan continued under the first President Bush, and the state and local governments had to operate in the context of what has been called "fend-for-yourself federalism." Whatever changes the Clinton administration tried to make in the intergovernmental relations faded into obscurity with the coming of a Republican-controlled House of Representatives and Senate in

January 1995. Newt Gingrich, the first Republican Speaker of the House of Representatives in 40 years, made shrinking the role of the national government and giving increased responsibilities to the states an important part of his campaign promises in the November 1994 congressional elections.

In the mid-1990s, the House of Representatives passed a number of bills fulfilling Gingrich's campaign promises. One such bill was designed to make it very difficult for the Congress to mandate the state and local governments to do something without providing the necessary funding. The Welfare Reform Bill of 1996 rewrote the welfare system that began in the 1930s, as part of the New Deal. At its core, lay the devolution of all sorts of responsibilities for providing government assistance to the needy to the state governments. While the national government remained responsible for funding the welfare system, the state governments were given increased responsibility for determining and implementing welfare policies. In the last two decades of the twentieth century, the United States seemed to have begun a new era of intergovernmental relations that would result in substantial increase of the power and autonomy of state and local governments. Then came the terrorist attacks of September 11, 2001. The resulting focus on the war on terror and homeland security may well lead to a long-lasting increase in national government power, with a corresponding decline in state and local responsibilities.

Selections in this unit discuss various dimensions of the relationship between the national, state, and local governments.

Federalism at a Crossroads

States must do their part to define federalism and shape the future.

WILLIAM T. POUND

The U.S. federal system is the most vibrant and effective federal system in the world. It is always dynamic, always evolving.

In large part, the success of federalism is a result of the creativity and innovation of the states. Yet the federal balance today is placing enormous strain on state budgets as the national government enacts initiatives and tells the states to pay for them. From the No Child Left Behind Act, to Medicaid reform, clean air and water, the federal government is asking states to do more—and come up with the money to do it.

Phases of Federalism

It wasn't always that way.

America began with a state-based federalism where the states wielded most of the power and initiated nearly all domestic policy. That began to change with the Civil War. It shifted even more with World War I, the Great Depression and World War II, and evolved into its second phase—a clearly Washington-dominated federalism where Congress and the administration became the principal players. Relative to the federal government, the states became weaker. In fact, an observer of federalism commented that by the late 1950s, the states had become mere administrative arms of the national government.

The federal government is asking states to do more—and come up with the money to do it.

Washington, D.C.-dominated federalism began changing around 1980, however, when President Ronald Reagan took office. Responsibilities and authority became much more balanced between the states and the national government, with both playing significant roles. State governments, and particularly state legislatures, had modernized in the 1960s and 1970s— from professionalizing their staffs to enhancing their research, bill drafting and budget capabilities. It wasn't very long before every legislature had its own fiscal staff to strengthen its role in the state budget process. Legislatures also created the National Conference of State Legislatures in the mid 1970s to make the states more active players on the national scene.

Fiscal Federalism

One of the distinctive features of U.S. federalism is that it is the only major federal system in the world in which the national government doesn't systematically share revenues with state government. In the past, the federal government shared revenues with the states to overcome regional disparities. But that doesn't happen in a single program today. Revenue sharing occurs to some extent through Medicaid and in a few formula programs, but the funds are tied to a specific outcome. It's not general purpose aid.

Just as general purpose aid has all but disappeared, there also has been a decline in federal support for state and local programs. Three significant changes have occurred:

- More federal money goes to individuals today than to state or local governments. Federal money is targeted to entitlement programs much more than before, with Medicaid being the primary example.
- Federal assistance to the states requires a significant match when compared to the 1950s to the end of the 1980s or early 1990s. For example, Medicaid is almost an equal split, although the very poorest of states can provide as little as a 20 percent contribution. And the highway program has a rough 80/20 to 75/25 split, with a 20 percent match being the general standard to receive federal money. But perhaps even more important than the size of the match is that federal action drives state decisions and determines what the states have to do with those programs.
- Programmatic responsibilities have shifted to state and local governments. In this period of balanced federalism, the federal government has devolved responsibilities to the states. The Medicaid program that began at the federal level has become a shared program and is the second largest component of state budgets. It's also the fastest growing one.

Local government responsibilities in environment, health care and education have been transferred to the states, too. It wasn't very many years ago when the states had very little responsibility over air and water quality. They also had very little to do with garbage and waste management. Now, many of those are state-run programs, partly because their complexity increased and partly because they exhausted the ability of local jurisdictions to deal with them—especially in some of the eastern states. Other areas have been affected as well. States have assumed a greater role in supporting K-12 education, and now fund about 51 percent of K-12 education costs.

In fact, states have assumed a greater funding role for many programs traditionally funded by local governments, in large part to support property tax relief efforts. By moving funding to a state's broader tax base, financial pressure at the local level is relieved.

But states also have taken on the responsibility for funding K-12 education because of the demands for educational equity and adequacy. More recently, there are federally imposed standards that states must meet.

The federal No Child Left Behind Act illustrates the relationship between decision-making at the national level and the impact at the state level. The law clearly has driven state funding increases, much more than the federal government has contributed to its cost. There's simply no question about that—state legislators have seen new funding demands generated by the implementation of the act.

There's another twist. States already are experienced with litigation around providing public education, but now the adoption of minimum federal standards is creating the basis for a whole new kind of lawsuit. States, not local school districts, are being sued over the standards. Kansas and Texas certainly can attest to that from their recent special sessions in which they wrestled with the question of educational adequacy and how to defend it. This is one direct way that a federal decision establishing a set of standards is now being used to guide some decisions in state government.

Medicaid is another area of concern in this latest phase of federalism. Medicaid funding, including both federal and state revenues, represents about 22 percent of total state spending and could rise to 24 percent by the end of 2006. States are virtually being taxed under the Medicaid "clawback" provision. This poses long-term and serious fiscal consequences for states. Some argue that it simply cannot continue.

Although the annual growth rate in Medicaid expenditures has been as low as 3.5 percent to 4 percent, in more recent years it has reached nearly 13 percent. But whatever the rate, Medicaid growth consistently outpaces the growth rate in state revenues. Last year, in fact, overall state revenues grew about 2.5 percent to 3 percent, while expenditures grew between 4 percent and 4.5 percent. Medicaid spending was a primary cause.

The Revenue Mix

From the mid 1990s to 2000, federal government revenue grew about 8 percent to 10 percent annually; state government revenues, about 5 percent to 6 percent a year; and local government revenues, about 2 percent to 3 percent. This is instructive for considering the capabilities of the various revenue systems.

The federal government has the largest share of income tax revenues, so these varying percentages suggest that the income tax is the most effective tax at raising revenue. States vary in the extent to and percentages at which they tax income. They also rely heavily on sales and use taxes. Telecommunications taxes and other similar levies traditionally are within the purview of local governments, much more than they are for either the federal or state governments, which place locals in the weakest position of all.

The capacity of the federal system to produce revenue has been reduced since the year 2001, when President Bush initiated federal tax cuts. Over time, the states generally have increased their revenue capacity, although they cut taxes during the late 1990s when revenue growth was booming. Notwithstanding those reductions and subsequent fiscal stress, state revenues now are doing as well as or better than they were in 2000, just before the economic downturn hit.

Today's Tax Challenges

We live in a rapidly changing economic environment and fiscal fortunes can turn quickly. State lawmakers not only need to be concerned about the health of the economy, but also the structure of their tax systems and the effects of federal tax policy decisions.

State tax systems do not capture economic activity to the extent they did 30 years ago. State sales taxes are primarily on goods, with only three states applying their taxes to a broad range of services. Yet the U.S. economy is now primarily service based.

Federal government decisions that may be made in the next two or three years also will have considerable impact on state revenues. President Bush's Commission on Tax Policy produced a report in October 2005 that had several recommendations. One that would affect state governments most would remove the deductibility of state and local taxes from federal income tax calculations. If implemented, that recommendation probably would make it more difficult to raise taxes at the state level.

Moreover, most state revenue systems are tied to the federal revenue system, particularly the income tax. States use the same definitions as the federal government and usually assess state income taxes based on a certain percentage of the amount paid in federal income taxes, with adjustments. That means that any federal income tax changes would have a subsequent effect on state tax collections.

That illustrates another interesting feature about today's federalism: The federal government has shown little concern for state and local governments in recent revenue decisions.

Two past examples are accelerated depreciation and the estate tax. Raising the rate of accelerated depreciation drove down state revenues because most states were tied to it. Federal estate tax changes were made with virtually no consideration of how this affected the state portion of the tax.

This concern also extends to future federal policy. A proposal to enact a federal value added tax is still pending.

One reason for the exploration of new federal levies is the national deficit. It is so large (the equivalent of $156,000 for every resident of the United States or $411,000 for every household) that many believe that the federal government will have to increase revenues. In fact, a former Reagan administration official was quoted as saying that federal taxes would have to be raised to address the deficit. And the value-added tax is the most likely way to do it.

The value-added tax has huge implications for state governments, particularly for the 45 that levy sales taxes. Can state sales taxes and a federal value-added tax coexist and, if so, at what level? What collection tool would be used? The easiest way for the federal government to collect a value-added tax would be to let the states collect it because they already have collection mechanisms in place.

Federalism's Future

The state-federal partnership largely is defined by which level of government provides services and which one funds them. As demonstrated over the past decade and longer, the federal government's pattern is to enact national policy initiatives but ask the states to pay for them. These unfunded and underfunded mandates are placing enormous strain on state budgets. Concurrently, federal revenue decisions are affecting, and even undermining, state tax collections. And future federal revenue actions could be even more alarming. In combination, federal policy is threatening long-term state fiscal stability.

But today's situation is not set in stone, and much change is likely in federal and state revenues and expenditures. State legislatures must do their part to define federalism and shape the future.

If they fail to do so, it will be at their peril.

WILLIAM T. POUND is NCSL's executive director.

From *State Legislatures*, June 2006, pp. 18-19. Copyright © 2006 by National Conference of State Legislatures. Reprinted by permission.

Leaving "No Child Left Behind" Behind

Our No. 1 education program is incoherent, unworkable, and doomed. But the next president still can have a huge impact on improving American schooling.

RICHARD ROTHSTEIN

The next president has a unique opportunity to start from scratch in education policy, without the deadweight of a failed, inherited No Child Left Behind (NCLB) law. The new president and Congress can recapture the "small d" democratic mantle by restoring local control of education, while initiating policies for which the federal government is uniquely suited—providing better achievement data and equalizing the states' fiscal capacity to provide for all children.

This opportunity exists because NCLB is dead. It will not be reauthorized—not this year, not ever. The coalition that promoted the 2001 bipartisan law has hopelessly splintered, although NCLB's advocates in the administration and the Congress continue to imagine (at least publicly) that tinkering can put it back together.

NCLB, requiring annual reading and math tests in grades 3 through 8 (and one such test in high school), represents an unprecedented federal takeover of education. It punishes schools not making "adequate yearly progress" toward having all students proficient at "challenging" standards by 2014, regardless of students' socioeconomic disadvantages or even of their cognitive disabilities.

Many Republicans supported NCLB out of loyalty to President Bush and because Karl Rove assured them that their vow to improve minority achievement would entice African Americans away from the Democrats. But now, with Democratic congressional majorities and a possible presidency, Republicans have rediscovered their belief in local control of education. Few now support reauthorization.

Many Democrats were equally cynical in supporting NCLB. Some believed a law demanding unrealistic achievement targets would justify big boosts in federal spending when targets proved unattainable. Others, arguing that low minority scores result mainly from poor teaching ("low expectations"), expected that federal demands for higher achievement would whip teachers into shape, even if the mandated goals were fanciful.

What few Democrats understood, however, was that test-based accountability might spur teachers but would also corrupt schooling in ways that overshadowed any possible score increases. Excessive testing is now so unpopular that Congress' newly elected Democrats campaigned in 2006 against NCLB and now won't support reauthorization. Senior Democrats are also hearing from parents, teachers, school boards, and state legislators.

Sen. Edward Kennedy of Massachusetts and Rep. George Miller of California, who sponsored the original legislation, promise colleagues that they can fix NCLB. But no fixes are possible. Weakening rigid testing requirements provokes denunciation from President Bush and Secretary of Education Margaret Spellings, who unabashedly calls the law "99.9 percent pure."

But NCLB was flawed from the start. The 2001–2002 stampede ignored well-established statistical and management theories predicting perverse consequences for test-based accountability.

Goal Distortion

One such consequence is goal distortion, the subject of extensive warnings in the economics and management literature about measuring any institution's performance by quantitative indicators that reflect only some institutional goals. Management expert W. Edwards Deming urged businesses to "eliminate management by numbers, numerical goals" because they encourage short-, not long-term vision. Peter Drucker gave similar advice. Today, management consultants urge "balanced scorecards" using qualitative judgment, as well as financial indicators, to measure corporate success.

Schools have many goals for students: basic math and reading skills but also critical thinking, citizenship, physical- and emotional-health habits, arts appreciation, self-discipline, responsibility, and conflict resolution. Schools threatened with sanctions for failure in only one goal will inevitably divert attention from others. One NCLB consequence has been less social studies, science, art, music, and physical education—particularly for low-income children, whose math and reading scores are lowest and for whose teachers the consequences of spending time on, say, history, rather than more math drill, are most severe.

Goal distortion has been particularly troubling, as it should be, to conservatives. Two former assistant secretaries of education (under Ronald Reagan and Bush père), Chester Finn and Diane Ravitch, once prominent NCLB advocates, now write:

> We should have seen this coming . . . more emphasis on some things would inevitably mean less attention to others. . . . We were wrong.

They conclude:

> [If NCLB continues,] rich kids will study philosophy and art, music and history, while their poor peers fill in bubbles on test sheets. The lucky few will spawn the next generation of tycoons, political leaders, inventors, authors, artists and entrepreneurs. The less lucky masses will see narrower opportunities.

Test Reliability

NCLB relies on an annual test, but single tests can be misleading. Every parent knows children have good and bad days. Every teacher knows particular classes can be talented or difficult. Entire classes can be attentive or distracted. So accurate measurement requires multiple retesting. Most schools are too small for statistical confidence that children's good and bad days will average out on one test. Because a school's subgroups (blacks, Hispanics, or low-income children) are smaller than a full-grade cohort, the margin of error for subgroup achievement is even larger. The more integrated a school, with more subgroups, the more inaccurate accountability becomes.

When the Bush administration and Congress were designing NCLB, two economists (Thomas Kane and Douglas Staiger) demonstrated that many schools would be rewarded or punished solely because of these statistical challenges. Their paper derailed NCLB for six months while administration and congressional experts tried to finesse the problems. They couldn't but enacted NCLB anyway, which engendered remarkable anomalies: schools rewarded one year and punished the next despite identical levels of effectiveness; schools rewarded under a state's system and simultaneously punished under the federal one, or vice versa. Some states

dodge these absurdities by reporting large error margins with test scores, but this hides poorly performing as well as misidentified schools, and draws the wrath of accountability enthusiasts.

The Proficiency Myth

Even with inordinate attention to math and reading, it is practically and conceptually ludicrous to expect all students to be proficient at challenging levels. Even if we eliminated all disparities based on socioeconomic status, human variability prevents a single standard from challenging all. The normal I.Q. range, 85 to 115, includes about two-thirds of the population. "Challenging" achievement for those at 115 would be impossibly hard for those at 85, and "challenging" achievement for those at 85 would be too easy for those at 115.

The law strongly implies that "challenging" standards are those of the National Assessment of Educational Progress (NAEP), periodic federal tests of national student samples. But while NAEP tests are excellent, their proficiency cut-points have no credibility. Passing scores are arbitrary, fancifully defined by panels of teachers, politicians, and laypeople. Many children in the highest-scoring countries don't achieve them. Taiwan is tops in math, but 40 to 60 percent of Taiwanese students are below proficient by NAEP standards. Swedish students are the best readers in the world, but two-thirds are not NAEP-proficient.

Expecting all Americans to perform at this level can only set them, their teachers, and schools up for failure. (Actually, this charge is slightly exaggerated: NCLB exempts the most severely disabled, requiring only U.S. children with I.Q.s above 65 to be as proficient as the top half of the Taiwanese.)

In a rare bow to local control, NCLB doesn't enact NAEP's proficiency definitions but permits states to invent their own. Not surprisingly, some define proficiency far below "challenging" expectations, and the Department of Education has little choice but to let this pass; if it enforces high standards, the already unacceptably large number of failing schools would be astronomical. But low state passing points are a sore spot for NCLB advocates, who propose to correct this with high national standards. Their demand makes reauthorization even less probable.

The Bubble Kids

Any single proficiency standard invites sabotaging the goal of teaching all children, because the only ones who matter are those with scores just below passing. Educators call them "bubble kids" a term from poker and basketball, where bubble players or teams are those just on the cusp of elimination. Explicit school policies now demand that teachers ignore already-proficient children to focus only on bubble kids, because inching the bubbles past the standard is all that matters for "adequate yearly progress."

Less obvious are incentives also to ignore children far below proficiency, whom even constant drilling won't pull across the finish line. Because all must eventually (by 2014) pass, ignoring poorer performers should, in the long run, be counterproductive. But NCLB places no premium on the long run. Educators can't worry about possible distant punishment. And since most consider the 2014 goal absurd, they have good reason to expect it to be abandoned, further reducing incentives to worry about the lowest achievers. What's more, the higher the standard, the more children there are who are too far below proficiency to worry about. So the law guarantees that more disadvantaged children will be left further behind, especially in states with higher standards.

For bubble kids, schools have substituted test prep for good instruction. With test development costly, states use similar tests repeatedly, guiding teachers to stress content they suspect will reappear. Teachers impart test-taking skills (like how to guess multiple-choice answers) that don't deepen understanding of math and reading. In the weeks before testing, schools step up drilling; this does little to help children retain what they learned. Thus, student scores on state tests are not duplicated in NAEP, which is less subject to test-prep corruption. Administered only to representative samples of schools and students, with more emphasis on critical thinking, NAEP scores have not shot up along with state test results. NAEP math scores have increased a little, but at about the same rate as before NCLB's adoption—suggesting that, for all its other problems, NCLB has also been an utter waste of time.

Schools and Social Policy

In one respect, NCLB betrays core Democratic principles, denying the importance of all social policy but school reform. Inadequate schools are only one reason disadvantaged children perform poorly. They come to school under stress from high-crime neighborhoods and economically insecure households. Their low-cost day-care tends to park them before televisions, rather than provide opportunities for developmentally appropriate play. They switch schools more often because of inadequate housing and rents rising faster than parents' wages. They have greater health problems, some (like lead poisoning or iron-deficiency anemia) directly depressing cognitive ability, and some causing more absenteeism or inattentiveness. Their households include fewer college-educated adults to provide rich intellectual environments, and their parents are less likely to expect academic success. Nearly 15 percent of the black-white test-score gap can be traced to differences in housing mobility, and 25 percent to differences in child- and maternal-health.

Yet NCLB insists that school improvement alone can raise all children to high proficiency. The law anticipates that with higher expectations, better teachers, improved curriculum, and more testing, all youths will attain full academic competence, poised for college and professional success. Natural human variability would still distinguish children, but these distinctions would have nothing to do with family disadvantage. Then there really would be no reason for progressive housing or health and economic policies. The nation's social and economic problems would take care of themselves, by the next generation.

Teachers of children who come to school hungry, scared, abused, or ill, consider this absurd. But NCLB's aura intimidates educators from acknowledging the obvious. Teachers are expected to repeat the mantra "all children can learn," a truth carrying the mendacious implication that the level to which children learn has nothing to do with their starting points. Teachers are warned that any mention of children's socioeconomic disadvantages only "makes excuses" for teachers' own poor performance.

Of course, there are better and worse schools and better and worse teachers. Of course, some disadvantaged children excel more than others. But NCLB has turned these obvious truths into the fantasy that teachers can wipe out socioeconomic differences among children simply by trying harder.

Denouncing schools as the chief cause of American inequality—in academic achievement, thus in the labor market, and thus in life generally—stimulates cynicism among teachers who are expected to act on a theory they know to be false. Many dedicated and talented teachers are abandoning education; they may have achieved exceptional results with disadvantaged children, but with NCLB's bar set so impossibly high, even these are labeled failures.

> **NCLB insists that teachers can wipe out Socioeconomic differences among children simply by trying harder.**

The continuation of NCLB's rhetoric will also erode support for public education. Educators publicly vow they can eliminate achievement gaps, but they will inevitably fall short. The reasonable conclusion can only be that public education is hopelessly incompetent.

"Fixing" NCLB

Few policy-makers have publicly acknowledged NCLB's demise. Instead, they talk of fixing it. Some want to credit schools for student growth from year to year, rather than for reaching arbitrary proficiency levels. Clearly, adequate progress from different starting points leads to different ending points, but growth-model advocates can't bring themselves to drop the universal-proficiency goal. Doing so would imply lower expectations, on average, for disadvantaged children—

too much for unsophisticated policy discussion to swallow. Consequently, the "fix" is incoherent.

Growth models have even larger error margins than single-year test results because they rely on two unreliable scores (last year's and this year's), not one. And accountability for math and reading growth retains the incentives to abandon non-tested subjects and skills. So some NCLB loyalists now propose accountability for "multiple measures," such as graduation rates. But presently quantifiable skills are too few to minimize goal distortion—the federal government is unprepared to monitor, for instance, whether students express good citizenship. Further, any mention of diluting a math and reading focus elicits the wrath of "basics" fundamentalists, such as the president and his secretary of education.

Although NCLB will not be reauthorized, the underlying Elementary and Secondary Education Act (ESEA), with funding for schools serving low-income children, will continue. NCLB will remain on the books, increasingly ignored. Virtually every school with minority, low-income, or immigrant children will be labeled a failure; the federal government will be hard-pressed to punish all. Eventually, under a new administration, ESEA will be renewed, perhaps including vague incantations that states establish their own accountability policies, once Washington abandons the field.

States will do so. Some, not having learned NCLB's lessons, will retain the distortions and corruption that NCLB established. Others, more creative, will use qualitative as well as quantitative standards, relying on school inspections as well as test scores.

Renouncing federal micromanagement will require liberals to abandon a cherished myth: that only the federal government can protect disadvantaged minorities from Southern states' indifference. The myth is rooted in an isolated fact: In the two decades following *Brown v. Board of Education*, the federal government forced states to respect rights not only of African Americans but of disabled and immigrant children.

But at other times, the federal government has been no defender of the oppressed. In the early 20th century, state governments enacted minimum-wage, health, and safety laws, only to see them struck down by the Supreme Court. Today, Southern states' attempts to improve education are often impeded by federal policy. Only last year, school integration efforts of Louisville, Kentucky, were prohibited by federal courts, while federal administrative agencies block efforts at integration and affirmative action. In recent decades, states like North Carolina and Texas have been innovators in school improvement. North and South Carolina and Arkansas have had nationally known "education governors" (Jim Hunt, Richard Riley, and Bill Clinton). The greatest potential for greater education improvement in the South lies in boosting African American voting participation, not more federal mandates.

What the Next President Can Do

With the federal government proven incapable of micromanaging the nation's 100,000 schools, what education roles remain for a new administration? There are two.

One is to provide information about student performance, not for accountability but to guide state policy. NAEP should be improved. Now given regularly at the state level only in math and reading, such coverage should expand to include history, civics, and the sciences, as well as art, music, and physical education. For example, NAEP could provide state-by-state data on physical education by sampling students' body mass index numbers and upper body strength, characteristics for which standardized tools are available.

When NAEP was first designed in the 1960s, it included important elements that were soon abandoned under cost pressures. While employing paper-and-pencil tests, early NAEP also dispatched field assessors to observe, for example, how young children solved problems in cooperative groups. NAEP assessed representative samples of adolescents, whether in or out of school, as well as of young adults in their mid-20s. Assessors tracked down 17-year-olds and young adults, administering tests to determine if their schooling had lasting impact.

A dramatic expansion of NAEP, covering multiple skills and out-of-school samples, with state-level reporting, would be expensive, multiplying by several times the current NAEP budget of $90 million. But this would only slightly increase the roughly $45 billion in federal funds now supplementing state and local school spending. Provision of state-by-state data on a balanced set of outcomes should be a federal responsibility.

The other new federal role should be fiscal equalization. New Jersey now spends about $14,000 per pupil, more than twice what Mississippi spends. Adjusting for the dollar's purchasing power still leaves New Jersey spending 65 percent more than Mississippi.

This cannot be attributed to New Jersey caring more about children than Mississippi. New Jersey's fiscal capacity, its per capita personal income, is over 70 percent greater than Mississippi's. And Mississippi's needs are greater: 10 percent of New Jersey's children live in poverty, compared to Mississippi's 29 percent. Again, after adjusting for the value of the dollar, Mississippi still faces greater educational challenges, with less ability to meet them.

Washington now exacerbates these inequalities. Federal school aid—ESEA aid to districts serving poor children—is proportional to states' own spending. So New Jersey, which needs less aid, gets more aid per poor pupil than Mississippi, which needs more.

It will be politically tough for a Democratic Congress and administration to fix this, because sensible redistribution, with aid given to states in proportion to need, and in inverse proportion to capacity, will take tax revenues from states like

New Jersey (which sends liberal Democrats to Congress), and direct them to states like Mississippi (which sends conservative Republicans). Funding equalization requires political courage not typically found in either Washington party. There's a role here for presidential leadership.

Narrowing huge fiscal disparities will take time. Whether the next Democratic Congress and administration—if they are Democratic—take the first steps will test whether the party is truly committed to leaving no child behind.

Abandoning federal micromanagement of education has a hidden benefit: helping to reinvigorate American democracy in an age of increasingly anomic and media-driven politics.

Local school boards in the nation's nearly 15,000 school districts (but not in the biggest cities) can still provide an opportunity for meaningful citizen participation. Debating and deciding the goals of education for a community's children is a unique American privilege and responsibility. Restoring it is a mission worthy of a new administration.

RICHARD ROTHSTEIN (riroth@epi.org), a *Prospect* senior correspondent, is a research associate of the Economic Policy Institute and the author of *Class and Schools: Using Social, Economic, and Educational Reform to Close the Black-White Achievement Gap.*

Eminent Domain— For The Greater Good?

The U.S. Supreme Court decision in *Kelo v. New London* has prompted states to look at their own eminent domain practices

GARRY BOULARD

When Suzette Kelo received a notice from the city of New London, Conn., to vacate her property, little did she or the city know that they were about to embark upon an historic journey that would wend its way to the U.S. Supreme Court. And little did she know that the case that ensued, *Kelo v. New London*, would prompt legislatures in several dozen states to look at their eminent domain practices.

The New London Development Corporation, a public/private effort promoting mix-used developments, wanted Kelo's property in order to redevelop some 90 acres of her mostly working-class neighborhood. Employing the use of eminent domain, they were trying to make way for a multi-million dollar conference center and hotel complex designed to complement a new $270 million global research facility owned by Pfizer Incorporated.

The city argued that the proposed redevelopment served a "public purpose" by creating new jobs, increasing tax revenue and leading to urban revitalization that would benefit the entire community. Kelo countered that condemning private property for economic development did not qualify as a "public use" under the state and federal constitutions.

But the Supreme Court, in a 5 to 4 vote in June, decided in favor of New London. The Court determined that the comprehensive nature of the city's redevelopment plan, which was adopted pursuant to a state statute, served a public purpose that satisfied the public use requirements of the constitution. It deferred to legislative judgment in defining public use, as it had in previous court decisions. At the same time, the Court invited more state legislation by emphasizing that nothing in its decision precluded a state from restricting the use of eminent domain for economic development purposes.

Lawmakers Step In

Legislatures are following suit. At least 12 states that were in session following the Court's decision considered bills to restrict the use of eminent domain for economic development purposes.

Four of them—Alabama, Delaware, Ohio and Texas—passed laws.

For critics of eminent domain, Kelo represents a practice that has become increasingly prevalent. "By our own count, over a 5-year period, we have found about 10,000 instances where a local government either used or threatened to use eminent domain in order to take a home or parcel of property from one person and give it to another," says Dana Berliner, a senior attorney with the Institute for Justice, a property rights group that represented Kelo and her fellow New London homeowners before the Supreme Court.

"It is obviously more widespread and commonly practiced than most people could ever imagine," she says. "And it is a power that essentially allows a government entity to take any person's home away from them, to ruin their business or destroy their lives, whatever the case may be."

Has a Purpose

But for city and state officials across the country, eminent domain is a vital tool, and in some cases the only tool left when it comes to improving a blighted area, transforming dangerous, abandoned and oftentimes drug-infested neighborhoods into modern mixed-use retail and residential complexes that not only create new jobs but also generate tax revenue.

"I can't even imagine how bad it would be if this tool was taken away from us," says William J. Kearns, the general counsel to the New Jersey State League of Municipalities.

"Every city has within its borders large areas of land that are sitting there unused or are in a deteriorated or dangerous condition," says Kearns.

"It would be nice if the owners of these kinds of properties would step forward and arrive at a fair market price for what they own and then sell it," Kearns says. "But all too often, owners can't be found or have no concern about the condition the property is in, and feel no responsibility to the surrounding area.

What's Up In Congress?

Congress didn't ignore the Kelo case. Bills were introduced that would withhold some sort of federal funding if a state or locality uses eminent domain for economic development purposes. Most of them do not define economic development.

The most important to watch:

HR 3058, the Transportation, Treasury, Housing and Urban Development, the Judiciary, the District of Columbia and Independent Agencies Appropriations Act of 2006. This bill passed both houses of Congress and is awaiting President George Bush's signature. It will prohibit transportation funds to be used to support state or local projects that seek to use eminent domain powers unless they are for public use. The bill defines public use as mass transit, rail, seaports or airports, utility projects and brownfields. It also calls for a state-by-state study on the nationwide use of eminent domain. Bill sponsors are New Jersey Representative Scott Garrett and Missouri Senator Kit Bond.

HR 4128, the Private Property Rights Protection Act of 2005. It passed the House by a margin of 376–38, and prohibits a state or locality from using eminent domain for economic development or subsequent economic development if the state or locality gets federal economic development funds. So even if the taking is completely in accordance with the state's own statutes and ordinances, the state will lose all federal economic development funds for a period of two fiscal years after a court determines there has been a violation.

HR 4128 also revokes states' constitutionally granted 11th Amendment sovereign immunity and permits private rights of action in state or federal court. Wisconsin Representative James Sensenbrenner is the sponsor.

HR 3405, the Strengthening the Ownership of Private Property Act of 2005. Approved by the House Agriculture Committee by a vote of 40-1, it withholds federal economic development funds if a state or locality uses eminent domain for private commercial development or fails to pay relocation costs to displaced property owners. An amendment limits penalties for two years and allows municipalities to "cure" the violation by returning the properties. The bill's sponsor is Texas Representative Henry Bonilla.

S 1313, the Protection of Homes, Small Businesses and Private Property Act of 2005. This bill would preempt state eminent domain authority by permitting it to be used only for a "public use." It applies to all state and local eminent domain authority that involves federal funding. The bill is in committee. Texas Senator John Cornyn is the sponsor.

There are other bills out there: HR 3083 from Montana Representative Dennis Rehberg, HR 3087 and HR 3268 sponsored by Georgia Representative Phil Gingrey, HR 2980 from Colorado Representative Tom Tancredo and HR 3315 sponsored by California Representative Maxine Waters.

—Susan Parnas Frederick, NCSL

To take away a city's power to change that means huge areas of blight would remain just that, and would probably only grow larger."

Eminent domain as a tool has been around since the beginning of the Republic. "It is hard to imagine how we would have grown and expanded as a country without eminent domain," says Jon Santemma, the author of "Condemnation Law and Procedures in New York," who also served on the commission that wrote the eminent domain procedure law for the state.

"The growth of the railroad industry would probably never have taken place in the 1800s had it not been for eminent domain, which gave it land to build on," Santemma says. The same can be said of the Tennessee Valley Authority and the first interstate highway network.

But these were public projects, and using eminent domain to acquire property was usually an orderly process with owners selling at a fair market price or through a process of just compensation.

"For years most people really have not paid much attention to this process," says Richard Epstein, a professor of law at the University of Chicago and the author of *Takings—Private Property and the Power of Eminent Domain.*

"Those who were subject to eminent domain accepted the reasons the government gave for wanting to acquire their land," says Epstein. "If there was a battle it had to do with how much the property was worth."

Los Angeles attorney Gary Kovavic says he's been practicing eminent domain law in relative obscurity for 29 years. "Most of that time litigation has centered around things like what is the fair market value of the property or what is the fair market value of the improvements to the property."

But in recent years, Kovavic says a growing percentage of litigation revolves around challenges to the practice of eminent domain. "That was almost unthinkable a generation ago."

Success and Failure

Along its historic waterfront, beginning in the late 1970s, the city of Baltimore launched what has been since hailed as one of the most successful uses of eminent domain. The city acquired some 150 acres of blighted and abandoned properties, including existing businesses, to make way for an urban renovation that included the Rouse company's Harborplace, which would go on to win applause from city planners around the world.

Baltimore was not only able to open up large swaths of land—some of which contained houses from the 18th century—for redevelopment, it was also able to realign city streets so that they would create an easy access to the waterfront.

"The amazing story of Baltimore's revitalization would never have taken place had it not been for the city's willingness to use eminent domain," says Rob Puentes, a fellow with the Brookings Institute's Metropolitan Policy Program.

"In fact, the challenges faced by Baltimore were typical of the challenges faced by many cities in the east and both the older suburban areas and the small towns of the Midwest that have simply run out of room to grow," says Puentes. "The only way they can get a handle on blight and limited growth is to target large sections of the city where redevelopment can only take place if what is already there is removed."

A less successful use of eminent domain, coming just as Baltimore unveiled its Harborplace, occurred in Poletown, a section of Detroit. Some 1,000 homes and 600 businesses in a predominantly Eastern European community were razed to make way for a new General Motors plant.

In 2004 the Michigan Supreme Court, reviewing the process by which eminent domain was used, agreed in a unanimous decision that the local government was "without constitutional authority to condemn the properties." Hundreds of residents said they did not want to leave Poletown and were forced out. But the court decision was too late for them. Most of Poletown's houses and businesses had long since been destroyed.

What separates Baltimore and Poletown from New London, contends New York attorney Jon Santemma, is that "the property in New London was not really blighted or debilitated at all. It was a low-income but stable neighborhood on the waterfront with families who had lived in the same house for generations."

"If eminent domain can be used in a place like New London," says Santemma, "does that mean it can be used almost anywhere else? What are the limits to its use? Is any house safe?"

Even before the *Kelo* decision, some states had been asking themselves those very questions. Arkansas, Florida, Illinois, Kentucky, Maine, Montana, South Carolina and Washington all have court decisions forbidding the use of eminent domain when the purpose is not to eliminate blight.

Since *Kelo*, Alabama, Delaware, Ohio and Texas have passed laws that restrict the use of eminent domain for private development. Alabama Senator Jack Biddle says he was inspired to propose legislation after eminent domain was used in his legislative district: "They just came in and put a bunch of individual stores out of business so that they could make way for a Wal-Mart," Biddle says. "And I didn't like that. None of these stores even had a choice and some of them had been there for 15 or 20 years."

Passed unanimously, Biddle says his bill means that "eminent domain can no longer be used for any for-profit business. It can only be applied to a genuinely declared area of blight—and it has to be that."

In Kansas, Senate Majority Leader Derek Schmidt and Senator Greta Goodwin have proposed a constitutional amendment guaranteeing that private property cannot be taken through eminent domain except for a public use.

"I think the whole issue of eminent domain has become scary to people," says Goodwin. "And this being a rural state where people greatly value their land makes the issue even more important to us."

In Maryland, Delegate David Boschert also is backing a constitutional amendment limiting the state's ability to seize private property for public use only.

"This is becoming one of the most hot-button issues I have ever seen at the state level," says Boschert. "We are hearing more and more about it from our constituents who are upset and angry. And I think they have a right to be."

But others urge caution.

In Connecticut, which generally has been supportive of the use of eminent domain for private development, Representative Michael Lawlor says lawmakers should proceed carefully when it comes to getting rid of a power that can be used for revitalizing economically depressed neighborhoods.

"You want to have the ability to take property if it is necessary to achieve a greater goal," says Lawlor. "But the process by which you accomplish that and the amount of money you have to pay in order to do it ought to be carefully thought out."

Lawlor said he is particularly concerned about public projects that may include private development. Should eminent domain be prohibited in such cases?

"A public economic development project is a lot different than a private developer trying to put in something like a mall," says Lawlor. "Should we really allow one or two property owners to hold out and demand a price so high that they could stop a project altogether? Should we risk creating opportunities for speculators to come in and buy up property and then hold out for top dollar when they sell? I think the potential for abuse exists on both sides."

Caught between trying to promote economic development, particularly in blighted areas, and protecting the rights of homeowners, some lawmakers have decided to take a second look at the process of eminent domain in their states. It is a move that is winning the support of advocates on both sides of the issue.

"It would be wrong to take away the power of eminent domain completely," says Los Angeles attorney Kovacic, who also sits on the city council of Arcadia, Calif. "But I don't think there is anything wrong with inserting as many protections into the process as you can. We can develop rules for making certain the property in question is really blighted. We can require such decisions be made by only a supermajority of the public body that votes on it."

Making certain the process is more open, thinks Puentes of Brookings' Metropolitan Policy Program, "will actually in the long run be good for both sides. It will mean that everyone will have been listened to. It will make it more likely that solutions can be found through negotiation rather than the court room."

GARRY BOULARD, a frequent contributor to *State Legislatures* magazine, is a freelance writer from Albuquerque, N.M.

A Patchwork of Immigration Laws

Conflicting state and local policies complicate federal action, some say.

ANTHONY FAIOLA

In New York, state officials are about to offer driver's licenses to illegal immigrants and already have extended limited medical coverage to those battling cancer. In Illinois, the state legislature just passed a law forbidding businesses there from using a federal database to check the legal status of employees.

Oklahoma, meanwhile, recently passed some of the toughest immigration laws in the nation, including one making it a felony to "transport" or "harbor" an illegal immigrant—leading some to fear that people such as school bus drivers and church pastors may be at risk of doing time. Tennessee's legislature this year revoked laws granting illegal immigrants "driving certificates" and voted to allow law enforcement officers to effectively act as a state immigration police.

As the Bush administration and Congress sit gridlocked on an immigration overhaul, states are jumping into the debate as never before. In the process, they are creating a national patchwork of incongruous immigration laws that some observers fear will make it far more difficult to enact any comprehensive, federally mandated bill down the line.

The number of states passing immigration-related bills has skyrocketed this year. No fewer than 1,404 pieces of immigration-related legislation were introduced in legislatures during the first half of 2007, with 182 bills becoming law in 43 states. That is more than double the number of immigration-related state laws enacted during all of 2006, according to the National Conference of State Legislatures.

Some observers are alarmed by the trend, calling the widely divergent laws further evidence of America's cultural divide and saying they could pose new hurdles in reaching a national consensus on immigration. Piecemeal policymaking is opening the door to a flurry of legal battles–the Department of Homeland Security, for instance, is suing Illinois for banning businesses there from confirming an employee's legal status through the federal E-Verify database, which state officials have called flawed and unreliable.

Others argue that the inability to reach a national solution has left states no choice. Governors are grappling with cities and towns that, in the absence of a national or state policy, have taken it upon themselves to pass local immigration laws either protecting or cracking down on illegal immigrants. This has occasionally led to radically different regulations within individual states.

Still others assert that the rush of state activism has created an unforeseen opportunity. By viewing states as laboratories and studying the successes and failures of their various policies, Americans may find useful information, even a road map, for developing a national strategy.

Perhaps the most compelling current example is Oklahoma, where a package of tough new laws will not only make it a crime to transport or harbor illegal immigrants, but will also strip such immigrants of any right to receive most health care, welfare, scholarships or other government assistance; penalize employers who hire illegal workers; and force businesses to verify the legal status of new hires.

That "comports with my philosophy that illegal aliens will not come to Oklahoma or any other state if there are no jobs waiting for them," said Randy Terrill, a Republican state legislator and the author of the bill. "They will not stay here if they know they will get no taxpayer subsidy, and they will not stay here if they know if they ever come into contact with one of our fine law enforcement officers, they will stay in custody until they are physically deported."

Hispanic business groups, citing school enrollment losses and church parish figures, say the laws, which start going into effect later this year, have caused as many as 25,000 undocumented workers to flee the state in recent months. The loss is being decried by the Oklahoma State Home Builders Association.

"In major metro areas we are seeing people leave based on the perception that things are going to get bad for them and that this state doesn't want them here," said Mike Means, executive vice president of the association. "Now we're looking at a labor shortage. I've got builders who are being forced to slow down jobs because they don't have the crews. And it's not like these people are going back to Mexico. They're going to Texas, New Mexico, Kansas, Arkansas, anywhere where the laws aren't against them."

Means said that while construction wages haven't yet gone up in Oklahoma, they are likely to do so if the shortage worsens. Advocates of such laws say that is precisely how strict regulations on illegal immigration can help American workers—by forcing wages higher. But construction industry leaders counter that a wage increase in Oklahoma, where builders are already paying $15 to $20 an hour for labor in a state with low unemployment, would lead to a net loss of jobs as some businesses are forced to close, particularly if other states allow less stringent hiring practices.

"This is what happens when you don't have a national policy," Means continued. "If I'm an Oklahoma builder on the border with Texas, you're going to face unfair competition because they don't have the laws we do. This needs to be standardized."

While local governments have been enacting a growing number of pro- and anti-immigration ordinances, states, with notable exceptions such as California, have until recently been more cautious. Experts say that is partly because achieving consensus on a state level is far harder than in smaller communities, but also because many states have awaited guidance from the federal government.

But as state officials have concluded that they can no longer afford not to act, they are often finding that doing so is an invitation for discord.

That is particularly true in New York, where Democratic Gov. Eliot L. Spitzer, the former attorney general who championed labor rights for immigrants, touched off a firestorm after announcing last month that he was reversing pre-Sept. 11 rules that had made it virtually impossible for illegal immigrants in the state to obtain a driver's license.

"The federal government has failed to establish a coherent or rational policy, and as a consequence, we are left to deal with this on a state level," Spitzer said in an interview with *The Washington Post.* "We're left dealing with the reality of up to 1 million [illegal] immigrants in New York. . . . I would prefer to have [them] carrying a legitimate form of identification, a driver's license that allows them to get insurance, allows our law enforcement to track their driving records and brings these drivers out of the shadows."

The ruckus over the policy change has been particularly heated because several of the Sept. 11, 2001, hijackers used illegally obtained driver's licenses as identification when renting vehicles or boarding flights. Spitzer argues that his plan will make it harder to get a license illegally, by requiring new electronic equipment in motor vehicles offices across New York to verify foreign passports and other documents used to obtain a license.

But many here counter that no matter what equipment is used, granting driver's licenses with a foreign passport as a primary proof of identity constitutes a significant security threat. Still others argue against the notion that illegal immigrants should be awarded any kind of government-issued identification.

Opposition is so fierce, particularly among state Republicans, that a handful of county clerks have publicly rebelled. Several have said they will instruct their driver's license offices—many of which are staffed by county, not state, employees—to disregard the new guidelines. And the Monroe County government, near Rochester, has gone as far as voting to continue making a valid Social Security number a requirement for a driver's license, setting up a potential legal showdown with the state.

"The government is trying to bring them into the fold, but how can you extend a privilege to drive legally in the United States to someone who is here illegally?" asked Frank J. Merola, the Republican clerk of Rensselaer County, near the state capital, Albany. "I'm not saying, 'Let's go out there and round them up,' but I am saying that it's wrong to reward them for breaking the law."

Not surprisingly, the plan, to go into effect in phases within eight months, is being hailed by New York's thriving immigrant community. A 33-year-old Manhattan lounge singer who would provide only his first name, Amilcar, because he arrived in the United States illegally from Mexico, said he has had to turn down numerous offers for work in New Jersey and elsewhere because he could not drive himself and was unable to afford the cost of transporting his equipment.

"But this is going to open new doors for me now," he says excitedly, noting that he has already made plans to buy a car. "I feel like having a driver's license is a going to be a great new freedom. It's why I came to America in the first place."

ANTHONY FAIOLA is a *Washington Post* staff writer. *Washington Post* staff writer Robin Shulman in New York contributed to this report.

Devolution's Double Standard

Alan Ehrenhalt

Somewhere in America, I suppose, there is a public official who believes unreservedly in devolution—believes that power, autonomy and flexibility should reside as far down in the governmental system as practically possible—and is willing to act on the basis of those beliefs, even at the expense of his own political authority.

I have a pretty clear sense of how such a politician would behave; I just never seem to come across one, no matter where in the hierarchy of government I happen to look.

An honest devolutionist would be a president who refused to impose billion-dollar burdens on the states without offering any money to pay for them. Or a governor who didn't find it clever policy to avoid a tax increase at the state level by forcing one on localities. Or a Supreme Court justice who made it a consistent practice to let legislatures enact pretty much any statute they wanted, as long as it didn't involve a blatant violation of the U.S. Constitution. We have no shortage of politicians in America who profess to believe in devolution, and invoke it regularly. What we don't have are public figures willing to follow the concept wherever it might lead.

When it's just a matter of theory, devolution commands virtually unanimous acceptance, all across the ideological spectrum. Devolution has a rich intellectual history in the Roman Catholic Church, where it goes by the name of "subsidiarity"—the principle that, as Pope John Paul II once put it, "a community of a higher order should not interfere with the life of a community of a lower order." There is language endorsing subsidiarity in virtually every document and treaty drawn up to create the current European Union.

On the American left, devolution was an article of faith in the 1960s for the radical Students for a Democratic Society, who saw it as a route to a new kind of participatory democracy through which "our monster cities...might now be humanized, broken into smaller communities...arranged according to community decision."

Much more familiarly, the Reagan administration in the 1980s, and most conservative Republicans in the years since, have taken it as a similarly self-evident truth that the best government is government close to the people, that the states are closer to the people than Washington is and the localities closer still. The 2000 Republican Party platform vows to restore the force of the 10th Amendment to the U.S. Constitution—the amendment that says any powers not specifically granted to the federal government belong to the states. The platform calls that amendment "the best protection the American people have against federal intrusion and bullying."

The Republicans made this vow just a few months after their House and Senate majorities passed a bill forbidding states to collect sales tax on Internet transactions, without a fig-leaf of an explanation why this was any of the federal government's business. It was a devolution-professing Democratic president, a former governor himself, who signed this measure into law.

One might have expected something different from George W. Bush, a conservative governor of Texas who spent six years in Austin bristling at federal intrusion into his state's affairs. But no such outburst of intellectual consistency was forthcoming.

The Bush administration's No Child Left Behind Act, passed with bipartisan support in 2001, imposes on state and local school systems the burden of administering millions of standardized tests whose cost may eventually be as high as $8 billion. A true believer in devolution might wonder what the federal government is doing in the pupil-testing business. Even an innocent reader of the Republican platform would be entitled to ask why, if the feds think such a burdensome mandate upon the states is really in the national interest, they don't at least have the courtesy to pay for it.

Those arguments didn't gain much headway when the nation's governors showed up in Washington earlier this year to plead for help with their own state deficits, caused to a significant degree by a long list of federal mandates and by the soaring expense of Medicaid, which is a joint state-federal responsibility. "We've got an issue with our own budget," the president told the governors. In other words: You're on your own. Deal with it. But keep those multiple-choice tests coming.

It's enough to make you feel genuinely sorry for the states—until you see them treating their own cities and counties the same way. Last year, North Carolina Governor Mike Easley closed a hole in the state budget by seizing more than $200 million in tax money that had been legally earmarked for local health care, education and criminal justice needs. Wisconsin Governor Jim Doyle proposed last month to cut state aid to localities by nearly $100 million, arguing that cities and counties should find a way to provide police and fire services at lower cost.

Doyle claimed credit for avoiding the humiliation of a state tax increase and warned the localities not to try any tax increases of their own. But the likelihood is that the locals will have to increase property taxes this year just to pay for the services they are required to deliver. They have no choice.

This doesn't just apply to fiscal issues. In Colorado, one of the states most fiercely protective of individual rights and state prerogatives, pro-gun legislators have been trying for the past four years to pass a law requiring local communities to legalize the carrying of concealed weapons, whether the local governments want it legalized or not. What right does the state have to preempt local gun laws? None of the proponents of this change have developed much skill at answering this question. Sam Mamet, a lobbyist for the Colorado Municipal League, has it just about right: "When Congress preempts the states," he says, "these state lawmakers squeal like stuck pigs. And in many cases they're right. And now they're doing it to us."

Nobody is innocent here. The feds stiff the states. The states stiff the cities and counties. Whenever one layer of government can push an unpleasant or costly responsibility down to the level below, it nearly always does so. The cities and counties would do it too, except they are on the bottom rung. They can't cut taxes and services and then pin the responsibility on the Salvation Army. Or at least they haven't thought of that yet.

I suppose if there is one public official in America who deserves to be taken seriously as a consistent devolutionist, it is William Rehnquist, the chief justice of the U.S. Supreme Court. Rehnquist has been a vocal advocate of states' rights since his days as a law clerk in the early 1950s, when he argued that the court's decision in *Brown v. Board of Education* went too far in imposing federal power in defiance of the 10th Amendment.

Nobody can accuse Rehnquist of forgetting about devolution once he acquired a robe of his own. In the past decade, he has ruled against a whole series of congressional statutes, in areas as diverse as gun regulation and sexual abuse of women, on the grounds that the "interstate commerce" language used to justify them provided insufficient reason to constrict state authority.

I'm willing to take Rehnquist seriously as a man who believes in devolution and wants to implement it. Still, when he steps down as chief justice, what will he be best known for: his narrow construction of federal regulatory power, or his court's vague, partisan and dubious use of the federal Equal Protection Clause to overrule the Florida Supreme Court and award the 2000 presidential election to the popular-vote loser, George W. Bush?

It is easy to portray all of these ironies as yet another example of the strong picking on the weak. But there's a dirty little secret here: In a federal system, unreasonable demands from above aren't a sign of strength. They're a sign of weakness.

When the system actually works, as it occasionally does, the leaders at the top of the pyramid do one of two things. They take up a problem, conceive a solution and figure out a way to pay for it—as the feds did with Social Security in the 1930s. Or they withdraw completely and allow lower-level governments to launch the experiments and make the rules. This is essentially what happened with welfare reform, arguably the most successful public policy initiative of the past decade.

When neither of these things happens—when one level of government simply dumps a problem on the level below, it's usually because underneath the bluster, those at the top are clueless about what to do. If the feds had any clear idea how to improve the performance of American education, they'd be promoting it. They wouldn't be telling state and local school systems to spend billions of dollars on standardized tests and then to punish the slackers.

If the U.S. Department of Homeland Security had a coherent vision of what a secure homeland actually was, it would be issuing precise directives to local responders and letting them know how much the work would cost. It wouldn't be barking out useless warnings and issuing color-coded alerts and promising that a check would be in the mail sometime in the future.

And when governors and legislatures boast about holding the line on taxes—when the truth is they are merely forcing higher taxes on those below—that's a form of weakness as well. It's a failure of the political will that democratic governments are supposed to have.

Any mandate from above, unaccompanied by the resources to help comply with it, is a scary experience for those on the receiving end. But it can also be an opportunity: to experiment, innovate and discover that there might be a way to get the job done more efficiently after all. Sometimes it turns out that the forces at the top aren't as powerful as they pretend to be.

UNIT 3
Linkages Between Citizens and Governments

Unit Selections

Key Points to Consider

- If you were the head of an interest group, would you use different techniques to try and influence the state government office-holders rather than try and influence their local government counterparts? Why or why not? How would the techniques differ according to the level you choose to influence?

- How do you think running for elective office in a small town differs from running for a seat in a state legislature or running for a seat in the U.S. Congress?

- Do you think people are more or less knowledgeable when they vote in state and local elections than in national elections? Why?

- Which level of government seems most responsive to citizens—the national, state, or local? Why?

- Do you think citizens should be allowed to participate in policy making through the initiative and referenda processes? Why or why not? What do you think about allowing citizens to recall officials during their term in office?

Student Web Site
www.mhcls.com/online

Internet References
Direct Democracy Center
http://www.realdemocracy.com/
PEJ Local TV News Project
http://www.journalism.org/resources/research/reports/localTV/default.asp
U.S. Federalism Web Site
http://www.usconstitution.net/consttop_fedr.html

The American political system is typically classified as a representative democracy. Top officials are elected by the people and, as a result, government is supposed to be responsive and accountable to the citizens. Both the theory and the practice of representative democracy are of interest to students of American politics. Political scientists study various features that seem essential to the functioning of a representative democracy: political parties, interest groups, election laws, campaign techniques, and so forth. Attention is not limited to the national government alone, the state and local governments are also examined in order to assess their responsiveness and accountability.

State and local governments operate under somewhat different institutional arrangements and circumstances than the national government. In many states and some localities, voters can participate directly in the policy process through mechanisms known as initiatives and referenda. In addition, some state and local voters can participate in removing elected officials from office by a procedure called recall. In many localities in the New England states, an annual open meeting of all local citizens, called a town meeting, functions as the local government legislature. These mechanisms provide additional avenues for citizens to influence the state and local governments.

Generally speaking, party organization is strongest at the local level and weakest at the national level. Party "machines" is a well-known feature of the local political landscape in the United States, and colorful and powerful "bosses" have left their mark on the local political history. While the heyday of bosses and machines is past, examples of contemporary political machines still exist. National elections, especially for the presidency, are usually contested vigorously by the two major parties and, over the long haul, the two parties tend to be reasonably competitive. This is less true in the states and localities, because voters in some states and many localities are decidedly oriented toward one party or the other. Thus, in some states and localities, closer and more significant competition can occur within the nominating process of the dominant party than between two parties as in general elections.

Party labels do not appear on the ballot in many localities, and this may or may not affect the way elections are conducted. In "nonpartisan" elections, candidates of different parties may, in fact, openly oppose one another, just as they do when party labels appear on the ballot. Another possibility is that parties field opposing candidates in a less than open fashion. As yet another alternative, elective office may actually be contested for without the parties or the political affiliations of candidates playing any part in it. One cannot assume that formally nonpartisan

© Stockbyte/Getty Images

elections are accompanied by genuine nonpartisanship, nor can one assume that they are entirely not.

One last feature of the political processes at the state and local level deserves mention here. While members of the Senate and the House of Representatives in Washington, D.C., hold well-paid, prestigious positions, their state and local counterparts often do not. Many state legislators are only part-time politicians who earn the bulk of their livelihoods from other sources. This is also true of most general-purpose local government officials. In addition, most local school board members are unpaid, even though many devote long hours to their duties. That so many elected state and local officeholders do not get their primary incomes from their positions in government may well affect the way they respond to constituents. After all, while they and their families typically live in the community that they are representing, their livelihoods do not depend on being re-elected.

Selections in the first section of this unit focus on elections, parties, and interest groups. The second section treats referenda, initiatives, and recalls—the three procedures that give voters in many states and localities a direct role in determining government policies and overseeing the performances of elected officials during their terms in office—as well as public meetings at which citizens can voice their views. The third section covers news media in the context of the state and local governments.

On the Oregon Trail

In a backlash against new electronic calamities, vote by mail spreads far beyond its roots, one county at a time.

SAM ROSENFELD

Oregon's statewide vote-by-mail system remains unique—for now. But with little fanfare, liberalized absentee balloting laws elsewhere have prompted a steady expansion of mail voting. In the process, popular support is growing, from the ground up. States are following the gradualist pattern of expansion first set in Oregon. Laws permitting at-will absentee registration in dozens of states, and permanent absentee registration policies in California and elsewhere, are expanding the pool of voters who know and like the process.

Meanwhile, in Arizona, Colorado, and Washington, municipalities and counties have won the option to run all vote-by-mail elections for various contests. More local election administrators are opting for mail balloting to save money and simplify the process. Oregon eventually reached a tipping point of popular support that pushed the entire state to vote by mail; most observers think Washington state has now reached the same point, and other western states are close behind.

This election year may turn out to be the catalytic moment for the expansion of mail voting. Pressure from looming Help America Vote Act (HAVA) and state-level compliance requirements, combined with the continued headaches associated with implementing and securing electronic voting systems, are provoking registrars and election officials in many states to advocate switching to a system that simplifies the process, saves money, and addresses major logistical and security concerns. Meanwhile, for the first time, advocates are organizing nationally and providing cross-state support and coordination for efforts to spread mail voting. Given the ground-level trends, vote-by-mail proponents feel the wind at their backs.

Electoral Quakes

California represents the biggest and least noticed expansion of absentee balloting. The turning point for the Golden State was 2001's enactment of permanent no-excuse absentee voting. Between 2002 and 2005, use of mail voting shot up statewide by more than a million votes, with absentee ballots accounting for 27 percent of votes cast in 2002, 33 percent in 2004, and 40 percent in 2005's special election. As use has expanded especially quickly in liberal counties, absentee voting's traditional Republican tilt has diminished. (The GOP-Democratic share of the absentee ballot vote was 47 to 41 percent in 1992; in 2005 it was 41 to 41 percent.)

While voters value the convenience, registrars actively encourage absentee voting to relieve administrative costs. "The voters are flocking to voting by mail in droves," reports Elaine Ginnold, registrar of voters for Alameda County, population 1.5 million, which includes the cities of Berkeley and Oakland. Absentee ballots accounted for 36 percent of Alameda's votes in 2004 and 47 percent in 2005's special election.

A state law passed in 2004 requires that electronic machines be equipped with paper trail printers for contemporaneous ballot verification by the voter. Counties across California had already procured machines that lacked such printers, and this year the secretary of state's office took too long to certify new machines for several counties to complete the procurement process in time for June. ("It's $12.7 million down the toilet," remarks Ginnold, referring to 4,000 noncompliant Diebold machines sitting in a warehouse in Alameda County.) Meanwhile, a lawsuit filed this year by California voters and activists seeking to block use of Diebold equipment in the June primary reflects the continued unease electronic machines inspire among significant numbers of voters.

Absentee ballots could well surpass 50 percent of the total California vote share in November. Ginnold sees 60 percent mail voting—which California might reach by the 2008 election—as a tipping point, when popular support will finally prompt either a ballot initiative to make the state all vote by mail or the reticent state legislature to give counties the option to run all-vote-by-mail elections. Either option, Ginnold says, would lead to universal vote by mail statewide. "I think what happened in Oregon is eventually going to happen here."

Going National

Oregon's neighbor to the north, meanwhile, is set to attain all vote-by-mail status imminently, having granted counties the option of choosing comprehensive vote by mail. Permanent-registration absentee balloting was first introduced in Washington state for disabled and elderly voters in the mid-1980s. It was expanded as an option for all voters, with no excuse required, early in the 1990s. "Many counties started having 75 to 85 percent of their voters choosing it," recalls Sam Reed, Washington's Republican secretary of state and a longtime proponent of vote by mail. "So last year I requested a bill to allow counties to exercise an option to go all vote by mail."

So far 34 out of 39 counties have opted for the system, and King County, encompassing Seattle and a full third of the state's registered voters, will likely do so by mid-2007. Most observers predict the remaining four counties will follow suit, and that by 2008, Washington will be the second state in the country to conduct all statewide elections by mail.

Until this year, no national advocacy outfit existed to help accelerate such absentee voting trends and leverage them to boost support for all-vote-by-mail systems. Political consultant Adam J. Smith has stepped into the organizational breach with the Portland-based Vote By Mail Project. Oregon Secretary of State Bill Bradbury serves on its board, and the outfit receives institutional and financial backing from the National Association of Letter Carriers (for obvious reasons, a major proponent of mail voting).

"We're going to support the whole continuum of vote by mail," says Smith, "from no excuse permanent absentee registration, to county option vote by mail, to statewide vote by mail. The natural progression seems to be you need to introduce the issue to people and give them the opportunity to vote this way, and inevitably the majority of people will decide they like it better." States in his sights include not only California but also Arizona, Colorado, and New Mexico—all places where liberalized absentee laws have sparked expanded use of mail balloting in recent years. Meanwhile, the recently formed Progressive Legislative Action Network is also planning to push for liberalized absentee and universal vote-by-mail laws.

Recorders in Arizona's two biggest counties estimate that 60 percent of their ballots for the 2006 midterms will be cast by mail. Phoenix and Tucson will also be holding all-vote-by-mail local elections. Meanwhile, a movement to put a statewide vote-by-mail initiative on the 2006 ballot was born when Rick Murphy, an Arizona Republican businessman, lost a congressional primary challenge in 2004 to Christian right darling Trent Franks. "It became quite obvious to Rick that the system was broken," says Fred Taylor, state director of Your Right to Vote and Murphy's partner in the vote-by-mail ballot initiative. "With a very small minority of the voters, you can win a primary election when there's such a low turnout. Rick wants to see a system that boosts engagement and dilutes the power of interest groups."

It's still early to gauge Murphy and Taylor's prospects in Arizona, but Colorado's experience in 2002 amply illustrates the pitfalls of moving too quickly for statewide change. That year, Democrat Rutt Bridges campaigned for a ballot initiative to make the entire state all vote by mail at a time when counties did not have the option to use the system and voters generally lacked experience with it. Like the majority of ballot initiatives on any issue in any election, it failed. Bridges now reflects that

states should follow a more gradualist strategy for achieving vote by mail, something Colorado has demonstrated since the 2002 loss.

Beginning in 2004, counties gained the option to run all non-partisan elections by mail in Colorado. This year, as in California, federal HAVA requirements for voting machine standards and accessibility are putting a crushing bind on county election officials and provoking requests—initiated by Denver County in February—for waivers to run vote-by-mail elections.

According to a survey of election clerks and counters, counties representing more than 80 percent of the voters in Colorado support switching to vote by mail for the midterm elections to avoid the regulatory chaos of HAVA compliance. If granted by the legislature, these would be onetime emergency waivers, but the record in other states demonstrates that further experience with mail voting invariably boosts public support for expanding the system.

Electronic Hell

Thirty states have spent more than $300 million since 2002 in federal funds to replace punch-card and lever machines with updated voting technology. Certainly there are places where the shift to direct recording electronic (DRE) systems occurred early, went smoothly, and met with general public satisfaction. And, as defenders of electronic voting technology like Ohio State's Daniel Tokaji emphasize, DRE machines do constitute a net improvement over punch-card and lever voting in terms of promoting accessibility and lowering miscount rates. But overall, the process of implementing the system in localities across the country has been marred by more difficulties than most could have imagined, contributing to a debilitating crisis of public confidence in electronic voting technology.

A 2004 North Carolina election for state agricultural commissioner, which collapsed in the wake of a major DRE programming glitch in Carteret County, served as a rallying cry for critics of electronic voting. Last December, election officials and computer experts in Florida's Leon County tested machines provided by Diebold and showed that election results could be manipulated from within the Elections Office with relative ease—and with no one knowing. Diebold responded by cutting off any communication with the county elections supervisor who'd instigated the test. Primary elections this March in Texas and Illinois, where DRE machines were used for the first time on a large scale in many localities, were the latest to be marred by major glitches in the tabulations, due to both machine errors and inadequate poll-worker training.

Also in March, Maryland made the stunning decision to dump its $90 million investment in Diebold machines due to the lack of a paper-auditing trail that could facilitate recounts. The paper-trail issue is a key fulcrum for organized resistance to electronic technology. Twenty-five states now have requirements for voter-verified paper audit trails (VVPAT) like the one in California, which are provoking major bureaucratic complications as officials attempt to graft printing technologies on to pre-existing electronic machines.

Problems with compliance provide the context for lawsuits against electronic voting machine vendors in five states beyond

California. Meanwhile, a lobbying coalition of DRE skeptics gathered on Capitol Hill the first week of April to push for Democrat Rush Holt's bill mandating VVPAT for all electronic machines, programming that allows for independent audits, and hand-counted verification for 2 percent of all ballots cast.

HAVA Heart

As Tokaji himself has demonstrated, grafting VVPAT technology on to existing electronic systems is not only proving to be cumbersome and logistically problematic, it also doesn't provide the panacea to security concerns that advocates think it does. VVPAT provisions heighten the complexity of the voting process, and handcount audits of select ballots have proven to be enormously time-consuming for election officials in places like Nevada, where it has been attempted.

Unfortunately, the response to these dilemmas by many election experts and consultants, invested as they are in the push to "make HAVA work," has been to try to reform electronic voting by plunging ever deeper into the logistical weeds of DRE compliance. Speaking at an American University conference on election reform held in late March, Tokaji listed at least four different teams of researchers and consultants, spanning various universities as well as the National Science Foundation and the National Academy of Sciences, who would be monitoring the 2006 elections and proposing further reforms.

HAVA has spawned a whole techno-academic-industrial complex. At the same conference, voting security expert Avi Rubin of ACCURATE (A Center for Correct, Usable, Reliable, Auditable, and Transparent Elections) proposed a truly daunting array of new reforms to ensure the integrity of electronic voting, from rendering all electronic systems interoperable and their coding open source, to mandating regular "threat analysis, code review, architectural analysis, and penetration testing"—so as to ensure that the system "can be trusted to the same degree as critical military, medical, and banking systems."

But this endless regress, reminiscent of *Mad Magazine's* "Spy vs. Spy," may only be leading experts and officials deeper into electronic Rube Goldberg territory and further away from the basic election reform principles HAVA was meant to address in the first place. And this reality is a big part of the context for the expansion in the ranks of officials and voters on the ground, in state after state, who are coming to prefer a simpler, lower-tech balloting method—snail mail.

Back To The Future

The local and county-level stirrings in Colorado, Arizona, and California are precisely what the Vote by Mail Project hopes to identify and catalyze nationally. But chicken-and-egg questions about process and political culture linger: Does vote by mail work in Oregon and Washington because it's a universally desirable system or because the Pacific Northwest's historic tradition of clean elections allows it to work? Is vote by mail a desirable alternative for, say, a state like Ohio or Illinois—or might it provide new opportunities for fraud and suppression in states lacking clean civic cultures?

There's no real consensus among election experts on this question, but the record of expanded mail balloting in California, Colorado, and elsewhere is virtually free of fraud or major glitches. Leading critics of mail voting, like Curtis Gans, director of the Committee for the Study of the American Electorate, cite the heightened potential for vote buying in the mail-voting process, given the lack of a truly secret ballot. (Gans can, indeed, point to a local vote-buying scandal involving absentee ballots in 2003 city elections in northern Indiana.) But Oregon, Washington, and California have not reported any vote-buying incidents during the years that vote-by-mail use has expanded there, and sustaining such fraud on a large scale without detection would likely be prohibitively difficult. Moreover, to the extent such dangers and potential unknowns remain troubling, the gradual, locality-by-locality expansion of vote by mail thus far will help observers detect problems and make proper adjustments *before* a system is implemented across the board in a given state. "We're not comparing this against 'the perfect system'—that doesn't exist," Adam Smith points out. "Possible problems that might arise can be addressed through best practices."

Proponents note the procedural safeguards built into the Oregon system—most importantly a full registry of digitized signatures that election officials cross-check against voters' signatures on ballot envelopes—that neither exist in the traditional system nor depend for their effectiveness on the honesty and civic virtue of voters. "There are a number of ways to make vote by mail more secure than polling places," says Ann Martens, Secretary of State Bradbury's communications director in Oregon. "Our county elections officials are trained by former state police forensics experts in handwriting analysis ... [The signature cross-checking] goes through a number of levels where it's either accepted or we eventually contact the voter."

Indeed, the time and ability that vote by mail affords officials to actually contact voters about questionable ballots address a more typical progressive election concern than voter fraud—the prospect of indirect voter suppression by politicized election officials applying deliberately onerous standards to targeted demographics. What if a vote-by-mail official in, say, Ohio, was tempted to reject a significant number of ballots on spurious grounds that the envelope signature didn't match the digitized registration signature? "Checking the signatures is such a process, involving so many workers, it would be really hard to do something like that," says Smith. "Even if you could systematically weed out certain groups, all you're going to do at that point is not in fact disqualify those ballots but force people to prove that they're actually who they say they are. So there are ways to safeguard against that."

Advocates hasten to highlight the real-world polling-place scenarios that have played out in elections past, where perfectly legal neglect and shortchanging of resources on the part of election officials led to logistical bottlenecks in various localities—leading, in effect, to de facto voter suppression. The prospects of such Ohio-style scenarios recurring in future elections would be eliminated with vote by mail—as would the dangers, posed by electronic voting, of a logistical screw up or security breach without the capacity for a recount.

For More Information

Oregon Secretary of State Elections Division (www. sos.state.or.us/elections/). Also housed here: several independent evaluations of voting by mail. See: www.sos.state.or.us/executive/policy-initiatives/vbm/execvbm.htm.

BlackBoxVoting.org provides consumer protection for elections.

VoterAction.org opposes privatized, electronic voting systems.

VoteTrustUSA.org promotes election integrity nationally.

VoteByMailProject.org provides state-by-state updates on vote-by-mail options.

Electionline.org offers news and analysis on election reform.

FairVote.org promotes inclusion, turnout, fair practices.

League of Women Voters (lwv.org) provides citizen education.

Demos.org promotes broad participation and fair elections.

Another criticism of vote-by-mail systems (also voiced in opposition to early voting provisions) is that the greatly expanded period for voting leads to "differentials in knowledge" among voters. Some might send in their ballot a week and a half prior to Election Day, and an ensuing dramatic event or development may change the dynamics of the race, leaving those early voters unable to change their decisions. But any voting date, whether it lasts one day or two weeks, is arbitrary, and may occur immediately prior to major occurrences that would have changed the electoral result in retrospect. And to the extent that a longer period for voting discourages the late-breaking artificial gimmickry and vicissitudes of political campaigns (as transmuted through media narratives and political advertising), that's more of a plus than a minus. Certainly Oregon's experience hasn't shown much voter discontent with the time differentials in voting, just as the state's experience hasn't revealed any major problems with fraud or logistics. Nor have citizens among the swelling ranks of mail voters in states outside of Oregon.

Indeed, the movement for mail voting represents a striking reversal in a nation that has always been infatuated with new technology. It is proceeding through firsthand experience, county by county, voter by voter, in a fascinating democratic rebellion against both the traditional complications of poll-site voting as well as insecurities associated with newfangled electronic technology imposed from above.

Locking Up the Vote

Disenfranchisement of former prisoners was the real crime in Florida.

NICHOLAS THOMPSON

Rosetta Meeks lives in Florida's Miami-Dade County, but she didn't get to vote in the presidential election. Nobody scrutinized her ballot for hanging chads or screamed himself hoarse trying to prevent officials from counting it. An African-American woman who has devoted her last six years to teaching computer skills to low-income people, Meeks wanted to vote and knew whom she wanted to vote for. But she was locked out of the mayhem.

Rosetta Meeks was convicted of a drug felony seven and a half years ago and, under Florida law, every felon is permanently barred from the voting booth unless the governor and at least three of his cabinet members decide to restore her civil rights. Thirteen other states have similar laws: If you commit any felony—be it murder or lying on a customs form—you never again get to have a say in the election of the president or the town selectman. According to the best available estimates, this law kept 525,000 people in Florida, most of them poor and a great many of them black, away from the polls in a presidential election decided by just a few hundred votes.

Like most ex-felons, Meeks didn't meet all 23 of the qualifications for Florida's process of fast-track enfranchisement. The qualifications range from the type of crime you committed (you can't, for example, have been found guilty of battery of a public transit official) to your financial status (you can't owe the state more than $1,000, not uncommon for poor ex-felons who are often subjected to large fines and restitution payments, or required by judges to pay the fees of their state-appointed attorneys.)

So, to start her application for clemency, Meeks had to fill out a convoluted 16-page form with questions ranging from the invasive, like the date of birth of any person with whom she had a child out of wedlock, to the irrelevant, like the cause of death of her parents, to the potentially invidious, like the name and purpose of any organization she belongs to. Then on page 14 it asks "Have you ever been a defendant in civil litigation? Y/N—. If Yes, please describe in details." Directly below, it repeats the exact same question without the "please."

The state clemency board uses the form to conduct an investigation into the applicant's past. It then makes a recommendation on whether clemency should be granted and forwards the investigative report, which the applicant is never allowed to see, to Governor Jeb Bush. The governor, according to Florida law, has "unfettered discretion to deny clemency at any time for any reason."

According to Meeks, "They wanted to know my mother and father's names. They wanted to know what my parents died of. Does that really matter?" Apparently it does because the Florida Parole Commission recommended against her. "I made a mistake. I'm sorry. I abused the system by using drugs. When you are young, you do things that you shouldn't do. Do I have to pay for this for the rest of my life?" Meeks asks before adding: "I'm very proud of myself now. If I don't get the right to vote this time, I'm going to continue to try."

Meeks was persistent, and her story has a happy ending. She paid off her fines, and a local civil-rights organization lent her a car so she was able to drive nine hours north to appeal directly to the governor. Finally, the day after Al Gore conceded the election and more than two and a half years after she began her quest, Jeb Bush waved his hand and magically returned Meeks her right to vote.

But most other ex-felons are shut out. The Sunshine State restored civil rights to only 1,832 ex-felons last year, about 1 out of every 300 in the state. Florida officials say that they do not have this data broken down by race or class, but, pre-election at least, it didn't seem to hurt to be a white Republican. Chuck Colson, who had proposed that the Nixon administration firebomb the Brookings Institution and went to prison for his role in the Watergate scandal, was pardoned by Bush and, unlike Meeks, allowed to vote in November. A supporter of the governor's brother, Colson now runs a ministry to bring Christianity to inmates. "He's a great American," said Gov. Bush.

In Alabama, one out of every three black men is barred from voting for life.

Extended Sentence

The United States is virtually the only industrialized country that denies former prisoners the vote, though the rules vary by state. In Maine and Vermont, convicts can vote even when behind bars. In 34 states, felons are not allowed to vote until they leave parole. Maryland and Arizona permanently disqualify two-time felons; Washington bans felons convicted before 1984, and Tennessee bans felons convicted before 1986. And in 10 states, if you commit a single felony you are essentially walled off on Election Day until you die.

The result is that about one million Americans who have completed their sentences are disenfranchised. Nationally, one out of seven adult black men will never again get to vote. In Alabama, which permanently denies felons the right to vote, about one out of every three adult black men is barred for life. In an extensive study of two poor and mostly black communities in Tallahassee, Florida, criminal justice professor Todd Clear was unable to find a single family without at least one disenfranchised man—making it unlikely that the community will be able to band together when, for example, a state senator proposes locating a toxic waste dump nearby.

Felons, of course, aren't just murderers and muggers. Three out of every five felony convictions don't lead to jail time, and there's no clear line you have to cross to earn one. Being convicted for driving while intoxicated three times bans you from voting for life in numerous states. Stopping payment on a check of more than $150 with intent to defraud makes you a felon in Florida. Being caught with one-fifth of an ounce of crack earns you a federal felony, but being caught with one-fifth of an ounce of cocaine only earns a misdemeanor.

Having a good lawyer can get you off the hook or at least knock the charges down to a misdemeanor. But most poor people get stuck with overworked public defenders who don't make the grade. Last year, for example, the four public attorneys in Hernando County, Florida had to handle 1,568 felony cases. That's slightly better than the even more appalling numbers from years past, but Governor Bush has proposed a funding cut that threatens the promising trend, according to Florida Public Defender Association President Howard Babb, Jr..

Ball and Chain

Felon disenfranchisement doesn't fit any of the standard justifications for criminal punishment. It doesn't rehabilitate, no one has ever argued or found evidence that it deters crime, and it's an odd form of retribution. Unlike, say, taking someone's license away when he's caught driving drunk, there's no clear link between the punishment and the crime.

Advocates usually argue from moral grounds, beginning that voting is actually a privilege not a right. Next, they argue that people who have broken the laws shouldn't be involved in making them, and that ex-felons will vote in ways that harm society and influence criminal justice policy for the worse. But only the most rehabilitated felons are likely to choose to exercise their right and there is no evidence that they choose harmful policies, even in states that allow convicts to vote while in prison.

There's also a case that restoring voting rights helps ex-felons in at least a small way to restore dignity and sense of community. According to ex-felon Heywood Fennell, such denial is "a way of preparing the guillotine of despair and hopelessness for people coming out of prison into community. If you don't vote, you don't have any say on when the trash man is going to pick up the garbage. A vote is power, a way to be involved in the process and it helps give you the opportunity to rebuild your life."

To put it another way, denying the right to vote is just one more slap in the face to the 95 percent of prisoners who complete their sentences and eventually return to their communities. Despite our nation's sky-rocketing prison population, investment in rehabilitation has dropped. Numerous prisoners now finish their sentences without parole and are released with just a bus ticket home and about $150—no skills and no assistance finding employment. Giving them the right to vote alone won't save them from returning to crime, but it's free and it can't hurt. According to Alex Friedmann, recently released from jail in Tennessee: "If society doesn't care enough about former prisoners to treat them as citizens, with the voting rights of citizens, then why should former prisoners care enough about society to act like law-abiding citizens?"

Reconstruction Never Ended

As with so much of this country's past, a large part of the history of felon disenfranchisement hangs on the issue of race. It's no coincidence that blacks are harmed the most by felon disenfranchisement; many of the laws seem to have been drawn up for that purpose.

Many states disenfranchised criminals even before the Civil War. But in the South, after the Civil War and Reconstruction, legal codes were crafted to countermand the 14th and 15th amendments, which gave blacks equal protection under the law and gave black men the right to vote. In Mississippi, the convention of 1890 replaced laws disenfranchising all convicts with laws disenfranchising only people convicted of the crimes blacks were supposedly more likely to commit. For almost ar century thereafter you couldn't lose your right to vote in Mississippi if you committed murder or rape, but you could if you married someone of another race.

In Virginia, U.S. Senator Carter Glass worked to expand the disenfranchisement laws along with poll taxes and literacy tests. He described the state's 1901 convention as follows: "Discrimination! Why that is precisely what we propose. That, exactly, is what this Convention was elected for—to discriminate to the very extremity of permissible action under the limits of the Federal Constitution, with a view to the elimination of every Negro voter who can be gotten rid of legally, without materially impairing the numerical strength of the white electorate."

In Alabama, the criminal code in the constitution of 1901 was, according to the chair of the convention, designed to "ensure white supremacy," and crimes worthy of disenfranchisement were classified depending in large part by whether delegates thought blacks were likely to commit them. The state though was additionally focused on excluding poor whites. Delegates "wished to disfranchise most of the Negroes and the uneducated and propertyless whites in order to legally create a conservative electorate," wrote historian Malcolm McMillan.

In Florida, the constitution drafted in 1868 disenfranchised ex-felons as well as anyone convicted of larceny, a crime that courts were given special jurisdiction over in 1865 because of "the great increase in minor offenses, which may be reasonably anticipated from the emancipation of former slaves." The 1868 constitution only passed when conservatives took over the convention and annulled a constitution passed by blacks and radical Republicans which did not include a disenfranchisement clause.

The provisions that came out of those conventions, from poll taxes to grandfather clauses to literacy tests were almost all struck down by the Warren Court and the Civil Rights Act of 1965. The only one still standing is the felony provision—which isn't surprising since, as historian Morgan Kousser testified before the Supreme Court in 1985, the disenfranchisement laws provided Southern states with "insurance if courts struck down the more blatantly unconstitutional clauses." Of course, the literacy test resembles Rosetta Meeks' 16-page form, and the poll tax isn't a great deal different from Florida's requirement that felons pay off money owed to the state—potentially including the cost of a public defender provided them because of their poverty.

Of course, not all felon disenfranchisement laws originate in clearly racist movements, but the impact always falls disproportionately on blacks. Even in Iowa and Wyoming, for example, one in four black men is permanently disenfranchised. Blacks do commit a disproportionate share of the crime in this country. But they also suffer disproportionately from incompetent public defenders and discriminatory sentencing practices, such as the disparate penalties given to crack and cocaine possessors. Cocaine is the drug of choice in corporate bathrooms and blacks and whites are convicted of possession at about the same rate. Crack is the drug of choice in inner cities and blacks are about 25 times more likely to be arrested for possession, and thus to receive felony convictions and be barred from voting—a legal oddity which would undoubtedly have delighted Carter Glass.

Votes They Really Don't Want to Count

Regardless of intent, the disenfranchisement of felons seems to be successfully keeping politicians disliked by a majority of blacks in office. According to Jeff Manza and Christopher Uggen, sociologists who have done the most thorough studies available of ex-felon voting patterns based on class, income, geography, race, and scores of other factors, giving ex-felons the right to vote would have swung several races away from conservative Republicans over the past two decades. Conservative Senator John Warner (R-Va.) would never have entered office; Mitch McConnell (R-Ky.) wouldn't have been elected in 1988; Connie Mack (R-Fla.) would have been defeated in 1988. Phil Gramm (R-Tex.) and Craig Thomas (R-Wyo.) might

also never have been elected since their Republican predecessors would have lost. These five Senators received an average grade of 25 percent out of 100 on the NAACP's most recent voting scorecard.

Manza and Uggen also estimate that Al Gore would have defeated George W. Bush by between 10,000 and 85,000 votes in Florida—unsurprising since Bush only earned six percent of the black vote in that state. The ironic result is that a man who ran partly on the theme of redemption, and turned his life around at age 40, may well be president because civil redemption wasn't offered to more than 500,000 ex-felons in the state his brother governs.

Not surprisingly, in a number of states, legislators are working to restore voting rights to ex-felons. But potential supporters always run into the same political problems: By definition, the people who stand to benefit the most can't vote, and no politician wants to be called soft on crime. Also, the advantage for Democrats of enfranchisement has pushed the issue into the coarse partisan realm.

The only way that state legislatures have been able to progress has been through bipartisan deals. In Alabama for example, Republicans and Democrats drafted a compromise bill that combined felon enfranchisement with a voter ID bill which Republicans supported. The bill sailed through the Alabama House of Representatives and was only derailed in the Senate when one powerful supporter tried to pile on a five-year death penalty moratorium. Another possibility for coalition building could occur by linking the restoration of voting rights to the restoration of the right to own guns. Just as the punishment doesn't fit the crime to deny the right to vote to felons who haven't been convicted of election fraud, it doesn't fit to deny the right to own a gun to felons, such as devious accountants, who have not committed violent crimes.

Closed Chambers

The easiest way to change the law would be for Congress to wipe the slate clean and standardize state rules. This would be particularly useful because the confusion over who can and cannot vote is a deterrent itself. At the Louisiana prison where he is incarcerated, Norris Henderson has started a civic engagement program because most ex-felons just don't know that they actually can vote in that state. "They don't even know that they can be part of the decision making that is governing their lives," he says. A woman currently bringing suit against Florida, on disability for blindness caused by diabetes and hepatitis, voted regularly in Florida for 25 years before being informed that she was disqualified because of a felony committed when she was 19. Worst of all, in Florida this year, Secretary of State Katherine Harris contracted out the job of scrubbing Florida's voting lists of all previously convicted felons to a Texas company called ChoicePoint. It apparently did a little too good a job and scrubbed out 8,000 people convicted of misdemeanors, blocking legitimate voters during the presidential election.

Unfortunately, however, the one effort to pass a federal initiative, proposed by John Conyers (D-Mich.) has both lacked bipartisan support and been scuttled by constitutional issues. At the convention in 1787, surprisingly little attention was given to the question of who determines the right to vote. The Articles of Confederation had left complete control of franchise to the states and the Constitutional Convention only considered the issue late in the drafting process, in a committee that met while George Washington went fishing. The result was a confusing mandate that gives states the authority to determine who votes while giving Congress the authority to make law regarding the "Times, Places, and Manner" of elections. Subsequently, issues such as the right of women to vote have only been resolved with constitutional amendments. That same result seems likely today, particularly as the Rehnquist Court devolves more and more power to states and whittles down the authority granted the federal government.

But it is possible that constitutional justification for Conyers' bill could be found in the 14th and 15th Amendments which give Congress the power to enforce the equal protection and suffrage provisions by "appropriate legislation." Recent case law has given Congress the power to use this justification to supersede state law only when it can prove that there was racist intent in the original drafting of the laws in question. A disparate racial impact is not sufficient—which is why the Supreme Court recently ruled that the disparate sentences given to crack and cocaine offenders are constitutional.

> ## "A perpetual loss of the right to vote serves no practical or philosophical purpose."
> —James Q. Wilson

Felon disenfranchisement laws, however, were clearly structured with racist motives in the post-Reconstruction conventions of Virginia, Mississippi, Florida, and Alabama. Congress and then the courts will have to determine however whether racist intent in some states is enough to justify a law superseding state laws nationally. Again the odds are limited by the Rehnquist Court which has not been particularly friendly to issues of civil rights.

Democracy in America

Since the nation's founding, we've moved forward, enfranchising more and more groups: from people who didn't own property and immigrants in the mid-19th century, to blacks after the Civil War, to women in 1920, to 18-year olds and blacks in a real sense again in the 1960s. In the past three decades, 15 states have restored voting rights to felons. But none of that progress has come without blood and years of work.

The arguments against enfranchisement are always the same: Voting is a privilege; the people who can't vote aren't competent or independent enough to make fair voting decisions; chaos will result if everyone gets to vote. But those arguments rest on very thin ice which eventually breaks. Alexis de Tocqueville wrote in 1835: "The further the limit of voting rights is extended, the stronger is the need felt to spread them still wider; for after each new concession the forces of democracy are strengthened ... Finally, the exception becomes the rule; concessions follow one another without interruption and there is no halting place until universal suffrage has been attained."

There have obviously been bumps on the road since de Tocqueville. But felons are now the only people over the age of 18 still denied the right to vote, with the exception of the insane. As prominent neoconservative social theorist James Q. Wilson says, "A perpetual loss of the right to vote serves no practical or philosophical purpose."

Denying felons the right to vote after they have served their sentences and done their time runs against both the idea that people can redeem themselves and one of the nation's most important principles, the right to choose who governs you. The laws are anachronistic remnants of the hideous post-Civil War Reconstruction. As Faulkner described the protagonist of Absalom! Absalom! living in Mississippi after the Civil War: "He was a barracks filled with stubborn back-looking ghosts still recovering ... from the fever which had cured the disease."

There are politicians today who know that their power depends on keeping these back-looking ghosts alive. And that turns what it should mean to be American upside down.

Research assistance provided by Joe Dempsey and Corine Hegland

From *Washington Monthly*, January/February 2001, pp. 18–21. Copyright © 2001 by Washington Monthly. Reprinted by permission.

Justice for Rent

The Scandal of Judicial Campaign Financing

ALEXANDER WOHL

During a recent campaign for a seat on a local Ohio Domestic Relations Court, a lawyer from a small firm ran up against a political, ethical, and financial dilemma. His predicament began innocently enough when he was solicited for a campaign contribution by supporters of the Democratic incumbent. The lawyer, a longtime Democrat, willingly put his signature on a $250 check to the judge's campaign. Soon, however, he was contacted by the campaign of the Republican opponent. Would the lawyer be willing to contribute to their candidate's campaign as well? The lawyer, who almost never gave to Republican candidates, nonetheless wrote out a matching check. His rationale was simple: His legal practice involved frequent appearances in family court, and he simply could not afford to risk offending whichever judge was eventually elected.

The Ohio lawyer's story highlights an increasingly common and troublesome phenomenon: the dramatic rise in costly, privately financed judicial campaigns wherein the preponderance of money comes from lawyers and others with a direct stake in the judge's decisions. This trend not only poses a danger to the independence of judges across the nation; it also encourages the politicization and potential corruption of the branch of government that should remain most immune from such influences. The real irony, though, is that this problem is going unattended just as our national campaign system, including constitutional limits on political contributions, is receiving increasing scrutiny.

Judicial campaigns date back to the first years of our national history but now involve far greater sums of money than ever before. Consider, for example, last year's campaign for chief justice of the Wisconsin Supreme Court. Spending totaled $1.3 million, nearly double the previous spending record set just two years prior and more than 10 times the spending of a campaign 20 years earlier. Or take the 1996 race for the Alabama Supreme Court, in which the two candidates together spent more than $2 million, about 10 times as much as was spent for a seat 10 years earlier. In Texas the seriousness and duration of the problem—even after the institution of reforms in 1995—have led to the recent filing of a lawsuit by Public Citizen challenging the constitutionality of the system. The lawsuit, which has the potential to affect campaign finance systems in other states, argues that a system that allows and encourages candidates for state court judgeships to solicit campaign funds from individuals and lawyers who appear before them violates the Due Process clause of the U.S. Constitution.

Some elected state judges are shaking down attorneys who appear before them for campaign contributions.

Much of this trend toward increasing expenditures in judicial campaigns dates back to a 1978 Calitornia judicial election in which Los Angeles deputy district attorneys recruited candidates to oppose unchallenged incumbent trial judges. The effort resulted in a significant turnover of judicial personnel, but more importantly, it marked the beginning of a movement that eventually led to one of the most prominent, controversial, and expensive judicial races ever: the 1986 recall election in which Californians voted out State Supreme Court Chief Justice Rose Bird and two associate justices. More than $11 million was spent by both sides on a campaign that centered on a single issue—Bird's refusal to enforce the death penalty in California.

By contrast, the federal judiciary is structured to avoid precisely this sort of politicization of the bench. Under the U.S. Constitution, members of the federal bench are appointed by the president and confirmed by the Senate, and they receive lifetime tenure—a prize intended to ensure judicial independence and fealty to the supreme law of the land over any partisan attachment. The federal system is certainly not without its underlying political influences: Presidents appoint judges with a view to their judicial and political philosophy. Judges may sometimes tailor decisions with an eye to advancement to higher courts. But on the whole, federal judges remain quite insulated from extra-judicial and political pressures.

States, on the other hand, have historically been far more reluctant to grant judges so much freedom from public accountability. Judicial elections are intended in part to ensure that judges do not become too independent. Not all states use elections as their primary tool of judicial selection, but most do. According to a recent study conducted by an American Bar Association (ABA) task force, almost 87 percent of the nearly 10,000 state trial and appellate court judges in the country face some kind of election. And even states that have merit selection systems often involve retention elections.

Pleasing the Court

Today, big money is distorting even the sometimes questionable goals judicial elections were initially intended to serve. The issue is not simply whether state and local judges will be elected or whether campaigns for these seats will cost money. The question is whether abuses of the system of elections and campaign finance have upset the critical balance between the competing values of judicial independence and public accountability. Instead of offering an opportunity for the majority to bring judges to account, "justice" is increasingly being slanted toward the wishes of a minority of the wealthiest citizens whose role in funding elections is disproportionately large. A recent study of Wisconsin State Supreme Court elections of the past 10 years found that candidates depend overwhelmingly on large individual contributions from a tiny number of well-off and nonminority contributors, most of whom are lawyers and lobbyists from a small number of large law firms. The study also found that personal wealth is among the most important factors in a candidate's success since the fastest-growing category of contributions is from candidates to their own campaigns.

Equally troubling, the breakdown of contributors is increasingly identifiable in terms of party alignment and single-issue advocacy. Many judicial candidates are identified with and endorsed by political parties. And even in those jurisdictions where judicial races are supposedly nonpartisan, judges are frequently grouped on ballots with candidates who are identified by party affiliation, thus making associations and decisions easy for voters, who are usually uninformed about judicial candidates.

The first amendment should not prohibit measures to prevent judges from being corrupted by campaign donations.

The driving force of single-issue contributions and voting also distorts the functioning of judicial elections. In the 1994 campaign for chief justice of the Alabama Supreme Court, the two candidates received nearly $1 million in campaign contributions. The Republican challenger received the bulk of his funds from business groups seeking caps on punitive damage awards, while the Democratic incumbent, a former trial lawyer who opposed the caps, took most of his funds from fellow trial lawyers.

And this kind of activity seems likely to grow. A recent report in *The Wall Street Journal* noted that Koch Industries

rates judges on their views concerning the business community. These ratings, in turn, have then been used to attract donations to supreme court candidates in a number of states including West Virginia, Kansas, Louisiana, Alabama, Mississippi, and Texas.

Single-issue judicial politics, especially on highly charged public questions, also reduces the public's trust in and respect for the judiciary. Such attacks, which often take an individual judicial decision out of context or without regard for the complex legal issues involved, both distort the public perception of judicial accountability and jeopardize judicial independence. In Pennsylvania last year, for instance, Superior Court Judge Kate Ford Elliott lost a race for the state supreme court after her opponent filled the last four days of the campaign with advertisements accusing her of having "let criminals loose on technicalities." In Georgia, Supreme Court Justice Leah Sears, the state's only African-American woman to serve on the high court, was attacked by Atlanta lawyer George Weaver for her views on the electric chair and other issues. In fliers he stated that "her views are a direct attack on our basic moral standards." Weaver was sanctioned by the state Judicial Qualifications Commission, which criticized his ads as "false, deceptive and misleading." His response was to file a federal lawsuit against the commission. What is especially noteworthy about this case is that the commission's regulations were themselves the result of a nasty campaign for the Georgia Court of Appeals a few years earlier. Such tactics may be par for the course in legislative and executive elections. But their very questionable appropriateness in a judicial context highlights the tensions inherent in electing judges.

Judicial Independence and the First Amendment

A natural response to any excess is to place limits on it. Unfortunately, when this excess involves political contributions, there is a significant obstacle—the First Amendment. In its 1976 decision in *Buckley v. Valeo*, the U.S. Supreme Court held that limitations on campaign expenditures may violate the Constitution because they "reduce the quantity of expression by restricting the number of issues discussed, the depth of their exploration, and the size of the audience reached." A number of recent rulings indicate that this holding, which has bedeviled national campaign finance reformers for years, is alive and well as it applies to the judiciary. In Ohio last year, a federal appeals court ruled unconstitutional a 1995 law that attempted to impose spending limits on judicial campaigns. The court rejected the argument, offered by the Ohio attorney general, that judicial campaigns should be exempt from certain First Amendment protections because states have a compelling interest in preserving the impartiality and appearance of impartiality of elected judges. The state's petition to the U.S. Supreme Court to hear its appeal, which might have served as a vehicle to begin whittling down the *Buckley* standard, was rejected by the Court earlier this year.

A challenge to a second Ohio law, passed in 1997, which sets higher campaign spending limits, is pending.

The issue, as noted by the Ohio attorney general, is not just the money—even when it is doled out in record-setting amounts—but the ethical dilemmas these contributions create for judges, the potential taint they may cast over subsequent decisions, and the appearance of impropriety that accrues to lawyers who appear before judges to whose campaigns they have contributed. As U.S. Supreme Court Justice Stephen Breyer said in 1998, "Judicial independence is in part a state of mind, a matter of expectation, habit, and belief among not just judges, lawyers, and legislators, but millions of people." When judges are viewed as little more than politicians who wear robes, that public perception can be dramatically altered. Not surprisingly, a recent Wisconsin poll found that more than three-quarters of those surveyed believe that campaign contributions from lawyers and plaintiffs in high-profile cases influence the decisions of these judges in court. The poll also found that 81 percent of the population believe that because of campaign contributions, special-interest groups get better treatment in our courts than do regular people. A similar study conducted by the Texas State Bar and Texas Supreme Court—which found that 83 percent of the public and 79 percent of lawyers believe that campaign contributions have a significant influence on a judge's decision—was the motivating factor and primary evidence in the filing of the current lawsuit challenging the constitutionality of that system.

So what is to be done? Over the years, there have been a number of suggestions for how to correct the system, both for how to combat the excessive influence of money and for how to limit negative and one-issue campaigning. Merit selection of judges, which is now used in 15 states and the District of Columbia, comes closest to achieving the goals of quality personnel, public accountability, and judicial independence. Candidates for the bench in such a system generally are screened by a nonpartisan committee composed of judges, lawyers, and laypeople. The committee reviews applications and sends a list of qualified individuals to the governor or legislature, who then selects one individual. In this system too, the judge usually must face voters in a retention election, thereby fulfilling the need for public accountability.

But after nearly 100 years of efforts to put merit selection systems in place, even the most committed advocates realize that there may need to be a less sweeping solution, one that focuses not on adopting a new system of selection, but on refining the current rules of campaign finance, disclosure, and disqualification of judges. And as long as the Buckley standard remains in force, public financing of judicial elections seems the obvious answer.

By establishing a floor of financial support that allows candidates to communicate with the voters, a state or locality can increase public debate and reduce both the frequency and the problems of candidates raising additional funds. In this way, the political speech that is at the core of First Amendment protection is maintained but does not fall victim to the skewing of the playing field that comes when unlimited wealth is injected into the equation. In Wisconsin, for example, an anonymous person or group paid $135,000 to send 450,000 postcards to voters just before the Supreme Court election. That kind of activity is one reason a coalition of judges, legislators, and grass-roots organizations is now working to pass an "impartial justice" bill that would expand the partial public funding that already exists in that state (the only state with active public financing of judicial elections) and eliminate special-interest contributions to participating candidates.

But along with elimination of campaign finance inequity that public financing works to stem, there is the related problem (unique to the judiciary) of undue influence that lawyers can have on judges through their contributions and, at least equally significant, that judges can have on lawyers who appear before them, through implicit and explicit pressures to contribute. Unlike lobbyists and others who give campaign contributions to legislators in order to gain access and influence, lawyers should have neither with the judges before whom they appear. At present, however, the restrictions on both lawyers and judges are relatively limited. Judges are bound by the Code of Judicial Conduct, which bars them from making "pledges or promises of conduct in office" or "statements that commit or appear to commit the candidate with respect to cases, controversies or issues that are likely to come before the court, or knowingly misrepresent the identity, qualifications, positions or other fact concerning the candidate or opponent."

But this moral bar does not always eliminate the potential for, or appearance of, impropriety by judges who can and frequently do receive contributions from parties or attorneys who appear before them. In Texas, for instance, the law specifically authorizes judicial candidates, including sitting judges, personally to solicit contributions and does not require them to recuse themselves even in cases in which parties, lawyers, or friends of the court have contributed, according to Allison Zieve, lead counsel in Public Citizen's suit against the Texas system. Other states, such as Alabama, have no limits on contributions but require attorneys to identify contributions they made to that judge and then offer the other party an opportunity to ask the judge to step aside.

Toward Reform

The ABA recently took a major step forward to enhance regulations relating to judicial campaign contributions. In rules adopted at its annual meeting, the Code of Judicial Conduct was amended to recognize that some jurisdictions may wish to enact strict campaign contribution limits for judicial elections and that a judge should disqualify himself or herself if a campaign contribution is made by a party or its lawyer in excess of local limits. The ABA also approved an amendment that prevents a judge from appointing a lawyer to perform legal services or serve in other official capacities if the lawyer has contributed a certain amount to the judge's campaign. As Georgetown University Law School Professor Roy Schotland, the head of an ABA task force on this issue, explains, it is now up to states to adopt or adapt these new rules and make them applicable to their judiciaries. One further issue that states will need to focus on, because the ABA does not specifically address it, is the aggregation of contributions—the possibility that, for instance, many lawyers from one law firm could contribute to one judge.

Ultimately, the solution must involve a combination of strategies: public financing of elections, modifications in disclosure and recusal rules for judges and lawyers, merit selection, and the final piece in the campaign finance puzzle—the creation of a more educated electorate. As Charles Price, a political science professor at California State University, Chico, notes, "Judicial races are like stealth candidates. They are barely above the radar."

There are a number of promising practices already in place. Missouri has developed an initiative that includes the distribution of brochures about voting for judges, establishment of a judicial speaker's bureau, a statewide survey of lawyers to evaluate the judiciary, and the enlistment of the media to write informative stories about the judiciary. And in recent elections in Washington, voter guides to judicial primary elections were included in the Sunday newspapers. These efforts, which have met with some success, indicate that when linked to other reforms, public education offers the promise of state judicial systems that ensure integrity, independence, and real accountability to all citizens.

Chief Justice John Marshall once wrote that "the greatest scourge an angry Heaven ever inflicted upon an ungrateful and a sinning people, was an ignorant, a corrupt, or a dependent judiciary." Marshall understood that judicial independence—whether guaranteed through life tenure in the case of qualified federal judges, or through the meritorious and fair selection of judges within the state systems—is the core of an effective judiciary and a foundation of our democracy. Until states begin to address these issues comprehensively, it will likely be politics as usual—a distressing indictment of our state judiciaries, and a continuing dilemma for those lawyers and citizens who want justice but don't want to have to buy it.

Electoral Overload

ALAN EHRENHALT

The most ridiculous elective office in American state government is about to pass out of existence.

As the result of a law that cleared the legislature in June, Louisiana voters will no longer be asked to vote every four years on who should be entrusted with the job of maintaining the state's voting machines. When the current term is over, at the beginning of 2004, this awesome responsibility will be given to a civil servant working under the Secretary of State.

That's actually where it resided until the late 1950s, when Governor Earl K. Long, embroiled in a feud with then-Secretary of State Wade O. Martin, decided to teach Martin a lesson by taking his jurisdiction away. Long created a position called Custodian of Voting Machines and made it an official state office with a comfortable salary and a four-year term.

Reformers, embarrassed by the triviality of the title, managed in the 1970s to change the name to Commissioner of Elections. But they didn't change the duties much: Louisiana's citizens continued to go to the polls every four years to pick a constitutional officer whose job consisted largely of buying and repairing machinery and remembering to deliver it to the right polling place when it was needed.

It was not only a cushy job, it was also the personal possession of a single family. When Long created the post, he promoted the candidacy of a loyal crony, Douglas Fowler, who held it from 1960 until his retirement in 1979. Then Fowler's son, Jerry, a former lineman for the Houston Oilers, took over and won reelection four times.

The odds are the job would still be a Fowler fiefdom if the second occupant of the office hadn't been caught looting the till in 1999. A legislative auditor found that Jerry Fowler had been taking kickbacks on the purchase of voting machines and occasionally paying friends of his to haul them around even when there was no election scheduled. Fowler was indicted on eight counts of malfeasance in office, entered a guilty plea and was sentenced to prison for five years.

In between, he was defeated for reelection by a challenger who said she would have no objection if the office were simply abolished. A state legislator who had been introducing bills to abolish it for years finally succeeded in getting one through, and Governor Mike Foster signed it into law June 25. So it's virtually a done deal that the current commissioner, Suzanne Haik Terrell, will be the last.

No other state has a political culture remotely resembling Louisiana's, so no other state faces a challenge anything like the one that confronted the Louisiana legislature in mustering the political support to undo Earl Long's office-creating constitutional mischief. But there are some lessons in this bizarre tale for state governments just about anywhere.

One is that mixing up politics and election administration is a dangerous risk to take at any level of government. Florida proved that last year; Louisiana has proved it more than once. Even if Jerry Fowler had been as honest as George Washington, he was still a partisan Democrat who ran for office on a partisan ticket and involved himself in the campaigns of other politicians whose votes he was supposed to count. Republicans still insist that in 1996, when a U.S. Senate election depended on the tabulation of a final few hundred votes, Fowler's employees tampered with the result by breaking the seals on the voting machines. Nobody has ever proved that. But the whole unpleasant business was the direct result of partisan management of the election process—whether you call the person in charge a custodian, a commissioner, or any other name.

It won't happen anymore in Louisiana. Attached to the new law eliminating the post of election commissioner/voting machine custodian is a provision barring any official in charge of future election management from raising political funds, assisting any candidate, or participating in party activities of any kind. Secretaries of State will remain elected officeholders, but they will be able to campaign only for themselves. This will be, in a sense, the positive legacy of both Jerry Fowler and Katherine Harris.

An even better legacy would be a nationwide reexamination of all the other offices in states throughout the country that are filled on a partisan elective basis and don't need to be. The vast majority of states have elected lieutenant governors and attorneys general, and a good case can be made for that. One of these is normally second in line to the governorship, and the other is the state's chief legal officer. Probably the voters are entitled to some say in who holds those offices.

But voters also choose agriculture commissioners in 12 states, education commissioners or superintendents in 14, and insurance commissioners in 11. In Louisiana, voters elect not only a governor and secretary of state but also a lieutenant governor, attorney general, treasurer, and commissioners of insurance and agriculture. The insurance job, another elected post created by Earl Long to punish his rival, Wade Martin, has generated even more embarrassment than the voting-machine job. Three commissioners in a row were sentenced to prison.

Not that there's any consistent relationship between the number of constitutional executive officers a state elects and the quality of the government it gets. North Dakota elects more of them than any state in the country—a dozen, not counting the governor—and it has a long history of honest and competent leadership. It is the only state that has an elected tax commissioner (arguably just the sort of position that should be divorced from politics), but the tax commissioner's office has been a springboard to leadership, producing both current U.S. senators and the most recent nominee for governor. Maine, on the other hand, has the smallest possible number of constitutional officers—only the governor is chosen by the voters—and, it too, has a history of being relatively well governed.

But structure does make a difference. A state that elects a large slate of executive branch officials is opting for a system of diffused power, multiple checks and balances, and numerous restrictions on the governor's ability to create a program and implement it. A state that elects only the governor often is opting to place its entire executive branch more or less under his personal control.

It's possible to make intelligent arguments either way. What seems beyond dispute is that the stated rationale for creating multiple offices—the need to give voters more of a say in the way they are governed—doesn't really hold up. The elected insurance commissioners and agriculture commissioners that still serve in capitols around the country are mostly a legacy of Progressive-era reforms meant to take power out of the hands of political bosses and promote direct democracy.

But let's face it: Not one voter in a thousand has any clear idea of the kind of job his auditor or insurance commissioner is actually doing. Placing these offices on an election ballot doesn't empower the electorate—it empowers the regulated interests that finance the campaigns.

State Representative Chuck McMains, who has been trying unsuccessfully to abolish Louisiana's elected insurance commissioner post for years, puts it this way: "You've got a statewide office that takes a million dollars to run for, and the only place somebody can go for campaign funds is to the people they regulate or the people they do favors for. It's not an appropriate position that should be elected." He's right.

Abolishing elected treasurers, auditors and commissioners would probably do more good than harm.

Admittedly, doing away with elected treasurers and auditors and commissioners does run the risk of giving the governor more authority than some will feel appropriate. But given the realities of our current political system, it's a choice that for many states probably carries with it more good than harm.

New Jersey is a good object lesson. As everybody knows, it's a state with an endemic political-corruption problem, one where the past few decades have witnessed the indictment and conviction of mayors, legislators and other elected officials in both parties. But the state executive branch, all of whose leaders are appointed by the governor rather than elected, has been by comparison a model of honest administration. That may not be entirely because the executives don't have to run for office, but somehow I doubt that it's a coincidence.

Of course, a system such as the one in New Jersey generates its own dilemmas. Early this year, when Governor Christine Todd Whitman resigned to join the president's cabinet, there was no statewide elected official who could take her place. The succession devolved on Senate President Donald DiFrancesco, who had to serve as a legislative leader and as acting governor at the same time, creating an obvious separation-of-powers problem.

Still, if states are moving in any direction, it is toward the New Jersey model, not the North Dakota model. They are eliminating superfluous constitutional offices, not creating new ones.

Florida is one of those. The statewide referendum that abolished the Secretary of State's position also did away with the elected education commissioner and combined two elected financial posts, reducing the number of independent constitutional offices to three. There are those who say that will give too much power to Governor Jeb Bush, but most voters seem to go along with the argument Bush himself made when the issue was on the ballot in 1998: "Most people in this state believe the governor is accountable for all this anyway, and he might as well get the power to be able to carry out what people expect him to do."

As with everything in government, there's no perfect system. Some states no doubt have the right number of elective offices to make things function smoothly. Some could use one or two more. But most would probably be better off getting rid of some of the constitutional baggage they have grown accustomed to carrying around. Louisiana is definitely one of those

Bada Bing Club

How Democratic machines keep women out.

ALEXANDRA STARR

Oftentimes, the women who gain access to New Jersey's behind-the-scenes political gatherings aren't wearing much in the way of clothes. That, at least, is the impression James McGreevey imparts in his memoir, *The Confession*. Strip clubs, he explains, play an integral part in the Garden State's power culture. "We used to order beer after beer at Cheeques," McGreevey writes, "watching the dancers twirl on their poles while debating everything from local policy initiatives and tax ratables to the merits of silicone breast enhancement." Presumably this ritual didn't hold much appeal for the gay future governor. Still, for the sake of political ambition, McGreevey didn't dare forgo it. Strip clubs, he writes, are the "fraternal lodges" of New Jersey politicians, places where "lasting and productive connections" are forged.

New Jersey is one of the country's most reliably liberal states. It has favored the Democratic candidate in the last four presidential elections and hasn't elected a Republican senator since 1972. Yet its political culture is also among the country's most sexist. It ranks in the bottom third of states in proportion of legislators who are women, while its congressional delegation contains no females. And New Jersey isn't the only state with deep-blue political tendencies and a virtually all-male power structure. Massachusetts and Rhode Island don't have any women in their congressional delegations, either, and Pennsylvania has one of the lowest percentages of female state legislators outside the South. In Rhode Island, female delegates make up a paltry 19.5 percent of the legislature—placing the state behind such liberal bastions as Kansas, Nebraska, and Idaho.

Indeed, if many left-leaning Northeastern states have proved surprisingly inhospitable to female politicians, the reverse is true of many conservative Western states. In 1999, women held the top five statewide offices in Arizona, which is also the only state where female governors have served back-to-back. Meanwhile, Colorado has the fifth-highest percentage of female legislators in the country and is one of only six states where a woman serves as speaker of the state Senate.

Why do so many liberal states lag behind conservative states in female representation? It's a puzzling question with a simple answer: machines. Northeastern states may be some of the most liberal in the country, but they are also the most likely to have political cultures shaped by bosses. In New Jersey, county chairmen (and they are pretty much all men) still decide who will receive official party support in primaries and reap financial backing. "Those decisions are generally made behind closed doors," says Debbie Walsh, director of the Center for American Women and Politics at Rutgers University. "It makes it harder for women, and outsiders in general, to get involved."

McGreevey's methodical rise through the state's political ranks sheds light on the phenomenon. As he writes in *The Confession*, he paid numerous visits to the powerful county bosses to beg for their support and unleashed charm offensives on their closest allies. He patiently listened to a political operative's description of his fiftieth birthday party, which had taken place in a whorehouse in the Dominican Republic, and, on another occasion, enlisted the owner of an Irish bar he patronized to plead his case to a powerful boss. Other glimpses of the Northeast's frat-like political culture have occasionally spilled into public view: In 2000, during an all-night budget session in Massachusetts, legislators chanted "Toga! Toga!" and rumors circulated that a freshman member who had fallen asleep woke up to find his leg shaved. The House speaker later compared the evening to a "keg party."

In the West, political conventions are very different. Claudine Schneider, who represented Rhode Island in Congress for ten years before relocating to Colorado, offers this comparison: "You don't have the old boys' club inner circle here, which is almost institutionalized on the East Coast. Here, it is wide open spaces. If you can build a constituency, you can run." And women have: Not only were Western states the first to grant women suffrage, they were also the first to send a congresswoman to D.C. and to elect a female governor.

The part-time political culture of the West—where elected office can seem more like a hobby than a job—also tends to favor women. As Alan Ehrenhalt pointed out in the late '80s, when he investigated why Colorado's state legislature had the highest percentage of female delegates in the country, the Colorado legislature only meets part-time (which makes it more family-friendly) and doesn't pay much (which may dissuade some male breadwinners from running). "While men tend to get involved in politics as a premeditated career option," says Walsh, "women often run because they want to *fix* something."

In the Northeast, bosses long had an interest in making government service a profitable profession. As a result, many legislatures pay a sizable salary—and demand a full-time commitment. "In a part-time legislature, service can be an extension of volunteerism," says Jennifer Mann, a Democratic state legislator from Allentown, Pennsylvania. "In a place like Pennsylvania, you don't fall into a political career by happenstance. It's not something you add to your life—it really replaces what you used to do."

The machine culture of many liberal states helps explain another odd phenomenon: why so many of the women who *have* succeeded at high levels of state politics in the Northeast—think governors Christine Todd Whitman (New Jersey), Jane Swift (Massachusetts), and Jodi Rell (Connecticut)—have been liberal Republicans. Schneider, who is pro-choice, was an environmental activist before she ran for Congress and probably would have been a more natural ideological fit in the Democratic Party. "But, when I looked at Rhode Island's Democratic politicians, all I saw were white Catholic males," she says. "And I thought, 'Whatever party the incumbents are, I am not.'" If the majority party appeared unreceptive to women, the state GOP welcomed her with open arms. Republicans in the Northeast are often so outmatched that they are happy to have just about anyone run. And, in Schneider's case, attempting to depose an incumbent with sky-high approval ratings *did* seem like a fool's errand. But, after a failed first attempt, she snagged the seat and was sworn into Congress at the age of 31.

That's not the only time allowing a woman to embark on a kamikaze mission ended up paying off handsomely for the GOP. Whitman challenged Senator Bill Bradley in 1990 because no one else wanted to take on the giant of New Jersey politics. After unexpectedly coming within a few points of toppling him, she emerged as the obvious choice to run for governor three years later.

Beyond Whitman, there are signs that women are finally beginning to circumvent the New Jersey machine. Two state senators, Nia Gill and Loretta Weinberg, have managed to serve as Democrats while simultaneously cutting ties to county bosses. Gill ran without the support of the Essex County organization in 2003 and stunned party officials when she eked out a victory against their anointed candidate. Weinberg landed in the Senate only after a bitter public fight with the Bergen County boss, who wanted to install the local sheriff instead. Both women champion independent legislative agendas, which is one reason they have feuded so publicly with the chairmen. "When women exercise discretionary power, an uproar ensues," says Gill.

Because they won't play by the traditional rules of New Jersey politics, and because they have an incentive to expose the foibles of the old boys' network, women like Gill and Weinberg are a threat to the long-term dominance of the machines. And so, while it isn't likely that New Jersey female politicians will match the level of representation that women have achieved in a state like Arizona anytime soon, they may be accomplishing something even more important: hastening the day when the bosses--and their strip-club political culture—are finally things of the past.

ALEXANDRA STARR, who writes frequently for *Slate*, is a 2007 Milena Jesenská journalism fellow.

California, Here We Come

Government by plebiscite, which would have horrified the Founding Fathers, threatens to replace representative government.

PETER SCHRAG

This June marks the twentieth anniversary of the passage of Proposition 13, the California voter initiative that has in many respects had a political and social impact on this era—not just in California but across much of the nation—almost as profound and lasting as that of the New Deal on the 1930s, 1940s, and 1950s.

The effect on California—which had been well above the national average in what it spent to educate its children, to provide free or nearly free higher education to every person who wanted it, for highway construction, and for a range of social services for children and the needy—was traumatic. Cutting local property taxes by more than 50 percent and capping the tax rate at one percent, Proposition 13 and the various initiatives that followed in its wake forced California to a level of spending far below the national average for such things as K–12 schooling, public-library services, the arts, and transportation. The respected journal *Education Week* said last year of California schools, "a once world-class system is now third rate." Even with a booming economy, California remains in the bottom third among the states, and far below the other major industrial states, in what it budgets per pupil.

Just as important, the march of ballot initiatives, the attack on legislative discretion, and the related acts of "direct democracy" that Proposition 13 helped to set in motion—involving taxes and spending, affirmative action, immigration, school policy, environmental protection, three-strikes criminal sentences, term limits, campaign reform, insurance rates, and virtually every other public issue—continue with unabated force, in California and beyond. In November of 1996 voters in twenty-three states were polled on a total of ninety initiatives, the most in more than eighty years (a decade ago there were forty-one), on everything from hunting rights to gambling to logging regulations to sugar production to the legalization of medical marijuana use (which was approved in Arizona and California).

This June, as if to honor the anniversary of Proposition 13, Californians will again confront a large array of sometimes nearly incomprehensible ballot measures, among them yet another one on term limits and one that would all but end bilingual educa-

tion. Each proposed reform further restricts the power of the legislature and local elected officials to set priorities, respond to new situations, and write budgets accordingly. When half of the state's tax-limited general fund must, under the terms of one initiative, be spent on the schools; when a sizable chunk must, under the mandate of the state's three-strikes measure, be spent on prisons; and when lesser amounts must, under the terms of still other initiatives that have been approved in the past decade, be spent on the repayment of bonds for parkland and transportation projects, the amount left over for everything else shrinks with Malthusian inevitability—as does the state government's capacity to cope with changed circumstances. When cities and counties are prohibited from raising property-tax rates beyond Proposition 13's one percent, and when it is difficult to raise other revenues without a vote of the electorate (in many instances a two-thirds vote) or of the affected property owners, local control is drastically reduced.

Just as inevitably, public policy is increasingly distorted by the shifting of costs from the general fund to the Byzantine system of fees, assessments, and exactions that local governments have devised in their attempts to get around tax limits and other restrictions. This reinforces the larger shift from a communitarian to a fee ethic—in the support of parks and playgrounds, in the construction of new schools, and in financing a range of other services that used to be funded entirely from general taxes. As one California letter writer complained to a newspaper, why should citizens contribute to "the methodical pillaging and plundering of the taxpayer, forcing those who have no kids to pay through the nose for someone else's"?

Direct democracy is an attractive political ideal, as close to our own experience as the New England town meeting. It has never worked, however, in large, diverse political communities, and the belief that electronics, direct mail, and televised slogans can replace personal engagement has so far looked far more like fantasy than like anything derived from hard political experience. In the case of the initiative, the new populism—unlike the reform movement that wrote the initiative into the constitutions of nineteen states around the turn of the century—seems to want greater engagement in government less than it wants an auto-pilot system to check government institutions with little active involvement by the citizenry beyond occasional trips to the polls to vote on yet more initiatives.

Nothing in California's initiative process presents the downside or the implications of any issue.

California sparked the anti-government, anti-tax mood that has gripped the nation for most of the past two decades, and it remains the most extreme illustration of that mood, a cautionary tale for those enamored of plebiscitary democracy. But it is now hardly unique. Virulent anti-institutionalism, particularly with respect to government, has become a prevailing theme in our national political discourse. A decade after Ronald Reagan left office, his facile dismissal of government as "the problem," not the solution, remains a talk-show staple, a posture that serves to exonerate both civic laziness and political ignorance. And this attitude, which has become banal toward representative government, now also encompasses the related institutions of constitutional democracy: the courts, the schools, the press. Voting and serious newspaper readership are declining together. The communitarian civic ideal that they represent is giving way to "markets," a fee-for-service ethic, and the fragmented, unmediated, unedited exchange of information, gossip, and personal invective.

The media—new and old alike—may ensure against the power of Big Brother to dominate communications, but they also proliferate shared ignorance at an unprecedented rate: what used to be limited to gossip over the back fence is now spread in milliseconds to a million listeners during the evening commute, and to thousands over the Internet. And at the fringes are the militias and the "patriots," collecting weapons and supplies, training in the hills, and hunkering down against the black helicopters and the coming invasion of United Nations troops. That kind of ignorance and extremism, the new media, and the surrounding paranoia about government have all become commonplace in the past decade. Oliver Stone's *JFK* and the videos promoted by Jerry Falwell about the alleged murder of Vincent Foster work the same territory.

Tracy Westen, the president of the foundation-funded Center for Governmental Studies, in Los Angeles, has constructed a "digital scenario" for the election of 2004—a not altogether wild fantasy about thirty-five California voter initiatives on various subjects, all of which have been circulated for "signatures" online, along with a spectrum of arguments pro and con, available at the click of a voice-activated mouse, from every conceivable source. In combination with a number of new elective offices, including drug commissioner and gay-rights commissioner, those measures contribute to a total of 200 ballot decisions for each voter to make.

Among Westen's futuristic initiatives is one urging Congress to approve an amendment to Article V of the U.S. Constitution

such that the language guaranteeing every state a "Republican form of government" is modified to permit the states to replace representative democracy with direct democracy. Westen points out that most of the technology for this politopia—individually targeted campaign ads, interactive "discussions" with candidates, electronic voting—already exists. Since "state legislatures seem to be fighting more and doing less... and leaving the real legislation to the people," the scenario continues, "it seems the trend toward 'democracy by initiative' is inevitable." A few years ago the Canadian fringe Democratech Party wanted to submit all government decisions to the public through electronic referenda. An official Democratech statement said,

> Representative government assumes that the people need to elect someone to represent them in a faraway legislative assembly. But with modern, instantaneous communications, the people can directly make their own decisions, relegating politicians to the scrap heap of history.

Three years ago The Economist mused about the possible benefits of replacing representative democracy with Swiss-style direct democracy, in which the voters "trudge to the polls four times a year" to decide all manner of plebiscitary questions. This process would prevent lobbyists and other special interests from buying the outcome, because "when the lobbyist faces an entire electorate... bribery and vote-buying are virtually impossible. Nobody has enough money to bribe everybody."

California shows that the process of bedazzling voters with sound bites, slogans, and nuanced bias works as effectively in the initiative process as it does in electoral politics. Offers that sound like something for nothing (a 50 percent property-tax cut, or a guaranteed level of education funding, or a state lottery offering a payoff for schools as well as for the lucky winners) may not be bribes, but they are the nearest thing to them. And when they work at the ballot box, their effects may last far longer than those of conventional legislation.

The larger danger, of course, is precisely the nondeliberative quality of the California-style initiative, particularly in a society that doesn't have the luxury of slow alpine trudges during which to reflect on what it's about to do. Nothing is built into the process—no meaningful hearings, no formal debates, no need for bicameral concurrence, no conference committees, no professional staff, no informed voice, no executive veto—to present the downside, to outline the broader implications, to ask the cost, to speak for minorities, to engineer compromises, to urge caution, to invoke the lessons of the past, or, once an initiative is approved by the voters, to repair its flaws except by yet another ballot measure (unless the text of the initiative itself provides for legislative amendment). Indeed, if the past decade of initiatives in California demonstrates anything, it is that the majoritarianism essential to the ethos of direct democracy almost inevitably reinforces an attitude of indifference if not hostility toward minority rights. All these dangers would be exacerbated, of course, by electronic or other forms of absentee balloting, whereby voters would no longer be required to go to the local school or church or social hall and encounter their fellow citizens participating in the same civic ritual—and thus be reminded that they are, after all, part of a larger community.

To say all that, probably, is merely to say awkwardly what the Framers of the Constitution said better in Philadelphia, what Hamilton, Madison, and Jay said in *The Federalist*, and what scores of delegates said in 1787–1788 at the various state conventions leading up to ratification, even before the Terror of the French Revolution: unchecked majorities are a danger to liberty almost as great as oligarchs and absolute monarchs.

Among the most common measures, put on the ballot by the organization U.S. Term Limits in fourteen states and passed in 1996 by voters in nine, is the "Scarlet Letter" initiative, also known as the "informed voter" initiative, which instructs a state's elected officials to support a constitutional amendment limiting members of the House of Representatives to three two-year terms and members of the Senate to two six-year terms, and which requires state election officials to indicate on the ballot next to the name of each congressional incumbent and each member of the legislature whether he or she "disregarded voters' instruction on term limits." It also requires nonincumbents to indicate whether they have signed a pledge supporting the amendment; those who have not will be similarly identified on the ballot. For Paul Jacob, who heads U.S. Term Limits, no compromise is acceptable. The watchword is "No Uncertain Terms" (which also happens to be the name of the organization's newsletter).

Jacob's very inflexibility helped to derail a more moderate term-limits amendment when it came up in the House (for the second time) early last year. It would have allowed six two-year terms in the House and two six-year terms in the Senate. By denouncing it as a sellout, U.S. Term Limits helped to ensure that no term-limits amendment was approved, and thus that the organization would enjoy a long, healthy life. The large turnover in Congress in 1994 probably took enough steam out of the movement to reduce its chances of success, but not enough to end it.

Ballot initiatives reduce the power and accountability of legislatures—and thus the ability to govern.

The Scarlet Letter initiative is probably unconstitutional. (U.S. Term Limits is now asking individual candidates to pledge to serve no more than three terms in the House or two in the Senate.) In Arkansas, one of the nine states that passed it in 1996, the state supreme court struck it down, as a violation of the procedures set forth in the U.S. Constitution for amendment. Because the drafters of the Constitution, in the words of the Arkansas court, "wanted the amending process in the hands of a body with the power to deliberate upon a proposed amendment... all proposals of amendments... must come either from Congress or state legislatures—not from the people." The U.S.

Term Limits measure was "an indirect attempt to propose an amendment... [that would] virtually tie the hands of the individual members of the [legislature] such that they would no longer be a deliberative body acting independently in exercising their individual best judgements on the issue."

There are scattered indications that the rabid anti-government fervor of the early nineties may have peaked. (One of those indications, in the view of Nancy Rhyme, who tracks the issue for the National Conference of State Legislatures, is that only nine passed the Scarlet Letter initiative.) Certainly, term limits are not likely to be written into the Constitution any time soon.

But the issue will not go away, either in national politics or in the eighteen states that now have term limits for their legislatures written into their constitutions or otherwise written into law. On almost the same day that term limits failed (again) in the House early last year, the Scarlet Letter, funded largely by U.S. Term Limits and a handful of out-of-state term-limits organizations, qualified for the next California ballot. (U.S. Term Limits kicked in about $300,000 to the campaign to qualify the California "informed voter" measure but won't, of course, disclose where its money comes from. The organization is willing to provide a list of its National Finance Committee members, all of whom are said to have contributed more than $1,000, but will not specify which among them are its largest contributors.) A few months later the long-established California organization Field Poll reported that voter support of term limits, which stood at roughly two thirds, remained just as strong as it had been in 1990, in the months before California approved term limits for legislators and other state officials.

Nor has the initiative process lost its allure. Twenty-four states have some form of initiative in their constitutions, most of them dating from the Progressive Era. Recently there have been moves in a number of other states—including Rhode Island and Texas—to write the initiative process into their constitutions.

The pressure does not come from Hispanics or other newly active political groups, who tend to vigorously oppose these constitutional changes as openings to yet more measures like California's Proposition 187—which, until it was blocked by a federal court, sought to deny schooling and other public services to illegal immigrants. Rather, the impetus is from Ross Perot's United We Stand America and other organizations that are overwhelmingly white and middle-class. And in the states that already have the ballot initiative, there is increasing pressure to use it, sometimes generated by the dynamics of political reform itself. In California, political officeholders, from the governor down, have become initiative sponsors as a means of increasing name recognition and raising or stretching political campaign funds. And as initiatives circumscribe the power and discretion of legislatures, often the best way of responding to new circumstances—and sometimes the only way—is through yet another initiative. The result, for better or worse, is an ongoing cycle of initiative reform, frustration, and further reform.

Yet despite all the unintended consequences and the inflexibility of the initiative and other devices of direct democracy, they seem to have one thing in common, whether they are used by liberal environmentalists or by tax-cutting conservatives: they are the instruments of established voter-taxpayer groups, particularly the white middle class, against urban politicians and political organizations that represent the interests and demands of minorities, immigrants, and other marginal groups. At the turn of the century the Yankee establishment in Boston and other cities sought to create political institutions and devices to dilute the power of the upstart Irish. In its impulse and spirit the current pressure for plebiscitary solutions driven by the general electorate, in which the white middle class can still dominate, is not all that different.

The celebratory history of direct democracy centers on its inclusiveness, but in our politically more sophisticated (and no doubt more cynical) age there is a need to understand that defense of the initiative may be less disinterested than it seems. The groups that embrace and cheer it are not just "the people" fighting "the interests" or "the politicians," much less battling "Satan" and "Mammon," as the editor of the Sacramento Bee put it in the heyday of the Progressives. They are often established political interest groups trying by extraordinary means to further a cause or repulse the advances of other groups. More important, each initiative reduces the power and accountability of legislatures—and thus the general ability to govern, meaning the ability to shape predictable outcomes. And whereas the initiative may well further the Jeffersonian objective of tying government down, and thus preventing mischief, it also vastly reduces the chances that great leaders, and the visionary statecraft with which they are sometimes associated, will arise. In the battle over the initiative the Framers would be the first to recognize that our politics, rather than being too conservative, are in the Burkean sense not nearly conservative enough.

PETER SCHRAG writes frequently on education and politics. His article in this issue appears in somewhat different form in his book *Paradise Lost: California's Experience, America's Future*, published by The New Press

The Initiative—Take It or Leave It?

Citizens are using the initiative like never before. Some think that's good for democracy. Others worry it undermines our representative government.

JENNIFER DRAGE BOWSER

Initiative and referendum lurked quietly in the background of state politics for much of the 20th century, but over the last 12 years they've come back strong.

Consider the numbers: There were 183 statewide votes on initiatives in the 1970s, 253 in the 1980s, and 383 in the 1990s—more than double the total from the 1970s. And California alone accounts for 130 of the total 819 measures during that 30-year period; Oregon can lay claim to 107. Between them, those two states account for nearly 30 percent of all initiatives from 1970 to 1999. It's no wonder people there are beginning to say initiatives are a problem.

Supporters say the resurgence of initiatives is great—it means citizens are using them as a tool to implement new laws and make reforms legislatures are unwilling or unable to enact. Besides changing policy, supporters also say initiatives increase citizen engagement with government—people are not only more aware of state policy issues, but are more likely to go out and vote.

In some states where the initiative is used heavily, however, people are beginning to speak out against it. And it's not just legislators. The governors in Arizona and Maine call for reform, and a wide range of citizen and business groups have offered their ideas. The California League of Women Voters submitted a menu of suggested reforms in 1999, and the City Club of Portland proposed changes for Oregon's initiative process in 1996.

Task forces are looking at the issue in several states. A group in Colorado called Save Our Constitution includes voices from just about every spectrum of the political rainbow—a wide range of citizen, business and local government groups, as well as current and former legislators.

One of the biggest problems in the minds of many lawmakers is that initiatives only ask voters to make simple yes or no decisions on very complex issues. "Voters don't have to make the same kinds of tough decisions legislators face in balancing competing needs with limited resources," says Oregon Representative Lane Shetterly, a member of NCSL's I&R Reform Task

Force. "The legislature may acknowledge an issue as a priority, but, in the face of an upcoming revenue shortfall and with existing programs and services to fund, it just isn't always possible to fund a new program. Then the initiative comes along and does it anyway. It puts the legislature in a box, having to meet newly mandated needs as well as existing ones," Shetterly says.

He favors reforms that would give voters better information about the fiscal impacts of initiative proposals and put that information into context with the fiscal resources of the state.

But reform won't come easy. Legislatures are struggling to find ways to prevent fraud in the signature-gathering process, disclose who pays for initiative campaigns, and add flexibility to the process to accommodate more debate, deliberation and compromise than presently exists. But the courts have made regulating petition circulators and initiative campaign finance very difficult. And almost any changes to the process can be a political hot potato because proponents of the initiative are generally hostile to legislative attempts to change it.

Others Want the Initiative

At the same time as some states are desperately seeking solutions for reining in an initiative process run amok, a few states without the process are thinking about implementing it for the first time.

Seventeen states have seen legislation to implement I&R procedures during the 2001–2002 biennium, but it's gathered the most momentum in Minnesota and New York.

The initiative had its heyday during the Populist and Progressive movements around the turn of the last century with 19 states adopting the process between 1898 and 1918. Since then, only five states have adopted the initiative and referendum, most recently Mississippi in 1992.

If Representative Erik Paulsen has anything to do with it, Minnesota will be next. He's the sponsor of an I&R bill that's already passed the Minnesota House (and a similar bill in the last biennium that also passed the House). He says Minnesota needs the initiative and referendum process as a "safety valve" for situations when government fails to act.

"I've always been a believer in trusting the people to make decisions. The legislature doesn't always act responsibly, and voters need an extra tool to deal with those situations," Paulsen says.

He says he's crafted his proposal carefully, trying to avoid some of the pitfalls other states have encountered with their processes. For instance, his measure calls for a so-called "geographic distribution requirement." Instead of gathering all their signatures during the lunch hour on the busiest corner in downtown Minneapolis, initiative proponents would have to fan out across the state, gathering signatures in at least three-fourths of the state's congressional districts.

I&R has gotten a lot of attention in New York recently, too. Governor George Pataki voiced support for it in his state-of-the-state address this year. At least 10 bills to implement the process have been introduced in the Legislature this biennium.

Improving On the Initiative

There have been numerous reports about the initiative and referendum process in California, Oregon and Nebraska, and many recommendations. The most recent report is from the Speaker's Commission on the California Initiative Process issued in January. Members suggest that California adopt an indirect initiative process, allowing the legislature an opportunity to review, amend and possibly enact an initiative before it goes on the ballot. The commission also recommends increasing public information about initiatives and who sponsors them. Similar suggestions from this and other reports include:

- Increase the requirements for disclosure of money spent on initiatives.
- Adopt an indirect initiative process and create incentives to encourage its use.
- Provide incentives for using volunteer signature-gatherers, such as requiring fewer signatures.
- Improve voter education on initiatives, including ballot pamphlets and public hearings.
- Impose a single subject requirement for initiative proposals.

"Initiative and referendum represents the very core of democracy," says Senator Michael Nozzolio, who has supported the implementation of I&R throughout his legislative career. "It ensures that all people have a voice in the democratic process. It is an idea grounded in the belief that power ultimately rests in the hands of the people," he says.

Whether Minnesota or New York will join the list of initiative states remains to be seen and is ultimately up to voters in those states. Paulsen is confident that Minnesota will eventually become an I&R state, in spite of the fact that voters have turned down the issue three times in the past. Most recently, they declined to pass a 1980 constitutional amendment to implement the initiative. The vote was close in all three cases, though. Representative Paulsen is certain that if voters knew more about it, they'd support I&R.

Controversy Continues

The only thing that is certain is that I&R will continue to be controversial in the states where it is heavily used. Legislatures in Arizona, California, Colorado and Oregon face an uphill battle in their efforts to make the initiative and the legislative process work together effectively.

JENNIFER DRAGE BOWSER is NCSL's expert on initiatives and referendums.

Total Recall

In the wake of California's attempt to recall Governor Gray Davis, it seems likely this tactic will be tried in other states.

ALAN GREENBLATT

The purported sins of Gray Davis are not unique to him. Plenty of other governors have been blamed this year for enormous budget deficits, even if none could rival California's $38 billion shortfall. And many have been accused of masking the size and scope of budget problems during their reelection campaigns. It would be ridiculous to assert that Davis is the only politician who deserves to be called "arrogant" or derided for his heavy fundraising. What's more, examples abound of executives who have lost popularity by bungling through a crisis, as Davis did with California's electricity deregulation fiasco.

Indeed, many pundits have argued that because Davis' failings are so common, he doesn't deserve the special ignominy of a recall election on October 7*. But such considerations of fairness beg a more important question: If so many politicians make the kinds of mistakes that Davis has, why aren't more of them facing recalls?

No governor has been recalled since 1921, but recall attempts are more common than you might think. Only 18 states allow recalls of state officials, but fully double that number allow recalls of local officials. Sixty-one percent of U.S. localities can hold recall elections—a higher percentage than allow initiatives or referenda. According to surveys by the International City/County Management Association, in the five-year period ending in 2001, recall elections or mayors or city council members took place in nearly 10 percent of U.S. cities. "Before people sneer at California, they should look at their own city charter and see how often their own guys have been recalled," says Shaun Bowler, a political scientist at the University of California, Riverside.

Given the worldwide publicity garnered by the California recall, interest in pursuing this particular tactic against disliked politicians will only increase. M. Dane Waters, who runs the Initiative and Referendum Institute in Northern Virginia, says that he normally receives only about one phone call a month asking about recall procedures. Since the attacks on Davis began, however, Waters says, "we've received literally hundreds of calls from activists who have suddenly awakened to the recall device. People are saying, 'Hey, maybe this is available and I should think of using it.' "

With California Democrats already threatening to run a recall campaign against any Republican who might win the election to replace Davis, which will also be held October 7, recalls are more likely than not to become a regular blood sport in the state. Recalls, like so many other policy ideas first tried out in California, may then spread into the nation's political mainstream. Ballot initiatives were out of fashion until the passage of Proposition 13, an anti-property tax measure approved by California voters in 1978, demonstrated their power and renewed their popularity. The recall of Davis could have a similar effect. "I think that it is possible, if this one succeeds, that politicians and parties may feel this is fair game and it could become a regular part of the process," says election expert Dan Lowenstein, of the UCLA law school.

The hurdles for placing a recall of a statewide official on the ballot are generally much higher in states other than California, requiring a larger percentage of voters in the state to sign onto the idea. Still, threatened recalls are likely to become much more common. And the mere threat may cow some officials into avoiding unpopular decisions, such as raising taxes. *The Milwaukee Journal Sentinel,* for instance, ran a column in July warning Governor Jim Doyle that he should start feeling nervous about a potential recall, given his veto of a property-tax limitation bill. (Milwaukee voters will have the chance to recall state Senator Gary George on September 16.) "In the past, you could do something unpopular at the beginning of your term in hopes that memories would decay and there would be perspective by the end of your term," says Bruce Cain, director of the Institute of Governmental Studies at UC, Berkeley. "Now what we have because of the recall is more of a permanent campaign. The threat of a recall is very powerful, and in policy debates you can keep the heat on a governor."

Hard to Recall

Recalls of delegates were allowed under the pre-1789 Articles of Confederation, but the first recall law of the modern era was introduced in Los Angeles in 1903. Oregon took up the idea five years later, and it spread to about a dozen states over the next few years, championed by progressives who saw it as a

Recall Rules

Eighteen states permit the recall of elected officials. The requirements to recall statewide officials are below. (Rules for recalling legislators and judges may differ.)

	Specific Grounds for Recall	Signature Requirement	Petition Circulation Time	Election for Successor
Alaska	Yes	25%	Not Specified	Successor appointed
Ariz.	No	25%	120 days	Simultaneous[5]
Calif.	No	12%	160 days	Simultaneous[6]
Colo.	No	25%	60 days	Simultaneous[6]
Ga.	Yes	15%[1]	90 days	Separate special
Idaho	No	20%[1]	60 days	Successor appointed
Kan.	Yes	40%	90 days	Successor appointed
La.	No	33.3%[1]	180 days	Separate special
Mich.	No	25%	90 days	Separate special
Minn.	Yes	25%	90 days	Separate special
Mont.	Yes	10%[1]	3 months	Separate special
Nev.	No	25%	60 days	Simultaneous[5]
N.J.	No	25%[2]	320 days[4]	Separate special
N.D.	No	25%	Not Specified	Simultaneous[5]
Ore.	No	15%[3]	90 days	Separate special
R.I.	Yes	15%	90 days	Separate special
Wash.	Yes	25%	270 days	Successor appointed
Wis.	No	25%	60 days	Simultaneous[5]

Notes: Signature requirement is % of votes cast in last election for official being recalled. Exceptions: [1] % of eligible voters at time of last election; [2] % of registered voters in electoral district of official sought to be recalled; [3] % of total votes cast in officer's district for all candidates for governor in last election. [4] Applies to governor or U.S. senator; all other 160 days. [5] Recall ballot consists of a list of candidates for the office held by the person against whom the recall petition was filed. The name of the officer against whom the recall was filed may appear on the list. [6] Recall ballot consists of two parts: The first asks whether the officer against whom the recall petition was filed should be recalled. The second part lists candidates who have qualified for the election. The name of the officer against whom the recall was filed may not appear on this list.
Source: National Conference of State Legislatures

tool for citizens to wrest control from banks, railroads, mining companies and other interests they saw as having a stranglehold on state capitols. Most of the state recall laws date back to the early part of the 20th century, although Minnesota, New Jersey and Rhode Island passed theirs during the 1990s.

Ironically, the first statewide officials to be recalled were progressives themselves. North Dakota Governor Lynn Frazier, along with the state attorney general and agriculture commissioner, was the subject of a recall election in 1921. Under their leadership, the state had founded a bank and a grain silo business as a way of helping North Dakota farmers. Republicans who considered these operations to be socialist led the recalls. They were successful, but there was not much lingering political damage. Frazier was elected to the first of three U.S. Senate terms a year later, and the state of North Dakota has remained in the banking and silo businesses to this day. The only other governor who faced a scheduled recall election was Evan Mecham of Arizona, until the legislature saved voters the trouble by impeaching him in 1987.

At the local level, the success rate for recall elections is less than one-third. Most of the municipal recalls have taken place in jurisdictions with populations under 25,000, where practically anyone with a grievance or a grudge can gather the requisite few

signatures. In 1959, Little Rock voters recalled the segregationist majority from the school board after its members had resisted federal pressure to allow nine black children to enter Central High School. Over the past quarter century, there have been recall elections in Cleveland, Los Angeles, Omaha and Colorado Springs. U.S. Senator Dianne Feinstein—who many California Democrats hoped would run to replace Davis—turned back a recall attempt 20 years ago when she was the mayor of San Francisco.

Most of the 18 recall states have more stringent requirements than California. That state demands petition signatures equal to 12 percent of the registered voters who participated in the previous election for the office in question. Most states require twice as many signatures (25 percent); Kansas mandates 40 percent. California is not unique in allowing for recalls for any reason whatsoever, but half a dozen states require specific grounds, such as malfeasance, corruption or lack of fitness. Georgia, Minnesota and Washington State subject such charges to a form of legal review before a recall can go forward. The states vary in terms of how often they will allow recalls to occur, how much time petitioners have to gather signatures (as few as 60 days in four states) and whether there must be waiting periods for a time after, or leading up to, a regularly scheduled election.

Because of the legal hurdles, recalls have been rare. Over the past hundred years, there have been fewer than two dozen recall elections involving state officials, including legislators. Even after Louisiana Governor Edwin Edwards was indicted on federal racketeering charges, a recall effort fell 200,000 signatures short in 1984. Louisiana requires a higher number of signatures than California, even though its population is only one-seventh the size. "There's a reason why it's been 80 years since it's been successful," says Tim Eyman, who has run several successful anti-tax initiative campaigns in Washington over the last several years. "The hurdle you have to clear for signatures is just tremendously high." Even in California, recalls have been a tough sell. There had been 31 attempts at recalling California governors prior to this year, including a 1968 campaign against Ronald Reagan that gathered more than 550,000 signatures. All failed to make it onto the ballot. But, regardless of whether Davis is tossed out of office, this recall is likely to have what political scientists call a demonstration effect.

Admittedly, the circumstances have to be right. You have to have a governor who just rubs hundreds of thousands of people the wrong way, as Davis does. You have to have someone with deep pockets to fund a signature-gathering campaign. (Congressman Darrell Issa put up $1.7 million of his own money to jump-start the Davis recall process.) California does make the process easier than most states, both in terms of its lighter legal requirements and the fact that it has such an active initiatives industry set up to help hopeful petitioners along their way. All of these factors, though, can be replicated elsewhere—maybe not every year, but certainly in less than 82 years. "This is a consultant's dream," says Cain, "to be able to run a campaign in the off season and generate business."

The Politics of Spite

We are living, after all, in a time of "slightly unhinged partisanship," in the words of University of Kansas political scientist Burdett Loomis. The nation is split almost down the middle politically, which is why the two major parties exploit their every advantage in an almost Hobbesian fight for power. Consider, for example, the legal wrangling over the 2000 presidential election results in Florida. Or the current efforts by Republicans in Colorado and Texas to redraw congressional maps to create more districts to the GOP's advantage. Or Gray Davis' own $10 million ad campaign last year against former Los Angeles Mayor Richard Riordan in the GOP primary, helping to deny the nomination of the candidate he least wanted to face in November—part of a growing trend of candidates interfering in the other party's primary. Formerly extreme and extraordinary political and legal tactics are being used with increasing regularity. There's little reason to think that recalls will be an exception.

It's possible that some state legislators, after watching the circus in California, with its many uncertainties about when and how to call the recall election, will want to tighten up recall laws. After a Kansas judge threw out a recall petition against three Kaw Valley school board members last November because "the law needs clarity," some state legislators talked about clearing up some of the confusion about the law's intent. Waters, of the I&R Institute, warns that legislative "tinkering with the recall device will lead to additional restrictions, making it more difficult to use." If that is the case, there may be a backlash. Voters may decide they like having the recall available. It's a means of keeping capitol elites in line. Michigan state Representative Charles LaSata has been trying for several years to overhaul the state's recall laws to require petitioners to come up with signatures equal to 100 percent of the number of people who participated in the last election, plus one. His bill is routinely derided as an "incumbent protection act," or worse.

The lack of trust implied by recall attempts is in keeping with the spirit behind voters' imposing term limits on legislators and supporting initiatives that cap state taxes or spending. The "recent popularity [of recalls] coincides with a rise in political cynicism, or distrust of government institutions and their elected leaders," Central Michigan University political scientist Lawrence Sych wrote in a 1996 Comparative State Politics article. Certainly much of movie actor Arnold Schwarzenegger's rhetoric in announcing his candidacy in August was based on a sense that politics-as-usual could not be trusted and that Sacramento needed an outsider such as him to clean things up.

Loomis says that the recall was meant as a tool for getting rid of particularly egregious offenders who refused to leave office on their own legs, but in California it's currently being used for partisan political reasons. "You end up with a politics that is continually contentious, and there's almost no time to sit down and deliberate your way out of a difficult situation," he says. "Rather than having an election and saying, 'Okay, for the next two years or four years, this is the way it's going to be,' you politicize everything: We will redistrict because we can, we will impeach because we can, we will recall because we can."

If California voters put Schwarzenegger or any other Republican atop the throne of a state where Democrats control both houses of the legislature and every other statewide office, that will be proof enough of the efficacy of the recall as a political tool. "It puts it into the category of a more routine political technique," says Lowenstein, the UCLA law professor. "My concern is that it will feed into this trend away from civility."

---

*About 61% of California's registered voters participated in the recal vote on October 7, 2003, and 55% voted to remove Governor Davis from office. In the so-called "replacement election" held at the same time as the recall vote, Arnold Schwarzenegger received the most votes, about 49% of the total votes cast. Thus, on November 17, 2003, Governor Davis was removed from office and was succeeded by Governor Schwarzenegger.

From *Governing*, September 2003. Copyright © 2003 by Congressional Quarterly, Inc. Reprinted by permission.

Public Meetings and the Democratic Process

Public meetings are frequently attacked as useless democratic rituals that lack deliberative qualities and fail to give citizens a voice in the policy process. Do public meetings have a role to play in fostering citizen participation in policy making? While many of the criticisms leveled against public meetings have merit, I argue that they do. In this article, I explore the functions that city council and school board meetings serve. While they may not be very good at accomplishing their primary goal of giving citizens the opportunity to directly influence decisions made by governing bodies, they can be used to achieve other ends, such as sending information to officials and setting the agenda. As a complement to deliberative political structures, public meetings have a role to play by offering a venue in which citizens can achieve their political goals, thereby enhancing governmental accountability and responsiveness.

BRIAN ADAMS
San Diego State University

Most local governments hold regularly scheduled meetings to discuss and decide public issues. Opportunities for citizens to voice their opinions are usually a part of these meetings. Public input may take the form of comments on specific issues before the governmental body, or it may be general comments on issues that citizens care about. In either case, citizens are given a specified period of time (frequently two to three minutes) to state their opinions and are usually prohibited from engaging other citizens or officials in dialogue.

In this article, I examine city council and school board meetings in a mid-sized city (Santa Ana, California) and ask what role public meetings have in the participatory policy process. Can they play a constructive role by allowing citizens to voice their concerns and influence policy decisions, or are they a hollow ritual that merely provides a facade of legitimacy? If we want to incorporate greater public participation into the policy process, is there a place for public meetings? I add to the literature that examines the role of public participation in policy analysis (Thomas 1990; Walters, Aydelotte, and Miller 2000) by exploring what function public meetings serve and how they fit into the larger institutional context of citizen input into the policy process.

I argue that public meetings serve an important democratic function by providing citizens with the opportunity to convey information to officials, influence public opinion, attract media attention, set future agendas, delay decisions, and communicate with other citizens. Meetings are a tool that citizens can use to achieve political objectives. This tool is ill-suited for fostering policy deliberations or persuading officials to change a vote on a specific issue. But meetings serve another purpose: By giving citizens a venue in which they can achieve political goals, public meetings can enhance the political power of citizens and, consequently, improve governmental responsiveness to citizens.

If we keep in mind the functions that public meetings can and cannot perform, their role in the participatory policy process becomes clearer. Public meetings can complement the structures that foster citizen deliberation (such as citizen panels, forums, and roundtables) by providing citizens with the opportunity to engage in the political process before deliberations commence and after citizens have developed a set of recommendations or a consensus policy position. Even though public meetings themselves are not deliberative, they can facilitate citizen participation and the development of good policy by assisting citizens in achieving their political goals. In this article, I hope to show the purposes that public meetings serve and how they fit into a larger scheme of citizen input into policy making.

Institutional Design and Citizen Participation

In recent years, many scholars have argued for an enhancement of the extent and quality of citizen participation in policy making (Fischer 1993; deLeon 1995, 1997; King, Feltey, and Susel 1998; Roberts 1997; Schneider and Ingram 1997; Dryzek 1990). They contend that we need to develop structures and institutions to provide citizens with opportunities to participate effectively. But how do you design institutions to allow citizen input into the policy process? There are many ways that citizens can be brought into the policy process: Public hearings, citizen juries, roundtables, and electronic town meetings are examples of institutions meant to create opportunities for citizen participation.

One of the most common methods of citizen participation is the public hearing: A survey of city managers and chief administrative officers found that over 97 percent of cities use it as a strategy for dealing with citizens (Berman 1997, 107). Public hearings, which are usually required by law, allow citizens to comment on a specific issue or proposal before a governmental entity makes a decision. Despite its widespread use, public hearings are not held in high esteem. The most common critique—made by participants, academics, and governmental officials alike—is that citizen comments do not influence policy outcomes (Cole and Caputo 1984; Checkoway 1981). Citizens march up to the podium, give their two-minute speeches, the presiding official says "thank you very much," and then officials proceed with their business irrespective of the arguments made by citizens. Citizens may speak their mind, but officials do not listen and usually have their minds made up before the public hearing. Hearings, in this view, are mere democratic rituals that provide a false sense of legitimacy to legislative outcomes: Officials can say they received input from the public, and it can give their decisions the respect afforded to democratic processes, even though citizen input has no impact. Rather than a means for citizen input, hearings allow officials to deflect criticism and proceed with decisions that have already been made (Rowe and Frewer 2000; Kemp 1985; Checkoway 1981).

A second critique of public hearings is that they are a poor mechanism for deliberation (King, Feltey, and Susel 1998; Kemmis 1990, 51–53; Checkoway 1981). Citizens go to the podium, speak their peace, and then sit down. There is rarely dialogue between citizens and officials; in fact, such dialogue is usually forbidden. While citizens have a chance to state their position and support it with a reasoned argument, public hearings do not allow them to engage elected officials or other participants in a dialogue to try to persuade them to change their opinions. Public hearings do not afford citizens a venue where they can engage in public discussions about common problems and try to reach understanding with their fellow citizens and elected officials. Further, public hearings frequently degenerate into the worst sort of debate: Rather than citizens stating their opinions and offering supporting argumentation, they will employ sound bites, hyperbole, and falsehoods to criticize and demonize opponents—hardly a model of citizen deliberation.

Hearings are also criticized for attracting an unrepresentative sample of the population (McComas 2001a; Gastil and Kelshaw 2000). People who show up to meetings are more likely to be extremists on the issue being discussed because they have greater personal incentives to participate. Hearings may be dominated by those with very strong views on the subject being discussed, crowding out moderate voices that may represent large segments of the community. This dynamic has two repercussions: It undermines the legitimacy of the hearing as a venue for assessing public opinion, and it provides officials with an excuse to ignore public comments (because they believe they are not representative of what the public really thinks).

While even defenders of public hearings acknowledge they are a poor venue for deliberation, some research indicates that hearings can be an effective form of citizen participation and citizens can, at times, be representative of the public at large. In studies of the California Coastal Commission, Mazmanian and Sabatier (1980) and Rosener (1982) found that citizen participation at public hearings had an impact on the denial rate of permits under consideration by the board. Others have argued that under the right conditions (for instance, meetings held at a convenient time and advertised extensively), hearings can be effective at influencing policy and attracting a representative sample of the citizenry (McComas 2001b; Chess and Purcell 1999; Gundry and Heberlein 1984; Gormley 1986).

Dissatisfaction with public hearings as an outlet for participation has led many scholars and practitioners to develop alternative methods for involving the public in policy making. One alternative has been to modify the format of public meetings, discarding the structured and nondeliberative hearing format in favor of a roundtable or small group setting. These settings differ from traditional public hearings in that citizens have an opportunity to discuss the issue at hand and deliberate with fellow citizens and officials. Roberts (1997) argues that the public deliberation occurring at these meetings should be the foundation of an alternative way to solicit public input, and Weeks (2000) describes successful attempts to integrate meetings into a deliberative policy process.

National Issues Forums, a network committed to enhancing civic life and public involvement in politics, has experimented with alternatives to the traditional public hearing for almost 20 years. Here, citizens deliberate over public problems with the goal of developing a plan of action to address the issue (for descriptions of the type of deliberation fostered in such forums, see Mathews 1999; Doble Research Associates 2000a, 2000b, 2001). America Speaks, a nonprofit organization, promotes and organizes electronic town hall meetings that allow citizens to deliberate over policy issues. Using a mix of face-to-face deliberation and communication through technology, America Speaks attempts to empower citizens to voice their opinions and inform governmental action (America Speaks 2002).

One common obstacle to public meetings concerns size: The more people who show up at the meeting, the more difficult it is to have the type of face-to-face interaction and discussion that deliberation proponents desire. While America Speaks and other organizations have addressed some of the logistical problems caused by size, fostering deliberation in large groups is still problematic. One response has been to convene citizens panels or citizens juries to deliberate on issues (Crosby, Kelly, and Schaefer 1986; Kathlene and Martin 1991; Haight and Ginger 2000). These panels are representative samples of the public, and thus can act as a proxy for deliberation among the entire public; because it is not feasible for everyone to deliberate on an issue, selecting a representative sample to do it for them is the next best thing. Fishkin's (1991, 1995) deliberative opinion polls are a variation on this theme: Select a random sample of the public to deliberate on an issue (or an election), and their recommendations will reflect what the public at large would have decided if they had deliberated themselves.

Finally, surveys and focus groups are often considered to be a form of participation, although a qualitatively different form than those already listed. Surveys do not allow for any deliberation, nor do they allow citizens to express their individual voices, as hearings do. While focus groups allow for greater voice and deliberation, they are still limited by a structure that is meant to solicit opinions, not form them. Even though surveys and focus groups by themselves do not offer much opportunity for citizens to participate in policy making, they can be used to enhance other participation tools, such as the ones described earlier, making for a more meaningful and rich participatory structure (for examples, see Weeks 2000; Kathlene and Martin 1991).

I have described various mechanisms by which citizens can provide input into the policy process. The question I pose is this: Where, in this landscape of meetings, panels, surveys, and forums, do local city council and school board meetings fit? What role can they play?

Data and Methodology

The arguments presented in this article are based on research conducted in a mid-sized city, Santa Ana, California. Located just south of Los Angeles, Santa Ana has a population of about 320,000. At one point in its history, Santa Ana was a suburb of Los Angeles, but its links to Los Angeles (in terms of its reliance on Los Angeles for employment, shopping, and entertainment) have diminished over the past few decades, and now it can be considered a city in its own right. Fifty-five interviews with citizen participants were conducted between March and July 2001. Respondents were selected through a variety of means: Some names were gathered through newspaper reports of citizen activities, some were culled from the minutes of city council and school board meetings, and other names were given to the researcher by respondents already interviewed. Through these methods, a list was compiled of these citizens who were most active in Santa Ana politics. Most respondents were involved in civic organizations, such as neighborhood associations, PTAs, and city advisory committees. While many held formal positions (president, treasurer, etc.) within these organizations, few could draw upon extensive institutional resources to achieve political ends, and thus were relatively less powerful than many other political actors, such as union leaders and developers.[1] Generally, the respondents were citizens who were highly involved in local politics but could not be considered "political elites." There were four exceptions: three former elected officials (one city councilman and two school board trustees) and the president of the Santa Ana Chamber of Commerce.

Interviews were semistructured and asked participants about their activities in trying to influence city and school district policy (the city and school district are separate entities, but both were included in this study). After some general questions about the activities they engage in when trying to influence public policy, respondents were asked to list two or three policies they had personally been involved with, and then were asked follow-up questions on each, including questions about their strategy and effectiveness.

Attending city council and school board meetings is a very common form of participation: 98 percent of respondents reported having attended at least one meeting during the past 10 years, and most indicated they attend meetings on a regular basis.[2] Even though almost everybody stated they went to public meetings, there was some disagreement about their effectiveness. While a few respondents said that attending meetings was the most effective form of participation, most did not (the most frequent response was talking or writing to elected officials directly). Many echoed the common complaint that elected officials already have their minds made up before the meeting. Despite this widespread belief, many respondents offered other reasons why attendance at public meetings is effective. These explanations form the basis for the findings that follow. These are not meant to characterize the aggregate opinion of the respondents, as opinion varied too much to reach any firm conclusion about the attitude of respondents toward public meetings. Rather, the findings that follow describe some functions that public meetings perform and offer reasons why we should maintain this institution.

I do not present Santa Ana as a typical or representative city. Future research on other cities may find that citizens go to meetings for different reasons than they do in Santa Ana, and thus the findings that follow may not be generalizable to other cities. That said, they are valuable because they offer insight into the potential for public meetings to have a constructive role in the policy process. The findings that follow are evidence that public meetings can serve a valuable function for citizens, not that they serve those functions in all contexts or situations.

The Functions of Public Meetings

Public meetings of city councils and schools boards in California are governed by the Brown Act, which requires that all meetings of local governments be open to the public and allow for public participation. The Brown Act gives the public the right to comment on items before the legislative body, and it also stipulates that "time must be set aside for the public to comment on any other matters under the body's jurisdiction" (California DOJ 2002, vii). Thus, citizens have an opportunity to speak about agenda items, as well as any other local issues they feel are important. There are six ways that citizens can use these opportunities to accomplish their political goals.

Provide Information

Public meetings can be an effective way to convey information about public opinion to officials. One piece of information that needs to be communicated is interest in a particular issue: Letting officials know that you are out there is a necessary first step to participation. One respondent stated that attending public meetings was important because "it seems like if you don't show up at the Council meetings, the council says 'well, maybe this is a non-issue.'" Another participant made a similar point, arguing that getting a lot of people to a council meeting is critical to showing that people care about an issue (in this case, a traffic issue). There are, of course, other ways to let officials know that a particular issue is important to citizens: They may circulate petitions, write letters, or call officials directly. In some circumstances, however, attending a meeting can be the most effective way of indicating interest. Gathering a group of citizens to go to a meeting not only is relatively easy, but also clearly communicates to officials that there is interest in an issue.

Some respondents also felt that attendance at meetings was important to counterbalance opposing views and to get their message out. A common theme among respondents was that there is power in numbers, and turning out the masses at city council or school board meetings provides a political advantage by adding force to their message. This dynamic was evident on both sides of a highly contentious debate over the siting of a new school. A supporter of the school stated that "we wanted to have a lot of parents with school children there [at the public meeting] because otherwise you were going to have an imbalance." School opponents also noted their attempts to bring out large numbers to meetings, and both sides claimed they had outnumbered their opponent. Having numbers turn out for meetings is important because one common discourse in local politics concerns which side of the debate has more popular support. Absent scientific polls, actual levels of support are not known, leaving participants free to convince elected officials that they, in fact, have more support. Turnout at public meetings may be seen by officials as evidence of popular support (although frequently weak support, given the unrepresentativeness of those who attend), and thus can be used as a debating point. Lacking other information sources, elected officials may rely on turnout at public meetings, however unrepresentative, to gauge public support for or opposition to a given policy.

The comments of two former elected officials indicate they use public meetings as a source of information. One former school trustee said she kept tallies of supporters and opponents on an issue to get a feel for what the community thought. A former city councilman, talking about a proposal for a permit-parking district in a residential neighborhood, told this story:

> We were told that this was going on and the neighborhood is happy with it and the staff was happy with it, and they worked it out and it was all ready to go. Then it came before us to vote on it, all of the sudden we had a swarm of people who were against it.… I was prepared to go ahead and vote with it from the information I had, but then when this large constituent [sic] of business owners came out I said this is something I hadn't planned on. I can't vote on it. We need to sit down and work this through to see if we can't make both sides a little bit happier. Those groups of people got to me.… I would do my homework, and my colleagues—we did our homework.… We may have had our minds made up with the facts that we had been given, but when we would have a group come and speak against it, I wouldn't ram it on through, but make a motion to continue it. Let's hear more of what the people are trying to say and sit down and talk to them, again get that dialogue going so we can really find out what their concerns are and what we can do to alleviate it.

For this city councilman, a public hearing provided information about where his constituents stood on an issue. He did not state that public comments had persuaded him to change his thinking on an issue by offering new ideas or new interpretations. He did not say the citizens appearing at the hearing had changed his mind on an issue, or persuaded him that he was mistaken in his support for the proposal. He did, however, change his actions based on the opposition to the proposal that was evident at the public hearing. The public hearing provided new information that altered the actions he took, even if it did not persuade him that his views were mistaken. Rather than acting as a deliberative forum where ideas are exchanged and people's opinions change based on rational persuasion, the view of meetings that emerges here is of a forum in which constituents provide their elected officials with new information about their views on an issue, prompting altered behavior on the part of officials.

Officials, of course, may have other sources of information about public opinion, such as surveys, focus groups, forums, letters and phone calls from constituents, conversations with others, and media reports. Some of these, such as surveys and focus groups, reflect public opinion more accurately because the participants are more representative of the population as a whole. Despite this shortcoming, public meetings have some benefits as a vehicle for voicing public opinion. First, public meetings are useful in measuring the strength of opinion on a particular issue. Officials know that citizens who take the time to come to a meeting care about the issue under discussion, while surveys make no such indication. Further, meetings are open to anyone who wishes to speak, while surveys, focus groups, and advisory panels have restricted participation. While not having restrictions may introduce bias into the opinions presented, the open meeting has an advantage in terms of legitimacy: Citizens who feel their voices are not being represented in survey results or panel recommendations have an opportunity to express views that may be a bit off the beaten path. By providing a venue for citizens who wish to present alternative opinions, meetings can add legitimacy to the policy process. By themselves, public meetings do not provide an accurate picture of public opinion on local issues, but they can act as a valuable and important supplement to other forms of public opinion, providing both additional information and legitimacy.

A Show of Support

One recurring theme among respondents was the importance of supporting friendly elected officials who take controversial policy stands and expressing displeasure with officials who take stands they disagree with. On controversial issues, elected officials are forced to take a position that may alienate some constituents—not a desirable position for politicians who prefer to please everyone. When an elected official takes a position that is unpopular with some, his or her supporters will frequently make a point of coming to a meeting to agree with the stand taken, in a show of support for a politician in an uncomfortable situation. For example, one participant made this comment about supporting a decision on a new school: "We certainly gave Rob and Audrey [two school board members] counter high-ground to stand on. They could say, 'look. These people, our constituents, the parents of the children, they are here to support.' This gave them a public high ground to stand on to shape the argument.…

It didn't change anybody's mind, but it certainly helped to direct the flow of discussion."

Sometimes, officials need political cover for taking unpopular stands, which can be provided by supporters at a public meeting. If a politician is supporting the view of a small minority (for example, of one particular neighborhood) that is highly unpopular, he or she could take a major public relations hit; he or she could be characterized as out of step with the majority, catering to special interests and the like. These characterizations can be even more potent if they are out there all alone, without any support, while opponents are banging away. Citizens at public meetings, however, can provide some cover by showing public support for an unpopular position. For example, one participant explained why he had attended a meeting in support of a restaurant desiring a liquor license: "It makes it easier for them [the city council] to make a decision if they have support, rather than you making that decision on your own because you know it's right and its best for the community. It takes some of that burden, some of that responsibility, from the Council if there's public support." While the politicians supporting the liquor license might still take some political heat (there was opposition from nearby businesses), at least they can point to a group of citizens and say, "I have some support in the community for my position." From a public relations standpoint, a show of support can be critical, providing cover for a politician in a tight spot and diffusing some of the criticism. Public meetings are an excellent venue to provide this support because they are usually televised and sometimes covered by local newspapers, allowing supporters to get their message out.

Supporting sympathetic officials does not affect votes on issues, nor is it meant to. But it does have an impact. First, it strengthens the relationship between a politician and his or her supporters and creates channels of communication. Elected officials, seeing who supports them during the tough times, will be more likely to return phone calls, arrange face-to-face meetings, and listen to those constituents. Politicians appreciate support on controversial issues and, as a consequence, will be more willing to listen to their constituents on other issues. In other words, public meetings allow citizens to identify themselves as supporters, giving them an opportunity to create relationships with officials. Second, it provides an avenue by which citizens can help officials whom they want to remain in office. Popular support for a controversial vote is an important political cover: Without it, elected officials are susceptible to accusations during the next election that they are out of touch with their constituents and out of step with public opinion. Public meetings provide a means by which citizens can provide political cover for supportive politicians, thus reducing their exposure during the next election.

Shaming

Most citizens at public meetings are not there to support, but to criticize. Elected officials frequently complain about citizens who are silent until they want to vent about a decision they disagree with. At first blush, this type of behavior may seem futile. Yelling and screaming at a meeting is not likely to change the votes of elected officials, so why do citizens go to meetings

to complain? One function it serves is to shame elected officials for disagreeable actions. As I have mentioned, support at a meeting can provide political cover for officials; the converse is also true. Criticizing officials in a public forum can create the perception they are out of touch with the community. This is particularly important from a media perspective: The local newspaper or television newscast is likely to report that officials were criticized by their constituents at a meeting, particularly if it is a highly controversial issue. Even if the citizens at the meeting are not representative of the community at large, the image of an official being hammered by his or her constituents is a powerful one, and one that may have important electoral implications.

One example of the shaming dynamic was seen when a group of parents went to a city council meeting to criticize a councilwoman. The issue was a proposed school that was generating a lot of controversy due to its location: The wealthy white neighborhood next to the proposed school opposed it, while many citizens in other parts of the city supported it. The decision to build or not to build was a school district decision (which is a separate entity from the city), but one councilwoman, Lisa Mills, was at the forefront of the opposition to the school. A group of school supporters went to a city council meeting to complain about Councilwoman Mills's activities on the issue and her divisive comments. One leader of the group explained why it was necessary: "[Lisa Mills] was very divisive … it was really a lot of lies that were coming down the pipe. A lot of people that weren't involved with the school district, that's all they were getting. So it was very important to counterbalance that. And you had to do it with numbers, you had to do that with a lot of people." Another leader of the group made this comment: "When [Mayor] Dan Young said after the meeting that he'd never ever seen anything like that before in his life, it was like 'ok, we got our message across.' To get up there and publicly censure Lisa Mills for her activities. That was something that … it was a distraction and a lot of energy that we didn't need to continue to fight that so we went in and we hit hard and she wasn't really heard from much on that issue after that."

Since the council had no authority over the issue, school supporters were not trying to change the outcome of any policy decision: Their only purpose was to shame Councilwoman Mills. This served two purposes. First, it swayed the terms of the debate and public perceptions by indicating the amount of support the school had. Also, it gave Councilwoman Mills a political black eye, which could have been a liability during the next election (she decided not to run for a second term).

Another example illustrates the effectiveness of shaming officials at public meetings. The issue was a proposed park and community center for Delhi, a working-class Latino community. The city had been promising to build the park for years but never came forward and provided the funding. After repeated stonewalling and delays by the city, supporters decided to force the issue by going to a city council meeting. Here's how a supporter relates what happened:

So we organized a meeting at City Council, we took about 150 people to that meeting. … And the questions were very simple. They were like: why haven't you kept your promises? And I think in many ways, we sort of shamed people, we shamed them because, you know, why haven't you kept your promises?... And so what happened was that was aired on Comcast [the local cable company] throughout Santa Ana. ... [S]o before you know it, I had people calling [me] ... they were saying "they can't do this to you guys. They can't just put all the money into north Santa Ana. They have to pay attention to all these neighborhoods." People starting coming out of the woodworking, you know, they said they have to make this project for this community. So I think they [the City Council] were probably receiving those kind of calls. And the day after the meeting ... at the meeting, the Mayor and the rest of the Council, they were kind of cool about things, very evasive, didn't act like they were disturbed in any way. But I'll tell you, the next morning, the Mayor was begging me to meet with him. He said, "please, let's sit down and let's try to work something out."

The value of this shaming strategy lies not in its capacity to persuade the council that the park was a good idea; accusing the council of lying and breaking promises is hardly the way to accomplish that goal. Rather, by embarrassing the council, it was forced to pay attention to the issue and take action (the council eventually did provide some funds for the park, although not as much as requested). A public meeting was the ideal venue for carrying out this shaming strategy. It was televised, and thus many people in the community heard the park supporters' message, placing additional pressure on the city council.[3] For council members, having to sit through a meeting at which 150 angry residents are accusing you of lying and breaking promises while other constituents watch on television is hardly an enticing prospect. We should not be surprised that this strategy bore fruit and got the city to move on the park project.

The capacity to publicly attack officials is an important aspect of democratic governance: Citizens need a venue in which they can counter what their elected officials are doing or saying. Public meetings provide that venue. They give citizens the ability to gather in one place and express opinions that run counter to what officials are saying. While citizens have other venues in which they can criticize officials—such as writing letters to the editor, staging street protests, or voting against officials in the next election—public meetings present a unique opportunity because they are public, easily accessible, and allow citizens to speak their minds. Elected officials never look good when they are being yelled at, and thus venting at public meetings can undermine and weaken the positions of elected officials. Much of the criticism that officials receive may be unjustified and unfair, and I certainly do not mean to imply that citizens are always correct or that elected officials always deserve derision. Fair or not, the ability to criticize elected officials is a cornerstone of democratic politics, and public meetings provide an excellent opportunity for citizens to do so.

Agenda Setting

The power of elites to set the agenda is well documented in the urban power literature (Bachrach and Baratz 1962; Crenson 1971; Gaventa 1980; see Polsby 1980 for a critique). Much less studied is how and under what conditions citizens can influence the agenda. We generally think of public meetings as venues where policy decisions are made, not where agendas are formulated. While in most cases this is true, meetings do provide opportunities for agenda setting by citizens. In Santa Ana, both the city council and school board allow for public comments on nonagenda items, allowing citizens to discuss issues that have not yet been formally taken up by officials. Some participants, when asked whether speaking at public meetings is effective, stated that attending a meeting the day an issue is going to be decided is useless, but going earlier in the process is very effective as an agenda-setting device. One respondent, who was both president of her neighborhood association and president of the library board (a city advisory board), has this to say about whether meetings are valuable:

You have to be smart when you do it. Like we started speaking a while ago about the library budget because they won't make their decision, they're starting to make their decisions now [March], but they'll make final decisions in June and July. I think they're thinking, too, if you speak on the agenda items, well no, its totally done before it comes to the committee. So you have to speak now about. ... Like we spoke about CenterLine [a light rail proposal]. ... We spoke about CenterLine before it even came up at all. And they said "why are you talking about this today?" and we said "because we know you are going to make a decision on it soon. We know you are. We've heard the buzz. So we are going to get a voice now, even though its not an agenda item or anything." I think that's where you have to be smart.

The respondent is making two interrelated points about the value of speaking at public meetings on nonagenda items. First, she is highlighting the importance of early participation. By the time a decision reaches the city council or school board, it has already been in the works for quite some time, with advisory committees, staff, and interested parties providing input. Compromises may already be built into the policy, with the key players working out agreements among themselves. Further, supporters or opponents of a policy may be able to convince elected officials of the merits of their position well before it ever gets to a formal vote. Participation, therefore, is most effective before positions harden, compromises are worked out, and advisory committees make recommendations; showing up at a city council or school board meeting on the day a policy is scheduled to be approved is, in many cases, too late in the process to make an impact. Thus, speaking on an issue to be decided that night is not the most effective way to influence decisions. Speaking at a public meeting well before a decision is made, however, can be effective: By speaking early in the process, citizens are able to get their opinions heard while officials are still deciding how they want to resolve the issue. This is why it was smart to comment on the CenterLine proposal well before it came up for a formal vote (at the time, it was unclear how the city council was going to vote).

Speaking at public meetings can also influence the agenda by making officials pay attention to issues they ordinarily would not. The respondent just quoted illustrates this with her comment about the library budget. Usually, the city does not pay much attention to the library budget and rarely provides additional funding. By speaking up early at a public meeting, citizens can establish an issue (in this case, library funding) as one that needs to be addressed. Another respondent, when asked why speaking at budget hearings is effective, said that it has some impact because "even though they've already made up their minds, it could stay up in their minds for the next budget meeting."

Agenda-setting effects tie into my first point about public meetings sending information to officials: The reason speaking at meetings may help set the agenda is that elected officials may use it as a measure of citizen interest in a topic. If citizens are coming to meetings to talk about the CenterLine proposal months before a decision is due, officials may conclude it is a highly controversial issue that deserves more attention than they are giving it. Conversely, if nobody raises the library budget as an issue, it will likely be ignored by officials (as it usually is). Not only can officials use public comments at meetings to gauge where their constituents stand on the issues of the day, but they can also use them to determine which issues are important and deserve their attention. With limited time at their disposal (elected officials in Santa Ana work part-time), they need to pick and choose the issues that get on their agenda, and citizens showing up to discuss an issue at a meeting may influence those decisions.

That said, public meetings are not the most effective way to influence governmental agendas. Motivating a group of citizens to attend a meeting to discuss an issue that will be decided far in the future is difficult. Further, elected officials may forget about public comments by the time decisions need to be made. Other forms of participation, such as writing letters, circulating petitions, or speaking directly to officials may be more effective at getting them to pay attention to certain issues. Public meetings, however, can be used in conjunction with these other methods and can further advance the agenda-setting goals of citizens. They are particularly useful in making demands on officials public. More private forms of participation, such as letter writing and speaking directly to officials, may get some attention, but they are likely to get more attention if they are coupled with a public display. One chief virtue of public meetings is that they are public, and thus can reach a larger audience than just officials and a small group of participants. They may not be a very effective method by themselves, but they can serve an important agenda-setting purpose if used along with other methods.

Many of the other participatory structures discussed previously, such as citizens' panels, forums, and roundtables, already assume an agenda that is decided by officials. Sometimes, officials use these structures to define agendas (Weeks 2000), but usually the issue to be discussed is identified and framed by officials beforehand. Citizen comments at public meetings can play a role in deciding which issues to convene panels or roundtables for and how those issues will be framed. Public meetings can provide the raw opinions and ideas that can start more deliberative (and ultimately constructive) processes to address public issues.

Delay

While it is rare for elected officials to change their votes based on citizen comments at a public meeting, it is much more common for votes to be delayed because of public outcry, especially if it is unexpected. In some cases, officials may delay to avoid making unpopular decisions with people present, hoping fewer people will be present at the next meeting. In other instances, citizens may desire a delay. One respondent told of a planning commission meeting that was discussing a development mitigation plan. A neighborhood resident, seeing the planning commission was prepared to vote against the plan, stated, "We told them we need to know what our rights are, and we asked them for a 30-day extension, and they granted it to us." This gave the neighborhood residents time to develop a strategy for accomplishing their goals. In some cases, citizens may not find out about an issue until the last minute, and thus they may not have time to take actions such as circulating petitions or organizing a letter-writing campaign which could apply pressure on officials. A delay may create time to work over officials or to gather more support in the community.

Public meetings are an excellent venue for asking for a delay: Elected officials may find it hard to ignore citizens who are merely asking for more time to study an issue, try to reach a compromise, or (as in the previous example) figure out what actions they can take. Asking for a delay is not an unreasonable request, increasing the pressure on elected officials to accommodate it. The ability of citizens to publicly ask for a delay and to provide reasons why the delay is necessary adds to the force of the request. Privately requesting a delay (in a letter or in a phone conversation) does not allow citizens to publicly state their argument in favor of a delay, and thus it is not as politically forceful. Public meetings provide the best opportunity for citizens to ask elected officials to delay a decision because they can publicly present arguments that attest to the reasonableness and wisdom of the request.

Networking

While the primary channel of communication at public meetings is from citizens to elected officials, citizens can also use meetings to communicate with each other. Communication among citizens is not easy because they usually lack the money to send out mailings and frequently lack the time to knock on doors or organize phone trees (although citizens do engage in these activities on occasion). Public meetings allow citizens to get their message out to other citizens relatively cheaply and without a significant time commitment. Usually, only citizens who are active in local politics attend or watch the meeting on television, so they are not a good venue for communication to the citizenry at large. But they are good for communicating with other citizens who are active. Public meetings can create and maintain social networks among active citizens by allowing them to let others know what they are doing. We saw one example of this with the citizen who was advocating a new park for the Delhi neighborhood. She mentioned that after the public meeting, people from other parts of the city called her about the park issue, fostering networks between her group and other neighborhoods and organizations. Of course, citizens have other ways to communicate with each other, and I do not mean to imply that public meetings are a primary, or even an effective, means of building networks. But they can help citizens get their message out and reach out to other citizens in the community.

Influencing Votes

Public meetings can serve other functions in addition to influencing the votes of officials. The six functions just listed are examples of how citizens can use meetings to achieve political goals that may indirectly influence votes by altering the political context in which the votes are taken, but they do not directly change a specific vote. Whether public meetings are effective at the latter is a point of contention in the literature. To round out my picture of the role and place of public meetings, in this section I will discuss the conditions under which meetings may be effective at directly influencing votes. Rather than claim that meetings are effective or not effective, I will explore under what conditions meetings might be influential and why.

My research uncovered one case in which a public meeting unequivocally changed the outcome of a city council decision. The issue was a citywide redevelopment project that, according to its supporters, was proposed to raise money for needed infrastructure projects such as parks and schools. Going into the meeting, most observers expected it to pass. In the weeks before the meeting, a few activists who opposed the redevelopment plan rallied citizens to go to the meeting to voice their opposition. Their efforts worked better than they had hoped: According to newspaper accounts, more than 2,000 citizens showed up to protest. After hearing a handful of irate speakers, the city council voted unanimously to table the item, and it was never brought up again. According to all sources, the redevelopment plan would have passed if it had not been for the outpouring of opposition at the meeting.

This incident illuminates some conditions in which public meetings can effectively change votes. First, elected officials were surprised at the turnout and the opposition.[4] If they had known it would generate so much opposition, they likely would have postponed the decision until they could marshal more support. Or, if they had had the resolve, they might have voted for it despite the opposition. Here we have a case in which meetings conveyed new information to officials (that is, the amount of opposition in the community) that had a direct impact on the vote. The reason it had such a profound impact was that officials did not have the luxury of a public opinion poll to gauge opposition, and thus were blindsided at the meeting. The conclusion to draw is this: If elected officials misjudge public support or opposition, meetings may change votes because they provide new information that changes officials' political calculations.

Two other conditions contributed to the public's ability to change the vote: the sheer numbers of people who appeared, and the absence of supporters. An attendance of 2,000 at a public hearing is phenomenal, particularly in a city of 320,000 people. This unusual show of force must have indicated to officials that the vote could have serious political ramifications and prompted them to change their votes on the spot. Further, the fact that all present were opposed, made a yes vote politically dangerous. As I have mentioned, having support provides political cover. None was present here, making an affirmative vote more difficult.

One more condition may have contributed to the vote change which was not present during the redevelopment incident: the ambivalence of elected officials. Some issues may be more important to citizens than to elected officials, and the latter may be willing to change their votes based on comments at a hearing because they do not have strong feelings either way. This is not likely because elected officials are usually in tune with the wishes and demands of their constituents. But it may happen on occasion.

Whether public meetings are more effective than other forms of participation at influencing the votes of elected officials is a research question that is beyond the scope of this article. My point is not that attending meetings is the most effective strategy for changing legislative decisions, but that, under some circumstances, meetings can be used to accomplish this goal. Adding this argument to the previous section's description of other functions that meetings serve illustrates the usefulness of meetings for citizens. They may not be the best tool for accomplishing political goals, but they do add a weapon to the citizen's political arsenal which can be marshaled to enhance the effectiveness of citizen participation.

Conclusion

At the core of democracy is citizen deliberation and rational persuasion: Citizens deliberate over pressing public issues and make arguments to persuade officials (and each other) to take desired actions. Public meetings do not contribute to either of these goals: They are not deliberative, and they are not an effective vehicle for rational persuasion. Public meetings, however, have a role to play in maintaining a democratic system. Around the core of deliberation and rational persuasion is a democratic periphery of political maneuvering and pressure tactics that are essential parts of a democratic process, and this is where public meetings come into play. Meetings are a tool in the citizen's participatory toolbox that can help them accomplish political objectives—such as supporting allies, embarrassing enemies, setting the agenda, and getting their voice heard—which can add to their influence and effectiveness. The findings from Santa Ana demonstrate some ways that meetings can be used to citizens' advantage.

How do public meetings fit into the overall scheme of citizen participation and policy making? Public meetings do not directly contribute to the process of formulating effective policy solutions to public problems; other devices, such as roundtables, forums, and citizens' panels, are more effective at this task. But meetings, by helping citizens to be more effective, can enhance the responsiveness and accountability of government. Citizen deliberation and discussion on tough policy choices may lead to the formulation of better policy but, by itself, does not make government any more responsive to citizens. If citizen recommendations go unheeded, then the whole process is for naught. This is where public meetings fit in: They provide a venue for citizens to carry out a political struggle to have their voices heard and recommendations heeded. After citizens deliberate on an issue, weigh policy choices, and make recommendations, they can go to a public meeting to make their case. This is not the current role that meetings play, as most speakers at public meetings argue for their personal opinions, not collective opinions derived through deliberation. But, if additional deliberation structures are put into place, public meetings could have a valuable role by enhancing the political power of citizens and, consequently, increasing the chances that government will be responsive to their recommendations.

Public meetings can also assist citizens at the front end of the policy process by providing a venue for citizens to set the agenda and frame policy issues. In many participatory venues, the issues to be discussed are identified beforehand and a framework for discussing the issue is set. While this may be necessary to foster constructive deliberation, it limits the voice of citizens, preventing them from altering the structure of the conversation or changing how an issue is framed. At public meetings, citizens are free to identify issues that need to be discussed and offer new frameworks for understanding issues already under discussion. Before deliberation in forums, panels, or roundtables commences, citizens should have the opportunity to propose what issues need to be discussed, how the issue should be understood, and the manner in which the process should work. Public meetings could give citizens the opportunity to influence the way citizens participate, rather than having government officials decide for them.

Thus, public meetings have a role to play at the beginning and the end of participatory processes. Designing institutions that allow for citizen participation in the policy process requires us to create deliberative and constructive outlets for citizen input. But this positive political power needs to be supplemented by other forms of participation that allow citizens to flex their political muscle (see Rimmerman 1997 for a description of different forms of political participation). Both types of power are needed for a healthy democratic policy process. A process that lacks opportunities for constructive citizen deliberation will lead to disillusionment among citizens and reinforce the disconnect between citizens and their government. On the other hand, a process that allows citizens constructive input but limits their capacity to fight political battles, influence legislative votes, or criticize officials will reduce governmental responsiveness. Without the political power to back up citizen input, much of it will be duly filed, never to see the light of day again. The power to pressure, lobby, and cajole government officials is an essential complement to positive power, as constructive citizen deliberation is only valuable if officials pay attention to it. Thus, public meetings, as a venue where this can occur, cannot be replaced by more deliberative or constructive venues.

In this article, I have explored the value that public meetings have for citizens. But why would local officials want to hold them? By giving citizens an opportunity to accomplish their political goals, public meetings reduce the power and control exercised by officials. There are, however, two reasons why officials would desire to keep public meetings. First, they can provide information to officials about public opinion, particu-

larly which issues citizens feel are important and the strength of their opinions. Second, because public meetings are an open forum in which any citizen can speak, they provide a measure of legitimacy to the policy process. As many scholars have noted, citizens are cynical about politics and government (Rimmerman 1997; Berman 1997; Harwood Group 1991), and thus likely to approach a roundtable, forum, or other project with a wary eye. By providing an open forum for citizens to express their opinions, public meetings enhance the legitimacy of the policy process, a desired commodity for public officials. While public meetings benefit citizens more than they do officials, the latter do derive some benefit and would be wise to maintain the institution.

Notes

1. Political actors commanding significant resources were intentionally excluded. The study was limited to focus on how citizens without institutional power or other resources can use public meetings as a political tool.

2. While this number is high, other forms of participation also ranked very high: 92 percent reported having circulated a petition, and 100 percent reported having spoken to an elected official. Because respondents were chosen based on the fact that they were active, we should expect such high numbers.

3. I do not know the television ratings for city council meetings, but I imagine very few people watch them. That said, those who do watch are most likely politically active, which explains the significant reaction to this meeting.

4. This observation is based on the comments of opponents who were interviewed for this study.

References

America Speaks. 2002. Taking Democracy to Scale: Reconnecting Citizens with National Policy through Public Deliberation. Paper presented at the Taking Democracy to Scale Conference, May 8– 10, Warrenton, VA.

Bachrach, Peter, and Morton S. Baratz. 1962. Two Faces of Power. *American Political Science Review* 61(4): 947–52.

Berman, Evan M. 1997. Dealing with Cynical Citizens. *Public Administration Review* 57(2): 105–12.

California Department of Justice, Office of the Attorney General. 2002. *The Brown Act: Open Meetings for Local Legislative Bodies.* Informational pamphlet.

Checkoway, Barry. 1981. The Politics of Public Meetings. *Journal of Applied Behavioral Science* 17(4): 566–82.

Chess, Caron, and Kristen Purcell. 1999. Public Participation and the Environment: Do We Know What Works? *Environmental Science and Technology* 33(16): 2685–92.

Cole, Richard L., and David Caputo. 1984. The Public Hearing as an Effective Citizen Participation Mechanism: A Case Study of the General Revenue Sharing Program. *American Political Science Review* 78(2): 404–16.

Crenson, Matthew A. 1971. *The Un-Politics of Air Pollution: A Study of Non-Decisionmaking in the Cities.* Baltimore, MD: Johns Hopkins University Press.

Crosby, Ned, Janet M. Kelly, and Paul Schaefer. 1986. Citizens Panels: A New Approach to Citizen Participation. *Public Administration Review* 46(2): 170-78.

deLeon, Peter. 1995. Democratic Values and the Policy Sciences. *American Journal of Political Science* 39(4): 886–905.

———. 1997. *Democracy and the Policy Sciences*. Albany, NY: State University of New York Press.

Doble Research Associates. 2000a. Public Schools: Are They Making the Grade? Report prepared for the Kettering Foundation, Dayton, OH.

———. 2000b. Our Nation's Kids: Is Something Wrong? Report prepared for the Kettering Foundation, Dayton, OH.

———. 2001. Money and Politics: Who Owns Democracy. Report prepared for the Kettering Foundation, Dayton, OH.

Dryzek, John S. 1990. *Discursive Democracy*. Cambridge: Cambridge University Press.

Fischer, Frank. 1993. Citizen Participation and the Democratization of Policy Expertise: From Theoretical Inquiry to Practical Cases. *Policy Sciences* 26(3): 165–87.

Fishkin, James S. 1991. *Democracy and Deliberation: New Directions for Democratic Reform*. New Haven, CT: Yale University Press.

———. 1995. *The Voice of the People: Public Opinion and Democracy*. New Haven, CT: Yale University Press.

Gastil, John, and Todd Kelshaw. 2000. Public Meetings: A Sampler of Deliberative Forums that Bring Officeholders and Citizens Together. Report prepared for the Kettering Foundation, Dayton, OH.

Gaventa, John. 1980. *Power and Powerlessness: Quiescence and Rebellion in an Appalachian Valley*. Urbana: University of Illinois Press.

Gormley, William T. 1986. The Representation Revolution: Reforming State Regulation through Public Representation. *Administration and Society* 18(2): 179–96.

Gundry, Kathleen G., and Thomas A. Heberlein. 1984. Do Public Meetings Represent the Public? *Journal of the American Planning Association* 50(2): 175–82.

Haight, David, and Clare Ginger. 2000. Trust and Understanding in Participatory Policy Analysis: The Case of the Vermont Forest Resources Advisory Council. *Policy Studies Journal* 28(4): 739–59.

Harwood Group. 1991. Citizens and Politics: A View from Main Street America. Report prepared for the Kettering Foundation, Dayton, OH.

Kathlene, Lyn, and John A. Martin. 1991. Enhancing Citizen Participation: Panel Designs, Perspectives, and Policy Formation. *Journal of Policy Analysis and Management* 10(1): 46–63.

Kemmis, Daniel. 1990. *Community and the Politics of Place*. Norman: University of Oklahoma Press.

Kemp, Ray. 1985. Planning, Public Meetings and the Politics of Discourse. In *Critical Theory and Public Life*, edited by John Forester, 177–201. Cambridge, MA: MIT Press.

King, Cheryl Simrell, Kathryn M. Feltey, and Bridget O'Neill Susel. 1998. The Question of Participation: Towards Authentic Public Participation in Public Administration. *Public Administration Review* 58(4): 317–26.

Mathews, David. 1999. *Politics for People: Finding a Responsible Public Voice*. 2nd ed. Urbana: University of Illinois Press.

Mazmanian, Daniel A., and Paul A Sabatier. 1980. A Multivariate Model of Public Policy-Making. *American Journal of Political Science* 24(3): 439–68.

McComas, Katherine A. 2001a. Public Meetings about Local Waste Management Problems: Comparing Participants to Nonparticipants. *Environmental Management* 27(1): 135–47.

———. 2001b. Theory and Practice of Public Meetings. *Communication Theory* 11(1): 36–55.

Polsby, Nelson W. 1980. *Community Power and Political Theory: A Further Look at Problems of Evidence and Inference*. New Haven, CT: Yale University Press.

Rimmerman, Craig A. 1997. *The New Citizenship: Unconventional Politics, Activism, and Service*. Boulder, CO: Westview Press.

Roberts, Nancy. 1997. Public Deliberation: An Alternative Approach to Crafting Policy and Setting Direction. *Public Administration Review* 57(2): 124–32.

Rosener, Judy B. 1982. Making Bureaucrats Responsive: A Study of the Impact of Citizen Participation and Staff Recommendations on Regulatory Decision Making. *Public Administration Review* 42(4): 339–45.

Rowe, Gene, and Lynn J. Frewer. 2000. Public Participation Methods: A Framework for Evaluation. *Science, Technology and Human Values* 25(1): 3–29.

Schneider, Anne Larason, and Helen Ingram. 1997. *Policy Design For Democracy*. Lawrence: University Press of Kansas.

Thomas, John Clayton. 1990. Public Involvement in Public Management: Adapting and Testing a Borrowed Theory. *Public Administration Review* 50(4): 435–45.

Walters, Lawrence C., James Aydelotte, and Jessica Miller. 2000. Putting More Public in Policy Analysis. *Public Administration Review* 60(4): 349–59.

Weeks, Edward C. 2000. The Practice of Deliberative Democracy: Results From four Large-scale Trials. *Public Administration Review* 60(4): 360–72.

A Shift of Substance

Changes in local media ownership have largely led to a decline in radio news.

BONNIE BRESSERS

When Jim Schuh was a commercial radio station manager and owner in the central Wisconsin city of Stevens Point (population: 25,000), local radio reporters covered the school board, city and county government, the surrounding towns and villages, the university, the police, local sports and two high schools. On heavy news days, a newscast scheduled to run five minutes could run nearly twice that.

There are about a dozen radio stations that serve Stevens Point today, but none offers local radio news.

"It's kind of sad, really," said Schuh who, after a 41-year-career in broadcasting, was inducted last year into the Wisconsin Broadcasters Association Hall of Fame. "I looked at it this way: It was the responsibility of the broadcast licensee to do this. You used the public airwaves and, in return, you provided your community with more than what most broadcasters are doing today. Having a contest with the local car dealer isn't local broadcasting."

Chris Allen, now an associate professor of communication at the University of Nebraska in Omaha, remembers his days as one of six local journalists at KRNT in Des Moines in the late 1970s and early 1980s. A competing station had seven local news people; even the rock-and-roll station had three.

But there is only one station making a serious attempt at local news in Des Moines today. In Omaha, which at one time had three or four radio stations providing local news, there are none.

Local news on commercial radio, once a competitive information lifeline for millions of Americans, has been on a steady path of decline caused by what more than one expert calls the "Perfect Storm" of trends and events that started some 20 years ago and peaked with the Telecommunications Act of 1996.

"I'm really depressed about what's happened," said John Vivian, a journalism professor at Winona (Minn.) State University and author of the popular textbook, "The Media of Mass Communication." "Years ago radio had immediacy, it was exciting, it was a priority. There were reports from the scenes where things were happening. You got a news update every hour—or more when something was breaking."

But commercial radio is no longer a reliable source of local information, even during times of breaking news and major emergency, says David Rubin, dean of the Newhouse School of Public Communications at Syracuse University in New York.

Rubin said he turned to the longtime local AM radio news leader for its emergency broadcasting when the series of electrical failures that crippled parts of the Northeast, Midwest and Canada last August left his home in Fayetteville, N.Y., without power.

"If you don't have electric power, and you need to know what's happening, television, the Internet, the local newspaper—none of them are of any use to you," he said.

Rubin knew what a radio station dedicated to local news would do: The news crew would report to work en masse regardless of prearranged shifts and schedules. The station's disaster coverage plan would be implemented and reporters would he dispatched to gather information at key sites. Local officials would be in the studio taking questions from anxious callers. Commercials would be suspended. A community that was literally in the dark would get information and, thus, the assurance that it had the information it needed to respond.

But the longtime local news leader is now owned by broadcasting conglomerate Clear Channel which, Rubin said, did a "particularly poor job of covering the impact of the outage on the community" despite its assertions that by consolidating local broadcast stations it could pool resources to provide better local coverage than before.

To its credit, Rubin said Clear Channel made some changes as a result of Aug. 24, including replacing the news director, adding newsroom staff and developing a coverage plan for disasters.

"It's been healthy from that perspective," Rubin said. "There's been a little progress. But it will take continued vigilance and a national effort."

Bob Betcher, who has covered radio and television for 15 years for the Scripps Treasure Coast Newspapers in Florida, shares Rubin's concerns. For example, he says some local radio stations have an agreement with the CBS network television station in West Palm Beach to simulcast its audio coverage in the event of an emergency. But the television station is 40 to 70 miles from the coverage areas of the radio stations. In addition, many stations are automated overnight, they operate with skeletal staffs on weekends, and AM stations—typically the "talk" band—are required to reduce their signals at night.

"God forbid that anything should happen at 10 a.m. on a Sunday or after 7 p.m. on weeknights," Betcher said. "I wonder where and how I would learn that information."

It is no small issue: What does the public-interest standard, long the guiding principle under which broadcasters operated, mean in an era when broadcast consolidation and monopoly ownership make it unlikely that local radio can adequately cover the community—from city councils, school boards and local controversies to emergencies, disasters and threats to national security?

Indeed, the decline of local radio news most greatly affects its historic stronghold: small-town and rural America, where television coverage was not universal and people depended on the ubiquitous radio for everything from tornado warnings to agricultural alerts, says Ed Staats, whose 41-year career in 10 offices of The Associated Press included overseeing broadcast services. And as small-town newspapers cut staff—or closed their doors altogether—the civic life of entire communities has been left unexamined.

"Radio news was bubbling all over America," Staats said. "Now there's nobody out in the 3,000-plus counties in the United States covering local news the way they were. That's a major loss. That's at the heart of what the impact has been."

But there are some bright spots on the local news landscape, Staats and others agree. The University of Nebraska's Allen sees annual broadcast contest entries as a member of the Board of Directors of the Northwest Broadcast News Association, a six-state regional news organization. He says some small-market stations in rural communities still do excellent reporting on city government, school boards, the environment, local controversies and human-interest stories.

"But almost all of the stations we're talking about are operations with one and two people who work 20 hours a day," Allen said. "They're invisible. York, Nebraska, has 4,000 people. They have a great radio station there, but it's not a huge market."

Another of those bright spots may be KORN Radio, a station with a long-held commitment to local news that serves a 70-mile radius of Mitchell, S.D. News director J.P. Skelly covers government bodies such as city council, school board and county commission and generates local talk programming that examines community issues and often features local newsmakers.

"If there's news to be found, I'll find it," Skelly said. "But I also have to be very selective."

Still, many media observers say, the overall role of local radio news has been seriously eroding for decades and the future is unclear. Deregulation, consolidation, economics, technology, demographics and declining audience interest are among the trends that coalesced to move local commercial radio news away from its historical position as pivotal in meeting the information needs of the local citizenry.

Deregulation

Many media observers lay blame for the current state of local radio news with the Telecommunications Act of 1996, which increased the number of stations a broadcast group can own in a market to up to eight, depending on the market size, and eliminated the rule that capped the number of stations one company can own at 40. But the 1996 Act, passed in the Clinton administration, was the outcome of a steady erosion of broadcast regulations that actually began a quarter of a century earlier under the Carter administration.

"The genie had been out of the bottle," said Man G. Stavitsky, associate dean and professor at the University of Oregon School of Journalism and Communication in Eugene, Ore., and a reviewer for The State of the News Media 2004 report released in March by the Project for Excellence in Journalism. "If you trace the deregulation flow, it began with Carter FCC when we first chipped away at ownership and content rules. It kept gaining momentum and, in 1996, the dam burst."

The Carter administration likely did not foresee the outcome when it launched its government-wide initiative against bureaucratic red tape and burdensome paperwork. But in its attempt to "pare away the regulatory underbrush," as Stavitsky puts is, the Federal Communications Commission began reviewing regulations that had been enacted decades earlier when radio was in its infancy. The broadcast industry, which chaffed under the regulations, saw an opening with the Carter FCC and began a massive and ongoing lobbying effort. The Reagan FCC followed with its philosophy that TV was more akin to an appliance— nothing more than a "toaster with pictures." One regulation after another that had defined "public interest" was eliminated and, by the late 1980s, the requirement that broadcasters applying for license renewals report how many hours they would devote to public affairs programming was gone.

"But you don't leave the public-interest standard out until you have something to replace it with" said Syracuse University's Rubin. "The last time I looked, the public still owned the airwaves."

Public ownership notwithstanding, radio stations throughout the country cut their local news operations in favor of far less costly fare, including entertainment programming and often "lowbrow" talk shows.

In addition to eliminating public affairs content requirements, the Telecommunications Act of 1996 allowed multiple-station ownership, which exacerbated the problem and contributed to the decline of local commercial radio news.

Consolidation and Economics

According to the Project for Excellence in Journalism's State of the News Media 2004 report, broadcast groups Clear Channel, Cumulus Broadcasting and Citadel Communication Corp. owned fewer than 1,000 stations in 1999. They now own about 1,600 stations, with Clear Channel owning 1,207. The 1996 Act, the report says, allowed Clear Channel, which had owned only 43 stations, to buy the 460-station AMFM Inc. The five largest broadcast groups now own more than 14 percent of the total number of stations in the United States.

But the debt involved with consolidation encourages broadcast owners to cut jobs and costs to pay the debt service and make the networks profitable. Most of the companies are publicly owned, which experts suggest encourages their allegiance to Wall Street and corporate stockholders rather than a public that owns the airwaves. General managers who historically have become rooted in the community as they worked their way up the station ladder increasingly are being replaced with corporate managers who have little loyalty and commitment to the locality.

"It's all designed to produce as cheap a product as possible and to appeal to as many people as possible in your demographic niche and to squeeze out all competition so the public doesn't have a place to go except to, maybe, the satellite networks which, of course, are not local," Rubin said.

Wisconsin broadcaster Schuh, who was general manager of one station and owner of another, acknowledges that "wall-to-wall music" has a greater profit margin than news, but he doesn't agree the stations that provide good local news coverage can't make handsome profits. And it's important, he says, to look at the psychographics of the listenership rather than the demographics.

"The listeners are the 40-plus or 50-plus people, but they're community leaders and business owners," he said. "They are the ones who are generally your sponsors, and that ties in with good community involvement. The decision-makers listen to your product to keep up with things in the community."

Even with groups that retain a barebones commitment to local news, the University of Oregon's Stavitsky says reduced staffs now produce news for multiple stations.

"Before you had six news people, with six takes on local news, working at six different stations," he said. "Now you may have one or two people providing the same news product across all six stations. You ask if they're doing local news and they say 'Yes, absolutely, we're doing six newscasts during morning drive-time.' But there's less diversity of voices."

And those six people are stretched so thin, experts say, they must rely on press releases, telephone interviews and stories lifted from the local newspaper rather than attending city council meetings, going to news conferences and covering local events.

Commercial stations committed to cost reductions turned to another source of programming in the 1980s and 1990s that was cheaper than local news: the so-called news/talk format. At one end of the spectrum, news/talk shows include programs such as National Public Radio's "Talk of the Nation," which provides serious—albeit not local—programming. But while some stations point to news/talk programming as evidence they have not abandoned the local news market, media observers are quick to point out that taking stories from the local newspaper and inviting often vitriolic local listeners to voice their opinions is a far cry from doing serious, in-depth reporting on the local issues of the day.

Regardless of the level of quality, news/talk was the most common format on AM radio in the 1990s, and Rush Limbaugh is still the most-listened to talk show in the nation with an audience of more than 14 million people a week.

Radio, sandwiched in the evolutionary media timeline between newspapers and television, is experiencing what newspapers experienced before and what local television news has started experiencing since, says Bob Priddy, chairman-elect of the national Radio Television News Directors Association and news director of MissouriNet, a statewide commercial network that provides primarily state government reporting and political news to 65 Missouri radio stations.

"What we have seen in radio in the last 20 years we will see in television: the consolidation of more and more newsrooms, doing news for more than one station without many additional resources, reduced commitment to news, fewer people being

spread thinner," Priddy said. "What we have seen in radio in the last 20 years we will see in television. We have been seeing it already in the last 10 years."

Technology

Technological advances also have contributed to the homogenization of local news, media observers say. Satellite and broadband delivery now enables broadcast companies to generate programming from a central hub for distribution throughout the network of radio stations. Pieces of local information can be transparently spliced into generic news broadcasts, giving listeners the erroneous impression that local newscasters within their local communities generate the newscasts.

Finally, the University of Oregon's Stavitsky says, the latest technological phenomenon—satellite networks such as Sirius Satellite Radio and XM Satellite Radio—offers "anti-local" radio programming that allows listeners to access the same radio station from New York City to San Francisco.

But, like a pendulum that has swung too far, anti-local programming may offer a solution to the current state of local radio news.

"Some people in the industry are saying the only way we can compete against satellite and the Internet is to rediscover our local roots," Stavitsky said. "That will be what differentiates us. The problem is news is expensive. But if they continue to get their lunch eaten by satellite and the Web and young people abandoning radio, that may be the only way to survive."

Demographics and Audience Interest

Local commercial radio news is following a pattern first seen in the local newspaper industry as circulations started declining 30 years ago, largely because of the industry's failure to attract younger readers for whom local news is not a top priority.

Local radio, both local news and music, is less a part of the "media diet" of young people, says Stavitsky. For one thing, he says, young people today have portable music players that contain their complete CD libraries. For another, commercial talk radio, which requires less fidelity, is on the AM band, "which young people ignore."

Indeed, Winona University's Vivian and other academicians point to a gradual disengagement of young people in the civic affairs of the community.

"Civic affairs," Vivian said simply, "is a gigantic tune-out."

But, media observers say, the problem extends well beyond the younger generation and involves a society that seems to place less value on news and information.

"Look at some of the political issues," said RTNDA's Priddy. "People clamor for better roads but they reject fuel tax increases when fuel taxes are the only way to pay for better roads. They don't have to watch politicians because, with term limits, the politicians will be gone. You have a certain amount of public irresponsibility. Lethargy and irresponsibility are combined to bring a slump in the service they get. They don't demand better. And federal deregulation has played a role in this."

The Case for Public Radio

Kevin Klose, president and chief executive officer of National Public Radio, sees a far different confluence of coincidental phenomena that he says have contributed to huge increases in audiences for NPR and its member stations: As commercial radio stations consolidated and gutted their local news offerings in the 1980s and 1990s, public radio's evolving capacity to produce national news programming was followed by its extension into local news. The second- and third-most-listened-to programs on both commercial and noncommercial radio— "Morning Edition" and "All Things Considered," respectively—were both formatted to encourage local member stations to generate local news programming that can be added to the national mix.

Of the 275 mother ship stations, about 150 produce local news, a total that Klose says is increasing. And the signals from those 275 stations are "repeated" to 475 other stations throughout the country.

Twenty years of evolution in the production of news and information programming were capped by two events early in the 21st Century that caused a dramatic surge in NPR's already growing audience. The 37-day end to the 2000 presidential election between George W. Bush and Al Gore became riveting news of continuous interest for more than a month. And less than a year later, the terrorist attacks on Sept. 11, 2001, produced an audience desperate for in-depth and high-quality, credible news.

"NPR and the local stations mixed up a marvelous tapestry of authentic local news, local hosts, local perspectives, interwoven with superb national and foreign coverage from us," Klose said. "And NPR audiences don't spike—once they start listening, they keep listening."

Indeed, Klose says, Abitron statistics bear that out. In 1999, 13 million of the 20 million people who listened to NPR stations each week listened to NPR-generated programming. That 13 million had increased to 16 million on Sept. 10. 2001, and to 20 on Sept. 12. Today, 30 million people listen to NPR stations, with 22 million listening to NPR-generated programming.

Steve Chiotakis, who is the local "Morning Edition" host and a producer with NPR's member station WBHM in Birmingham, Ala., has split his 16-year career equally between public and commercial radio.

Like Klose, he sees public radio as the last bastion for people serious about local radio news.

"I love my medium," he said. "I love radio. People want news and they want it now. Who better than radio? We've been doing it for 80 years."

But commercial radio news, Chiotakis says, "is dying a really fast death."

The Future

Without doubt, NPR is attracting larger and larger audiences as commercial radio moves away from news, says the University of Oregon's Stavitsky, but the bottom line remains: Local news is expensive. Two-thirds of the NPR member stations are licensed to universities, many of which are questioning where to put increasingly scarce resources in the face of colossal state budget deficits. Declining local economies may affect the level of underwriting available to the member stations.

"A lot of them are struggling to keep the local news there," Stavitsky said. "But overall, public radio is still a much more hospitable place for local journalism than commercial radio is."

So if a windstorm of trends and events contributed to the current state of local commercial radio news, what is the possibility that forces can be reversed or, at the least, moderated? Many media observers are not optimistic.

Stavitsky and the University of Nebraska's Allen agree that there are pockets of good local news programming in both small and large markets, but both question a future for local radio news in the face of public indifference to news in general.

And while RTNDA's Priddy argues that radio has reinvented itself many times in many ways—and will do so again—others suggest a more systemic problem that will require significant public will to reverse. Syracuse University's Rubin, for example, says change needs to come from a federal government willing to confront the broadcast industry's powerful lobby.

Inroads could be made, he says, under scenarios such as these:

- Broadcast groups that didn't meet revenue targets decided to sell stations, and the FCC, in an effort to prevent station-trading among big chains, enacted rules to encourage local ownership.
- Congress and the FCC recognized the results of their actions and rolled back the number of stations an owner could own, although that's admittedly unlikely.
- The FCC enacted regulations that made chain ownership more expensive and more accountable to the public in hopes of encouraging chains to divest. For example, if the FCC re-enacted the Fairness Doctrine, which had required that broadcast stations air all sides of public issues, so talk show programming such as Rush Limbaugh and Michael Savage could be challenged station-by-station, market-by-market.
- The FCC returned to license renewal every three years and, as part of the renewal process, required that stations ascertain whether they were meeting the public interest and report their findings in an open forum as they did in the past.
- The FCC again required public affairs programming.
- Commercial broadcasters were taxed, and the tax revenues were used to support robust noncommercial local news operations.

"If I can think of this sitting here in Syracuse, why can't the people in Washington? This will take a national effort, a new administration, a new FCC and a new FCC chairman" Rubin said. "Am I optimistic? No, I'm not."

BONNIE BRESSERS is an assistant professor of journalism at the A.Q. Miller School of Journalism and Mass Communications at Kansas State University.

Cross Examination

**Local prosecutors are the last sacred cow in journalism.
But some journalists have found the value of a more thorough.**

STEVE WEINBERG

Some journalistic epiphanies take a long time to form. In my case, 30 years. That is how long it took me to realize somebody needed to conduct a systematic examination of the nation's 2,341 local prosecutors' offices.

During an era when journalists tend to be skeptical about the performance of elected and appointed government officials at all levels, prosecutors qualify as the last sacred cow: assumed to be acting in the public interest, rarely scrutinized and, if covered at all, covered favorably.

In lots of newsrooms, the shorthand for the criminal justice beat is "cops and courts." That traditional label says a lot by what it fails to mention—the prosecutor. My painfully slow epiphany is that prosecutors are the linchpin of the criminal justice system. They receive information from the police about an alleged crime before any defense attorney or judge receives information, and information is power. No case can move forward without the prosecutor's assent. In most jurisdictions, about 95 percent of the crimes charged never reach trial; that means 95 percent of the time, prosecutors are acting as judge and jury combined, all behind closed doors. Furthermore, when a case does reach trial, no matter how wisely or unwisely judges, defense attorneys and juries act, it is usually won or lost because of the way the prosecutor presents the evidence.

Every day, prosecutors in district attorneys' offices throughout the United States decide if people arrested by local police should be:

- Charged with a crime.
- Placed back on the streets, or jailed.
- Allowed to sign a plea agreement, or proceed to trial.
- A candidate for the death penalty if the law permits that outcome.
- Heard after imprisonment because new evidence suggests a wrongful conviction.

Counting the elected district attorney at the top of the office pyramid and the lawyers appointed by the district attorney to serve justice, there are about 30,000 prosecutors working in the United States. Many of these prosecutors are dedicated, skilled public servants. Many others are mediocre. Some should never have been allowed to wield power. But few people know much about their local prosecutors. Most of the time, in most of those 2,341 jurisdictions, journalists are nowhere to be seen as new prosecutors are hired, as veterans are promoted, as other veterans retire or are forced out.

The sacred cow syndrome blessedly appears to be fading in some newsrooms, however. One factor: In cases with DNA evidence, the number of documented wrongful convictions is approaching 200. They demonstrate like nothing else the fallibility of prosecutors. Everybody makes mistakes. But in a system supposedly devoted more to serving justice than to winning at all costs, in a system supposedly loaded with safeguards, how do prosecutors allow innocent people to be charged with a crime, indicted by a grand jury, incarcerated for months or years while awaiting trial, convicted and sentenced?

The Center for Public Integrity Comes Through

Hoping to find somebody to support a national examination of prosecutors, I approached Charles Lewis at the Center for Public Integrity in Washington, D.C. Lewis is a former CBS 60 Minutes producer who had his own epiphany about 15 years ago. He left his job to start an organization that would conduct investigative journalism in the public interest, in-depth, on topics normally ignored. Against gigantic odds, the Center for Public Integrity has not only survived, but thrived.

Lewis and his staff raised money from foundations and individuals to make my idea a reality. The Center hired two individuals to work with me—Neil Gordon, a Baltimore lawyer who wanted to change careers, and Brooke Williams, a recent University of Missouri Journalism School graduate.

For three years, we gathered information about the performance of every local prosecutor's office in the United States and about as many of the individual district attorneys as we could identify. In several dozen newsrooms, reporters have used our specific findings about the local prosecutor's office, posted at www.publicintegrity.org at the "Harmful Error" icon, to produce insightful follow-ups. In addition to our specific findings, our general conclusions ideally will inform future coverage of prosecutors in every newsroom.

Maurice Possley's Epiphany

To some degree, we stood on the shoulders of giants while conducting our research. Chicago Tribune reporter Maurice Possley is renowned today for his coverage of Cook County prosecutors who break the rules to convict the guilty, and sometimes the innocent. Possley, with colleagues Ken Armstrong and Steve Mills, changed the world in ways most journalists only dream about: Because of their prosecutorial misconduct exposes, first the Illinois governor and legislature, followed by officials in other states, imposed a death penalty moratorium as well as spearheading procedural reforms to the criminal justice system.

But until a few years ago, Possley was part of a widespread newsroom problem—indifferent coverage of prosecutors. Possley saw them one-dimensionally, the way so many other journalists do—as good guys trying to put bad guys behind bars.

Possley covered federal courts in Chicago, first for the Sun-Times, then for the Tribune. He might evaluate a prosecutor's courtroom performance, but gave little attention to the decision-making outside of public view leading to the trial.

In 1995, Possley started covering local courts, which tend to be grittier than the federal system. He began to see the inflexibility of prosecutors as he honed his approach to trial coverage by telling each day as "a separate story with a beginning, middle and end. I tried to always balance the day with some flavor of cross-examination, sometimes saying it was unsuccessful. Sometimes the cross-examination became the lead.... Quite a few prosecutors would make remarks about my inclusion of cross-examination. They had seen (the questioning of prosecution witnesses by defense lawyers) as meaningless or not damaging their case and questioned why I would even report it."

Possley realized that "for most prosecutors, it is a one-way street—their way. And I understood that to be a condition of the beat. Along with these realizations came the knowledge that while the prosecution does usually win, that doesn't mean the truth got found out. There were cases where you couldn't really tell where the truth was, and I could see that for many prosecutors, it was all about winning. Still, I mostly thought they got the right guy—some cases were just closer than others. ... The thought that innocent people were being convicted or that justice was being undermined was really not on my radar."

The epiphany Possley needed arrived during the murder trial of Rolando Cruz in DuPage County, Ill. Police and prosecutors originally said Cruz and two other men killed a 10-year-old girl. Some police officers and prosecutors believed early on that the arrests were misguided—especially after a fourth man, a convicted murderer, confessed. The DuPage County prosecutor refused to credit the confession.

In 1995, Cruz won a directed acquittal from a judge in a trial covered by Possley. After the acquittal, a court-appointed special prosecutor recommended that seven DuPage County prosecutors and police be charged with criminal offenses for their conduct.

Possley received a question from an editor: How often does it happen that a prosecutor is indicted for misconduct? Possley had no idea, so he studied decades of reporting by the Tribune and other Chicago-area news organizations. He found himself "astounded to see how prosecutor-oriented the coverage was." During the early stages of the research, Possley continued to cover the Cook County prosecutor's office. "Many prosecutors still thought of the beat guy and the Tribune largely as their allies. ... I think many of them never imagined that the result of our reporting would be critical."

Armstrong joined Possley to document 381 cases back to 1963, the date of the U.S. Supreme Court decision Brady v. Maryland, in which the justices said convictions could be reversed if prosecutors presented evidence they knew to be false, concealed evidence suggesting innocence, or both. The Tribune's January 1999 series put prosecutors and readers on notice that a new era of coverage had dawned.

Then, in November 1999, Armstrong and Mills published a new revelatory series, examining murder cases in which Illinois prosecutors sought the death penalty. The journalists identified 326 reversals attributed in whole or in part to the conduct of prosecutors. Armstrong and Mills wrote themed articles as part of the series, examining how prosecutors use confessions extracted through police torture, perjured testimony of jailhouse informants seeking rewards and unreliable hair/fiber analysis from law enforcement forensic laboratories.

When interviewed in July, Possley was collaborating with Mills on a new project, preparing for the launch of his second book (about a Chicago murder case) and planning his fall teaching leave at the University of Montana journalism school.

Without question, Possley has become skeptical about prosecutors. Today, he says, "I try to persuade defense attorneys to provide discovery (from the prosecutor) to me. I try to actually interview witnesses before trials. I spend more time covering pretrial motions, when significant evidence often comes out and evidence that tends to contradict the prosecution often is aired. And I adhere to the belief that not everything said is the truth, even if it's under oath, and that many things are said as truth but with such semantic gymnastics as to be ridiculous."

It Takes a Village

Possley came to his epiphany alone. When he started acting on it, though, he shared it with two reporting partners, Armstrong and Mills, who helped mine the possibilities of prosecutor coverage.

Dallas Morning News reporter Holly Becka has teamed up professionally, too. In fact, she learned last year it takes a village of journalists to provide exemplary coverage of a scandal that crosses beat lines, involving prosecutors, police and judges.

Becka, a veteran cops and courts reporter, became one of those village members when a Dallas fake-drug scandal emerged: Defendants were being charged, convicted and imprisoned for possessing or selling what appeared to be narcotics, but in fact was billiards chalk planted by police informants or police themselves. Instead of asking the right questions to halt the scam, prosecutors proceeded against the hapless defendants.

"The story started on the police beat and spilled to the criminal courts beat and then to the federal beat," Becka said. "A senior general assignments reporter also pitched in during the early months of the scandal to look at policies in the district attorney's office that helped lead to the scandal. ... Most of the stories in the early months were written by the two then-criminal courts reporters because prosecutors were dismissing drug case upon drug case, and the effects were being felt by defendants-turned-victims, their lawyers and the court system in general. More recently, our federal beat reporter has handled the story ... because of the FBI investigation and the federal civil-rights lawsuit." Becka also credits a Morning News editorial writer, journalists at WFAA-TV and the alternative weekly Dallas Observer.

In an April 27, 2003, story that skillfully weaves together seemingly stray strands to create a new reality for readers, Becka and fellow reporter Tanya Eiserer explain how police blame prosecutors for the scandal, while prosecutors blame police. For example, prosecutors say police learned earlier than previously acknowledged that the primary drug informant lacked credibility. While corrupt informants were fooling police officers, prosecutors accepted the cases without asking the tough questions, then hammered out plea bargains with presumably guilty defendants without running the allegedly illegal seized substances through drug testing.

As stories about the scandal kept coming, Becka still had to find time to cover the routine aspects of the beat, such as profiling the Dallas assistant district attorney who was recognized as the top prosecutor in Texas. Becka used a feature lead, telling how the assistant district attorney saw prosecutors as heroes even when he was a child—heroes with the same stature as movie star tough-guy John Wayne. For 19 years, Becka explained, the child hero worshipper has been living his dream as a real-life prosecutor. Such stories inform readers of the positive and help build relationships on the beat.

Becka recently moved from the criminal courts beat to a newly created criminal justice enterprise role. "I've had so many people—members of the public, the criminal defense bar and even a few prosecutors—credit the media with forcing public officials here to do the right thing after the scandal erupted," she said. "... The sentiment I've heard is if the media had been asleep or uncaring, innocent people would have remained in jail."

The Value of Appellate Court Rulings

Rob Modic, a Dayton Daily News reporter since 1979, knows what the best beat reporters, including Becka, know: When keeping tabs on prosecutors, study every appellate court opinion that comments on their conduct.

The upside of studying appellate court rulings is huge: They are official records, they often contain nuggets of news amidst the normally dry prose of judges, and those rendering opinions are often former prosecutors who know first-hand what to look for when examining state conduct. An appellate ruling can be a platform for discussing a specific issue, such as whether local prosecutors regularly withhold evidence from the defense in violation of U.S. Supreme Court mandates; use jailhouse snitches as witnesses, without fully checking the snitches' accounts or fully disclosing the quid pro quo to the defense; coach state witnesses or discourage potential defense witnesses from cooperating; cross the line during trial, perhaps during opening statements, perhaps during cross-examination, perhaps during closing arguments.

Part of a three-person criminal justice team, Modic and colleagues "get together regularly to discuss filed cases at every stage," including the appellate stage. "We look at search warrants, motions to suppress (evidence), preliminary hearings. We talk to parties about overcharging and undercharging. We collect string, then put the twine together for a story."

Watch The Interactions Carefully

As a longtime St. Louis County courthouse reporter for the Post-Dispatch, Bill Lhotka knows almost all the prosecutors and defense attorneys who work opposite sides of criminal cases. Tuned-in reporters watch "for veteran prosecutors taking advantage of neophyte defense attorneys or public defenders. The reverse is also true: veteran defense attorneys running circles around new prosecutors." Neither scenario leads to the closest approximation of the truth. Winning is ingrained in prosecutors and defense counsel, but, Lhotka says, that is no excuse for cutting corners to win a case, to obsess over percentages of victory and defeat because of career advancement plans or personal vanity.

Tim Bryant covers the St. Louis City courthouse for the same newspaper. He and Lhotka sometimes compare notes, especially because the same defense attorneys often appear in both jurisdictions. The reputation of individual prosecutors among defense attorneys and judges is usually easy to learn after trust is built on the beat, Bryant says. That information can also be supplemented through close observation. "Attendance at court proceedings early in a case may be helpful," Bryant said. "For example, a prosecutor's performance in a preliminary hearing or an evidentiary hearing could likely provide clues to his effectiveness. Was he prepared? Did he show proper courtesies to the judge and the opposing lawyer, especially in a proceeding where jurors are not present? Does the prosecutor have the respect of his office's investigator and the police detectives on his case?"

Jury selection provides more evidence, but lots of reporters are absent from that stage of the trial. "Was jury selection contentious to the point that the prosecutor was accused of removing potential jurors because of their race or gender?" Bryant asked. "Then there is the trial itself. Did the defense lawyer make more than a typical number of objections? Were disputes serious enough to merit sidebar conversations with the judge, or even recesses in the trial?"

Seek Access, and You Might Find It

Access granted to journalists by district attorneys might increase understanding of the daily difficulties faced by prosecutors—and everybody wins when that occurs. But it appears that journalists rarely ask to be a fly on the wall.

Gary Delsohn of the Sacramento Bee asked. Elected district attorney Jan Scully said yes. The only restrictions: Delsohn could not write anything for his newspaper during his year inside; nobody would be quoted by name without consent; personnel matters could be ruled off-limits by Scully; Delsohn would provide periodic reports on his observations if requested. (Scully never made such a request.)

In return, Delsohn would be provided a semiprivate writing space, could wander freely, pose questions and attend meetings. "There were more than a few people in the office who thought Scully was insane," Delsohn said, "… but for the most part people were extremely open and accessible. Prosecutors and investigators freely discussed the most sensitive aspects of their cases in front of me. I was allowed to sit in on meetings with victims, defense attorneys, judges, police and witnesses. I was almost never told something was off limits, and after I had been showing up for a few weeks, most of the resistance that I was aware of had disappeared."

Much of what Delsohn learned appears in his book, published in August by Dutton. The book, "The Prosecutors," subtly emphasizes Delsohn's special access in the subtitle: "A Year in the Life of a District Attorney's Office." It is a primer for any outsider journalist who wants to think about how to cover prosecutors more effectively.

Prosecutors Rarely Admit Their Mistakes

Ofra Bikel is a producer of documentaries for the PBS program Frontline. After turning her attention to the criminal justice system 15 years ago, she produced the "Innocence Lost" trilogy about the mishandling of child sexual abuse cases in Edenton, N.C. In 1999, her documentary about three prison inmates exonerated by DNA testing aired as "The Case for Innocence." Last year, Frontline aired "An Ordinary Crime," Bikel's account of a North Carolina armed-robbery prosecution beset with problems.

Bikel says she is baffled by the refusal of the prosecutor to reopen the conviction of Terence Garner, given post-trial evidence that the wrong man is in prison. Baffled but not surprised, because Bikel has watched prosecutors in previous cases dig in.

"There are a few problems with prosecutors," she said. "First, because it is an adversarial system, and the defense's job is to defend their client in any way they can—within the boundaries of the law, which is quite flexible. The prosecution, as the adversary, wants to do just the opposite of the defense: Convict the defendant in any way they can. So it is a contest. The problem is that the prosecution has a double function. Besides being one side in a contest, they are supposed to represent the people and to see that justice is done. This double-headed function in a cutthroat adversarial system is very hard to maintain. Unfortunately, I have not met too many prosecutors who spend sleepless nights over the fact that they won a case but sent an innocent person to prison. The prosecutors are not villains, but they look at a case, and they see people who they think are guilty go free because of smart-ass, manipulative attorneys, and they are furious. So they, too, cut corners, and blind themselves many times to the truth, or at least to doubt."

Expect to Be Verbally Attacked by Prosecutors

Edward Humes wrote about prosecutorial error and misconduct in the office of the Kern County, Calif., district attorney. The incumbent responded with a 154-page document attacking the journalist and his findings. Both used incendiary words. Humes' book, published by Simon & Schuster, is "Mean Justice: A Town's Terror, a Prosecutor's Power, a Betrayal of Innocence." The district attorney's reply is "Junk Journalism: Correcting the Errors, False Claims and Distortions in Edward Humes' Mean Justice."

Humes, like Possley, took awhile to reach the realization that prosecutors are not always the good guys. First as a newspaper reporter, then as the author of high-end true crime books, Humes usually found defendants' claims of innocence filled with holes.

He began to change his attitude while investigating the conviction of Pat Dunn, a Bakersfield educator and businessman, for murdering his wife, Sandy. Convinced after extensive research that Dunn is innocent, and appalled at what he believed to be prosecutorial misconduct in the case, Humes examined the actions of the district attorney and his deputies over several decades. The research resulted in what appeared to be questionable patterns of behavior among specific prosecutors handling specific types of cases.

Humes possessed an advantage over Bakersfield-based journalists. He was writing a book, then would probably leave the jurisdiction to pursue a different book. Beat reporters, on the other hand, who examine prosecutor conduct sometimes see sources dry up not only in the district attorney's office, but also in other law enforcement quarters.

Investigative reporting about prosecutors' performance, Humes said, "is likely to be met with strong, even bizarre, resistance from prosecutors, who may be prone to suggesting that anyone who criticizes their actions must be a) in league with criminals; b) in league with criminal defense lawyers; c) are criminals themselves; or d) worst of all, political liberals."

The Horrible Power of Self-Delusion

Dorothy Rabinowitz has carved out a specialty in her place on the Wall Street Journal editorial board. That specialty: problematic prosecutions of alleged child molestation rings.

Her first Journal expose, published in 1995, centered on the Fells Acres Day School in Malden, Mass. Prosecutors charged Gerald Amirault, his sister Cheryl plus his mother, Violet, the founder of the day care center, with monstrous multiple molestations based on the word of preschoolers—and without a shred of physical evidence.

As Rabinowitz chronicled other fantastic-sounding child molestation cases in New Jersey, Florida, Washington State and California, an awful question occurred to her: What if the prosecutors did not believe in the guilt of those they brought to trial? What if they filed the charges to appease community outrage, to build support for a re-election campaign or a higher office? After all, the evidence of molestation seemed unbelievable when evaluated using common sense.

Rabinowitz worked up to raising her unpleasant question in her 2003 book "No Crueler Tyrannies: Accusation, False Witness, and Other Terrors of Our Times." What did the prosecutors think? she mused. "Did they actually believe in the charges they had brought, of naked children tied to trees in full public view and raped in broad daylight, as in the Amirault case; in the testimony of child witnesses who had recited obvious whoppers about robots, being stabbed with swords, and the like?"

Some prosecutors actually believe those seemingly ludicrous scenarios, and some do not, Rabinowitz concluded. Both patterns of thought are scary. One type of prosecutor cares nothing about the justice that is part of the office's sworn duty; won-lost records are paramount. The other type of prosecutor is blinded by passion, too close to the emotional residue of little children being victimized.

"The prosecutor's propensity to believe in the guilt of anyone accused of the crime of child sex abuse (is) overwhelming," Rabinowitz said. "That belief (is) fueled by investigators who share the same propensity and interrogated the children accordingly."

STEVE WEINBERG is a freelance magazine writer and book author in Columbia, Mo. He served as executive director of Investigative Reporters Editors, based at the Missouri Journalism School, from 1983–1990. He teaches from time to time at the Journalism School.

Bloggers Press for Power

Whether bloggers qualify for press credentials is getting a lot of attention in state capitols.

NICOLE CASAL MOORE

A "blog swarm" began shortly after Rob Weber told a blogger why he couldn't have a press pass to cover the Kentucky Legislature.

Weber, who is director of public information at the Kentucky Legislative Research Commission, told Mark Nickolas of BluegrassReport.org that he was welcome to watch from the gallery. But he couldn't have a seat with the journalists.

This is how Nickolas headlined his post about their exchange: "A Brave New World Hits the Old World Head-On."

And this is how Weber reacted: "I'm 35 years old," he thought. "I'm the Old World?"

It got worse. A few days later, Club for Growth's blog called for a swarm. "It's time for blogging barbarians to jump the moat and tear down the gate," the blog read. Seven or eight more blogs started writing about the issue, Weber says.

This is "likely an early skirmish in what will be a lengthy nationwide struggle," read Tapscott's Copy Desk.

Even National Journal's Beltway Blogroll mentioned the situation.

Weber was more famous than he wanted to be, but he and the Kentucky Legislative Research Commission stuck by their decision at the time. But the media landscape is evolving, he says, and the precise geography of blogger country is still unknown. The question of whether bloggers qualify for press credentials is one his state will undoubtedly revisit, and others are taking up.

Bloggers aren't taking "no" for an answer. Bluegrass-Report.org's Mark Nickolas found a loophole in the Kentucky policy and qualified for credentials. He started writing a column for a local paper. Bloggers in at least Texas and Tennessee plan to apply for press passes to cover the 2007 session.

"This is an issue that's going to keep coming up," Weber says. "Blogs are gaining power. They're influencing the way

stories are covered and they're revolutionizing the information distribution system. . . . There is a metamorphosis going on and nothing is the same as it was yesterday."

Into the Blogosphere

The web log was born around a decade ago. Its earliest genre, which is still its most popular, was the personal diary. Today, blog search engine Technorati.com tracks 57 million blogs, 11 percent of which discuss politics, according to the Pew Internet and American Life Project.

Although just 8 percent of American Internet users keep blogs, 39 percent of Americans read them, Pew found in a summer 2006 survey. The Blogosphere is part of the larger online media universe—a place 19 percent of Americans went for election news on a typical day in August 2006, according to another Pew study.

It's hard to count exactly how many bloggers write about legislatures, but NCSL's blog, The Thicket at State Legislatures, links to around 150 others with some connection to a statehouse. Many are part of the grassroots or citizen journalism movement like BluegrassReport.org.

State Legislatures doesn't know of any bloggers not affiliated with a print or broadcast news organizations who have credentials to cover a legislature. A majority of legislative communicators who responded to a quick survey said they would not be inclined to give a blogger the same credential status as a journalist. That's a sentiment reporters echo. But media experts say a blanket denial policy is not a good idea.

Of the 99 state legislative chambers (Nebraska is unicameral.), 81 have a process to give reporters credentials. The qualifications vary, as do the perks, which range from a parking space and a beeline through security to a desk in the building and floor access.

Reaching Out to Blogs

Even without press credentials, bloggers are writing about legislatures and their members in every state. You might want to watch what they're saying, and consider reaching out to them as a new part of public relations. Here are some ideas.

1. **Peer into the blogosphere:** If you don't already know, find out which blogs write about your legislature. You can use Technorati.com to search for who has mentioned you or your legislature in a blog post. NCSL's blogroll at The Thicket at State Legislatures (ncsl.typepad.com/thethicket) can tell you who's writing blogs in each state.

2. **Don't ignore bloggers:** "The real issue is whether legislatures and the executive branch will view bloggers as a legitimate part of the public discussion," says Tennessee politics and policy blogger Bill Hobbs, of BillHobbs.com. "Will they talk to bloggers? Will they respond to their Freedom of Information Act requests?" If you don't comment, bloggers will say so. And remember: reporters read blogs.

3. **Tip off bloggers:** Bloggers can use anonymous sources. Some of them are even anonymous themselves. If you've got an important news tip you don't feel comfortable telling a reporter, tell a blogger. Eileen Smith, of InThePinkTexas.com is all ears. "People send me stories, anonymous tips and suggestions," she says. "They share things with me that they wouldn't tell reporters."

4. **Talk to bloggers directly:** Pennsylvania Representative Mark Cohen, who blogs at repmarkbcohen. blogspot.com and occasionally at national political blog DailyKos.com, sends out special e-mails to his list of bloggers. "When we reach out to bloggers, we're reaching out to the people who also read the blogs. There's a large number of people who like to get their news just from blogs," Cohen says. Sometimes he turns to the blogosphere when the mainstream media aren't interested. And that has paid off. A blogger was the first to write about his 2005 bill to increase the use of hybrid electric vehicles. The newspaper came next.

5. **Post comments on blogs:** People are turning to more informal means of communication like blogs, and PR professionals should understand and embrace that, says Robert Niles, editor of the online journalism review at the USC Annenberg School for Communication. "You're not just working with reporters now," Niles says. "You have to get in and participate in the discussion with the communities."

6. **Start your own blog:** Legislative staffer Ric Cantrell started SenateSite.com, the unofficial voice of the Utah Senate Majority, as a way to engage the public. As a bonus, says the assistant to majority leadership, he discovered a thriving community. "We comment on other blogs every day, and they offer their comments on our site as well," Cantrell says. "It's like talking to your neighbors."

Why Bloggers Want Credentials

Credibility is another big boon, bloggers say.

Eileen Smith, who blogs on InthePinkTexas.com, believes treating "qualified" bloggers as press is in the best interest of the legislature. "A known, credible blogger on the floor is better (and far less dangerous) than an unknown anonymous blogger in the gallery," Smith says. She suggests considering a blogger's education, experience and even legislative background when deciding who is "qualified." Bloggers deserve consideration, Smith says, if for no other reason than their power.

"My statewide readership consists of influential political insiders, decision makers, motivated individuals, elected officials and their staff, lobbyists and voters," Smith says. "I would contend that the reason traditional media outlets are granted press credentials is not because of their inherent objectivity, but because they have political power, influence and a direct line of communication to the public."

Smith covered the 2006 session and plans to ask for credentials in 2007. At press time, Texas officials were working on a policy that would apply to bloggers.

Martin Kennedy, an economics professor at Middle Tennessee State University, will be new to legislative blogging this session with his Legislative Report. He, too, plans to request credentials. Why? "Credibility and access," Kennedy says. "To make contacts more easily, to spread the word about the blog."

Officials in the Tennessee legislature say he'll likely get his wish. It's easy in Tennessee. He just has to rent space in the press room.

Bill Hobbs, a media relations and blogging consultant who publishes the personal political blog BillHobbs. com, believes even Tennessee's policy should be updated to be fair to "grassroots journalists" who may not be able to afford to rent space.

Letting bloggers have credentials would give the public another way to follow the legislature, Hobbs says.

"Journalists covering the state capitol can't cover every piece of legislation that's filed, but bloggers can focus on specific topics. I cover tax-type stuff, and I don't cover legislation that may affect abortion rights," he says. "Bloggers provide a second, larger set of eyes and ears and can find stories the news media missed."

Like many other web logs that cover legislatures, Hobbs' blog contains original reporting. He digs up about 50 percent of the content himself. He has sources inside the dome, he says. He doesn't just comment on news articles.

Are Bloggers Worthy?

Based on the most common view of press credentialers, bloggers aren't worthy of press credentials. They don't subject themselves to the same ethics and accuracy standards as news reporters. They write mostly opinion. And press space is limited.

Where to Draw the Line

Based on what experts say, California has the right idea. Officials there are looking at its credentialing policy and may develop a process to let in some bloggers. All blogs shouldn't be credentialed just because they exist, experts say. But neither should all blogs be denied special access. Doing that, says Robert Niles, editor of the *Online Journalism Review* at the USC Annenberg School for Communications, is "a really good way to make your message utterly irrelevant."

"You have to decide what the new standard is going to be. If you credential everyone, you could be in a situation where you'd have to rent out the local stadium," Niles added. "You have to look at the publication."

Does the blog have a history? Niles says it's fair to say it should publish for a little while before legislatures grant it special access. Is the blog being used as ammunition for opposition research? If so, it might not qualify.

Does the blog do original research? That's the main question Mike McKean, chair of the convergence journalism faculty at the Missouri School of Journalism would ask.

"If all they do is comment upon the writings of others, maybe that's not journalism," McKean says. "If they're doing any type of original reporting, they're journalists like anyone else."

Credentialing only bloggers who are connected to mainstream media outlets is a comfortable fix, but it might be too narrow, Niles says. "They've already determined that print is inherently more legitimate than online. They need to get over that. You have to look at the publication."

Bloggers suggested looking at the number of hits a site gets. Lawyers said look at the blog's intent. If it is published to disseminate information to the public, then it just might fit under the umbrella of journalism.

And instead of renting a stadium, blogger Bill Hobbs suggests a rotating spot in the capitol press room for "citizen journalists."

Wyoming Legislative Information Officer Wendy Madsen says her office would likely provide press credentials only if the blogger was a member of a commercial media outlet. "Blogging is still the 'wild, wild west' of the journalism frontier and until there are standards for collecting, verifying, and editing information posted by bloggers, I think it is a stretch to even classify the phenomenon as journalism," she says. "That doesn't mean politicians should ignore the trend. They need to pay close attention to the blogging world to keep pace."

Allentown Morning Call reporter John L. Micek is president of the Pennsylvania Legislative Correspondents Association, which grants the long-term press passes to statehouse reporters there. He says bloggers might join the association as affiliate members, similar to membership held by journalism professors and retired reporters, but he doesn't believe they could get a full membership.

"A lot of these guys are fairly partisan, so I have concerns about opening the full membership to people who are not in a traditional sense objective reporters," says Micek, who added that this is his personal opinion; the association hasn't decided yet. "We could get into a days-long discussion of what is journalism and who is a journalist. Not to say that bloggers' work is any less credible than others but they have one point of view."

MediaNews reporter Steve Geissinger, president of the Capitol Correspondents Association of California, doesn't think it's a good idea to have partisan voices in the Capitol press corps. In California, certain press conferences aren't open to the general public, he says.

"On the officials' side, the governor and legislators don't want biased people skewing a news conference," Geissinger says. "And the media doesn't want valuable time taken up with biased questions."

The California Assembly is working with Geissinger's association to write new rules that apply to bloggers.

Scott Gant is a lawyer in Washington, D.C., whose book, *We're All Journalists Now: The Transformation of the Press and Reshaping of the Law in the Internet Age*, will be released in June. Are bloggers journalists? is a big question, but Gant takes a step further back and asks whether professional journalists should get preferential treatment at all.

Gant's argument goes back to the Bill of Rights. He says the Supreme Court has never found that the "freedom of the press" provision of the First Amendment grants any rights that "freedom of speech" doesn't apply to all citizens.

"Giving special privileges to established news organizations might violate the federal Constitution's guarantee of equal protection," Gant says. "There hasn't been enough attention to that issue."

Christine Tatum, national president of the Society of Professional Journalists, says newspapers are the "Fourth Estate"—another check and balance on our three branches of government. It would be wrong, Tatum says, not to save space for professional reporters.

"We're talking about helping advance and promote an informed citizenry, which I contend is one of the cornerstones of democracy," Tatum says. "We have to make room in these places for people who represent news organizations to be there. That's how news organizations have traditionally functioned. They're the ones who are willing to sit and listen to the blather and the grandstanding."

As for non-professional reporters, Tatum says it's hard to figure out where to draw the line. She's not alone. The Blogosphere is a murky place that can be scary, experts understand. And it's not the first time a new medium has produced confusion. In a talk to legislative communicators in October, Mark Senak, senior vice president at Fleishman-Hillard who blogs on EyeOnFDA.com, read some quotes about the dawn of television.

This one is from a New York Times editorial in 1939. "The problem with television is that people must sit and keep their eyes glued to the screen. The average American family hasn't time for this. Therefore, the showmen are convinced that for this reason, if no other, television will never be a serious competitor of broadcasting."

NICOLE CASAL MOORE is an editor and writer with NCSL's Communications Division. She contributes to the magazine's blog, *The Thicket at State Legislatures.*

UNIT 4

Government Institutions and Officeholders

Unit Selections

Key Points to Consider

- Compare and contrast the powers and responsibilities of the president of a school board, the elected chief executive of a small town, the city manager, the Mayor of a large city, the State Governor, and the President of the United States.

- Compare your State Constitution with the United States Constitution—in length, the subjects covered, ease of reading, and your familiarity with it.

- Is it better to have well-paid and prestigious, elected positions, as in the national government, or low-paid, part-time elected posts, as are common in local governments and many state legislatures? Which makes for better government? Which makes for more representative government?

- Do you think that it is a good idea to let citizens participate directly in the policy process by means of initiatives, referenda, or town meetings? Or should legislating be left to elected representatives only? Why or why not?

Student Web Site
www.mhcls.com/online

Internet References
Center for the American Women in Politics (CAWP)
http://www.rci.rutgers.edu/~cawp/
Council on Licensure, Enforcement and Regulation (CLEAR)
http://www.clearhq.org
EMILY's List of Women in State Legislatures
http://www.emilyslist.org/
National Conference of State Legislatures
http://www.ncsl.org/index.htm
NGA (National Governors Association) Online
http://www.nga.org

Government institutions are to state and local political systems what skeletons are to people. They shape the general outlines of policy processes in the same way that bones shape the outlines of the human body. For the state and local governments, as well as for the national government, institutions are critical factors in the governing process.

There are important state-by-state variations in the executive, legislative, and judicial structures and in the degree to which citizens have access to the policy-making process. In strong governor states, chief executives hold substantially greater appointive, budgetary, and veto powers than those in weak governor states. The roles of parties, committees, and leaders differ among state legislatures, as does the degree of professionalism among legislators themselves. The roles of the state courts vary according to the contents of the state constitutions, as well as the state political and judicial traditions. In some states, the state's highest court plays a role that is roughly comparable to that of the United States Supreme Court at the national level. The highest courts in most states, however, are generally less prominent. States also differ in whether judges are elected or appointed. With respect to policy making and government as a whole, some states allow for direct citizen involvement through the devices of initiative, referendum, and recall, while others do not. Many of these structural details of the state governments are spelled out in each state's written constitution, although state constitutions generally do not play as prominent or symbolically important a role in state government as the United States Constitution does in national government.

Local governments do not incorporate the traditional three-branch structure of government to the extent that state and national governments do. Legislative and executive powers are often given to a single governing body, with the members choosing one among them to be the nominal chief executive. For example, school boards typically elect their own board president to preside over meetings, but they hire a professional educational administrator, called a superintendent, to manage day-to-day affairs. What is true of school districts also applies to many other local governments. In contrast, the structures of some strong mayor cities do resemble the executive-legislative arrangements in the national and state governments. The traditional notion of an independent local judiciary as a third

© Brand X Pictures

branch does not apply in a straightforward way at the level of the local government. Local courts, to the extent that they exist, do not restrain the other branches of local government in the way that state and national courts are empowered to restrain their respective legislative and executive branches. As with state judges, some local judges are appointed and some are elected.

This unit on institutions is organized along traditional legislative, executive, and judicial lines. The first section treats state and local legislatures, with the latter including city and town councils, school boards, town meetings, and the like. The second section turns to governors and local government executives, while the third and last section treats state and local courts.

The Legislature as Sausage Factory

It's About Time We Examine This Metaphor

When you get right down to it, making sausage is a lot different than making laws, no matter what the old saw says.

ALAN ROSENTHAL

If you spend any time hanging around legislatures or around Congress for that matter, you will inevitably hear the expression, "There are two things you don't want to see being made—sausage and legislation." Attributed to Otto von Bismark (1815–1898), Germany's chancellor, the metaphor of sausage making and lawmaking has had a remarkably long run. But, I wonder, does it still apply or are today's sausages and legislation on separate tracks, unlike in the 19th century?

In connection with a book I am writing, I have been closely observing lawmaking in four states. So when I had the opportunity to observe sausage making at the Ohio Packing Company, I took it.

Established as a neighborhood butcher shop in 1907, Ohio Packing has two processing facilities in Columbus, one of which turns out 40,000 pounds of sausage a day. As sausage factories go, this is a medium-sized plant. Larger plants are more automated and have more bells and whistles, but the process is nearly the same. Rick Carter, the quality control manager in the facility, served as my guide.

The Guts of Sausage Making

Sausage making occurs in distinct stages, each of which takes place in a specified room or area. First comes the raw materials cooler, where sausage ingredients are mixed according to computer formulations. A vat will hold 2,000 pounds of one-quarter fat trimmings and three-quarters lean trimmings. At the second stage, the raw materials proceed to the sausage kitchen. A grinder processes up to 40,000 pounds per hour, a blender allows water and seasoning to be added, an emulsifier reshapes the content into a new form, and natural hog casings are stuffed with ingredients.

The Cooking Process Is The Third Stage. Huge Processing Ovens Dry, Smoke, Cook Or Steam The Sausage. A Gas Fire, Using Hickory Chips, Provides Natural Smoking. The Chilling Or Holding Area Is The Fourth Stage. Here, The Sausage Sits Around Waiting To Be Packaged, Which Comes Fifth And Is Accomplished By Three Large Machines. With The Assistance Of 10 To 15 Packagers, The Machines Wrap Multiple Sausages In Plastic Film. Sixth Is Storage In A Huge Freezer With A Capacity Of About A Million Pounds. Finally, Seventh Is The Shipping Area Where Wrapped, Packaged Sausage Waits To Be Loaded On Trailer Trucks.

The Sausage Link

At first glance, sausage making and lawmaking would appear to be a lot alike.

Just as pork, beef and chicken make their way stage by stage to the shipping docks, so a bill is introduced, reviewed by a committee, considered on the floor of one house and then further reviewed by committee and on the floor of the other house. The two houses have to concur before the bill proceeds to the governor for his or her decision to sign, not sign or veto. In sausage making what you see is what you get. However, the "How a Bill Becomes a Law" formulation that is supposed to describe the process in Congress and state legislatures is way off the mark. So, let's compare the processes of sausage making and lawmaking in some of their significant dimensions.

Accessibility. It is not easy to get into a sausage factory, unless you work there or are a raw ingredient. Because of the possibilities of liability and contamination, the public is barred. I could not get in on my own recognizance, but had to secure a letter of introduction from the president of the Ohio Senate. Such a letter is not needed to get into the legislative process. The statehouse is most accessible. Public tours are offered. More important, people can observe the legislature indirectly through the media and more directly through C-Span coverage, which is aired in almost half the states. Constituents can visit with their legislators at home or in the capital. Furthermore, members of the public not only are observers, but, mainly through interest groups and their lobbyists, are also participants. They can make demands and help shape what comes out. Contamination is welcome in the legislature; it is a major element of democracy.

From *State Legislatures*, September 2001, pp. 12-15. Copyright © 2001 by National Conference of State Legislatures. Reprinted by permission.

In Search of the Perfect Metaphor

The legislature has been compared in other metaphors as well as Bismark's—among others, to a circus, marketplace and zoo.

Two interesting metaphors are offered by John A. Straayer in his book, *The Colorado General Assembly*. First is the legislature as an arena in which "a score of basketball games are progressing, all at one time, on the same floor, with games at different stages, with participants playing on several teams at once, switching at will, opposing each other in some instances and acting as teammates in others."

Second is the legislature as a casino, where there are lots of tables, lots of games, the stakes are high, there are winners and losers, but the outcome is never final, for there is always a new game ahead.

Just because the legislature as sausage factory does not stand the test of empirical examination doesn't mean there isn't a metaphor that can do the job. State Legislatures invites legislators, legislature staff and other readers to offer metaphorical candidates, even ones that only apply to part of the process or apply only in part, but not entirely.

Mail your submissions to Sharon Randall, NCSL, 1560 Broadway, Suite 700, Denver, CO 80202 or fax to 303–863–8003 or e-mail to Sharon.Randall@ncsl.org.

Coherence. The 60 people of Ohio Packing who make sausage work in different areas and engage in different operations. But they are all part of one team, making a variety of products according to specification. No one tries to introduce a substitute sausage or attach a bratwurst amendment to a frankfurter. No one wants to prevent a sausage from coming out. In the legislative process, there may be as many teams as there are individual members of the particular legislature. There is a Republican team, a Democratic team, a House team, a Senate team, a liberal team, a conservative team, an urban team, a suburban team and so on. Often, as in Congress and many states today, these teams are quite evenly matched. These teams are not in the business of producing the same product, but often are competing with one another over legislation and over the state budget.

Regularity. Sausage making strives for uniformity. Constant testing takes place to ensure the proper measurement of ingredients—fat content, moisture, seasoning and so forth. The process is strictly regulated by the U.S. Department of Agriculture, whose applicable regulations currently run into thousands of pages (there were only 86 pages of federal regulations in 1914) and whose inspector makes at least one visit a day to check on the operations of the Ohio Packing Company. In addition, the process is monitored diligently in-house by quality control personnel.

Not so with the legislative process, where uniformity is virtually unheard of, measurement of content is illusory, and just about every bill—and certainly every important bill—gets individualized treatment. At the outset, one can predict what will come out of the sausage factory. It is impossible to predict what will come

out of the legislature. We are pretty sure that every year or two we will have a budget, but that is as far as certainty goes.

Efficiency. Sausage making has to be efficient if Ohio Packing is to survive and prosper. Only a few weeks elapse from the time the raw materials are unloaded at the shipping dock to the time when the finished products are loaded onto trucks bound for distributors and retailers. And most of that time is spent on a shelf, waiting for orders to arrive. Not so with the legislative process. Noncontroversial bills may be enacted within a month or so, but significant legislation may take years before enactment. Not infrequently, the legislature fails to meet its budget deadline, as New York has failed for 17 consecutive years, or fails to finish its budget before constitutional adjournment, as is the case of Minnesota this year. Legislatures are hardly efficient if any economic sense. Nor should we expect them to be.

Comprehensibility. The process of making sausage ought not be minimized; it is complex. But it is also comprehensible. In an hour-and-a-half tour, I could figure it out. I have been a student of the legislative process for more than 30 years, but I still can't figure it out. The legislature is too human, too democratic and too messy to be totally comprehensible.

Product. There is no denying that sausage comes in many varieties. Ohio Packing produces 250 different items, although most are variations on the same theme: breakfast and Italian sausage, bratwurst, frankfurters, bologna and salami are the major items under the sausage umbrella. The brand names that Ohio Packing supplies also vary. Harvest Brand is the company's own label. Through a license agreement with Ohio State University, it also manufactures and sells Buckeye Hot Dogs and Brutus Brats; and it is the coast-to-coast distributor of Schmidt's Bahama Mama (a spicy, smoked sausage).

Whatever the brand, however, the labeling required by USDA provides consumers with more information than they could possibly absorb: the brand name; product name; ingredients by proportion, including seasoning; nutrition facts; inspection legend; net weight statement; signature line (that is, who manufactured the sausage); and a handling statement.

New Metaphor Needed

Legislation is much more diverse than sausage, law is much greater in scope. And it is much more indeterminate. Consumers can read the enactment and the bill analyses leading up to it, but they can never be sure of how a law or program will be funded and implemented and how it will actually work. No accurate labeling system has ever been devised.

The products as well as the processes of sausage making and lawmaking are almost entirely different. Bismark has been at rest for more than a century; his metaphor ought to be laid to rest also. We can search for another metaphor, although I doubt that we will find one. The legislative process in Congress and the state is sui generis, incomparable, not like anything else in our experience—and pretty much the way it ought to be.

ALAN ROSENTHAL is a professor of political science at the Eagleton Institute of Politics at Rutgers University.

Legislative Pay Daze
CSG National Study Finds Legislators' Salaries Lag Inflation

A new CSG study has found legislative salaries haven't kept up with inflation. The salaries for lawmakers are influenced by type of legislature, frequency of sessions and the regions in which legislators serve.

JACK PENCHOFF

New Hampshire and California sit on opposite coasts. They also sit on opposite sides of the legislative pay scale. New Hampshire's lawmakers are the lowest paid in the nation at $100 per year. Legislators in California, however, are the highest paid in the 50 state capitols with annual salaries of $110,880.

Yet, lawmakers in both states share something in common with their brethren in the other 48 states—their pay has not kept pace with inflation nor the average salary increases among the general population.

Those are some of the findings in a new publication from The Council of State Governments, *State Legislator Compensation: A Trend Analysis.*

Dr, Keon Chi, editor-in-chief of CSG's annual *Book of the States,* wrote the 38 page report. Using data compiled from *Book of the States* over the past 30 years, Chi and his staff took a comprehensive look at state legislative compensation and the various factors that influence salaries for state lawmakers.

"To my knowledge, this is the first longitudinal analysis that focuses on legislative salaries broken down by types, frequency of sessions and regions," Chi said.

Even in California and other states with higher pay, compensation levels have an impact on recruitment, retention and the work of the legislature. If legislators are not paid adequately, then candidates are drawn from a smaller pool. High pay broadens that pool. You can't expect to attract good candidates with pay that is lower when compared to other jobs and professions.

—Dr. Keon Chi

Salaries Decline

Chi's trends analysis shows that since 1975, when adjusted for current dollars, legislators' pay in the majority of states—28—has actually declined. In 22 states, salaries over that same 30-year period increased.

But even in states where salaries increased, pay did not keep up with inflation.

Between 1975 and 2005, per capita income in the 50 states increased 50.62 percent.

Meanwhile during that same period, annual salaries for legislators declined nearly 7 percent when adjusted for inflation.

In New York, for example, where the legislature is full-time, the annual legislative salary declined 8.63 percent between 1975 and 2005. Meanwhile, per capita income for residents of the Empire State rose 56.92 percent.

Even in some states where legislators' salaries increased in current dollars, gains were much smaller than per capita income in the state.

An example is Massachusetts. Legislative pay for legislators increased 18.29 percent since 1975 when adjusted for inflation. Meanwhile, per capita income in the Bay State increased 85.19 percent when adjusted for inflation over the 30 years included in the report.

Although California's legislators are the highest paid, their inflation adjusted salary increased between 1975 and 2005 by 41.79 percent, about the same increase in per capita income for all residents, 40.41 percent.

Pay influences the interest level of potential candidates for legislative offices, said Chi.

"Even in California and other states with higher pay, compensation levels have an impact on recruitment, retention and the work of the legislature," said Chi. "If legislators are not paid adequately, then candidates are drawn from a smaller pool. High pay broadens that pool. You can't expect to attract good candidates with pay that is lower when compared to other jobs and professions."

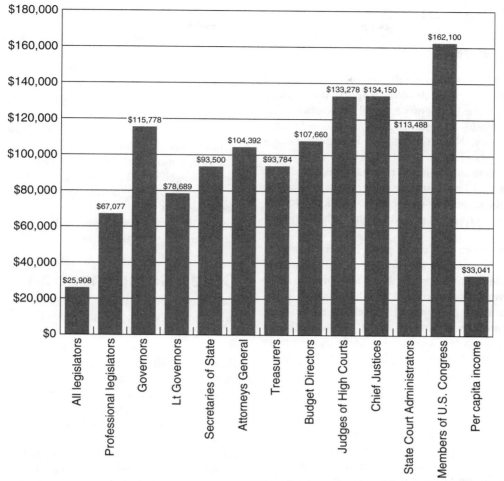

2005 Salary Comparison: Legislative, Executive and Judicial Branches

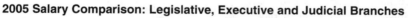

Professional Legislator Annual Salaries by State: 1975–2005 (CPI adjusted)

State	1975	1985	1995	2005	Percent change (%) 1975–2005
Professional					
California	$78,198.91	$62,437.93	$94,109.76	$110,880.00	41.79%
Illinois	74,052.00	60,157.50	55,243.74	57,619.00	−22.19
Massachusetts	46,978.59	55,530.00	60,661.58	55,569.39	18.29
Michigan	70,349.40	67,598.52	64,249.52	79,650.00	13.22
New Jersey	37,026.00	46,275.00	45,747.80	49,000.00	32.34
New York	87,011.10	79,593,00	75,157.10	79,500.00	−8.63
Ohio	64,795.50	58,600.81	55,454.18	56,260.62	−13.17
Pennsylvania	57,760.56	64,785.00	61,432.76	69,647.00	20.58
Wisconsin	58,049.36	50,350.90	49,742.24	45,569.00	−21.50
Average	63,802.38	60,592.07	62,422.07	67,077.22	5.13
w/o CA (a)	62,002.81	60,361.34	58,461.11	61,601.88	−0.65
Median	64,795.50	60,157.50	60,661.58	57,619.00	−11.08
w/o CA (a)	61,422.43	59,379.15	58,057.88	56,939.81	−7.30

Types of Legislatures

Among the factors that impact legislative compensation, according to the report, is the type of legislative body—professional, citizen or a hybrid of the two.

Professional legislatures are generally comprised of full-time legislators who have no legal limits on the length of their regular sessions. The nine states with professional legislatures also are the nine highest paid—California. Illinois, Massachusetts. Michigan. New Jersey, New York, Ohio, Pennsylvania and Wisconsin.

In 2005, the average salary in professional legislatures was $67,077.22. That's a 5.13 percent increase for those states since 1975. In four of those states—Illinois. New York, Ohio and Wisconsin—salaries during that period declined when adjusted for inflation.

Citizen legislatures are the lowest paid. Citizen legislators generally hold full- or part-time jobs outside the legislature and spend less time on legislative work. In 2005, legislators in those states earned an average salary of $9,158, which was 12.4 percent lower than the average for those 18 states 30 years earlier.

Hybrid legislatures possess some of the characteristics of professional and citizen legislatures, In 2005, legislators in those 23 states earned an average of $22,907, a 16.22 percent decline in pay when adjusted for inflation.

Regions

The report includes regional information. Tables in the re-port show that in 2005 legislators in the Eastern Region were the highest paid. At $35,833, their salaries were nearly double the average legislators in the South are paid. Three states in the East, however, had an inflation-adjusted net decrease in pay between 1975 and 2005. Those were Maine, New Hampshire and New York.

In the Midwest, average salaries in 2005 were $30,442.82, a 14.14 percent decline from 1975 when adjusted for inflation. That decline is reflected in the fact that there were no increases in eight of the 11 Midwest state legislatures between 1975 and 2005 when pay is adjusted for inflation.

In the South, basic compensation for lawmakers between 1975 and 2005 declined in 11 of the 16 states. In Alabama and Texas, there was no change in legislative salaries between 1975 and 2005, resulting in a 73 percent decline when adjusted for inflation. The five states with increases, when adjusted for inflation, were Arkansas, Kentucky, Louisiana, Missouri and Oklahoma. Southern lawmakers earned an average of $17,957 in 2005. Overall, Southern legislatures' average pay declined 29.23 percent between 1975 and 2005 when adjusted for inflation.

In the West, legislators' average salary in 2005 was $24,222. However, remove California's salary figures and the rest of the West averaged only $17,000, below that of the South.

While average legislative pay in the West increased an inflation adjusted 8.98 percent between 1975 and 2005, the average pay for Western legislators actually declined 3.2 percent when California's figures are not used.

Other Compensation

The report includes tables and charts on other forms of legislative compensation, including expense allowances, per diems and retirement benefits.

"Some states are generous with their per diem expenses allowances, therefore salaries are not the only indicator of total compensation," Chi said. "Expenses, retirement and health care benefits are highlighted in the report."

Chi also uses data to compare legislative salaries with those of other elected and judicial officials. While acknowledging that most state legislators are part time, he uses for his comparison the averages of the nine professional legislatures. Stale high court justices, for example, earn a national average of $133,278, nearly double the salaries of the average lawmaker in professional legislatures.

Executive branch offices included for comparison, and all higher with higher salaries than legislators, are governors, lieutenant governors, secretaries of state, attorneys general, treasurers, budget directors and state court administrators.

JACK PENCHOFF is CSG associate director of communications and senior editor of *State News* magazine.

From *State News*, February 2007. Published by The Council of State Governments. Reprinted by permission.

Are City Councils a Relic of the Past?

One of America's oldest political institutions isn't adapting very well to 21st-century urban life.

Rob Gurwitt

You notice two things right off about the 19th Ward in St. Louis. The first is that pretty much everywhere there's construction, there's also a large sign reading, "Assistance for the project provided by Michael McMillan, Alderman." The second is just how limited Alderman McMillan's domain happens to be. Walk a few minutes in any direction, and you're out of his ward. You don't see the signs anymore. You also don't see as much construction.

Within the friendly confines of the 19th, St. Louis looks like a city busily reviving. There are new high schools being built, scattered apartments and loft projects underway, efforts to rejuvenate the historic arts and entertainment district, and a HOPE VI retrofit of an enormous public housing facility. While all this activity has some powerful people behind it, just one person has had a hand in all of it, and that is McMillan himself. Only 31, he has been on the St. Louis Board of Aldermen for six years, and in that time has made it clear that his ambitions for his ward—and by extension, himself—are high. "I don't have other obligations," he says. "I'm not married, I have no kids, I have no other job. It's one of my competitive edges."

Cross the ward boundary, and you find out what "competitive edge" means in St. Louis politics. North of the 19th, and for some distance to the east, stretch a series of neglected, depopulated neighborhoods that do not in any way suggest urban revival. This is, in part, a consequence of private market decisions: These neighborhoods don't have much clout within the corporate suites where such decisions are made. But equally important, they don't have much clout in local government, either—at least not when it comes to large-scale development projects.

That's because in St. Louis, each of the 28 ward aldermen is the gatekeeper of development in his or her little slice of the city. If they're shrewd and well connected, like Michael McMillan, the ward does fine. If they're inattentive, or maladroit at cutting deals, or on the outs with local developers, or just plain picky, which is the case in more than a few wards, hardly anything gets done. "You don't see a Mike McMillan coming out of some of these devastated wards," says one City Hall insider. "They have a voice, but if it's weak, what do they really get?"

To be sure, even the weak aldermen in St. Louis have their uses. They get potholes filled and streetlights fixed, offer advice on how to handle code violations or deal with housing court, and see that garbage gets picked up in alleyways where contractors dump it illegally. This hands-on attention is hardly a bad thing. In the words of Jim Shrewsbury, who as president of the Board of Aldermen runs at large and is its 29th member, the city's deeply entrenched system of political micro-management "protects neighborhoods and gives people a sense of influence." As members of a democratic institution, that's what city councilmen are supposed to do. But when that's about all many of them do, in a city that is struggling to emerge from years of economic debility, even Shrewsbury agrees that something is wrong. The system, he says, "creates a sense of parochialism and feudalism. We become the Balkans."

Feuding and Hot Air

The concept of balkanization could be applied these days to councils and boards of aldermen in many of America's biggest cities—perhaps most of them. Look around the country and you can quickly compile a dossier of dysfunction.

Sometimes it is a case of pursuing tangents, as the Baltimore City Council likes to do. In a recent commentary about what it called "the hot-air council," the Baltimore Sun suggested that frequent resolutions on foreign affairs, hearings on the differences between telephone exchanges, and debate about counteracting "the negative images of Baltimore, as portrayed in 'real-crime' fiction, TV dramas and movies" suggested that the members didn't have enough real work to do.

Other councils become so embroiled in internal maneuvering that they lose their relevance. In Philadelphia, where a former mayor once referred to the city council as "the worst legislative body in the free world," there was a brief period of council influence in the mid-1990s, when John Street was council president and worked closely with Mayor Ed Rendell. Now, however, Street is mayor and finds himself in regular tangles with various council factions. "It's like an opera where everybody has a different libretto," says Mark Alan Hughes, an urban affairs professor at the University of Pennsylvania and columnist for the *Philadelphia Daily News*. "The melodrama is clear, it's just the meaning that's completely obscure."

There are councils where bickering and infighting are so intense that the entire body acquires an image of irresponsible flakiness. In Detroit recently, one member charged that supporters of the city's mayor had sabotaged the electric massager in her desk chair to give her a jolt when she used it. Not surprisingly, the public's response was disdainful—what most people saw was a group of elected officials engaged in sabotaging its own reputation.

There are places where, if you want to find the future of the city being pondered, the council chamber is the last place you'd look. "What you have," says a close watcher of civic affairs in Pittsburgh, "is a group of people who primarily deal with very mundane, housekeeping things in their districts. That's what they do, it's what they're interested in, and it's the way they see their power." The real power lies in the mayor's office and with the city's still-strong civic and corporate leadership.

Finally, there are councils whose problem has not been an absence of energy but a hyperactive compulsion to argue over everyday management decisions and prevent important decisions from being made. In Hartford, Connecticut, the city charter for years gave most of the political power to the council, but the council had a long history of intervening in the day-to-day administration of city services and tying itself up in petty squabbles corrosive to the morale of residents, as well as city employees. In the 1990s, the council essentially torpedoed the program of Mayor Mike Peters, who appeared to have broad voter support for his economic reform and revival ideas. Small surprise that when they were finally given a straightforward chance last November to change things, the city's voters opted to create a new form of government that strengthened the mayor at the council's expense.

None of this is to say that councils in large cities never tackle important issues or play a key role in crafting policy. Council members in Los Angeles, for instance, have a great deal to say about basic infrastructure issues, in their districts and across the city. And for all its infighting, the Philadelphia City Council did help to re-shape Street's ambitious urban renewal program, the Neighborhood Transformation Initiative, to be more responsive to neighborhood concerns.

But in all too many large cities these days, the power of councils is, at most, the power to stop things. The wellsprings of citywide innovation and progress lie elsewhere. It is telling that until this past year, neither of the two major national organizations speaking for cities addressed the specific concerns of big-city councils. The National League of Cities is dominated by small- and medium-sized jurisdictions; the U.S. Conference of Mayors, which focuses on larger cities, doesn't address council members at all. "We're literally locked out of the one national group that deals with big cities," observes Nick Licata, a Seattle council member.

Licata, who was struck by the dearth of representation from places like his when he first attended a League of Cities meeting, has put together a new "Central Cities Council" at the League, for council members in the 100 or so largest cities to share information and strategies on common issues. "We're not communicating on a regular basis, we're not exchanging information on local programs we can learn from, and on the national level, when we should be lobbying, we don't have our act together," he says. "This should help us link up."

Still, the sense of floundering one often gets watching big-city councils isn't really a surprise. Over the years, as mayors have moved to get a handle on crime, economic development and even school management, and as semi-private institutions—redevelopment authorities, stadium authorities, transit authorities, convention center authorities, tax increment finance districts—have proliferated, the role of councils in the most critical issues of urban governance has atrophied. Individual council members, the Michael McMillans of the country, may still have a share of power and influence, but the bodies on which many of them serve have lost their identity. "I think city councils have been neutered in most cases," says Dennis Judd, an urban affairs specialist at the University of Illinois-Chicago. "They are engaging in the most trivial aspects of urban government rather than the most important aspects."

Under these circumstances, it is hard not to wonder whether city councils are becoming relics of the political past, poorly adapted to making the decisions of 21st-century urban life. In all too many cases, they seem in danger of becoming the dinosaurs of American local government.

Out of the Loop

There was a moment not long ago when the St. Louis Board of Aldermen managed to command national attention, but it's one local politicians would rather forget. In the midst of a tense and racially charged ward redistricting debate in 2001, Alderman Irene Smith was conducting a filibuster when she asked whether she could go to the bathroom. Told by Board President Shrewsbury that the rules required her to yield the floor to do so, she summoned her supporters, who brought in a trash can and surrounded her with improvised drapes while she appeared to urinate into the can. "I was mortified," says a St. Louis politician who happened to be watching on cable television at the time. "If you've been in the aldermanic chambers, they call to mind a time when the city was a powerful city, a grand place. To think of her staging that in there! The stock of the entire board of aldermen went down." Smith was later indicted on charges of public indecency but was acquitted in January on the reasoning that no one could know for sure whether she was actually urinating or simply pretending to do so.

To those who spend their time in City Hall, the incident was puzzling, because Smith, a lawyer and former judge, is generally seen as one of the more careful and thoughtful members of the board. "She's bright, she knows how to read the law, she asks tough questions in committee hearings," says one aldermanic insider. But to many in the city at large, there was little question about how to interpret her outburst: Not even its own members accord the board much respect any longer.

The fact is, for all the opportunities that ambitious aldermen have to promote development within their own neighborhoods, it's been a while since the board has played a significant role in shaping matters of vital interest to St. Louis as a whole. One of the biggest issues on the plate of Mayor Francis Slay—himself a former board president—is a new stadium for the St. Louis Cardinals baseball team, and while pieces of the complex deal he has put together will require aldermanic approval, the board itself has had very little role in constructing it.

"When I was in City Hall," says a former aide to one of Slay's recent predecessors, "I only went to the board if I absolutely had to. The truth is, I never felt the need to involve people there on the front end in order to get something passed on the back end. In the 1970s or '80s, if a mayor had a stadium project, he'd have had to line up five or six people on the board before he even went public with it." Because that didn't happen in the current situation, the aide argues, this stadium deal is just a stadium deal—it is not part of any broader city commitment to, say, refurbishing public sports facilities or community centers in the neighborhoods.

There are any number of theories about what has led the board of aldermen to its diminished citywide import, and many of them focus on its size. The 28 wards were created in 1914, when St. Louis had 680,000 people. They remained in place when the city reached its peak of 850,000 in 1950. And they're still there, half a century later, when it's down to 340,000. This means that each alderman represents about 12,500 people. Chicago's 50-member city council, which is one of the largest in the country, would have to grow to 200 members if its wards were the same size as those in St. Louis.

If all you expect of an alderman is close attention to garbage pickup and street repairs, of course, small wards are just fine. But they have a cost, as well. For one thing, they form a low barrier to political entry. In some wards, a politician needs as few as 800 votes to get elected. When the city was larger, says former Mayor Freeman Bosley Jr., "you had to be a real leader to get on the board, someone who could put together thousands and thousands of votes. That plays into your ability to put people together and pull them in a direction. So as the years have gone by, the number of go-to people has diminished."

To be sure, it's possible to overstate the case. "Just because we were once a city of 800,000 people doesn't mean we had rocket scientists serving on the board of aldermen," notes Jim Shrewsbury. "I don't think someone makes a decision between running a corporation and being an alderman." But it's equally true that city councils are, in essence, a political proving ground—former U.S. House Minority Leader Richard Gephardt, for instance, got his start on the St. Louis Board of Aldermen. The less skill and vision they demand of their members, the poorer a city's civic life is likely to be.

"If you can make the council a place where young people who are interested in public policy think they ought to be, then it serves as a farm system to create people who understand how local government works and who have sympathy for it," says Mike Jones, a former alderman who now runs the regional Empowerment Zone. "Because the real question is, Where do you get local leadership from? On a city council where you've got to work hard to get elected, it takes good political instincts and hones them into political and policy-making skills."

Ironclad Privilege

Over time, the small size of the constituencies and the rules of the institution itself have combined to make the lure of parochialism more and more irresistible. In the 1950s, following passage of the federal Urban Renewal Act of 1949, aldermen in St. Louis suddenly found themselves with real power in their neighborhoods as the arbiters of development. That law, says Lana Stein, a University of Missouri-St. Louis historian, "brought a huge pot of money, and the aldermen had to pass bills authorizing urban renewal projects and highway projects. They were courted by Civic Progress [the group of corporate movers and shakers at the time] and by the mayor. Even though there were working-class people and saloon keepers elected to the board, they became a much bigger deal because of what they were voting on."

But if the urban renewal money brought the board instant influence, it also led inexorably to parochialism. As requests grew for new housing or redevelopment in the wards, they ran into the ironclad principle of aldermanic privilege—the notion that no member of the board would interfere in matters affecting another member's ward.

Fifty years later, developers still need help from the city, and that usually means a vote from the aldermen, supporting a "blighting" provision or providing a tax abatement or creating a tax-increment financing district. If you happen to live in a ward with an active, responsive alderman who knows how to put together development deals, you're fortunate. But there's scarcely anyone left on the board looking at what makes sense for the city as a whole. Aldermen rarely feel any right or responsibility to look closely at deals being made in others' wards.

When a group of downtown residents recently challenged plans backed by their alderman to demolish a historic, marble-fronted building to make way for a parking garage, the board deferred to the alderman's wishes by essentially ignoring the protest. The demolition plans were backed by the mayor and by his allies, and the developers insisted that the garage was vital to their plans, even though there are underused garages within a block's walk.

The local residents, part of a small but growing group of loft dwellers who form one of the few tangible signs of hope for St. Louis' downtown, attended the one aldermanic hearing on the matter and found no one to talk to. "It was a farce," says Margie Newman, one of their leaders. "There was no opportunity to make our case. Literally, there was an alderman with the Sunday comics held up in front of his face, and of the six on the committee, three were wandering in and out. Remember, this was at our one opportunity to bring our case."

Indeed, confirms Matt Villa, a young alderman who represents the city's far southeast, there is little incentive on the board to pay attention to what others are doing when you don't have to. "In our neighborhood," he says, "there's a neighborhood association and a housing corporation, and we sit down to plan the next five years and never take into consideration what other wards are doing. I don't even know how a citywide plan would be embraced by 28 aldermen."

Bodies Large and Small

Size of selected city councils

City	Number of Districts	Average Size of District
Los Angeles	15	246,000
Phoenix	8	165,000
New York	51	157,000
Kansas City	6	74,000
Memphis*	9	72,000
San Francisco**	11	71,000
Milwaukee	17	35,000
Minneapolis	13	29,000
Richmond	9	22,000
St. Louis	28	12,000

*Two districts have three members each, the others each have one, for a total of 13 members

** City/county supervisors

Source: Governing research

And because the board itself doesn't have an independent capacity to look carefully at measures that come before it—it has very few staff members, and those who want help, such as Michael McMillan, raise funds on the side to pay for an assistant—it often approves important decisions with scarcely any scrutiny at all. "We give pay raises and pension raises and things like that," Villa says, "without really knowing the fiscal impact. The alderman who's sponsored it explains, we pass it, and years later it turns out it wasn't a $5 million impact, it was a $50 million impact."

Charter Changes

If there's anyone unhappy with this state of affairs, it's Jim Shrewsbury, who as president would like the board to become more independent and active. "The truth is, most legislation and ideas originate with the administration," he says. "The vast majority of bills are administration-sponsored bills; they have the resources and the interest and the concentration. Sometimes, I wish we were more careful and would scrutinize them more carefully. And I wish there were more innovation, that more legislation originated here." But he is also quick to point out that in the calculus of the 28 politicians who serve alongside him, that may be more of a risk than they want to take. "I know that on Election Day, the one thousand people who hate me will be there," he explains. "I don't know how many of the thousands who like me will be. I'm prepared to lose my office for something that was in *Profiles in Courage*. If it's not, you start to wonder whether it's worth getting involved."

Yet it's possible that change will come to the St. Louis Board of Aldermen anyway. Although St. Louis is technically a "strong mayor" city, the political reality is that the mayor is constitutionally among the weakest in the country for a city this size. Power has to be shared with a half-dozen other elected officials; the state controls the police through a board on which the mayor has only his own seat; budget decisions and city contracts have to be approved by two of the three members of the Board of Estimate and Apportionment, which is made up of the mayor, comptroller and aldermanic president. "St. Louis is probably the nation's best case of an unreformed government," says the University of Illinois' Dennis Judd, referring to the nationwide movement early in the last century to give mayors enhanced authority. "It's as if it never was touched by the reformers."

Like the board's awkward size, all of this is a result of the 1914 city charter, which is still in effect. But last November, voters statewide approved a home-rule provision for St. Louis that will allow it to take up charter change. Although most of the attention is likely to go to placing more power in the hands of the mayor, there is plenty of sentiment among civic leaders for shrinking the size of the board of aldermen.

This is happening in other big cities with similar problems. Contraction is on the docket in Milwaukee, where some aldermen themselves have proposed shrinking the Common Council from 17 to 15 members, and in Baltimore, where voters last November approved trimming the city council from 19 to 15. Baltimore's initiative, backed by a coalition of labor unions and community organizations, was opposed by most of the city's elected leadership, but it passed overwhelmingly.

It's unclear how much impact tinkering with council size will really have, in St. Louis or anywhere else. But it's clear that some fundamental changes will have to take place for city councils such as these to maintain any real relevance at all in coming years.

By any standard, there is still important work for these bodies to do. Cities need robust political institutions, and by all rights, city councils ought to be among them—they are, after all, the one institution designed to serve as the collective voice of residents and communities, whether their members are elected in districts or at large. But when little is expected of them, because a city's most important decisions are made elsewhere, it's no surprise that over time the ambitions of their members shrink to take in smaller and smaller patches of turf.

There are undeniable benefits to this. Two decades ago, voters in St. Louis overwhelmingly turned down an initiative to cut the number of wards. They felt, says Shrewsbury, "that government had gotten so complicated and big, the only way their voice could be heard was having an alderman who paid close attention." It may be that all most people really want from their city council is the kind of personal stroking that is often hard to come by elsewhere in a big city. But it's also hard to escape the feeling that, as Judd puts it, "when citizens are consulted these days, it's about things that are less and less consequential. What we're seeing is the slow strangulation of local democracy."

First, Kill All the School Boards

A modest proposal to fix the schools.

Matt Miller

It wasn't just the slate and pencil on every desk, or the absence of daily beatings. As Horace Mann sat in a Leipzig classroom in the summer of 1843, it was the entire Prussian system of schools that impressed him. Mann was six years into the work as Massachusetts secretary of education that would earn him lasting fame as the "father of public education." He had sailed from Boston to England several weeks earlier with his new wife, combining a European honeymoon with educational fact-finding. In England, the couple had been startled by the luxury and refinement of the upper classes, which exceeded anything they had seen in America and stood in stark contrast to the poverty and ignorance of the masses. If the United States was to avoid this awful chasm and the social upheaval it seemed sure to create, he thought, education was the answer. Now he was seeing firsthand the Prussian schools that were the talk of reformers on both sides of the Atlantic.

In Massachusetts, Mann's vision of "common schools," publicly funded and attended by all, represented an inspiring democratic advance over the state's hodgepodge of privately funded and charity schools. But beyond using the bully pulpit, Mann had little power to make his vision a reality. Prussia, by contrast, had a system designed from the center. School attendance was compulsory. Teachers were trained at national institutes with the same care that went into training military officers. Their enthusiasm for their subjects was contagious, and their devotion to students evoked reciprocal affection and respect, making Boston's routine resort to classroom whippings seem barbaric.

Mann also admired Prussia's rigorous national curriculum and tests. The results spoke for themselves: illiteracy had been vanquished. To be sure, Prussian schools sought to create obedient subjects of the kaiser—hardly Mann's aim. Yet the lessons were undeniable, and Mann returned home determined to share what he had seen. In the seventh of his legendary "Annual Reports" on education to the Commonwealth of Massachusetts, he touted the benefits of a national system and cautioned against the "calamities which result . . . from leaving this most important of all the functions of a government to chance."

Mann's epiphany that summer put him on the wrong side of America's tradition of radical localism when it came to schools. And although his efforts in the years that followed made

Massachusetts a model for taxpayer-funded schools and state-sponsored teacher training, the obsession with local control—not incidentally, an almost uniquely American obsession—still dominates U.S. education to this day. For much of the 150 or so years between Mann's era and now, the system served us adequately: during that time, we extended more schooling to more people than any nation had before and rose to superpower status. But let's look at what local control gives us today, in the "flat" world in which our students will have to compete.

The United States spends more than nearly every other nation on schools, but out of 29 developed countries in a 2003 assessment, we ranked 24th in math and in problem-solving, 18th in science, and 15th in reading. Half of all black and Latino students in the U.S. don't graduate on time (or ever) from high school. As of 2005, about 70 percent of eighth-graders were not proficient in reading. By the end of eighth grade, what passes for a math curriculum in America is two years behind that of other countries.

Dismal fact after dismal fact; by now, they are hardly news. But in the 25 years since the landmark report *A Nation at Risk* sounded the alarm about our educational mediocrity, America's response has been scattershot and ineffective, orchestrated mainly by some 15,000 school districts acting alone, with help more recently from the states. It's as if after Pearl Harbor, FDR had suggested we prepare for war through the uncoordinated efforts of thousands of small factories; they'd know what kinds of planes and tanks were needed, right?

When you look at what local control of education has wrought, the conclusion is inescapable: we must carry Mann's insights to their logical end and nationalize our schools, to some degree. But before delving into the details of why and how, let's back up for a moment and consider what brought us to this pass.

130,000 Little Red Schoolhouses

Our system is, more than anything, an artifact of our Colonial past. For the religious dissenters who came to the New World, literacy was essential to religious freedom, enabling them to teach their own beliefs. Religion and schooling moved in tandem across the Colonies. Many people who didn't like what the local minister was preaching would move on and found their own church, and generally their own school.

This preference for local control of education dovetailed with the broader ethos of the American Revolution and the Founders' distrust of distant, centralized authority. Education was left out of the Constitution; in the 10th Amendment, it is one of the unnamed powers reserved for the states, which in turn passed it on to local communities. Eventually the United States would have 130,000 school districts, most of them served by a one-room school. These little red schoolhouses, funded primarily through local property taxes, became the iconic symbols of democratic American learning.

Throughout the late 19th and early 20th centuries, nothing really challenged this basic structure. Eventually many rural districts were consolidated, and the states assumed a greater role in school funding; since the 1960s, the federal government has offered modest financial aid to poorer districts as well. But neither these steps, nor the standards-based reform movement inspired by *A Nation at Risk,* brought significant change.

Many reformers across the political spectrum agree that local control has become a disaster for our schools. But the case against it is almost never articulated. Public officials are loath to take on powerful school-board associations and teachers' unions; foundations and advocacy groups, who must work with the boards and unions, also pull their punches. For these reasons, as well as our natural preference for having things done nearby, support for local control still lingers, largely unexamined, among the public.

No Problem Left Behind

Why is local control such a failure when applied to our schools? After all, political decentralization has often served America well, allowing decisions to be made close to where their impact would be felt. But in education, it has spawned several crippling problems:

No way to know how children are doing. "We're two decades into the standards movement in this country, and standards are still different by classroom, by school, by district, and by state," says Tom Vander Ark, who headed the education program at the Bill and Melinda Gates Foundation from 1999 through 2006. "Most teachers in America still pretty much teach whatever they want."

If you thought President Bush's 2001 No Child Left Behind legislation was fixing these problems, think again. True, NCLB requires states to establish standards in core subjects and to test children in grades 3–8 annually, with the aim of making all students "proficient" by 2014. But by leaving standards and definitions of "proficiency" to state discretion, it has actually made matters worse. *The Proficiency Illusion*, a report released in October by the conservative Thomas B. Fordham Foundation, details how. "'Proficiency' varies wildly from state to state, with 'passing scores' ranging from the 6th percentile to the 77th," the researchers found:

> Congress erred big-time when NCLB assigned each state to set its own standards and devise and score its own

tests . . . this study underscores the folly of a big modern nation, worried about its global competitiveness, nodding with approval as Wisconsin sets its eighth-grade reading passing level at the 14th percentile while South Carolina sets its at the 71st percentile.

The lack of uniform evaluation creates a "tremendous risk of delusion about how well children are actually doing," says Chris Cerf, the deputy chancellor of schools in New York City. That delusion makes it far more difficult to enact reforms—and even to know where reforms are needed. "Schools may get an award from their state for high performance, and under federal guidelines they may be targeted for closure for low performance," Vander Ark says. This happens in California, he told me, all the time.

Stunted R&D. Local control has kept education from attracting the research and development that drives progress, because benefits of scale are absent. There are some 15,000 curriculum departments in this country—one for every district. None of them can afford to invest in deeply understanding what works best when it comes to teaching reading to English-language learners, or using computers to develop customized strategies for students with different learning styles. Local-control advocates would damn the federal government if it tried to take on such things. Perhaps more important, the private sector generally won't pursue them, either. Purchasing decisions are made by a complex mix of classroom, school, and school board officials. The more complicated and fragmented the sale that a company has to make, the less willing it is to invest in product research and development.

Incompetent school boards and union dominance. "In the first place, God made idiots," Mark Twain once wrote. "This was for practice. Then He made School Boards." Things don't appear to have improved much since Twain's time. "The job has become more difficult, more complicated, and more political, and as a result, it's driven out many of the good candidates," Vander Ark says. "So while teachers' unions have become more sophisticated and have smarter people who are better-equipped and -prepared at the table, the quality of school-board members, particularly in urban areas, has decreased." Board members routinely spend their time on minor matters, from mid-level personnel decisions to bus routes. "The tradition goes back to the rural era, where the school board hired the schoolmarm and oversaw the repair of the roof, looked into the stove in the room, and deliberated on every detail of operating the schools," says Michael Kirst, an emeritus professor of education at Stanford University. "A lot of big-city school boards still do these kinds of things." Because of Progressive-era reforms meant to get school boards out of "politics," most urban school districts are independent, beyond the reach of mayors and city councils. Usually elected in off-year races that few people vote in or even notice, school boards are, in effect, accountable to no one.

Local control essentially surrenders power over the schools to the teachers' unions. Union money and mobilization are often decisive in board elections. And local unions have hefty intellectual and political backing from their state and national affiliates. Even when they're not in the unions' pockets, in other words, school boards are outmatched.

The unions are adept at negotiating new advantages for their members, spreading their negotiating strategies to other districts in the state, and getting these advantages embodied in state and sometimes federal law as well. This makes it extraordinarily difficult for superintendents to change staffing, compensation, curriculum, and other policies. Principals, for their part, are compliance machines, spending their days making sure that federal, state, and district programs are implemented. Meanwhile, common-sense reforms, like offering higher pay to attract teachers to underserved specialties such as math, science, and special education, can't get traction, because the unions say no.

Financial inequity. The dirty little secret of local control is the enormous tax advantage it confers on better-off Americans: communities with high property wealth can tax themselves at low rates and still generate far more dollars per pupil than poor communities taxing themselves heavily. This wasn't always the case: in the 19th century, property taxes were rightly seen as the fairest way to pay for education, since property was the main form of wealth, and the rich and poor tended to live near one another. But the rise of commuter suburbs since World War II led to economically segregated communities; today, the spending gap between districts can be thousands of dollars per pupil.

But local taxes represent only 44 percent of overall school funding; the spending gaps between states, which contribute 47 percent of total spending, account for most of the financial inequity. Perversely, Title I, the federal aid program enacted in the 1960s to boost poor schools, has widened the gaps, because it distributes money largely according to how much states are already spending.

What Would Horace Do?

I asked Marc Tucker, the head of the New Commission on the Skills of the American Workforce (a 2006 bipartisan panel that called for an overhaul of the education system), how he convinces people that local control is hobbling our schools. He said he asks a simple question: If we have the second-most-expensive K–12 system of all those measured by the Organization for Economic Cooperation and Development, but consistently perform between the middle and the bottom of the pack, shouldn't we examine the systems of countries that spend less and get better results? "I then point out that the system of local control that we have is almost unique," Tucker says. "One then has to defend a practice that is uncharacteristic of the countries with the best performance.

"It's an industrial-benchmarking argument," he adds.

Horace Mann wouldn't have used this jargon, but his thinking was much the same. In his time, the challenge was to embrace a bigger role for the state; today, the challenge is to embrace a bigger role for the federal government in standards, funding, and other arenas.

The usual explanation for why national standards won't fly is that the right hates "national" and the left hates "stan-

dards." But that's changing. Two Republican former secretaries of education, Rod Paige and William Bennett, now support national standards and tests, writing in *The Washington Post*: "In a world of fierce economic competition, we can't afford to pretend that the current system is getting us where we need to go." On the Democratic side, John Podesta, a former chief of staff to President Clinton and the current president of the Center for American Progress (where I'm a senior fellow), told me that he believes the public is far ahead of the established political wisdom, which holds that the only safe way to discuss national standards is to stipulate that they are "optional" or "voluntary"— in other words, not "national" at all.

Recent polling suggests he's right. Two surveys conducted for the education campaign Strong American Schools, which I advised in 2006, found that a majority of Americans think there should be uniform national standards. Most proponents suggest we start by establishing standards and tests in grades 3–12 in the core subjects—reading, math, and science—and leave more-controversial subjects, such as history, until we have gotten our feet wet.

According to U.S. Department of Education statistics, the federal government accounts for 9 percent, or $42 billion, of our K–12 spending. If we're serious about improving our schools, and especially about raising up the lowest, Uncle Sam's contribution must rise to 25 or 30 percent of the total (a shift President Nixon considered). Goodwin Liu, a University of California at Berkeley law professor who has studied school financing, suggests that a higher federal contribution could be used in part to bring all states up to a certain minimum per-pupil funding. It could also, in my view, fund conditional grants to boost school performance. For example, federal aid could be offered to raise teachers' salaries in poor schools, provided that states or districts take measures such as linking pay to performance and deferring or eliminating tenure. Big grants might be given to states that adopt new national standards, making those standards "voluntary" but hard to refuse. The government also needs to invest much more heavily in research. It now spends $28 billion annually on research at the National Institutes of Health, but only $260 million—not even 1 percent of that amount—on R&D for education.

What of school boards? In an ideal world, we would scrap them—especially in big cities, where most poor children live. That's the impulse behind a growing drive for mayoral control of schools. New York and Boston have used mayoral authority to sustain what are among the most far-reaching reform agendas in the country, including more-rigorous curricula and a focus on better teaching and school leadership. Of course, the chances of eliminating school boards anytime soon are nil. But we can at least recast and limit their role.

In all of these efforts, we must understand one paradox: only by transcending local control can we create genuine autonomy for our schools. "If you visit schools in many other parts of the world," Marc Tucker says, "you're struck almost immediately . . . by a sense of autonomy on the part of the school staff and principal that you don't find in the United States." Research in 46 countries by Ludger Woessmann of the University of Munich has shown that setting clear external standards while granting real discretion to schools in how to meet them is the most effective way to run a system. We need to give schools one set of national expectations, free educators and parents to collaborate locally in whatever ways work, and get everything else out of the way.

Nationalizing our schools even a little goes against every cultural tradition we have, save the one that matters most: our capacity to renew ourselves to meet new challenges. Once upon a time a national role in retirement funding was anathema; then suddenly, after the Depression, we had Social Security. Once, a federal role in health care would have been rejected as socialism; now, federal money accounts for half of what we spend on health care. We started down this road on schooling a long time ago. Time now to finish the journey.

How to Win Friends and Repair a City

Atlanta needs all the help it can get. Luckily, it has a mayor who knows where to get it.

ROB GURWITT

Last fall, the president of the Georgia Senate, Eric Johnson, published a letter in the Atlanta Journal-Constitution. It was polite, as public rebukes go, but just barely.

The subject was Atlanta's sewers, or, more precisely, Atlanta's desperate need for help in fixing its sewers. After four decades of deferred maintenance and a federal consent decree that city officials had ignored for years, the bill had come due. Under its new mayor, Shirley Franklin, Atlanta was embarking on a $3 billion overhaul, but it was also staring at astronomical water and sewer rate increases for residents. The new rates promised much hardship for Atlanta's large population of poor people—who in a few years might be paying a total of $100 a month—and for its businesses, especially hotels, which in this convention-dependent city could be paying $100,000 a month by 2008. Not surprisingly, Franklin wanted help from the state and the federal government in defraying the cost.

Johnson's letter was his way of saying "forget it." Atlanta had repeatedly shrugged off its responsibilities, he said, and now had to pay the price. "I will fight any effort to shift the costs of Atlanta's sewer repairs onto the taxpayers of our state," Johnson wrote. "And I will not participate in any effort to ask that America's taxpayers share in your costs, either. ... Atlanta is already costing Georgia's taxpayers plenty. I will not ask them for any more."

As unsympathetic as the letter might have been, its symbolism was even more barbed: a white Republican from Savannah lecturing the black Democratic mayor of a majority-black city on its spendthrift ways. It's not hard to imagine a disastrous chain of events: fury in political circles, an angry press conference at City Hall and shattered relations between the state and its capital city.

And that makes what actually happened all the more interesting. Franklin and Johnson had a private meeting. Shortly afterward, the Republican governor, Sonny Perdue, stepped forward with a commitment to put together a $500 million loan package. Then the GOP-controlled Senate agreed to Atlanta's request that it be allowed to vote on a sales tax increase to defray the repair costs. That bill's sponsor was Eric Johnson himself. A *Journal-Constitution* reporter called these events "the biggest

Atlanta and Its Environs	
CITY OF ATLANTA: Mayor and 15-member council	
Area in square miles	132
Population	423,400
Average household income	$51,328
METRO ATLANTA: 28 counties and 110 municipalities	
Area in square miles	6,208
Population	4,262,584
Average household income	$58,568

Sources: Metro Atlanta Chamber of Commerce, *Atlantic Journal-Constitution*

pre-Christmas happy hour since Tiny Tim and Scrooge patched things up."

Actually, a lot of people are getting along surprisingly well with the city of Atlanta and its mayor these days. Since taking office in January 2002, Franklin has engineered a remarkable turnaround in the city's credibility and public demeanor. She is on friendly terms with the state's leaders. She has plunged into regional efforts to deal with metropolitan transportation, economic development and watershed dilemmas. She meets regularly with officials from the fast-growing suburban counties that surround her jurisdiction. And she has cajoled members of Atlanta's powerful corporate community into serving on task forces that deal with everything from expanding the city's park system to revising its ethics code to exploring the problems of the homeless. "She and I talk every week," says Sam Williams, president of the Metro Atlanta Chamber of Commerce. "If my phone rings at 7 in the morning, I know it's Shirley."

All this bonhomie is in large part the result of Franklin's political candor, nuts-and-bolts understanding of what makes her city tick and willingness to tackle Atlanta's problems head-on. "Before her," says Eric Johnson, "Atlanta hadn't been taking leadership, they were viewed as corrupt, no one trusted them. I think she has the highest integrity personally, but she has also gone out of her way to make everybody know there's a new atmosphere."

Yet what makes the 58-year-old Franklin one of America's most intriguing mayors isn't just her persona, it's her determination to master the trickiest balancing act in urban politics today. Franklin has decided that making progress on her city's challenges means working with everyone from the governor to suburban county commissioners to regional business leaders and nonprofit executives—as she says, "I'm looking for friends for Atlanta." At the same time, she admits it's far easier to enlist their help if the city can show it's willing to take responsibility for straightening out its own messes.

As reasonable as this may sound, it's a daunting task. To build the trust she needs among state officials and business leaders, Franklin has to bolster the political will within the city to make hard choices The state sewer deal, for instance, could not have been put together without the stunning rate increases Atlanta has asked residents and businesses to pay. Yet to sustain political support for such burdens, Franklin needs to show measurable progress in improving their lives—which she can only do with the help of people who want to see her city step up to the plate first. Franklin has juggled these demands with aplomb so far; the trick will be to continue doing so as the cost of putting Atlanta on a solid footing takes an ever bigger bite out of citizens' wallets.

Changing Direction

There was a time, of course, when a big-city mayor in search of "friends" generally looked in only one direction: toward Washington. Chasing federal largesse for everything from highways and sewers to anti-poverty funding was a way of life. In 1982, an uproar ensued when E.S. Savas, an aide to President Reagan, drafted a report taking cities to task for relying too heavily on federal programs. Support from Washington, Savas concluded, had transformed mayors "from leaders of self-reliant cities [into] wily stalkers of federal funds. All too often the promise of such guaranties has created a crippling dependency rather than initiative and independence." The report generated such a storm of protest that Reagan publicly distanced himself from it. He also, however, began the process of cutting and reshaping federal aid.

By the 1990s, it was becoming increasingly clear that pinning a city's fortunes on substantial money from Washington was a fool's game, and a different attitude began to take hold among many mayors: the sense that in effect Savas had been right, and they could do just fine on their own.

Milwaukee Mayor John O. Norquist argued that federal policies had actually hurt cities more than they had helped, and he pulled out of the U.S. Conference of Mayors, which he believed paid too much attention to Washington. "You can't build a city on pity," Norquist insisted. Meanwhile, in New York, Rudolph Giuliani was demonstrating that a mayor who focused on issues such as safety and clean streets could create a sense of dynamism and give urban life a chance to reassert itself.

In a sense, Franklin is amalgamating the two approaches, except that rather than looking to the federal government for help, she's looking everywhere else. This is a strategy that big-city mayors across the country may have little choice but to adopt, whether they recognize it or not.

In part, it's a simple function of money. Atlanta is hardly the only city facing extraordinary infrastructure costs, as local governments in every region confront deferred maintenance on bridges, roads and transit systems and federal environmental mandates on sewers. Indianapolis, Cleveland and Providence are all raising water and sewer rates as they struggle to come up with the hundreds of millions, if not billions, of dollars they each need to bring their sewer systems into compliance with environmental regulations.

So, too, with the costs of meeting demands for better public schools and for boosting homeland security—federal mandates may be plentiful, but federal money is not—and with the costs of improving parks, neighborhoods and other amenities that urban fortunes depend on these days. Finding the resources to meet all those needs demands creativity and an ability to build partnerships at every turn.

At the same time, it's more evident than it used to be that cities' fortunes are tied inextricably to the fortunes of the communities around them. Their economies are linked, their watersheds acknowledge no political boundaries, they inherit one another's air-quality problems, their residents' cars jam one another's streets. This is hardly news, but metropolitan political leaders haven't exactly built a strong track record of taking it to heart.

"For too long, the various counties and cities in the metro region spent all their time on their own governance issues and insufficient time on how their actions affected their neighbors," says Sam Olins, chairman of the commission government in Cobb County, the huge suburban jurisdiction to Atlanta's northwest. "This doesn't take a degree in public administration. It just takes common sense."

Out of the Red

That may be, but in the years before Franklin took office, there wasn't a great deal of common sense on display in Atlanta City Hall. Franklin's predecessor, Bill Campbell, was smart, articulate and impressive in person, but his two terms were also calamitous for the reputation of city government. In addition to possessing an argumentative and thin-skinned nature, Campbell paid attention to the wrong details: He micro-managed personnel decisions but ignored major budget issues. He got into constant spats with the business community, disregarded the city's regional profile and engendered a deep pool of ill will toward Atlanta among politicians around the state.

By the time Franklin took over, the city was on the fiscal ropes, although not many people knew it. One of the new mayor's first moves was to bring in several teams of consultants—some of them paid for by the Metro Chamber of Commerce—to get a handle on finances and to help reorganize the human resources, procurement and information technology systems. A group from Bain & Co., working pro bono on the city's finances, discovered that, instead of the $21 million surplus Campbell's last budget had shown, the city was actually deep in the red.

"It was a very intense process," says Franklin, "with a dozen people doing a 20-year analysis of the city's budget, revenues, expenditures. In the previous years, it had spent well over its revenue. So while the city was holding property taxes low, in fact we were spending ourselves into a hole." Franklin's team eventually announced a gap of $82 million for 2002—"because at some point you just had to settle on a figure," Franklin says—although it probably amounted to more than $90 million, or over a fifth of operating expenditures.

Franklin's response was to tell residents that in order for things to be fixed they were going to have to share the pain. She persuaded the city council to raise property taxes, cut nearly 1,000 jobs from the city payroll and, in announcing a series of other budget cuts, began by slicing her own salary. Since then, she has set out to overhaul everything from yard waste collection to the municipal courts and corrections systems.

Through all of this, Franklin has mastered the political art of appearing to be non-political. It is an art she learned over two decades as an aide to previous Atlanta mayors. Franklin was commissioner for cultural affairs under Maynard Jackson in the 1970s, then chief administrator for Jackson and his successor, Andrew Young, in the 1980s. Later, she spent five years helping to organize Atlanta's 1996 Olympic Games. In each job, she managed to maintain credibility among widely disparate interests and factions. She also benefited from a tendency of those in power to underestimate her.

"I always thought she was little and cute, but I'd say 'Beware!' that first impression," warns longtime Atlanta political figure Michael Lomax, who is now head of the United Negro College Fund. "She's a powerful intellect, a tough personality and a person of extraordinary integrity. She's become formidable in her mature years."

Franklin insists that in forging coalitions with unexpected partners, she is merely responding to what voters told her they wanted during the 2001 campaign. "They wanted a mayor," she says, "who could relate to the state leadership and relate to the region." But Franklin is also responding to reality: Without allies, it would be difficult to solve any of Atlanta's significant problems. "There is no issue the city faces that can be solved alone," says Bill Bolling, a longtime civic leader.

Meeting the Critics

There's no better example than the sewer crisis, which has forced the active involvement of an astounding array of players. At heart, the problem dates to several decades of infrastructure neglect, but the immediate catalyst was a pair of consent decrees, in 1997 and 1998, which the city agreed to after it was sued for violating the federal Clean Water Act. As is true in many other cities, the century-old sewer system in Atlanta combines sewage from households and businesses with runoff from the streets, and it has a tendency to overflow during heavy rainstorms, dumping raw sewage into the South and Chattahoochee rivers.

The consent decrees imposed deadlines for fixing the system, but very little had been done when Franklin took office, even though failure to meet the deadlines carried with it the threat of fines, contempt of court citations, and the very real possibility of a ban on new sewer hookups, which would effectively halt all development in Atlanta. Franklin created a task force, headed by Georgia Tech President Wayne Clough, to look at the city's options, then based the $3 billion overhaul plan on its work.

The challenge, of course, was how to pay for it. With the state and federal governments in fiscal distress, it became clear that help from those quarters would be limited, and the city's water and sewer rates would have to rise dramatically, if only to forestall court action. At the same time, the resulting rate increases were unsustainable for either the city's businesses or its residents, and the only way for the city to roll them back even in part was to get help from somewhere on the outside to underwrite the repairs.

For much of 2003, nothing seemed to be happening. A majority on the city council, worried about constituent anger, refused to pass the rate increase that Franklin was proposing. Governor Perdue and Senate leader Johnson ruled out any state grants, while other Republicans at the state capitol suggested that Atlanta ought to sell its international airport and use the proceeds for sewer repairs. Perdue did eventually offer a $100 million loan, but Franklin rejected it. "Though a generous offer compared to the zero we'd gotten before," she says, "$100 million wasn't going to significantly help the people or the ratepayers." And the Fulton County Commission, which had to approve any sales tax increase for Atlanta, voted against one three times.

Behind the scenes, however, progress was being made on two fronts. The Metro Chamber of Commerce, worried by the prospect of Atlanta failing to fix its sewers and appalled at the possibility that a federal court would shut down development, created a task force on the problem, headed by Lee Thomas, president of Georgia Pacific and EPA administrator under Reagan from 1985 to '89. And Franklin hired a lobbyist to represent the city at the state capitol: Linda Hamrick, an influential white Republican who was a friend of Eric Johnson's and a board member of the state's Christian Coalition.

The key breakthrough came after Johnson sent his letter to the newspaper, rebuking Franklin and the city's demands for money. Hamrick called to tell him he really ought to sit down with Franklin, that they would actually like one another. Johnson called Franklin, and she accepted his offer. "Her attitude is if people say nasty things about you, apparently they don't understand, so you better meet with them," says the Chamber's Sam Williams.

What had rankled Johnson most was that Franklin sent out a letter to close to 200,000 Atlantans recommending that they get in touch with everyone from President George W. Bush to state legislators asking for financial help for the city. "His complaint," Franklin recalls, "was that I didn't give him a heads up—I should have called him. I explained that the element of surprise was part of our plan, but I appreciated that he didn't like it. Then I said that just because it was part of our plan didn't make it right. So he and I began to talk about what it was we really needed."

Meanwhile, Lee Thomas was serving as a broker between Franklin and Governor Perdue. Once the governor had been convinced that the state had to act somehow, he settled on amending a loan program for localities so that Atlanta could qualify for the $500 million Franklin had been hoping for, albeit over a 10-year period. Senator Johnson, for his part, agreed to help Atlanta make an end-run around the Fulton County Commission and vote on its own local-option sales tax. And in January, the city council finally agreed to pass Franklin's rate increases.

"Once the governor said, 'I understand this is a Georgia problem and I'll step into it,' Lee Thomas explains, "he communicated with legislators to say, 'We have to step up.' But they had to see the city was going to pass the rate increase. At the same time, the governor coming in was probably the big thing in helping us with the city council." For her part, Franklin happily gives credit for the arrangement to everyone else. "All I did," she told local business leaders in January, "was hold on by my fingernails until everybody else realized I was about to fall off a cliff."

Richer and Poorer

With the sewer crisis largely behind her—"to say it's been smooth sailing is an overstatement," she confides, "but at least we're not bailing water"—Franklin has turned her attention to the broader issues facing Atlanta. Close to a quarter of the city's population lives below the poverty line, and although there are signs of gentrification dotted throughout the city's southern (read African-American) neighborhoods, there are still many places that look as though no one with any influence has paid attention to them for years. The city's overall population has been growing larger, wealthier and whiter. Demographic forecasts predict a metro region increase of 2 million people over the next 25 years, but not everyone is confident this will benefit the inner-city black community. Atlanta seems fated to endure a whole new round of stresses as it figures out how to apportion the benefits of its growth.

For a mayor who entered office facing a budget deficit, infrastructure crisis and economic downturn, Franklin provoked little overt opposition during her first year. But frustration is beginning to surface. The mayor's willingness to take uncomfortable measures to improve the city's image among outside power-brokers has raised questions in the poorer neighborhoods. Although the property tax increase, the water and sewer rate increases and a recent rise in property values haven't yet generated angry protests, they are becoming political issues. "She made a lot of people unhappy with some of the decisions she made," says Sandra Robertson, a longtime anti-poverty activist who runs the Georgia Coalition on Hunger, which sits in a depressed neighborhood in south Atlanta. Robertson is quick to add, however, that Franklin still enjoys not only her support but that of the people with whom her agency works.

For her part, Franklin has begun to talk about wealth-and-poverty issues. She has asked a cross-section of the community to advise her on homelessness, and on how the city ought to pursue a living wage for its residents. While the specifics haven't taken shape yet, she insists that they will. "The city of Atlanta's interactions with people of low income around issues of poverty are [limited to] law enforcement," she says. "That's how we interact with them. Well, we've got to shift that model." She is also looking for advice on persuading companies that fled to the suburbs to return to the city.

These are long-term strategies, and whether they'll pay off in time to forestall unrest among key portions of Franklin's constituency is anyone's guess. "The problem she faces is that Atlanta is a poor city," says Robertson. "It has this image as a prospering, glitter city, but it is a poor city. She does not have a large tax base to support the government. And then, there's a very strong, organized corporate community she has to deal with. So far, she's gotten a bye from the citizens, but it's not everlasting. Shirley is going to have to handle that, and that's why I keep her in my prayers."

Now This Is Woman's Work

There are more female governors in office than ever before, and they are making their mark with a pragmatic, postpartisan approach to solving state problems.

KAREN BRESLAU

In 1998, voters in a focus group were asked to close their eyes and imagine what a governor should look like. "They automatically pictured a man," says Barbara Lee, whose foundation promoting women's political advancement sponsored the survey. "The kind you see in those portraits hanging in statehouse hallways." They most certainly didn't visualize Alaska Gov. Sarah Palin, a former beauty-pageant winner, avid hunter, snowmobiler and mother of four who was elected to her state's highest office last November. Or Arizona Gov. Janet Napolitano, a badge-wielding former federal prosecutor and onetime attorney for Anita Hill who has redefined the debate over illegal immigration in her state.

While this year's political buzz has been about Hillary Clinton's run for the White House and Nancy Pelosi's ascension to Speaker of the House, women leaders like Palin, a Republican, and Napolitano, a Democrat, have gained significant power in the lives of millions of Americans at the state level. In addition to Alaska and Arizona, Michigan, Kansas, Washington, Hawaii, Connecticut, Louisiana and Delaware elected or re-elected women governors in the last year. That's a total of nine, the highest number to serve simultaneously. And next year women candidates will run for the statehouse in North Carolina and Indiana. A decade ago only 16 women in U.S. history had served as governor (four of them were appointed to replace their dead husbands or other ill-fated male predecessors). Today that number stands at 29. "The best way for people to believe in women as competent executives is by actually watching them govern," says Lee. "They find them likable, strong and effective."

New research shows that voters give female governors significantly higher marks than their male counterparts on such qualities as honesty, cooperation and caring—as well as toughness. And at a time when the national debate has become poisonously partisan, governors like Napolitano, 49, and Palin, 43, are making their mark with a pragmatic, postpartisan approach to solving problems, a style that works especially well with the large numbers of independent voters in their respective states.

Napolitano vetoed 127 bills proposed by Republican lawmakers during her first term. But she also went on to approve tax cuts opposed by some of her fellow Democrats while winning Republican support for her pet project, funding all-day kindergarten. She was the first governor of either party to demand that the federal government live up to its constitutional responsibility to secure her state's border with Mexico while at the same time fending off conservatives' efforts to deny social services to illegal immigrants. In 2006, President George W. Bush traveled to the Arizona border, where he publicly praised Napolitano's policies. She won re-election in a landslide, and in a state where Republicans still hold the majority. "Arizonans don't wake up saying, 'I'm a blue person' or 'I'm a red person'," Napolitano tells *Newsweek*. "They wake up saying, 'How is the governor dealing with my freeway problem, my school problem, my whatever issue it is of the day?'"

In Alaska, Palin is challenging the dominant, sometimes corrupting, role of oil companies in the state's political culture. "The public has put a lot of faith in us," says Palin during a meeting with lawmakers in her downtown Anchorage office, where—as if to drive the point home—the giant letters on the side of the ConocoPhillips skyscraper fill an entire wall of windows. "They're saying, 'Here's your shot, clean it up'." For Palin, that has meant tackling the cozy relationship between the state's political elite and the energy industry that provides 85 percent of Alaska's tax revenues—and distancing herself from fellow Republicans, including the state's senior U.S. senator, Ted Stevens, whose home was recently searched by FBI agents looking for evidence in an ongoing corruption investigation. (Stevens has denied any wrongdoing.) But even as she tackles Big Oil's power, Palin has transformed her own family's connections to the industry into a political advantage. Her husband, Todd, is a longtime employee of BP, but, as Palin points out, the "First Dude" is a blue-collar "sloper," a fieldworker on the North Slope, a cherished occupation in the state. "He's not in London making the decisions whether to build a gas line."

In an interview with *Newsweek*, Palin said it's time for Alaska to "grow up" and end its reliance on pork-barrel spending. Shortly after taking office, Palin canceled funding for the "Bridge to Nowhere," a $330 million project that Stevens helped champion in Congress. The bridge, which would have linked the town of Ketchikan to an island airport, had come to symbolize Alaska's dependence on federal handouts. Rather than relying on such largesse, says Palin, she wants to prove Alaska can pay its own way, developing its huge energy wealth in ways that are "politically and environmentally clean."

It's no coincidence that two of the nation's most popular women governors come from frontier states (Arizona and Alaska were the 48th and 49th, respectively, to join the Union) without established social orders that tend to block women from power. In Washington (the 42nd state), Gov. Christine Gregoire and both U.S. senators are women, a trifecta yet to be achieved by any other state. As women reach these top jobs, even more women enter the political pipeline. "When voters perceive things are bad, they expect a woman candidate to come in and create change," says Debbie Walsh of the Center for American Women and Politics at Rutgers University. "Voters give them license not to fit the mold."

They also are willing to embrace women in nontraditional roles as protectors or enforcers of the public interest. Napolitano, like Gregoire and Gov. Jennifer Granholm of Michigan, served as her state's attorney general. Granholm and Gregoire made national reputations helping the states win a record $200 billion settlement against the tobacco industry in the 1990s. Napolitano prosecuted human-smuggling rings as a U.S. attorney in the Clinton administration, and as state attorney general sued long-distance provider Qwest for consumer fraud. "It's a very authentic role for women to do that kind of caretaking and say, 'I am going to look after your interests'," says Walsh. "What makes them formidable as candidates is experience as the chief law-enforcement officer for their state, a role that exudes

strength. Which is always the question asked about a woman. 'Is she strong enough? Is she tough enough?'"

It's a question Napolitano doesn't bother with much anymore. Sitting in her Phoenix statehouse office, decorated with sports memorabilia, law-enforcement badges and the flags of Arizona National Guard units serving in Iraq, Napolitano is surrounded by a cluster of public-safety experts, reviewing preparations for next winter's Super Bowl, which will be played near Phoenix. "Who's in charge?" she demands, jabbing at an impossibly complex organizational chart listing dozens of law-enforcement agencies. "Who do I call if something goes wrong?" That practical approach has impressed lawmakers, even if they don't agree with her on the issues. "Her door is always open," says State Sen. Tom O'Halleran, a Republican, who has clashed with Napolitano over legislation but is also impressed by her negotiating skills. "She's not stuck to an ideology."

Although she has been in office less than a year, Palin, too, earns high marks from lawmakers on the other side of the aisle. During a debate earlier this year over a natural-gas bill, State Senate Minority Leader Beth Kerttula was astounded when she and another Democrat went to see the new governor to lay out their objections. "Not only did we get right in to see her," says Kerttula, "but she asked us back twice—we saw her three times in 10 hours, until we came up with a solution." Next week in Juneau, Alaska lawmakers will meet to overhaul the state's system for taxing oil companies—a task Palin says was tainted last year by an oil-industry lobbyist who pleaded guilty to bribing lawmakers. Kerttula doesn't expect to agree with the freshman governor on every step of the complex undertaking. But the minority leader looks forward to exploiting one backroom advantage she's long waited for. "I finally get to go to the restroom and talk business with the governor," she says. "The guys have been doing this for centuries." And who says that's not progress?

Rise of the Super-Mayor

How mayors of American cities are coping with suburban growth.

Jerry Abramson's domain is six times bigger and contains twice as many people as it did in 1985, when he first claimed his city's top office. The longest-serving mayor in Louisville's history now oversees not just urban areas, from the old rubber plants to the newly hip Butchertown, but suburban subdivisions and farms. And still Mr Abramson's influence grows. It now extends almost as far as it is possible to see from downtown's National City Tower; it even reaches across the Ohio river into southern Indiana.

Until recently Louisville seemed to be following the path of many industrial cities. Its factories were shedding workers. Middle-class whites were drifting to the suburbs and beyond. Between 1960 and 2000 the city's population dropped from 391,000 to 256,000. For the city to prosper, Mr Abramson realised, it must work with its neighbours. Ever since he took office the relationship has become closer.

In 2003 Louisville joined forces with surrounding Jefferson county in the biggest such merger since the 1970s (Indianapolis and Nashville, for example, also have consolidated city-county governments). Mr Abramson, who had served his three terms as city mayor, easily won the top job in the new "Louisville Metro". Since then he has streamlined public services and accelerated the redevelopment of downtown Louisville. The city's core is dotted with new museums. A planned cluster of towers designed by OMA, a fashionable architectural practice, will be Kentucky's tallest. In a forthcoming report for the Brookings Institution, a Washington, DC, think-tank, Carolyn Gatz and Edward Bennett commend it as a model for other recovering cities.

Most striking is the development of a shared economic fate. Greater Louisville Inc, the metropolitan chamber of commerce, has helped companies like Geek Squad, a computer-service outfit, move beyond the city's borders. "It's better that a company locate in the next county over," Mr Abramson says, "than we lose it to Chicago or Atlanta, Nashville or Cincinnati."

Increasingly, co-operation extends across the Ohio river. At present Louisville and Indiana are linked by two ageing, congested bridges—a big problem for a city that claims to be a logistics hub. Greater Louisville Inc has joined with its equivalent in southern Indiana to promote plans for two new bridges, and is considering whether, and how, to share revenue from a new industrial park in southern Indiana.

Mr Abramson is not the only regional power-broker to emerge from America's cities in the past few years. Richard Daley of Chicago and John Hickenlooper of Denver have both cultivated their fellow mayors in neighbouring suburban towns. Mr Hickenlooper secured their support for a big extension of commuter railway lines, which local voters (generally a tax-averse bunch) duly approved in 2004.

Mayors are forming alliances with nearby settlements mostly because they have to. Few cities can now expect to dominate their hinterlands simply by virtue of being big. Across America suburbs are strongly competing for people, offices and cultural centres. Many mayors quietly worry that their cities will turn into nightmarish Detroits, with a rotten core and a choice collection of the region's most troubled residents. The mayor of Tucson, in Arizona, has openly said so.

Trouble in Paradise

Tucson is one of the sunbelt's rustiest cities. Its population is growing much more slowly than that of Phoenix, to the north, or Albuquerque to the east. It is poorer and more Hispanic than its surroundings. Tucson accounts for just over half the population of 9,000-square-mile Pima county. But probably not for long: between 2000 and 2006 some 71% of the county's population growth and more than half of its job growth took place outside the city. "We get all the negative externalities and none of the positive ones, except for sales taxes," complains Mike Hein, the city manager.

Pima county's enormous size means a Louisville-style merger is out of the question. And suburbs have become wary of "annexation"— the legal incorporation of adjoining areas which is the traditional western method of coping with growth beyond city borders. Which leaves co-operation the only option. Bob Walkup, Tucson's mayor, has helped end a long struggle between the city and county governments. They now work closely to attract new businesses and write transport policy. In Arizona and elsewhere, suburbs may be unusually susceptible to courtship just now. Some are beginning to acquire urban traits: more Latinos now live in Chicago's suburbs than in the city proper. The foreclosure crisis has hit expanding suburbs hardest, wrecking their budgets. Meanwhile, cities have cleaned themselves up and cut crime. In Tucson, burglaries fell by a quarter between 2001 and 2006. In the surrounding suburbs of Oro Valley and Marana they more than doubled, though admittedly from a low base.

Like Mr Abramson, Mr Walkup is now focused on downtown. Tucson's core is singularly bleak and unimpressive. But the city has extracted tax concessions from the state that will help it to build a hotel and an arena, and expand its convention centre. Expect more of that, if Mr Walkup gets his way. City mayors have proved they can work with suburbanites to solve common problems. Their next challenge is to convince them that both will be stronger with a beating heart.

Take It to the Limit

As large-city mayors continue efforts to gain control of schools, the track record for takeovers remains mixed.

DEL STOVER

D oes stripping an elected school board of its authority—and giving control of the schools to a mayor or state-appointed administrator—make any difference in the quality of education that students receive? That question can be answered in a few simple words: Yes, No, and Maybe.

That's the clearest assessment one can offer given the mixed results of state and mayoral takeovers over the past two decades. Clearly, a change in governance can be a successful intervention for a troubled school system. In Boston, Chicago, and Philadelphia, such dramatic action led to increased financial stability, a greater clarity of strategic vision, and modest academic gains.

But sweeping aside an elected school board is no panacea. A few years back, for example, takeovers of the Detroit and District of Columbia schools proved a disruptive and ultimately unsatisfying experiment in reform. Other takeovers led to needed financial and management reforms but failed to improve upon the record of elected school boards in boosting student academic performance.

Even Kenneth Wong, director of Brown University's Urban Education Policy Program and author of a new book generally favorable to mayoral takeovers, says takeovers have a limited role to play—mostly in large urban school systems that are clearly struggling.

"It's a promising strategy," he says. But "a lot of other districts are functioning well and the way they select their school board members and how they identify their superintendents is fine."

Many agree with that assessment. But opinion is almost always divided on when such a bold intervention is appropriate. That certainly was the case in Los Angeles last year during Mayor Antonio Villaraigosa's highly politicized campaign to take over the Los Angeles Unified School District. School officials argued strenuously that a takeover made no sense given the school system's progress in improving test scores and tackling long-standing issues of overcrowding with a massive school construction effort.

After months of debate, state lawmakers ultimately scaled back Villaraigosa's proposal, and a state judge subsequently killed the plan altogether.

As *ASBJ* went to press, a legal battle also was under way in St. Louis, where the state legislature earlier this year installed a state-appointed board of education. Some groups contend the move disenfranchises city voters and that the newly elected board majority should be given a chance to end years of policy infighting. A court hearing in late September was scheduled to argue the legality of the state takeover.

Mixed Success

When a takeover attempt survives such challenges—and most do—the results of such initiatives can vary widely. In 1994, Chicago was considered the worst-run school system in the nation when the Illinois legislature turned over control to Mayor Richard M. Daley. A school board hand-picked by the mayor, along with Paul Vallas, Daley's former budget chief, as schools chancellor, made an impressive start at reform, ending years of budgetary turmoil, closing some of the city's worst schools, pushing out weak administrators, and easing labor strife that had closed the schools nine times in the 1970s and '80s.

What proved a harder nut to crack was student achievement. Gains certainly have been made at the elementary schools, says John Easton, executive director of the Consortium on Chicago School Research. But progress at the high schools has been spotty. Overall, test scores show many schools still score poorly compared to national averages, and overall academic gains, while promising at some grades, are not significantly different from many urban schools overseen by elected school boards.

This story is common to most takeovers, whether pushed by the mayor or the state. In 1989, Jersey City became the first school system in the nation to be taken over by a state, and in the early years officials boasted both operational and academic improvements. But, a decade and a half later, the city's students still score well below the state average on test scores. The same is true for Newark and Paterson, N.J., despite a substantial new investment in school funding for these targeted school systems.

For many, this track record suggests that a takeover can prove invaluable in shattering the political infighting, corruption, and bureaucratic intransigence that can stymie institutional reform in a seriously dysfunctional school system. And, as takeovers from California to Massachusetts have shown, a policy report by the Education Commission of the States notes, these interventions "seem to be yielding more gains in central office activities than in classroom instructional practices but . . . student achievement still oftentimes falls short of expectations."

Indeed, test score data suggest elected school boards can be just as successful as the mayor-appointed boards that have been put in the limelight by takeover advocates. The appointed Boston school board has been rightly honored with both the Council of Urban Boards of Education Annual Award for Urban School Board Excellence and the Broad Prize for Urban Education. Yet the elected Houston school board, also a Broad winner and a finalist for the 2006 CUBE award, has posted similar gains in reading and math, according to NAEP data between 2002 and 2005.

Perhaps that shouldn't be surprising, particularly given the fact that most takeovers are targeted at financially struggling urban school systems. Limited financial resources, coupled with the effects of poverty and high populations of limited English-proficient students, make significant academic gains challenging to any school leadership, regardless of its composition or governance structure.

No Great Bandwagon

At least 29 states now authorize the takeover of troubled school districts, and mayoral appointees have replaced elected school board members in at least a dozen cities in the past 15 years. One of the latest big-city takeovers came earlier this year when Washington, D.C., Mayor Adrian Fenty won authority to strip the elected school board of direct control of the schools and appoint a chancellor who reports directly to him.

The reality, though, is that the takeover bandwagon waxes and wanes. In 2002, for example, Detroit voters opted to replace its mayor-appointed school board with elected officials. This past year, interest in takeovers has peaked. In addition to Villaraigosa's takeover attempt, Missouri officials stepped forward to strip the St. Louis school board of authority, and some political leaders have raised the prospect of takeovers in Seattle and Richmond, Va.

Such discussions might well be strengthened by Wong's new book, *The Education Mayor*, which reviews data on 14 urban school systems and finds significant academic gains following the switch to mayoral control. "Roughly, that means students are able to learn a quarter to 30 percent more" in a school year, he says.

Most likely, the link between governance structure and student achievement will remain a topic of dispute for years to come. But past experience suggests, say educators, the political fuel behind future takeover attempts will depend a lot on public perceptions of the school systems targeted. Those plagued with political infighting among school board members or regularly reporting red ink in their budgets—anything that seriously undermines public confidence in the schools—are a potential target of a takeover. Indeed, most state takeovers have been largely focused on financial matters, not academic.

Many mayors are willing to work in partnership with the school board, such as San Francisco Mayor Gavin Newsom's efforts to put municipal resources into early education.

And that's usually the better alternative to a takeover, suggests NSBA Executive Director Anne Bryant. "Smart mayors know they have more on their plates than running schools," she says. "Mayors should work with the board of education on a regular basis in a shared relationship. Both mayor and school board should be asking of the other, 'What resources should be shared within the city so that the schools succeed?'"

The reality is that the school board can be the mayor's greatest resource to keep the community's educational interests front and center, she says, as well as "a vehicle to govern a huge enterprise focused on an important element in the future of that city—its children."

Building Partnerships

The bottom line is that almost all future takeover attempts will be determined at the local level—by the ability of school boards to build partnerships with municipal officials and community leaders, as well as to strengthen public confidence in the schools, observers say. State lawmakers are loath to intervene in school governance issues unless local community leaders put pressure on them.

"You really need mayors involved practically and consistently," says Suzanne Blanc, senior research associate for Research in Action, a Philadelphia-based nonprofit research group focusing on school improvement and equity. "Creating a process of increased civic engagement also is key."

That lesson is abundantly clear to the school board in Richmond, Va., where local business leaders recently proposed the switch to a mayor-appointed school board. Although that proposal is unlikely to move forward, school leaders are frustrated by their poor relationship with their mayor and a perception of the school system's progress that's based on outdated academic data and unrealistic comparisons to affluent suburban school systems.

Clearly, more community discussion will be helpful, says Richmond School Board President George Braxton. But the issues surrounding suggestions for a governance change are not as simple as some proponents might think.

"There are definite pluses and minuses to both elected and appointed school boards," he says. "And which one is worse or better I can't say. But many of the issues that have been brought out to bring business leaders to come forth like this will not be changed, solved, or even affected by the way school board members are chosen."

DEL STOVER (dstover@nsba.org) is a senior editor of *American School Board Journal*.

The Avengers General

**State AGs have accumulated an enormous amount of power.
Too much, some people think.**

ALAN GREENBLATT

Tom Miller, the attorney general of Iowa, is a genial sort of fellow, with sandy hair, a guileless face and a soft-spoken manner. But when he talks about suing corporations, he can sound a little menacing. Miller is convinced that, on many issues, attorneys general have become an almost unstoppable force. If the AGs get wind of a company engaging in illegal activities and join together against it, he boasts, there is nothing that company can do to head them off before justice has been meted out. "There's no political fix," he says. "They can't hire the right lawyers, they can't hire the right lobbyists. They can't go to the governors."

Few would dispute that, in the past five years, state attorneys general have altered the dynamics of corporate regulation in this country. They have taken on Microsoft and Merrill Lynch, Philip Morris and Household Finance. They have sued the manufacturers of compact discs and lead paint, footwear and George Foreman grills. And most of the time, they have won.

"In some ways, they're more powerful than governors," says Bob Sommer of MWW Group, a lobbyist for major corporate clients. "They don't need a legislature to approve what they do. Their legislature is a jury. That's what makes them frightening to corporate interests." And most attorneys general have not been shy about acknowledging their influence. Last fall, when a coalition of AGs reached a $484 million settlement with the parent company of Household Finance, Miller called it a "basis for reforming the [lending] industry." New York Attorney General Eliot Spitzer made similar claims about changing the behavior of Wall Street financial firms when he announced settlement deals with them last year in a conflict-of-interest dispute.

That a backlash against this power would ultimately emerge is no surprise. What is interesting is where the backlash is coming from—a dissident bloc of the attorneys general themselves. Four years ago, a group of Republican AGs created RAGA, the Republican Attorneys General Association, to stop what they called "government lawsuit abuse" and redirect state legal efforts away from national tort cases and back to traditional crime fighting. RAGA may not have slowed down the litigation process very much, but it has brought the office of state attorney general back into political play around the country. There were

only 12 Republican attorneys general in 1999, when RAGA was founded; today, there are 20.

One of the RAGA recruits is Phill Kline, who was elected attorney general of Kansas last November on a platform that accused his predecessor of presuming corporations to be guilty and treating justice as a revenue source. Kline says today's activist AGs have gotten "dangerously close" to an "addicting" cash-prize legal system reminiscent of the old territorial practice of paying judges for convicting defendants.

Like several of the other RAGA rookies, including Mike Cox of Michigan and Brian Sandoval of Nevada, Kline feels it is a mistake to spend too much time and energy pursuing consumer cases at the expense of criminal prosecutions. He says he will pursue any case where there is clear wrongdoing and will join with other states when a case warrants it. But, in general, he favors a less confrontational approach, hoping that his fellow AGs will be more willing to talk things through with a company before filing a suit. "There's a different threshold that has to be met," Kline says. "You have to prove legal violations, not just an unfortunate policy result." RAGA has received generous help in its bid to rein in the activists. Last fall, the U.S. Chamber of Commerce ran its own television campaigns against aggressive Democratic candidates for attorney general. So did the Law Enforcement Alliance of America, an arm of the gun lobby. In some states, these efforts generated million-dollar ad campaigns. In Texas, the Alliance's estimated $1.5 million late-season ad campaign helped keep the attorney general's office in Republican hands. This was an expanded version of the Chamber's effort in Indiana in 2000, when a $200,000 ad campaign was widely viewed as a leading factor in driving an incumbent Democrat out of office.

To some of the conservative AGs who are active in RAGA, winning elections is the one sure way to change the culture of the office. "Any time you've got more Republicans in any organization, it tends to be more conservative, more business-friendly and more antiregulatory," says Virginia's Jerry Kilgore, the current RAGA chairman.

Kilgore cites the issue of pharmaceutical pricing as one that would likely have been pursued by state AGs through the courts just a few years ago but is being addressed in much more quiet negotiations today. "Everything will be looked at more closely," Kilgore says, "to keep the balance between protecting consumers and allowing business to grow."

No Letup

Despite RAGA's successes, however, it is not at all clear that the activism of recent years is about to crumble away. Even the Republican attorneys general who have been most critical of the multistate cases have been happy to share in the wealth once a nationwide settlement agreement has been reached. True, they are less likely to generate such cases themselves. But there remain more than enough activist Democrats in office to keep the litigation going. "Even five to 10 AGs, if they have the resources and drive, can go ahead if they have a good case," says Tom Miller. "It was always a failed mission to get rid of the multistate cases by electing more Republican AGs, even a majority of Republican AGs."

The 58-year-old Miller, now serving his sixth term, is the dean of state attorneys general. He is happy to recite the history of the group, recalling the easy collegiality of the earlier years when few of the AGs even knew the party affiliation of their peers. The multistate approach, according to Miller, was born during the late 1970s, when several AGs wanted to pursue a case against General Motors Corp. They were afraid the carmaker would "out-resource us," and banded together to share their strength. "We started defensively," he says, "but then we understood there were some tactical advantages to joining together as well."

During the Reagan years, many of the state attorneys general felt that the Federal Trade Commission and the U.S. Justice Department's antitrust division were too wedded to laissez-faire regulatory dogma. (Connecticut Attorney General Richard Blumenthal has called the feds of that era "toothless and clueless … as a matter of ideology.") The AGs also noticed that many of the types of businesses they had sued in the past in their home states, such as pharmacists and funeral home operators, had become part of national chains. So they initiated a number of successful multistate consumer protection cases.

The combined weight of the AG offices, which range in staff size from about two dozen lawyers in South Dakota to more than 1,000 in California, was enough to take on even the most sophisticated corporations. Advances in technology—notably e-mail and conference calling—made it easier for state lawyers in disparate capitals to spread and coordinate their efforts.

By the end of 2000, various groups of AGs could boast of a long list of multimillion-dollar settlements. They had won $56 million in antitrust money from toy makers and retailer Toys "R" Us, and $16 million worth of settlements with Reebok and Keds to answer pricefixing complaints. They had forced Publishers Clearing House to pay $18 million to 24 states. They settled on favorable terms with retailers and consumer credit firms that had collected on debts discharged in bankruptcy and with pharmaceutical firms over complaints about the effectiveness of medicines and improper payments to pharmacists.

The pace has not slowed down since then. In the past few months alone, the AGs have claimed victory and $51 million in a case against Ford Motor Co. over SUV safety. They have settled two cases against Bristol-Myers Squibb, collecting a $155 million payoff, after claiming the company had blocked the introduction of generic alternatives to its drugs. Last year's litigation season brought the huge Household Finance settlement and Spitzer's series of agreements with Merrill Lynch and other Wall Street securities firms. Household will refund money to mortgage borrowers who were misled into paying extra charges, buying extra insurance or accepting unfair interest rates. The Wall Street cases turned on brokers recommending the stocks of companies their firms were doing business with (and issuing misleadingly cheery research about).

The granddaddy of all the AG successes, of course, is the crusade against the tobacco companies. When this case got underway in 1994, says Mississippi Attorney General Mike Moore, "I was alone. No one had a clue it was going on." But within four years, 19 other states had filed their own lawsuits. This led, after a period of delay in which Congress wrestled unsuccessfully with the issue, to the series of settlements with states initially estimated to be worth $246 billion over 25 years.

A few weeks ago, after Moore had announced he would not be seeking reelection this year, a group of contributors at a RAGA fundraiser in Washington lustily cheered. Moore calls that reaction "unseemly," but the more appropriate word might be "naïve." Moore may have started the ball rolling, but there are now at least a dozen attorneys general equally enthusiastic about launching anti-corporate lawsuits. And as critics continually point out, the attorneys general aren't a legislative body. They don't need a majority vote to proceed.

"If you assume over the next couple of cycles that this becomes a mature political office, meaning national interests are participating on both sides," says Sommer of the MWW Group, "you're never going to have more than 30 of one party and less than 20 of the other. You're always going to have plenty of AGs who are going to sign on to litigation."

Pursuing Power

Until recently, there has been no political cost imposed on an attorney general joining a multistate settlement—even if he didn't approve of bringing the case initially. The money is there on the table. Most AGs feel they wouldn't be doing their jobs if they didn't take it. Virginia's Kilgore, now the point man in the Republican drive to restrain AG activism, says that his decision to sign on to the Household settlement was easy: It represented $16 million for Virginia consumers.

The reality is that where there is money to be had from the work of others, virtually every state AG will come on board, regardless of ideology. "While they're getting a lot of funding from corporations to elect Republicans," says Lisa Madigan, the newly elected Democratic attorney general of Illinois, "the fact is that Republicans are participating in settlements. Essentially, you've got Republicans working both sides of the streets."

Democrats delight in pointing out such apparent contradictions. At an AGs meeting in Washington in March, Alabama Republican Bill Pryor introduced a constituent who runs a program designed to curb violence against women. Pryor is one of the leading conservative voices against AG excesses, but the Alabama program is funded by money from a multistate case against the women's footwear company Nine West—money that Pryor didn't mind accepting. California Democrat Bill Lockyer sarcastically commended Pryor "for his enthusiastic participation in the Nine West case. It made your outstanding initiative possible." Amidst the laughter of his colleagues, Pryor could say nothing but "thank you."

Free money aside, there is additional pressure on even reluctant attorneys general to join a multistate settlement. In many instances, the company involved in a case wants them to: The more AGs sign on to a settlement, the more protection the company has from future liability. Sometimes, a firm will demand as part of the settlement that states representing 80 percent of its customer base sign on before the agreement takes effect. Or that California and New York come on board, so it doesn't have to worry about suits from the big states down the road.

Pryor sees the wave of anti-corporate activism receding a bit now because Democratic AGs are fighting the Bush administration on issues such as environmental policy, leaving less time for private litigation than they had in the Clinton years. And he sees RAGA and its campaign assistance to be a further force that will restrain AG activism in the future.

But whatever the partisan or ideological makeup of the 50 AG offices around the country might be, it seems unlikely that a majority of them will want to renounce their influence now that they have attained it. Around the same time that RAGA was being formed, Spitzer, whose Wall Street investigations have largely been a one-man show, declared to a conservative audience that "there has been this tremendous redistribution of legal power away from Washington, and who better than state attorneys general to step into the void to ensure that the rule of law is enforced?"

In the long run, that is a proposition that attorneys general of all stripes are likely to find attractive, regardless of where their campaign money came from. "Like every officeholder, they want to enhance the importance of their office," concedes James Wooten, former president of the U.S. Chamber Institute for Legal Reform and a critic of the activists. "The trend will probably continue."

Article 30

Watching The Bench

Justice by Numbers

Mandatory sentencing drove me from the bench.

Lois G. Forer

Michael S. would have been one of the more than 600,000 incarcerated persons in the United States. He would have been a statistic, yet another addition to a clogged criminal justice system. But he's not—in part because to me Michael was a human being: a slight 24-year-old with a young wife and small daughter. Not that I freed him; I tried him and found him guilty. He is free now only because he is a fugitive. I have not seen him since the day of his sentencing in 1984, yet since that day our lives have been inextricably connected. Because of his case I retired from the bench.

Michael's case appeared routine. He was a typical offender: young, black, and male, a high-school dropout without a job. The charge was an insignificant holdup that occasioned no comment in the press. And the trial itself was, in the busy life of a judge, a run-of-the-mill event.

The year before, Michael, brandishing a toy gun, held up a taxi and took $50 from the driver and the passenger, harming neither. This was Michael's first offense. Although he had dropped out of school to marry his pregnant girlfriend, Michael later obtained a high school equivalency diploma. He had been steadily employed, earning enough to send his daughter to parochial school—a considerable sacrifice for him and his wife. Shortly before the holdup, Michael had lost his job. Despondent because he could not support his family, he went out on a Saturday night, had more than a few drinks, and then robbed the taxi.

There was no doubt that Michael was guilty. But the penalty posed problems. To me, a robbery in a taxi is not an intrinsically graver offense than a robbery in an alley, but to the Pennsylvania legislature, it is. Because the holdup occurred on public transportation, it fell within the ambit of the state's mandatory sentencing law—which required a minimum sentence of five years in the state penitentiary. In Pennsylvania, a prosecutor may decide not to demand imposition of that law, but Michael's prosecuting attorney wanted the five-year sentence.

One might argue that a five-year sentence for a $50 robbery is excessive or even immoral, but to a judge, those arguments are necessarily irrelevant. He or she has agreed to enforce the law, no matter how ill-advised, unless the law is unconstitutional.

I believed the mandatory sentencing law was, and like many of my colleagues I had held it unconstitutional in several other cases for several reasons. We agreed that it violates the constitutional principle of separation of powers because it can be invoked by the prosecutor, and not by the judge. In addition, the act is arbitrary and capricious in its application. Robbery, which is often a simple purse snatching, is covered, but not child molestation or incest, two of society's most damaging offenses. Nor can a defendant's previous record or mental state be considered. A hardened repeat offender receives the same sentence as a retarded man who steals out of hunger. Those facts violate the fundamental Anglo-American legal principles of individualized sentencing and proportionality of the penalty to the crime.

Thus in Michael's case, I again held the statute to be unconstitutional and turned to the sentencing guidelines—a state statute designed to give uniform sentences to offenders who commit similar crimes. The minimum sentence prescribed by the guidelines was 24 months.

A judge can deviate from the prescribed sentence if he or she writes an opinion explaining the reasons for the deviation. While this sounds reasonable in theory, "downwardly departing" from the guidelines is extremely difficult. The mitigating circumstances that influence most judges are not included in the limited list of factors on which "presumptive" sentence is based—that an offender is a caretaker of small children; that the offender is mentally retarded; or that the offender, like Michael, is emotionally distraught.

So I decided to deviate from the guidelines, sentencing Michael to 11-and-a-half months in the county jail and permitting him to work outside the prison during the day to support his family. I also imposed a sentence of two years' probation following his imprisonment conditioned upon repayment of the $50. My rationale for the lesser penalty, outlined in my lengthy opinion, was that this was a first offense, no one was harmed, Michael acted under the pressures of unemployment and need, and he seemed truly contrite. He had never committed a violent act and posed no danger to the public. A sentence of close to a year seemed adequate to convince Michael of the seriousness of his crime. Nevertheless, the prosecutor appealed.

Michael returned to his family, obtained steady employment, and repaid the victims of his crime. I thought no more about Michael until 1986, when the state supreme court upheld the appeal and ordered me to resentence him to a minimum of five years in the state penitentiary. By this time Michael had successfully completed his term of imprisonment and probation, including payment of restitution. I checked Michael's record. He had not been rearrested.

I was faced with a legal and moral dilemma. As a judge I had sworn to uphold the law, and I could find no legal grounds for violating an order of the supreme court. Yet five years' imprisonment was grossly disproportionate to the offense. The usual grounds for imprisonment are retribution, deterrence, and rehabilitation. Michael had paid his retribution by a short term of imprisonment and by making restitution to the victims. He had been effectively deterred from committing future crimes. And by any measurable standard he had been rehabilitated. There was no social or criminological justification for sending him back to prison. Given the choice between defying a court order or my conscience, I decided to leave the bench where I had sat for 16 years.

That didn't help Michael, of course; he was resentenced by another judge to serve the balance of the five years: four years and 15 days. Faced with this prospect, he disappeared. A bench warrant was issued, but given the hundreds of fugitives—including dangerous ones—loose in Philadelphia, I doubt that anyone is seriously looking for him.

But any day he may be stopped for a routine traffic violation; he may apply for a job or a license; he may even be the victim of a crime—and if so, the ubiquitous computer will be alerted and he will be returned to prison to serve the balance of his sentence, plus additional time for being a fugitive. It is not a happy prospect for him and his family—nor for America, which is saddled with a punishment system that operates like a computer—crime in, points tallied, sentence out—utterly disregarding the differences among the human beings involved.

The mandatory sentencing laws and guidelines that exist today in every state were designed to smooth out the inequities in the American judiciary, and were couched in terms of fairness to criminals—they would stop the racist judge from sentencing black robbers to be hanged, or the crusading judge from imprisoning pot smokers for life. Guidelines make sense, for that very reason. But they have had an ugly and unintended result—an increase in the number of American prisoners and an increase in the length of the sentences they serve. Meanwhile, the laws have effectively neutralized judges who prefer sentencing the nonviolent to alternative programs or attempt to keep mothers with young children out of jail.

Have the laws made justice fairer—the central objective of the law? I say no, and a recent report by the Federal Sentencing Commission concurs. It found that, even under mandatory sentencing laws, black males served 83.4 months to white males' 53.7 months for the same offenses. (Prosecutors are more likely to demand imposition of the mandatory laws for blacks than for whites.)

Most important, however, as mandatory sentencing packs our prisons and busts our budgets, it doesn't prevent crime very

effectively. For certain kinds of criminals, alternative sentencing is the most effective type of punishment. That, by the way, is a cold, hard statistic—rather like Michael will be when they find him.

Sentenced to Death

In the past two decades, all 50 state legislatures have enacted mandatory sentencing laws, sentencing guideline statutes, or both. The result: In 1975 there were 263,291 inmates in federal and state prisons. Today there are over 600,000—more than in any other nation—the bill for which comes to $20.3 billion a year. Yet incarceration has not reduced the crime rate or made our streets and communities safer. The number of known crimes committed in the U.S. has increased 10 percent in the last five years.

How did we get into this no-win situation? Like most legislative reforms, it started with good intentions. In 1970, after the turmoil of the sixties, legislators were bombarded with pleas for "law and order." A young, eager, newly appointed federal judge, Marvin Frankel, had an idea.

Before his appointment, Frankel had experienced little personal contact with the criminal justice system. Yet his slim book, *Fair and Certain Punishment,* offered a system of guidelines to determine the length of various sentences. Each crime was given a certain number of points. The offender was also given a number of points depending upon his or her prior record, use of a weapon, and a few other variables. The judge merely needed to add up the points to calculate the length of imprisonment.

The book was widely read and lauded for two main reasons. First, it got tough on criminals and made justice "certain." A potential offender would know in advance the penalty he would face and thus be deterred. (Of course, a large proportion of street crimes are not premeditated, but that fact was ignored.) And second, it got tough on the "bleeding heart" judges. All offenders similarly situated would be treated the same.

The plan sounded so fair and politically promising that many states rushed to implement it in the seventies. In Pennsylvania, members of the legislature admonished judges not to oppose the guidelines because the alternative would be even worse: mandatory sentences. In fact, within a few years almost every jurisdiction had both sentencing guidelines and mandatory sentencing laws. Since then, Congress has enacted some 60 mandatory sentencing laws on the federal level.

As for unfairnesses in sentencing—for instance, the fact that the robber with his finger in his jacket gets the same sentence as the guy with a semiautomatic—these could have been rectified by giving appellate courts jurisdiction to review sentences, as is the law in Canada. This was not done on either the state or federal level. Thus what influential criminologist James Q. Wilson had argued during the height of the battle had become the law of the land: The legal system should "most definitely stop pretending that the judges know any better than the rest of us how to provide 'individualized justice.' "

Hardening Time

I'm not sure I knew better than the rest of you, but I knew a few things about Michael and the correctional system I would be throwing him into. At the time of Michael's sentencing, both the city of Philadelphia and the commonwealth of Pennsylvania were, like many cities and states, in such poor fiscal shape that they did not have money for schools and health care, let alone new prisons, and the ones they did have were overflowing. The city was under a federal order to reduce the prison population; untried persons accused of dangerous crimes were being released, as were offenders who had not completed their sentences.

As for Michael, his problems and those of his family were very real to me. Unlike appellate judges who never see the individuals whose lives and property they dispose of, a trial judge sees living men and women. I had seen Michael and his wife and daughter. I had heard him express remorse. I had favorable reports about him from the prison and his parole officer. Moreover, Michael, like many offenders who appeared before me, had written to me several times. I felt I knew him.

Of course, I could have been wrong. As Wilson says, judges are not infallible—and most of them know that. But they have heard the evidence, seen the offender, and been furnished with presentence reports and psychiatric evaluations. They are in a better position to evaluate the individual and devise an appropriate sentence than anyone else in the criminal justice system.

Yet under mandatory sentencing laws, the complexities of each crime and criminal are ignored. And seldom do we ask what was once a legitimate question in criminal justice: What are the benefits of incarceration? The offenders are off the streets for the period of the sentence, but once released, most will soon be rearrested. (Many crimes are committed in prison, including murder, rape, robbery, and drug dealing.) They have not been "incapacitated," another of the theoretical justifications for imprisonment. More likely, they have simply been hardened.

Sentence Structure

Is there another way to sentence criminals without endangering the public? I believe there is. During my tenure on the bench, I treated imprisonment as the penalty of last resort, not the penalty of choice. And my examination of 16 years' worth of cases suggests my inclination was well founded. While a recent Justice Department study found that two thirds of all prisoners are arrested for other offenses within three years of release, more than two thirds of the 1,000-plus offenders I sentenced to probation conditioned upon payment of reparations to victims successfully completed their sentences and were not rearrested. I am not a statistician, so I had my records analyzed and verified by Elmer Weitekamp, then a doctoral candidate in criminology at the Wharton School of the University of Pennsylvania. He confirmed my findings.

The offenders who appeared before me were mostly poor people, poor enough to qualify for representation by a public defender. I did not see any Ivan Boeskys or Leona Helmsleys, and although there was a powerful mafia in Philadelphia, I did not see any dons, either. Approximately three fourths of these defendants were nonwhite. Almost 80 percent were high school dropouts. Many were functionally illiterate. Almost a third had some history of mental problems, were retarded, or had been in special schools. One dreary day my court reporter said plaintively, "Judge, why can't we get a better class of criminal?"

Not all of these offenders were sentenced to probation, obviously. But I had my own criteria or guidelines—very different from those established by most states and the federal government—for deciding on a punishment. My primary concern was public safety. The most important question I asked myself was whether the offender could be deterred from committing other crimes. No one can predict with certainty who will or will not commit a crime, but there are indicators most sensible people recognize as danger signals.

First, was this an irrational crime? If an arsonist sets a fire to collect insurance, that is a crime but also a rational act. Such a person can be deterred by being made to pay for the harm done and the costs to the fire department. However, if the arsonist sets fires just because he likes to see them, it is highly unlikely that he can be stopped from setting others, no matter how high the fine. Imprisonment is advisable even though it may be a first offense.

Second, was there wanton cruelty? If a robber maims or slashes the victim, there is little likelihood that he can safely be left in the community. If a robber simply displays a gun but does not fire it or harm the victim, then one should consider his life history, provocation, and other circumstances in deciding whether probation is appropriate.

Third, is this a hostile person? Was his crime one of hatred, and does he show any genuine remorse? Most rapes are acts of hostility, and the vast majority of rapists have a record of numerous sexual assaults. I remember one man who raped his mother. I gave him the maximum sentence under the law—20 years—but with good behavior, he got out fairly quickly. He immediately raped another elderly woman. Clearly, few rapists can safely be left in the community, and in my tenure, I incarcerated every one.

Yet gang rape, although a brutal and horrifying crime, is more complicated. The leader is clearly hostile and should be punished severely. Yet the followers can't be so neatly categorized. Some may act largely out of cowardice and peer pressure.

Fourth, is this a person who knows he is doing wrong but cannot control himself? Typical of such offenders are pedophiles. One child abuser who appeared before me had already been convicted of abusing his first wife's child. I got him on the second wife's child and sentenced him to the maximum. Still, he'll get out with good behavior, and I shudder to think about the children around him when he does. This is one case in which justice is not tough enough.

By contrast, some people who have committed homicide present very little danger of further violence—although many more do. Once a young man came before me because he had taken aim at a person half a block away and then shot him in the back, killing him. Why did he do it? "I wanted to get me a body." He should never get out. But the mandatory codes don't make great distinctions between him and another murderer who came before me, a woman who shot and killed a boy after he and his friends brutally gang-raped her teenage daughter.

I found this woman guilty of first-degree murder, but I found no reason to incarcerate her. She had four young children to support who would have become wards of the welfare department and probably would have spent their childhoods in a series of foster homes. I placed her on probation—a decision few judges now have the discretion to impose. She had not been arrested before. She has not been arrested since.

Of course, the vast majority of men, women, and children in custody in the United States are not killers, rapists, or arsonists. They're in prison for some type of theft—a purse snatching, burglary, or embezzlement. Many of these criminals can be punished without incarceration. If you force a first-time white-collar criminal to pay heavily for his crimes—perhaps three times the value of the money or property taken—he'll get the message that crime does not pay. As for poor people, stealing is not always a sign that the individual is an unreasonable risk to the community. It's often a sign that they want something—a car, Air Jordans—that they are too poor to buy themselves. Many of them, if they are not violent, can also be made to make some restitution and learn that crime doesn't pay.

Of course, to most of us, the idea of a nonprison sentence is tantamount to exoneration; a criminal sentenced to probation has effectively "gotten off." And there's a reason for that impression: Unless the probationer is required by the sentencing judge to perform specific tasks, probation is a charade. The probationer meets with the probation officer, briefly, perhaps once a month—making the procedure a waste of time for both. The officer duly records the meeting and the two go their separate ways until the probationer is arrested for another offense.

When I made the decision not to send a criminal to prison, I wanted to make sure that the probation system I sent them into had teeth. So I set firm conditions. If the offender was functionally illiterate, he was unemployable and would probably steal or engage in some other illegal activity once released. Thus in my sentencing, I sent him to school and ordered the probation officer to see that he went. (I use the masculine pronoun deliberately for I have never seen an illiterate female offender under the age of 60). I ordered school dropouts to get their high school equivalency certificates and find jobs. All offenders were ordered to pay restitution or reparations within their means or earning capacity to their victims. Sometimes it was as little as $5 a week. Offenders simply could not return to their old, feckless lifestyles without paying some financial penalty for their wrongdoing.

Monitoring probation wasn't easy for me, or the probation officers with whom I worked. Every day I'd come into my office, look at my calendar, and notice that, say, 30 days had passed since Elliott was let out. So I'd call the probation office. Has Elliott made his payment? Is he going to his GED class? And so on. If the answer was no, I'd hold a violation hearing with the threat of incarceration if the conditions were not met within 30 days. After I returned a few people to jail for noncompliance, both my offenders and their probation officers knew I meant business. (Few probation officers protested my demands; their jobs were more meaningful and satisfying, they said.)

Of course, probation that required education and work and payment plans meant real work for criminals, too. But there was a payoff both the probation officers and I could see: As offenders worked and learned and made restitution, their attitudes often changed dramatically.

Time and Punishment

My rules of sentencing don't make judgeship easier; relying on mandatory sentencing is a far better way to guarantee a leisurely, controversy-free career on the bench. But my rules are, I believe, both effective and transferable: an application of common sense that any reasonable person could follow to similar ends. What prevents Americans from adopting practical measures like these is an atavistic belief in the sanctity of punishment. Even persons who have never heard of Immanuel Kant or the categorical imperative to punish believe that violation of law must be followed by the infliction of pain.

If we Americans treated crime more practically—as socially unacceptable behavior that should be curbed for the good of the community—we might begin to take a rational approach to the development of alternatives to prison. We might start thinking in terms not of punishment but of public safety, deterrence, and rehabilitation. Penalties like fines, work, and payment of restitution protect the public better and more cheaply than imprisonment in many cases.

Mind you, sentencing guidelines are not inherently evil. Intelligent guidelines would keep some judges from returning repeat offenders to the streets and others from putting the occasional cocaine user away for 10 years. Yet those guidelines must allow more latitude for the judge and the person who comes before him. While some states' sentencing laws include provisions that allow judges to override the mandatory sentences in some cases, the laws are for the most part inflexible—they deny judges the freedom to discriminate between the hardened criminal and the Michael. Richard H. Girgenti, the criminal justice director of New York state, has long proposed that the legislature give judges more discretion to impose shorter sentences for nonviolent and noncoercive felonies. This common-sense proposal has not been acted on in New York or any other state with mandatory sentencing laws.

Current laws are predicated on the belief that there must be punishment for every offense in terms of prison time rather than alternative sentences. But when it comes to determining the fate of a human being, there must be room for judgment. To make that room, we must stop acting as if mathematic calculations are superior to human thought. We must abolish mandatory sentencing laws and change the criteria on which sentencing guidelines are based.

Why not permit judges more freedom in making their decisions, provided that they give legitimate reasons? (If a judge doesn't have a good reason for deviating—if he's a reactionary or a fool—his sentencing decision will be overturned.) And why not revise the guidelines to consider dangerousness rather than the nomenclature of the offense? If we made simple reforms like these, thousands of non-threatening, nonhabitual offenders would be allowed to recompense their victims and society in a far less expensive and far more productive way.

You may be wondering, after all this, if I have a Willie Horton in my closet—a criminal whose actions after release privately haunt me. I do. I sentenced him to 10 to 20 years in prison—the maximum the law allowed—for forcible rape. He was released after eight years and promptly raped another woman. I could foresee what would happen but was powerless to impose a longer sentence.

And then there are the other cases that keep me up nights: those of men and women I might have let out, but didn't. And those of people like Michael, for whom justice shouldn't have been a mathematical equation.

Lois G. Forer, a former judge of the Court of Common Pleas of Philadelphia, is the author, most recently, of *Unequal Protection: Women, Children, and the Elderly in Court.*

Keeping *Gideon's* Promise

How a victory for poor people's justice came about in an unlikely place.

EYAL PRESS

In 1987 a jury in Billings, Montana, convicted an 18-year-old man named Jimmy Ray Bromgard of raping an 8-year-old girl. At the trial the victim, who earlier had picked Bromgard out of a police lineup, said she was only "60–65 percent" sure he was the perpetrator. The next day in court, however, prosecutors introduced hair samples found at the scene of the crime that they said were indistinguishable from those provided by the accused. The director of the state's crime lab testified that the chances of this being a coincidence were one in 10,000. Bromgard's public attorney did not challenge this claim. He met with his client only once before the trial began, waived his opening statement and failed to investigate whether other evidence at the scene of the crime, such as traces of semen on the girl's dress, implicated his client. It took one hour for the jury to arrive at a guilty verdict; the judge, struck by Bromgard's lack of remorse, sentenced him to three concurrent forty-year sentences.

But there is a reason Bromgard wasn't sorry. As an investigation by the New York–based Innocence Project would eventually reveal, the semen found on the victim's dress did not match up with his. The scientific-sounding claims about the hair samples turned out to be baseless. In 2002 DNA testing cleared Bromgard of the crime, by which point he'd spent more than fifteen years in state prison—"hard years," stresses Ron Waterman, a lawyer now representing him in a civil suit. Like many presumed child molesters, Bromgard was beaten repeatedly while locked up. On one occasion his jaw was smashed. He left with a decade-plus gap in his employment history and no functional skills. "And, of course, there's still a stigma that follows him," Waterman told me when we met at his office in downtown Helena, the state capital.

Jimmy Ray Bromgard may have paid more dearly for the shoddy legal representation he received than most people who have shuffled through Montana's criminal justice system over the past few years, but his case was no anomaly. "Our estimate was that the system got roughly 100 people wrongfully imprisoned per year," said Waterman, a partner at one of Helena's most prestigious law firms. The problem was not just overzealous prosecutors, he explained. It was a public defender system that left poor people accused of crimes consistently shortchanged.

A few years ago investigators from the National Legal Aid and Defender Association (NLADA) fanned out across Montana to gauge the extent of problems like those Bromgard encountered. In some counties, they found, public defenders reported being so overloaded they spent forty-five minutes per felony. Others said judges pressured them to pursue plea bargains for their clients regardless of the circumstances, or that they had no money to purchase office supplies, much less to hire experts to contest the evidence prosecutors presented in court. In one instance a lawyer was unaware that his client was a schizophrenic; another characterized investigating the charges against the people he represented as "aspirational activities."

The NLADA investigation was carried out at the behest of the ACLU, which in 2002 had filed a lawsuit charging seven Montana counties with failing to fulfill their constitutional obligation to provide indigent residents with qualified legal counsel. Afterward lawyers on both sides set about preparing for a bruising legal battle. Depositions were taken; arguments were prepared. The matter seemed destined to be settled in court. In May 2004, however, perhaps sensing that a ruling might not go in the state's favor, Montana Attorney General Mike McGrath announced that instead of fighting the lawsuit, he would work with the ACLU to convince the legislature to pass a bill addressing its concerns.

It was a novel concept, one that, in a fiercely libertarian state where suspicion of government runs deep, many people doubted could succeed, which is one of the reasons the ACLU agreed to suspend its lawsuit for one year to see how things played out, not withdraw it altogether. In June 2005 Montana became the first state to enact legislation modeled on the American Bar Association's "Ten Principles of a Public Defense Delivery System," creating a new Office of the State Public Defender that, among other things, would provide indigent defendants with lawyers as soon as possible, keep attorney caseloads reasonable and rigorously supervise performance to insure that the constitutional rights of anyone accused of a crime in Montana are upheld. To the surprise of everyone, the bill passed with overwhelming support from Democrats and Republicans alike.

What makes the turnaround in Montana all the more noteworthy is that nationally, improving legal representation for indigent defendants has not exactly been a front-burner issue. Although Congress passed legislation addressing the lack of competent attorneys for poor people accused of capital crimes, the funds were never appropriated. The picture at the state level has not been much rosier. Three years ago, on the fortieth anniversary of *Gideon v. Wainwright,* the landmark Supreme Court decision establishing that states have a constitutional obligation to provide indigent defendants with counsel in felony cases—a right that subsequent rulings have extended to various other types of crime—the American Bar Association held a series of public hearings to examine whether its promise was being fulfilled. Its conclusion was grim. "Thousands of persons are processed through America's courts every year either with no lawyer at all or with a lawyer who does not have the time, resources, or in some cases the inclination to provide effective representation," the ABA report stated. "The fundamental right to a lawyer that Americans assume applies to everyone accused of criminal conduct effectively does not exist in practice for countless people across the United States."

David Carroll, director of research at the NLADA, says the crux of the problem is that since the *Gideon* decision so many states have left the task of implementation to counties, with predictably perverse results. "When you have counties funding the system, the ones that have higher crime, more poor people and the greatest needs tend to have the least tax base," he explained. "In a state like California, counties that have money—LA, Santa Clara—have really great systems and try to follow national standards. At the same time, the ones without tax revenue hire a single attorney for a flat fee. They have enormous caseloads with no supervision or training, and contracts that don't cover costs. The level of justice defendants receive depends on which side of the county line they live on."

Montana, before passage of the recent legislation, was a case in point. At the time the ACLU filed its lawsuit, only one of the seven counties it was suing even had a formal public defender office. There were no uniform training standards for lawyers representing poor people in different parts of the state, no rules limiting the caseloads they handled and no system to monitor performance, so that even the most basic functions, such as insuring that attorneys met with their clients, often were ignored.

While in Montana I drove one day to Missoula, a small city nestled in an old glacial lakebed in the western part of the state, to meet with Candace Bergman, one of the plaintiffs in the ACLU's suit. Bergman has curly brown hair, bright eyes and an attractive smile that disappeared when the subject turned to her experience with the criminal justice system. A few years ago she got arrested on a drug possession charge. A meth addict who knew she needed help but had never committed a violent crime and had two children to support, Bergman hoped that, with some guidance from the lawyer assigned to her case, she could get into treatment and turn her life around. For weeks, however, she sat in county jail without hearing from him. She wrote letters but received no reply. Bergman tried phoning, only to discover that collect calls from the detention facility weren't

accepted. As the weeks passed, her frustration mounted. One day, she opened the newspaper and spotted a notice in the classifieds indicating that her trailer home had been auctioned off without her consent.

Providing legal services for the poor is framed as a way to prevent wasteful spending—but creating a fair system may cost money.

"I felt discarded, abandoned, ashamed," she told me. When she finally met with the lawyer, he told her he was leaving the Public Defender Office and that another attorney would take over her case. Nearly two months passed before she saw that lawyer. When she went before a judge, she was handed a six-month sentence, four months fewer than she'd already served.

Locally as well as nationally, stories like Bergman's have generally failed to move politicians, not least because the people being shortchanged are poor and, disproportionately, members of minority groups (in Montana Native-Americans are 7 percent of the population but 17 percent of those in the state corrections system). Yet beginning in 2003, the Law and Justice Interim Committee, a twelve-member legislative body divided evenly between Democrats and Republicans, started hearing months of testimony about how the system worked: private attorneys who pulled out all the stops to keep clients out of jail while overburdened public defenders encouraged theirs to cop pleas; counties where judges hand-picked public defenders they knew wouldn't put up much of a fight for the people they represented. The testimony evidently swayed members of both parties, for the effort to overhaul the system was "astoundingly bipartisan," says Vincent Warren, a senior staff attorney with the ACLU who spearheaded the litigation effort. Indeed, the bill approved by the legislature last year was co-sponsored by Democrat Mike Wheat, a state senator from Bozeman, and Dan McGee, a Republican from Laurel known as one of the most conservative members of the legislature—a fervent opponent of abortion and an antitax crusader who came into office as "a hang-em-high anticrime guy," according to Scott Crichton, head of the Montana ACLU.

As McGee tells it, he and other Republicans supported reform because they were convinced by arguments that the old system was fundamentally unfair. "One of the hallmark principles of American jurisprudence is you are innocent until proven guilty," McGee told me in an interview, a principle he said should apply to everyone, not just the rich. But McGee went on to strike a more pragmatic note as well: By creating uniform performance standards and a state office to oversee counties, he suggested, Montana could reduce the glut of appeals and wrongful convictions, insure that people being paid to work as public defenders actually do their jobs, and improve efficiency. It is not an argument widely in dispute. "There was absolutely no accountability in the old system," Pam Bucy, who works in the Attorney General's office, told me. "We didn't say the new system was going to be cheap. We said, You don't even know what you're paying now. What you need is accountability. I think that moved county officials, and it certainly moved the legislature."

It didn't hurt, of course, that lawmakers understood that failure to act might mean being forced to do so by a judge, as happened in November 2004, when the Montana Supreme Court affirmed a lower-court ruling declaring the state's system of funding public education unconstitutional. "I told legislators, If you don't fix this and we go to court and we win, you'll have a train wreck that will make school funding look like a picnic in the park," Ron Waterman told me. "The day a judge declares the system unconstitutional, every prosecution that goes forward thereafter is under question. And everyone who is incarcerated can say, The system that convicted me is unconstitutional. You could have a rehearing on 2,000-plus cases."

In places where the movement for reform is making headway, it's likewise been for a combination of principled and pragmatic reasons. "Any time an innocent person is convicted of a crime that was committed, the perpetrator was not," noted Rhoda Billings, the former Chief Justice of North Carolina, in an interview. Billings, a Republican, is among the co-chairs of the National Committee on the Right to Counsel, a bipartisan group of judges and public officials headed by former Vice President Walter Mondale. It is preparing a report on the consequences of failing to fulfill the obligation spelled out in Gideon. Like many people with firsthand experience in the courts, Billings has seen how abdicating responsibility can overwhelm the correctional system. "If criminal prosecution is not done effectively and efficiently, the cost runs up," she explained.

There are, of course, risks to framing provision of legal services for the poor as a good way to prevent wasteful spending—creating an equitable system may, after all, cost money. In early February, at a Chicago summit on indigent defense hosted by the ABA, Michael Mears, director of the Georgia Public Defender Standards Council, told me that to get fiscally conservative Republicans behind the effort to overhaul the system there, advocates stressed "efficiency and effectiveness." But, he acknowledged, "the downside of dealing with fiscally conservative people is that they really mean it." If insuring that every poor person is represented by a competent attorney ends up being expensive, reformers may end up regretting the promises they made.

It's a scenario some fear will crop up in Montana, which will have its new system up and running in June, at which point politicians will be watching closely to see what the price tag is. In a state with a limited tax base that ranks forty-ninth in wages,

the hope many people have invested in the new law may come crashing up against the hard rock of fiscal reality. "What we have now is a wonderful piece of legislation," said Waterman. "But the day will come when we go back to the legislature and say, Here's what it will cost to fund it." At that point, he said, "there's going to be some struggle." Attorney General McGrath insisted to me that such concerns are overblown, since running a more accountable system will end up saving taxpayers money.

For now, anyway, it can at least be said that Montana has made a genuine commitment to change, which is a lot more than can be said of many other states. It has hired a Chief Public Defender, Randi Hood, who in 2004 was named Public Defender of the Year and who told me she intends to fire attorneys who fail to measure up. The state has created an eleven-member Public Defender Commission, staffed by attorneys with years of experience and headed by James Park Taylor, a former public defender and tribal attorney. Both Taylor and Hood acknowledge that implementing change will take time, but both also believe Montana may well serve as a model for other states looking to enact reforms in the years to come.

It is a point I heard echoed by Karla Gray, Chief Justice of the Montana Supreme Court. Gray was attending the ABA's Chicago summit to talk about the legislation Montana had passed, which she described to me as "visionary." When I mentioned that I was from New York, she told me that the Chief Judge there, Judith Kaye, was a friend of hers—a friend who's eager to see the Empire State follow in Montana's footsteps, it appears. A few months ago a commission examining New York's indigent defense system shared its interim findings with Judge Kaye. In her 2006 State of the Judiciary Address, she declared, "I have not seen the word 'crisis' so often, or so uniformly, echoed by all of the sources, whether referring to the unavailability of counsel in Town and Village Courts, or the lack of uniform standards for determining eligibility, or the counties' efforts to safeguard county dollars, or the disparity with prosecutors, or the lack of attorney-client contact, or the particular implications for communities of color." As the statement indicates, the assumption that indigent defendants are denied their rights only in the Deep South and in poorer states is wrong. The good news is that changing this is not impossible. As one person told me in Helena, if it can happen in Montana, it can happen anywhere.

DAVID MOBERG writes frequently for _The Nation_ on labor. Research support for this article was provided by the Investigative Fund of The Nation Institute. **EYAL PRESS**, a _Nation_ contributing writer, is the author of _Absolute Convictions: My Father, a City, and the Conflict That Divided America_, just published by Holt.

Who Needs a Bad Teacher When You Can Get a Worse Judge?

The courts are making a mess of America's schools.

One reason that America's public schools do badly in international rankings, despite getting more money, is that nobody is really accountable for them. The schools are certainly not run by Washington: the federal government pays only 8% of their costs. Most of their money comes from state and local government, but often responsibility for them lies with school boards. And within the schools themselves, head teachers usually have little power either to sack bad teachers or to expel rowdy pupils.

Until recently, the main villains of the piece had seemed to be the teachers' unions, who have opposed any sort of reform or accountability. Now they face competition from an unexpectedly pernicious force: the courts. Fifty years ago, it was the judges who forced the schools to desegregate through *Brown v Board of Education* (1954). Now the courts have moved from broad principles to micromanagement, telling schools how much money to spend and where—right down to the correct computer or textbook.

Twenty-four states are currently stuck in various court cases to do with financing school systems, and another 21 have only recently settled various suits. Most will start again soon. Only five states have avoided litigation entirely.

Nothing exemplifies the power of the courts better than an 11-year-old case that is due to be settled (sort of) in New York City, the home of America's biggest school system with 1.1m students and a budget nearing $13 billion. At the end of this month, three elderly members of the New York bar serving as judicial referees are due to rule in a case brought by the Campaign for Fiscal Equity, a leftish advocacy group, against the state of New York: they will decide how much more must be spent to provide every New York City pupil with a "sound basic" education.

The idea that the state must provide a "sound basic" education was laid down by New York's Court of Appeals in 1995. At first blush, the term sounds obvious and modest. In practice, it is anything but. The New York courts have since said that schools must provide an education that gives "the intellectual tools to evaluate complex issues, such as campaign-finance reform, tax policy and global warming". This is a standard most congressmen probably could not meet.

Trying to guess the amount of extra money the court will mandate has virtually become an industry in itself. State officials think the schools may need a top-up of $2 billion-5 billion a year; others say twice as much. Seeing that both the city and the state have large budget deficits, that will mean uproar (already there is talk of introducing slot machines to help meet the cost), followed by a fresh burst of litigation. The state and the city will also fight over who should contribute what to the settlement. Needless to say, talks with the teachers' unions have also stalled, as the unions wait to see how much extra money they can get for their members.

What is going on? *Brown v Board of Education* concerned a fundamental principle of racial equality. Although the current cases often refer back to Brown, they are to do with the far more complex issues of social class and educational excellence.

Traditionally, American schools have been funded by local property taxes, which inevitably meant that richer areas ended up with more lavish schools. In the 1970s, social reformers launched lawsuits to force states to equalise spending between rich and poor districts. Most were unsuccessful: the courts did not think they could mandate equality. But this changed in 1989 with a Kentucky case, *Rose v Council for Better Education*, where the court decided that education in poor school districts was inadequate, rather than merely unequal. The Kentucky court set specific standards that the children in state schools must reach.

In the wake of *Rose*, similar cases were brought across the country. In New York, the Campaign for Fiscal Equity seized on the phrase "sound basic" education, which had ironically been used by a state court in an earlier decision denying an attempt by Levittown, a Long Island school district, to equalise funding across the state. The case of *Campaign for Fiscal Equity v State of New York* was launched in 1993; so far, most of the decisions have gone the plaintiff's way.

Laying Down the Law

Rare is the politician willing to argue that more money for schools is a bad thing. But are the courts doing any good? Two suspicions arise. First, judges are making a lazy assumption that

More money, more drop-outs

New York City:

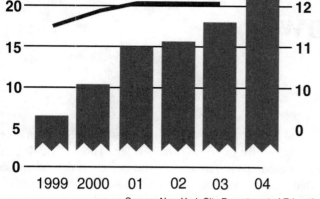

Source: New York City Department of Education

the average in any state with the exception of Connecticut, and more on average than the next 30-odd largest school districts. Despite this, New York City does not have good schools: more than half its pupils in grades three to eight fail to meet the city's standards for maths or English, a fifth of its high-school pupils drop out, and its buildings are falling to pieces.

As for complexity, back in 1979 the city was successfully sued for failing to meet the needs of a severely handicapped pupil. This well-intentioned litigation has since mushroomed into a vast, court-directed "special education programme" with 172,000 children, very few of whom are handicapped as badly as the original plaintiff. To satisfy its requirements, the court lays down innumerable mandates, rules and reporting requirements that are the bane of many teachers' lives.

The current case could be even worse. The courts have already said that, in order to determine the necessary spending, they may consider everything from class size to the availability of computers, textbooks and even pencils. This degree of intervention is all the more scandalous because the courts have weirdly decided to ignore another set of "inputs"—the archaic work practices of school teachers and janitors. David Schoenbrod and Ross Sandler of New York Law School reckon the demands of the court will simply undermine reform and transform an expensive failure into a more expensive one.

And of course, the litigation never ends. Kentucky, for example, is still in court 16 years after the first decision. A lawsuit first filed against New Jersey for its funding of schools in 1981 was "decided" four years later—but it has returned to the court nine times since, including early this year, with each decision pushing the court deeper into the management of the state's schools. Bad judges are even harder to boot out of school than bad pupils.

more money means better schools. As the international results show, the link between "inputs" and "outputs" is vague—something well documented by, among others, the late Senator Daniel Patrick Moynihan of New York. Second, the courts are muddling an already muddled system. Over time, they have generally made it harder to get rid of disruptive pupils and bad teachers.

New York illustrates both these points. Back in the 1980s, Kentucky ranked 48th among states on spending for each child. But New York City spends, on average, more on each child than

In Tiny Courts of N.Y., Abuses of Law and Power

WILLIAM GLABERSON

Some of the courtrooms are not even courtrooms: tiny offices or basement rooms without a judge's bench or jury box. Sometimes the public is not admitted, witnesses are not sworn to tell the truth, and there is no word-for-word record of the proceedings.

Nearly three-quarters of the judges are not lawyers, and many—truck drivers, sewer workers or laborers—have scant grasp of the most basic legal principles. Some never got through high school, and at least one went no further than grade school.

But serious things happen in these little rooms all over New York State. People have been sent to jail without a guilty plea or a trial, or tossed from their homes without a proper proceeding. In violation of the law, defendants have been refused lawyers, or sentenced to weeks in jail because they cannot pay a fine. Frightened women have been denied protection from abuse.

These are New York's town and village courts, or justice courts, as the 1,250 of them are widely known. In the public imagination, they are quaint holdovers from a bygone era, handling nothing weightier than traffic tickets and small claims. They get a roll of the eyes from lawyers who amuse one another with tales of incompetent small-town justices.

A woman in Malone, N.Y., was not amused. A mother of four, she went to court in that North Country village seeking an order of protection against her husband, who the police said had choked her, kicked her in the stomach and threatened to kill her. The justice, Donald R. Roberts, a former state trooper with a high school diploma, not only refused, according to state officials, but later told the court clerk, "Every woman needs a good pounding every now and then."

A black soldier charged in a bar fight near Fort Drum became alarmed when his accuser described him in court as "that colored man." But the village justice, Charles A. Pennington, a boat hauler and a high school graduate, denied his objections and later convicted him. "You know," the justice said, "I could understand if he would have called you a Negro, or he had called you a nigger."

And several people in the small town of Dannemora were intimidated by their longtime justice, Thomas R. Buckley, a phone-company repairman who cursed at defendants and jailed them without bail or a trial, state disciplinary officials found. Feuding with a neighbor over her dog's running loose, he threatened to jail her and ordered the dog killed.

"I just follow my own common sense," Mr. Buckley, in an interview, said of his 13 years on the bench. "And the hell with the law."

The New York Times spent a year examining the life and history of this largely hidden world, a constellation of 1,971 part-time justices, from the suburbs of New York City to the farm towns near Niagara Falls.

It is impossible to say just how many of those justices are ill-informed or abusive. Officially a part of the state court system, yet financed by the towns and villages, the justice courts are essentially unsupervised by either. State court officials know little about the justices, and cannot reliably say how many cases they handle or how many are appealed. Even the agency charged with disciplining them, the State Commission on Judicial Conduct, is not equipped to fully police their vast numbers.

But The Times reviewed public documents dating back decades and, unannounced, visited courts in every part of the state. It examined records of closed disciplinary hearings. It tracked down defendants, and interviewed prosecutors and defense lawyers, plaintiffs and bystanders.

The examination found overwhelming evidence that decade after decade and up to this day, people have often been denied fundamental legal rights. Defendants have been jailed illegally. Others have been subjected to racial and sexual bigotry so explicit it seems to come from some other place and time. People have been denied the right to a trial, an impartial judge and the presumption of innocence.

In 2003 alone, justices disciplined by the state included one in Montgomery County who had closed his court to the public and let prosecutors run the proceedings during 20 years in office. Another, in Westchester County, had warned the police not to arrest his political cronies for drunken driving, and asked a Lebanese-American with a parking ticket if she was a terrorist. A third, in Delaware County, had been convicted of having sex with a mentally retarded woman in his care.

New York is one of about 30 states that still rely on these kinds of local judges, descendants of the justices who kept the peace in Colonial days, when lawyers were scarce. Many states, alarmed by mistakes and abuse, have moved in recent decades to rein in their authority or require more training. Some, from Delaware to California, have overhauled the courts, scrapped them entirely or required that local judges be lawyers.

But New York has no such requirement. It demands more schooling for licensed manicurists and hair stylists.

And it has left its justices with the same powers—more than in many states—even though governors, blue-ribbon commissions and others have been denouncing the courts as outdated and unjust since as far back as 1908, when a justice in Westchester County set up a roadside speed trap, fining drivers for whatever cash they were carrying.

Nearly a century later, a 76-year-old Elmira man who contested a speeding ticket in Newfield, outside Ithaca, was jailed without even a warning for three days in 2003 because he called the sheriff's deputy a liar.

"I thought, this is not America," said the man, Michael J. Pronti, who spent two years and $8,000 before a state appeals court ruled that he had been improperly jailed.

'Justice in the Dark'

It is tempting to view the justice courts as weak and inconsequential because the bulk of their business is traffic violations. Yet among their 2.2 million cases, the courts handle more than 300,000 criminal matters a year. Justices can impose jail sentences of up to two years. Even in the smallest cases, some have wielded powers and punishments far beyond what the law allows.

The reason is plain: Many do not know or seem to care what the law is. Justices are not screened for competence, temperament or even reading ability. The only requirement is that they be elected. But voters often have little inkling of the justices' power or their sometimes tainted records.

For the nearly 75 percent of justices who are not lawyers, the only initial training is six days of state-administered classes, followed by a true-or-false test so rudimentary that the official who runs it said only one candidate since 1999 had failed. A sample question for the justices: "Town and village justices must maintain dignity, order and decorum in their courtrooms"—true or false?

The result, records and interviews show, is a second-class system of justice.

The first class—the city, county and higher courts—is familiar to anyone who has served on a jury or watched "Law

& Order": hardly perfect, but a place of law-schooled judges, support staffs and strict rules. The lower and far larger rung of town and village courts relies on part-time justices, most of them poorly paid, some without a single clerk. Those justices—two-thirds of all the state's judges—are not required to make transcripts or tape recordings of what goes on, so it is often difficult to appeal their decisions.

When they stray badly, the Commission on Judicial Conduct—a panel of lawyers, judges and others—can do little more than try to contain the damage.

Some 1,140 justices have received some sort of reprimand over the last three decades—an average of about 40 a year, either privately warned, publicly rebuked or removed. They are seriously disciplined at a steeper rate than their higher-court colleagues.

The Office of Court Administration, which runs the state court system, makes little pretense of knowing much about what happens in the justice courts. Beyond their names, ages and addresses, it has little information about the justices. Because they are paid by the towns and loosely tied into the court system, "we have limited administrative control, and very, very limited financial control," said Jan H. Plumadore, the deputy chief administrative judge for all courts outside New York City.

The courts also handle money—more than $200 million a year in fines and fees. But the state comptroller's office, which once conducted scores of justice-court audits every year, now does only a handful. When it looked most recently, auditing a dozen courts in May, it reported serious financial-management problems and estimated that millions of dollars a year might be missing from the justice courts statewide.

Norman P. Effman has been the public defender for 16 years in Wyoming County, where he said only one of the 37 justices was a lawyer. In testimony last year, he described the justice courts as a forgotten realm: a "closed door, back of someone's house, in the barn, in the highway department, no record" justice system.

"The reality is," he told a state commission, "if you keep justice in the dark, it stays in the dark."

That commission, which was studying how the court system treats poor people, issued a study in June saying the justice courts remained "a fractured and flawed system." And in recent days, the Office of Court Administration has said it plans to begin addressing some of those failings—for instance, taking steps to double the amount of initial training and to ensure that proceedings are recorded.

But those measures do not address some of the most serious problems: the use of justices who are not lawyers, and the state's weak oversight.

This is not the first time the justice courts have come under scrutiny. "Probably the most unsatisfactory feature of the administration of criminal law remaining in the state today is the obsolete and antiquated institution known as the justice of the peace," another state commission concluded.

The year was 1927.

A Record of Trouble

Certainly, there are worthy justices, and defenders of the system say the good far outnumber the bad. Those supporters, chiefly the justices themselves and the local political leaders who often select them, contend that hometown judges know the hometown problems—and the problem people—and can tailor common-sense solutions.

And, they have argued, putting lawyers in charge of all the courts could cost the state tens of millions of dollars.

"It is the most efficient, low-cost method of ensuring that the people of the state receive justice," said Thomas R. Dias, a town justice in Columbia County who is president of the State Magistrates Association, the justices' organization.

But the record shows otherwise in hundreds of disciplinary cases—most of them unknown to the public.

In the Catskills, Stanley Yusko routinely jailed people awaiting trial for longer than the law allows—in one case for 64 days because he thought the defendant had information about vandalism at the justice's own home, said state officials, who removed him as Coxsackie village justice in 1995. Mr. Yusko was not even supposed to be a justice; he had actually failed the true-or-false test.

Outside Rochester, in Le Roy, a justice who is still in office concocted false statements, state officials said, to help immigration officials deport a Hispanic migrant worker in 2003. Although the man had pleaded not guilty to trespassing, the town justice, Charles E. Dusen, issued a court order saying he had been convicted. In an interview, Justice Dusen said he tried to right his wrong after the worker's lawyer complained. But the man was still deported.

Last December, disciplinary officials disclosed that in a five-year period, a Rochester-area justice had mistakenly imposed $170,000 in traffic fines beyond what the law allowed. And in June, a justice in western New York was disciplined for threatening to jail a man—and warning him to "bring a couple thousand in bail money"—over a complaining phone message the man had left him.

Even the commuter towns around New York City, where the justices are typically lawyers, have endured the system's abuses.

In Mount Kisco, people who asked for the court's sympathy were treated to sarcasm: Justice Joseph J. Cerbone would pull out a nine-inch violin and threaten to play. Mr. Cerbone phoned one woman and talked her out of pressing abuse charges against the son of former clients, state records show. But it took eight years, and evidence that he had taken money from an escrow account, before the State Court of Appeals removed him in 2004 after a quarter-century in office.

In interviews, many of these justices disputed the findings against them, saying the Commission on Judicial Conduct was unfair and determined to end the justice courts.

Commission officials say they have no such agenda.

And the agency is struggling itself. Charged with policing all the state's courts, it can do no more than respond to complaints. Its staff has shrunk by more than half in the last two decades, with just two investigators for the western half of the state.

So commission officials were surprised to learn last year that a western New York justice who had resigned while facing disciplinary charges was back on the bench.

The commission twice disciplined the town justice, Paul F. Bender of Marion, for deriding women in abuse cases. Arraigning one man on assault charges, he asked the police investigator whether the case was "just a Saturday night brawl where he smacks her and she wants him back in the morning."

But the commission spared him removal in 1999 because he was not seeking re-election. Four years later Mr. Bender ran again anyway, unbeknownst to the commission, for a term that will not expire until 2007.

Robert H. Tembeckjian, the commission's administrator, said, "Our working assumption is, a judge who resigns while under disciplinary charges by the commission is not going to return to the bench." But he would not say whether his agency would—or could—take any action against Justice Bender.

'I'm Not a Lawyer'

A 17-year-old girl had stayed out all night, then fought with her family and wound up facing a harassment charge in court in Alexandria Bay, a busy tourist village on the St. Lawrence River. The justice, Charles A. Pennington, a boat hauler with 23 years on the bench, took her not-guilty plea on a Sunday in 2003.

But when told that the girl had no place to go, the judge did not send her to a women's shelter or alert social service officials, as local justices typically do. He took her home.

"I left the court kind of in shock," a police officer later testified. "I've never heard of anything like this before."

The girl's mother, Keitha Rogers, said in an interview that she was appalled to find her daughter at the home of the justice, then 61, as he sat drinking with another man. "Sure, he can tell the difference between the stern and the bow," Ms. Rogers said. "But what does that have to do with making major judgments about people's lives?"

The judicial conduct commission, which ordered Justice Pennington's removal last fall for this and other lapses, ruled that while there was no evidence he had made any improper advances toward the girl, who left after about an hour, he had shown "extraordinarily poor judgment."

And while Mr. Pennington argued that he had not been drinking, he did not entirely disagree with the findings. "Granted, there is mistakes," said the justice, who resigned before the commission ruled. "I'm not a lawyer."

Neither are most of his peers. And that is pretty much all the state knows about them. Office of Court Administration officials say the only way they usually find out a new justice has been elected is if local officials notify them.

For decades, the agency has asked justices to fill out modest biographical questionnaires, then filed away the answers. Under freedom of information law, The Times obtained questionnaires completed by more than 1,800 current justices; they portray a group that is often poorly educated and poorly paid, even though the law they are dealing with is increasingly complex.

Of those who are not lawyers, about a third—more than 400—had no formal education beyond high school. At least 40 did not complete high school, though several went on to earn equivalency degrees.

Interviews with more than 60 justices made it clearer who many of these people are: retirees, farmers, mechanics, former police officers and others with flexible schedules or seasonal work. Most look something like Mr. Pennington: white, and graying. At least 30 justices are in their 80's, well beyond the mandatory retirement age, 70, for other New York judges.

Though the justices' pay is often meager—as little as $850 a year—they can set bail, a basic legal safeguard. They hold crucial preliminary hearings in felony cases and conduct trials on misdemeanors. They preside over civil cases with claims of up to $3,000, and landlord-tenant disputes with no dollar limit, including commercial cases involving hundreds of thousands of dollars.

And then there are the powers they simply take.

In what the Commission on Judicial Conduct called "a shocking abuse of judicial power," Justice Roger C. Maclaughlin single-handedly went after a man he decided was violating local codes on the keeping of livestock in Steuben, near Utica. The justice interviewed witnesses, tipped off the code-enforcement officer, lobbied the town board to deny the man approval to run a trailer park, then jailed him for 10 days without bail—or even a chance to defend himself, the commission said.

In an interview, Justice Maclaughlin said the commission seemed to be chasing legal technicalities rather than real justice.

An Essex County town justice, Richard H. Rock, jailed two 16-year-olds overnight without a trial, saying he wanted "to teach them a lesson." They had been accused of spitting at two other people and charged with harassment. Then he sent them back for 10 more days, the commission said, without ever advising them they had a right to a lawyer.

In 2001, the commission punished him and Justice Maclaughlin with censure, the most serious penalty short of removal from the bench. Justice Maclaughlin is now in his 11th year in office. Justice Rock is in his 10th.

In Alexandria Bay, where Justice Pennington presided at a metal desk in a tiny room inside the police building, a quarter-century in office did not seem to deepen his understanding of his role. Just three days after he took home the 17-year-old girl, another case raised fresh questions about his familiarity with the law, or even the world outside his court.

Eeric D. Bailey, a 21-year-old black soldier from nearby Fort Drum, was facing a disorderly conduct charge after a tussle with a white bar bouncer. Sitting three feet from Mr. Bailey, the bouncer identified him as "that colored man." Mr. Bailey's jaw dropped.

The soldier, who did not have a lawyer, told the judge that the term was offensive. But Justice Pennington said that while certain other words were racist, "colored" was not. "For years we had no colored people here," he said.

The commission had heard worse. After arraigning three black defendants arrested in a college disturbance in 1994, a justice in the Finger Lakes region said in court, "Oh, it's been a rough day—all those blacks in here." A few years before that, a Catskill justice reminisced in court that it was safe for young women to walk around "before the blacks and Puerto Ricans moved here."

In an interview, Justice Pennington said the commission had treated him unfairly. But he may not have helped his case when he told the commission that "colored" was an acceptable description.

"I mean, to me," he testified, "colored doesn't preferably mean black. It could be an Indian, who's red. It could be Chinese, who's considered yellow."

Basic Training

As the blunders, and worse, have piled up over the years, so have the muffled complaints from within the system. Transcripts of the commission's disciplinary hearings, which are usually closed to the public, show that some justices have nearly begged for more training, or any kind of help.

Anthony Ellis, a meat cutter who routinely jailed defendants in Tupper Lake to coerce them into pleading guilty, neatly summed up his insecurities in one closed hearing: "I'm almost like a pilot flying by the seat of my pants."

William G. Mayville, a retired factory worker who turned his courtroom in nearby Fort Covington into a collection agency for local business owners, offered a quietly damning explanation: "I certainly am only a simple man doing a job that, you know, the very best I can do with a limited amount of education that they offered me."

Simple men, and their simple wisdom, are the whole idea behind the justice courts. A 13th-century English institution, the justice of the peace was imported to the colonies in the 1600's along with a fundamental notion: that laymen could settle small-bore cases with practical solutions grounded in local custom or common sense.

But as life, and the law, became vastly more complex by the mid-20th century, several states, including California, New Jersey and Connecticut, created more professional local courts.

In Delaware, where the appointed local magistrates have less authority than New York's justices, the state screens candidates with academic and psychological tests, and starts them off with 11 weeks of training. "It is a reflection of the view that when we're dealing with people's livelihood, when we're dealing with people's freedom, we're going to take this seriously," said the chief magistrate, Alan G. Davis, a lawyer.

In New York, the justice courts have been replaced by state-financed district courts, with lawyer judges, in Nassau County and western Suffolk County. But the last major calls for statewide reform sputtered out in the early 1980's, and the amount of training for justices has not changed. Those without law degrees must take six days of classes at the start. Lawyers do not have to attend, but all justices must take a 12-hour refresher course once a year.

Maryrita Dobiel, who runs the training program for the Office of Court Administration, said the classes provide an introduction to legal principles, but not much more, given a student body with such varying levels of education. "We have to teach to the lowest common denominator," she said. General principles of criminal law, a subject that takes up a semester or more in law school, gets about five hours.

At training's end, justices must score at least 70 percent on a test of 50 questions, all true or false. Those who fail can retake the course, and the test. "We don't decide whether they're qualified to be a judge," Ms. Dobiel said. "The people who have elected them have already made that decision."

The real test comes on the bench.

Several justices have threatened to arrest litigants in small-claims cases, showing they do not understand the difference between civil and criminal cases. Others have told the judicial conduct commission that they disagreed with the constitutional guarantee that a defendant is entitled to a lawyer.

John D. Cox, a quarry manager in Le Ray, near Watertown, summarily jailed people who were unable to pay fines, the commission said. But he received the lightest public penalty, an admonition, in 2002 after he explained that in 22 years in office, he had never been taught that state law allows defendants a new hearing and a lawyer when they say they cannot pay their fine.

The justices do have something of a lifeline: They can call a resource center near Albany where four lawyers field more than 18,000 questions a year. But there are limits on what the center tries to do.

"We tell them what their options are," said the center's supervisor, Paul Toomey. "We don't tell them they're wrong."

Power and Prejudice

Few people who came to his court ever told Donald R. Roberts he was wrong. A strapping former state trooper, he was working as a gas-company truck driver when he was appointed village justice in Malone, near the Canadian border, in 1993. When he was removed five years later, the Commission on Judicial Conduct dispatched him with a stinging description: "a biased, mean-spirited, bullying judge."

It was Justice Roberts who declared that women needed "a good pounding." He had already battled with the county district attorney over his resistance to granting orders of protection.

When a village resident asked that the dentist suing him be forced to come to court to prove his case, Justice Roberts told the man, who had a Hispanic surname: "You're not from around here, and that's not the way we do things around here." The justice did not mention that the plaintiff was his own dentist.

A common argument in favor of New York's justice courts is that local judges know the people and problems that come before them. But that can be a problem itself when justices use those prejudices to favor friends and ride herd over others.

"They have their own little fiefdoms," said Laurie Shanks, an Albany Law School professor. "Some are benevolent despots, but despots nonetheless."

Again and again, the commission's records show, justices have failed to remove themselves from cases involving their own families.

In this department, Pamela L. Kadur may hold a record. As town justice in Root, west of Schenectady, she presided over at least seven cases involving relatives, who often received lenient treatment, the commission said when it ordered her removal in 2003. Justice Kadur heard a speeding case against her son in her own kitchen, then tried to cover up their family relationship in record books, the commission said, by misspelling his last name.

One longtime town justice near Albany let a friend who owned a driving school sit with him at the bench; when the justice ordered anyone to take a driver-training course, only the friend's school was acceptable. Another justice, in Rensselaer County, told a trucker charged with drunken driving that he would not suspend his license because "I can't do that to a fellow truck driver."

Historically, large numbers of the justices have been former law enforcement officers, and lawyers complain that many have unfairly favored the police and prosecutors.

Some justices, unsure of the law, have also come to rely too much on the authorities. Elaine M. Rider, who presided in Waterville, near Utica, fretted that she did not "really have the time to puzzle this out" when a criminal defendant argued that evidence had been seized illegally. So she had the prosecutor write her decision, the commission said.

But one of the most common prejudices on view in the commission's files is far more basic, and it can be found as often in the big-city suburbs that have official-looking courthouses and lawyers on the bench.

In 20 years in office in Haverstraw, north of New York City in Rockland County, Justice Ralph T. Romano drew attention for his opinions on women, state files show. Arraigning a man in 1997 on charges that he had hit his wife in the face with a telephone, he laughed and asked, "What was wrong with this?" Arraigning a woman on charges that she had sexually abused a 12-year-old boy, the justice asked his courtroom, "Where were girls like this when I was 12?"

Across the Hudson, Joseph Cerbone, the Mount Kisco justice with the miniature violin, persuaded a young woman to drop her abuse case against the son of a couple he had done legal work for. She told the commission that while she did not believe the justice's claim that the son was "a decent guy" who had "made a mistake," she had no choice.

"I kind of felt I had no one behind me, no support," she said. "And by getting a phone call from a judge, I felt that maybe I was making a mistake by going through with these charges."

But the human damage can be much worse in the small communities where the justice is often the most powerful local official.

In 11 years as justice in Dannemora, in the North Country, Thomas R. Buckley had his own special treatment for defendants without much money: Even if they were found not guilty, he ordered them to perform community service work to pay for their court-appointed lawyers, although defense lawyers and the district attorney had reminded him for years that the law guaranteed a lawyer at no cost.

"The only unconstitutional part," he told the commission before it removed him in 2000, "is for these freeloaders to expect a free ride."

He twice jailed David Velie, a 19-year-old charged with a misdemeanor, even though the law required him to set bail. In an interview, Mr. Buckley explained that the young man had been a troublemaker "ever since he was born."

Like many small-town justices, he said many of his decisions were down-to-earth solutions. "You've got to use your own judgment," he said. "That's why they call us judges. The law is not always right."

Some residents say that without the law to protect them, they lived in fear. Debra E. Bordeau, the justice's neighbor, said she went into hiding after he threatened to jail her in a dispute over her dog, which he ordered destroyed.

And Carson F. Arnold Sr., a contractor from a nearby town, was jailed for five days after a woman who knew Justice Buckley complained that Mr. Arnold had threatened her, the commission said. There was no trial. The justice simply told Mr. Arnold to shut up, then sentenced him without bail.

"How many years did he treat people like this?" Mr. Arnold asked in an interview. "How many people did this affect?"

A Culture of Secrets

The feeling of powerlessness often begins at the courthouse door.

Many justices preside in intimidatingly tight quarters, admitting participants one by one. Many have heard testimony, settled claims or ruled in criminal cases without noti-

fying the prosecutor, lawyers or even the people directly involved. Some justices can be very selective, state records show: At a 1999 criminal trial in Kinderhook, south of Albany, Justice Edward J. Williams admitted everyone but the victim's lawyer.

Court sessions may be just as unpredictable—held infrequently or at odd hours, or canceled without notice. In 2004, the NAACP Legal Defense and Educational Fund found that people awaiting trial in Schuyler County in the Finger Lakes were jailed for months simply waiting for court to convene again. A high school student arrested on a minor drug charge in the summer of 2003, it said, was still sitting in jail in October.

But the biggest obstacle of all is pinning down what happens in the courtrooms.

A Rochester poverty lawyer, Laurie Lambrix, said that when she appealed the case of a mother of six—a black woman evicted in 1999 by a white landlord who she said had made racist comments—a justice in nearby Gates told her she could not examine the court file of her own client. "I knew court records were public records," Ms. Lambrix said. "I couldn't believe a judge would be ignorant of that."

She was lucky; at least there were records, which she eventually obtained. In many justice courts, it is next to impossible to reconstruct what happened. Some towns spring for a stenographer or taping system, and some justices try to scrawl notes while they preside. But in some cases, there are not even notes.

When someone does appeal, the law requires that justices write a summary of the case. Justices said in interviews that their decisions were rarely appealed, anyway, and even more rarely overturned.

The Commission on Judicial Conduct, then, remains the last line of oversight for justices, and only for those who have stirred up enough concern to be reported by a prosecutor, lawyer or citizen. But the panel is stretched thin—"persistently and acutely underfunded," as it lamented in one annual report. Its statewide staff, which numbered 63 in 1978 when it began, is down to 29.

Supporters of the justice courts have long maintained that they are no worse than the higher courts, citing commission statistics that show justices are disciplined at about the same rate as their higher-court colleagues. But responding to questions from The Times, commission officials studied the agency's three-decade record and found—to their surprise—that cases against local justices were more likely to result in serious punishments.

Although the justices make up about 66 percent of all New York judges, they constitute 76 percent of the 147 judges who have been removed from office.

Last year, six justices were publicly disciplined for the second time, more repeat offenders than ever. But Mr. Tembeckjian, the commission administrator, said the agency had no way to keep a closer eye on them.

"It would be in the public interest for the commission to make sure that a judge who was identified as having a problem has corrected it," he said. "But we simply don't have the resources to do it."

Lawrence S. Goldman, the commission's chairman until April, said all justices should be lawyers. His successor, the divorce lawyer Raoul Felder, would not discuss the quality of the justice courts, but predicted that a reckoning was at hand.

"This is something that's going to have to be addressed by the next governor," he said. "There is a controversy here, and this issue has not been addressed for many, many years."

Jo Craven McGinty contributed reporting.

Kids, Not Cases

Judges make better decisions when children and their families—with adequate legal representation—participate in child welfare proceedings.

SUSAN ROBISON

I never went to court. I have been in and out of foster care since I was a baby, and I really resent that I never got the chance to speak on my behalf or even be present when my future was being discussed." This South Dakota foster youth's experience is all too common. In addition to being excluded from the courts that make life-altering decisions, many children in foster care do not receive the legal representation that the rest of us expect as a fundamental, democratic right.

In Colorado, during 12 years in foster care, 19-year-old Andrew has been in 42 placements. And not once was he present for the numerous court hearings about his case. Despite state statutes requiring that all children with dependency cases have an appointed advocate, an "attorney guardian ad litem" who acts in the child's best interest, Andrew has met with his only a couple of times, and they have never had what he considers a meaningful, private conversation.

Access to court and legal representation for children who have been abused or neglected can vary from case to case and even from proceeding to proceeding. Both the decision-making process and the results for children can stray far from legislative intent, often without legislators even knowing it. The courts, the ultimate decision makers in these cases, are far removed from legislative scrutiny.

Instead of playing the blame game that seems to dominate child welfare discussions, a growing number of legislators are determined to forge a new, more informed and productive dialogue with the courts. And that includes shining a light on court performance.

Kids in Court

Although executive branch child welfare agencies are more often in the public and legislative limelight, the courts have a powerful role in the lives of children who have been abused or neglected.

"Once you are in the system, your life is in their hands, not yours," says a former foster child from California. Courts decide whether children are removed from their homes and families, how long they remain in the system, and what education and health care services they receive. Only the courts sanction foster care, terminate parental rights and grant adoptions.

Historically, children have been barred from the courtroom because of the belief that it was inappropriate and unhealthy for the young to hear bad things about their parents. Many young people in foster care see it differently. They want a choice. These youths report that by the time they enter foster care, they've already experienced trauma. Court participation helps them gain a realistic view of their family and a sense of control—both important for getting on with their lives.

In a 2006 California survey, youths in foster care who attended court reported real benefits. Some were able to take an active role in decisions about their lives, while others found it helpful to simply be present and see how the decisions were made. Young people and their legal advocates believe that better decisions result when the judge can interact with children face-to-face instead of only reading a case file. The judge can observe the child's appearance and interaction with others, hear firsthand the child's hopes and opinions, and see that the child is getting older and needs a permanent family. One lonely child in foster care was unable to convince her case worker, foster parents or guardian ad litem that she desperately needed to see her sister at least once a week—despite busy schedules and conflicting demands on the adults' time. When she presented her case directly to the judge, a visitation arrangement that met her needs was accomplished.

A Kinder, Gentler Court

In some states, legislators have required courts to notify young people about hearings and to consider whether their presence is appropriate. Minnesota and California lawmakers make participation in court proceedings a right. Recent federal legislation supports this approach. It makes court and agency consultation with children a requirement for states to receive Title IV-E foster care funding.

At the same time, foster youths and their advocates are not saying that it should be business as usual in the courtroom. Los Angeles County, home to 36,000 children in foster care, allows all children over 4 years of age to attend court. According to Leslie Heimov of the Children's Law Center of Los Angeles, children need support from a caring adult before, during and after the proceeding. They also need special kid-friendly waiting areas, opportunity for private discussions with the judges, and plain talk instead of legal jargon.

Many lawmakers are surprised when they learn that vulnerable children in their state do not receive adequate legal representation and are not given the opportunity to speak directly to judges. After all, every state has enacted statutes requiring appointment of an advocate to obtain firsthand understanding of the child's situation and to make recommendations to the court. Thirty-five states require an attorney to represent the child. But rarely do either statutes or court rules define the attorney's role, specify duties and responsibilities, or describe the necessary training. And there are few mechanisms for legislators to monitor the workings of the judicial and legal aspects of the child welfare system.

Lawyers and Courts

All too often, capable lawyers find little incentive to represent abused and neglected children or their parents. Attorneys object that they are not appointed in time to prepare a case or allocated the necessary time, resources and compensation to perform even the most basic legal services. In New York City, poor compensation accompanied by higher caseloads and court backlogs led to an exodus of attorneys. In turn, families were disrupted, and children remained longer in foster care.

In addition to numerous caseloads and low pay, lack of specialized training and performance standards for both attorneys and judges plague the judicial process. Not only are procedures for handling dependency cases unique, but they require skilled professionals who understand the complex dynamics of troubled families and the maze of resources and rules for responding to them. Only half of the 2,000 judges participating in a 2004 survey had received child welfare training before hearing child abuse and neglect cases.

Legislative Oversight

Ensuring that children's voices are heard in court is but one example of the need for greater oversight over courts and the critical decisions they make. Federal and state statutes make courts responsible for overseeing the actions of child welfare agencies in individual cases, but who oversees the courts? Although legislation and investment in the judicial system are necessary, some legislators are beginning to think they are not enough. With the public's eyes and ears on state government, legislators feel a responsibility to monitor court performance and its impact on children and parents.

This summer, NCSL took the unusual step of convening a group of lawmakers, judicial leaders and child welfare agency executives to examine how legislators can help strengthen the courts on behalf of vulnerable children. These leaders quickly cut to the heart of their dilemma: the risk that vulnerable children are caught in the middle of the constitutional separation of powers among the three branches of government.

To ensure an independent judiciary, courts traditionally resist legislative oversight. A Minnesota judge worried that legislators would attempt to manage the judiciary. Privately, judges admit their fear that legislators will try to influence the cases of individual constituents.

"We hold the public purse strings and are responsible for some oversight of how it's spent," says Washington Representative Ruth Kagi, chair of the House Early Learning and Children's Services Committee and member of the Appropriations Committee. Fellow Washington Representative and Human Services Committee Chair Mary Lou Dickerson agrees: "The Legislature funds state agencies and expects them to be accountable. The courts need to be accountable for taxpayers' money, too."

Sitting Down Together

Consensus among legislators was that it's up to them to improve communication and understanding as well as accountability. According to Fernando Macias, a former New Mexico legislator who now serves as a district Children's Court judge, "It isn't one branch of government ignoring another, but there is no transition." Texas Representative Harold Dutton, chair of the House Juvenile Justice and Family Issues Committee, agrees: "Judges don't feel included in the development of legislation, but legislators don't hear from judges upfront."

To receive new federal Court Improvement Grants authorized in 2005, state courts have developed multidisciplinary commissions, and they are ready-made vehicles for legislators to hear the judicial perspective. In some states, legislators themselves have created court commissions or other workgroups, and they serve on these bodies in Arkansas, California, New York, North Dakota, Utah, Vermont and Washington.

"It's a continuing process of court-legislative education—not just during session," says Arkansas Judge Joyce Williams Warren.

Lives Behind the Numbers

Legislators now have better tools for monitoring court performance. National judicial and legal organizations have joined together to develop performance standards for courts that handle child dependency cases. State courts are taking advantage of federal court improvement grants to ramp up data collection and analysis, so more courts are able to provide statistics about the cases they hear, how they are handled, and how they progress.

But legislators worry that courts will game their numbers, and Judge Macias, the former New Mexico legislator, says that caution is justified. "Everybody—the court, child welfare agencies, even the legislature—paints the most positive picture possible," he says. Instead of disregarding data, judicial expert Mark Hardin of the National Child Welfare Resource Center on Legal and Judicial Issues warns legislators, "Be careful when using statistics in connection with requests for funding or for the expansion or termination of programs." Hardin advises policymakers to ask impartial resource people to help them interpret court numbers.

New Mexico Representative Jim Trujillo speaks for other legislators who want to see beyond the numbers to ensure that individual children and families are getting fair treatment, "I'm worried about the quality, not just numbers." Experts suggest a method called quality service reviews to scrutinize performance of the child welfare system—agencies and courts alike. Independent reviewers randomly select a few cases to examine in depth, dig beyond case files to interview key parties (children, parents, teachers or others who know the family, case workers, attorneys, foster parents, court appointed special advocates and others), and carefully analyze actions. Findings can help identify and correct problems that affect both individuals' lives and child welfare system performance.

Holding Courts Accountable

Some legislatures have gone beyond shining a public light on the courts to make them more accountable. The Oregon legislature has directly imposed court performance measures and requires the judiciary to report on them. In both Idaho and Oregon, the legislature refuses to approve the judicial budget unless courts meet statutory guidelines.

Judge Nancy Sidote Salyers retired from the Cook County, Ill., bench where she was presiding judge of the Child Protection Division. At a time when foster care caseloads were growing unchecked, she worked with the state child welfare agency to reduce the court's dependency caseload from more than 58,000 to 19,000 and to quadruple the number of permanent homes secured for children.

She says the key to better performance for kids is getting beyond separation of power. "Incentives and outcome-based legislation can be tied to a shared vision when the powers come together."

Judge Salyers invokes the words of Andy Warhol—words that many youth in foster would no doubt find true: "They say that time changes things, but you actually have to change them yourself."

Representing Parents

Parents also face serious court obstacles that ultimately delay safe and permanent homes for their children—barriers that lawmakers often assume legislation has eliminated. Although 39 states require counsel for parents at some point during a child abuse and neglect case, representation is often too little and too late.

One parent described an experience that is not unusual: "When I arrived at court that morning, I was told this is my lawyer. My lawyer sat down with me for five minutes, asked me a couple of things, and told me to admit to drug addiction. I wasn't told the procedure of court. I didn't have any idea what was happening, and I was very much afraid, because the most important thing in my life had just been lost."

Many parents—especially absent fathers—aren't engaged until parental rights are being terminated. Parents' absence robs the court of the opportunity to correct case information that is all too often inaccurate, to give instructions and explain orders, and to have a direct impact on parents' behavior. In Washington, a cost study requested by the Legislature showed that family reunification rates improved after appropriations for legal representation of parents increased.

SUSAN ROBISON is a national consultant on child and family policies. A former NCSL staffer, she lives in Durango, Colo.

UNIT 5

Cities and Suburbs, Counties, Towns, and Homeowners Associations

Unit Selections

Key Points to Consider

- Do you prefer city, suburban, or rural life? What do you think are the key differences among these three different settings for the local government in the United States?

- Do you share the pessimism of many people who doubt the ability of the local governments in metropolitan areas to cope with the contemporary urban problems? Why or why not?

- Would it be desirable for suburban local governments to raise property taxes and provide better public transportation, more frequent garbage collections, and better recreational facilities from the revenues raised? Why or why not?

- Would major metropolitan areas be better served if they each had only one metropolitan-wide local government instead of a large number of local governments, as they currently come under? Why or why not?

Student Web Site
www.mhcls.com/online

Internet References
ICMA: International City/County Management Association
http://www.icma.org/othersites/
Innovation Groups (IG)
http://www.ig.org
National Association of Counties (NACo)
http://www.naco.org/
National League of Cities (NLC)
http://www.nlc.org

More than three-quarters of Americans live in cities or in surrounding suburban areas. In these densely populated settings, local governments face great challenges and opportunities. One challenge is to provide at a satisfactory level, services such as policing, schooling, sanitation, water, and public transportation at a cost that taxpayers can and will bear. An accompanying opportunity is the possibility of helping to create a local setting that improves the lives of residents in meaningful ways. The challenges and opportunities occur amid a formidable array of urban and suburban problems: crime, violence, drugs, deterioration of public schools, racial tension, financial stringencies, pollution, congestion, aging populations, decaying physical plants, breakdown of family life, and so forth.

Cities are the local government jurisdictions that generally exist where there is high population density. Major metropolitan areas usually have a large city at their center and a surrounding network of suburbs under a number of smaller local government jurisdictions. In smaller metropolitan areas, a single county often encompasses both the center city and the surrounding suburbs. Smaller cities may themselves be part of suburban rings, or they may exist independently of major metropolitan areas, with their own smaller network of surrounding suburbs.

Cities of all sizes generally provide more services to local residents than other kinds of local government jurisdictions. Thus, city residents generally expect their city governments to provide water, a sewer system, public transportation, a professional firefighting force, public museums, parks and other such recreational facilities, and various other amenities associated with city life. By contrast, local governments in rural areas are not expected to provide such services. Local governments in suburban areas typically provide some but not all of them. With the greater range of services provided in cities come higher taxes and more regulatory activities.

Like cities, suburbs come in various shapes and sizes. Some are called bedroom or commuter suburbs because people live there with their families and commute to and from the central city to work. Others have a more independent economic base. Local governments in suburbs have often emphasized quality education (i.e., good schools), zoning plans to preserve the residential character of the locale, and keeping property taxes within tolerable limits. Generally speaking, suburbs have a greater proportion of whites and upper-middle- and middle-class people than the cities.

© David Buffington/Getty Images

One problem facing suburban governments today stems from aging populations. Older people need and demand different services than the young families that used to occupy suburbs in greater proportions. It is not always easy to shift policy priorities from, for example, public schooling to public transportation and recreational programs for the elderly. A second problem is structural in nature and relates to the overlapping local government jurisdictions in suburban areas—school districts, sanitation districts, townships, counties, villages, boroughs, and so forth. The maze of jurisdictions often confuses citizens, and sometimes makes coordinated and effective government difficult.

The goals of small suburban local governments, one or more counties, and the central city government in a single metropolitan area often come into conflict in policy areas such as public transportation, school integration, air pollution, highway systems, and so forth. Sometimes common aims can be pursued through cooperative ventures between suburban and city governments, through counties, or through creation of metropolitan-wide special districts. Sometimes, through annexation or consolidation, a larger unit of general-purpose local government is formed in an attempt to cope with metropolitan-wide issues more easily.

Selections in this unit mainly discuss city and suburban governments and the problems and opportunities faced in metropolitan areas. Cities and suburbs, of course, typically face different sets of problems. Even so, it is important to note that not all cities face similar problems; nor do all suburbs or all counties.

How to Save Our Shrinking Cities

WITOLD RYBZYNSKI AND PETER D. LINNEMAN

The first half of the twentieth century saw the widespread emergence of large cities in the United States. In 1900, there were only six cities with more than half a million inhabitants; only 50 years later, there were 17 such cities. Much of this urban growth was stimulated by two world wars and the government-supported expansion of war-related industries, most located in big Northeastern and Midwestern cities. The largest cities also benefited from the fact that for more than a decade after the Second World War the United States was the only country in the world with its manufacturing facilities intact.

It was inevitable that eventually things would change. Europe and Japan rebuilt themselves and challenged the dominance of U.S. urban manufacturing. The previous rapid growth of large cities began to level out, and new urbanization patterns emerged. One of these patterns was a change in the kind of cities Americans chose to live in. We differentiate between small cities (100,000 to 500,000 inhabitants) and large cities (more than 500,000 inhabitants). In 1900, eight million Americans lived in large cities as compared to less than five million in small cities.

Over the next 50 years, the total population of the large cities increased at a faster rate than that of the small cities, and, by 1950, the large cities were home to more than 26 million people, compared to about 13 million for the small cities. However, after 1950, this pattern began to reverse, and the total population of small cities grew more quickly. By 1990, for the first time in the twentieth century, more Americans lived in small cities than in large ones. This situation is likely to continue for some time. For example, between 1980 and 1990, the total population of the small cities increased by a remarkable 17.3 percent, compared to 6 percent for large cities, and 9.7 percent for the nation as a whole.

Forces of Change

What drove this reversal? The growth of small cities and the decline of large cities in the postwar p eriod resembled the contemporary restructuring of the steel industry, where new small plants replaced old large mills. Technological advances made the old steel plants obsolete and took their toll on large cities. The confluence of river and barge commerce, railroads, and the telegraph fueled urban centralization throughout the nineteenth century. In the early 1900s, these forces were reinforced by the efficiencies of scale in urban infrastructure technology, such as water supply, sewage treatment, and streetcars. However, the post–World War II period witnessed the predominance of car and truck commerce, the expansion of air travel, the evolution of modern telecommunications, and massively improved efficiencies in the provision of sewer- and water-treatment facilities. All of these changes facilitated urban decentralization. Air conditioning opened up large parts of the country to year-round occupancy, just as heating technologies had done centuries before. Entertainment and communication technologies, including television, the VCR, and the personal computer, greatly reduced the sense of cultural inferiority and isolation that historically characterized life in small cities. Now, a small city with an airport and access to an interstate highway became just as good a place from which to conduct business as the downtown of a large city. Land economics allowed residents of small cities to enjoy larger (and newer) homes while still being able to see their favorite sports team, watch first-run movies, and enjoy concerts on cable TV.

These technological changes were fueled by the evolution of increasingly efficient capital markets. Capital markets actively sought out, and provided capital to, the best businesses, even if they were not in the biggest cities. Examples include: The Limited (Columbus, Ohio), WalMart (Bentonville, Arkansas), Microsoft (Seattle), and Turner Broadcasting (Atlanta). In addition, the municipal bond market increasingly provided equal access to capital (for public infrastructure) to cities and communities that had previously been too small to tap this source.

In older cities, an aging infrastructure imposed increasingly high capital and operating costs. In contrast, smaller cities had recently installed new infrastructure with low maintenance and operating costs. Older cities flourished when they were the newest, cheapest, and most modern. The mantel has now passed to a new set of cities and suburbs.

However, not all large cities were equally affected by these trends. Of the 77 cities with current (1990) population in excess of half a million, 51 actually grew by an average of 539 percent between 1950 and 1990. The nine largest of these (Los Angeles, Houston, San Diego, Dallas, Phoenix, San Antonio, San Jose, Jacksonville, and Columbus) grew from 1950 to 1970, and continued to grow during the next two decades. Nevertheless, 26 of the 77 cities shrank (by an average of 24 percent) between 1950 and 1990. Moreover, these shrinking cities include some of the largest in the country. Seven of the largest cities that declined (New York, Chicago, Philadelphia, Detroit, Baltimore, Washington, D.C., and Boston) have been doing so steadily since 1950. Indianapolis, Milwaukee, and Memphis declined in population between 1970 and 1990, although they grew between 1950 and 1970. Only one major city, San Francisco, reversed its 1950–70 decline during the following two decades.

Two facts stand out about the decline of the largest cities. First, the population losses have been significant. Chicago, New York, and Detroit have each lost about half a million people each since 1970 while Philadelphia has lost more than 350,000 over this period. Second, this decline is neither merely recent nor episodic. The cities that are shrinking have been doing so steadily for the last half of this century, and, according to the recent U.S. Census figures, the decline continues to the present day.

Some of the population increases in the growing cities have been the result of the aggressive annexation of surrounding cities and towns. Since 1950, the fastest growing seven major cities (Phoenix, San Jose, San Diego, Jacksonville, Houston, Dallas, and San Antonio) have each at least doubled their areas through annexation. In the case of Phoenix and Jacksonville, the increase in area has been more than twentyfold. Some of the urban growth, especially in California, Texas, and Florida, has been due to immigration. In fact, were it not for the steady flow of immigrants, cities like New York, Chicago, and Washington, D.C., would have experienced massive population losses.

Against this backdrop of the decline of the largest cities and the growth of our smaller cities, it is imperative to remember that every metro area has experienced population growth since 1950. Thus, although the cities of St. Louis, Cleveland, and Detroit lost about half their populations between 1950 and 1990, their metro areas each notably expanded. Similarly, while the city of Philadelphia lost about half a million people during this period, Philadelphia's metro area grew by more than a million. This means that the cities that shrank did so not because they were part of dying regional economies but, rather, in spite of strong regional growth.

Vertical Cities and Horizontal Cities

The cities that have declined can be called vertical cities while the growing ones are best thought of as horizontal cities. These two prototypes differ radically with respect to infrastructure, amenities, and housing stock. The vertical city, which evolved during the industrial era, has highway, mass transportation, and rail systems designed to link the suburbs to city center. Its population density is high, typically more than 10,000 persons per square mile. Its amenities include large public parks. And it is known for downtown offices, manufacturing, and shopping and cultural activities. Typically, about half of its housing stock was built before 1939. It is comprised primarily of rowhouses, walk-up flats, and apartment buildings that were located to permit walking (or riding mass transit) to work and play.

In contrast, the horizontal city evolved after World War II and is designed for rapid car and truck movement, not merely from suburb to city but also from suburb to suburb. There is very little mass transit or rail infrastructure. Instead, massive transportation expenditures have focused almost exclusively on facilitating auto travel. The density is low (typically less than 3,000 persons per square mile), and urban amenities are more private than public. Equally important is the fact that the housing stock is much newer, typically offering single-family houses with large backyards (and large garages to "house" cars). The horizontal prototype is not simply a newer or updated version of the vertical prototype—it is a different kind of city.

Much of the current interest in the historic preservation of old buildings and efforts to recreate the "old time" urban fabric romanticize cities of the past. The stark reality is that, for the majority of working people, the vertical city offered cramped and noisy housing, little privacy, and relatively crude public amenities. One only need stroll through Chinatown in New York on a hot summer day to get a sense of what everyday life was like for the common New Yorker 50 years ago. The vertical city was built to house immigrants who had little money and who could not afford cars. The horizontal city has been built for a society with much greater disposable income (as a result of real income growth and two-earner families) and different quality-of-life expectations. It is a city that owns (indeed loves) cars. It is a crude generalization, and one that the proponents of traditional urbanism resist, but the horizontal city seems to have provided a kind of life that the overwhelming majority of Americans consciously chose—in spite of their romantic image of the old vertical city.

Is population loss always a bad thing for a city? We think not. Cities with more than a million inhabitants were rare before the twentieth century. There is no reason to assume that a smaller city is worse than a large one. In fact, an argument can be made that when a city is smaller it is also more human in scale, more livable, less anonymous, with a more manageable and responsive government. The problem with the decline of U.S. cities is not a question of size but, rather, a question of who is leaving and who is staying.

The people moving out of our cities are predominantly middle-income families of all races while those remaining—and entering—are predominantly poor minorities. If the 77 largest American cities are evaluated in terms of a diverse set of social barometers, such as poverty and unemployment rates, the number of families on public assistance, infant mortality rates, and average household incomes, a clear pattern emerges. Comparing the cumulative average rates for the 26 cities that have shrunk since 1950, with the cumulative average rates for the 51 cities that have grown, the shrinking cities as a group are currently worse with respect to all of these social welfare indicators. Only crime levels appear to be comparable—and appallingly high—for both groups of cities, although even they are slightly higher in shrinking cities.

Cities with High Vacancy Rates

A city that has lost much of its population has—to borrow a real-estate phrase—a high vacancy rate. When a shopping mall has a high vacancy rate, the owner suffers not only because of the lost revenue on the empty space but also because the overall vitality and attractiveness of the center's shopping experience is diminished. This, in turn, makes other tenants more likely to vacate, depressing rents on leased space. So, too, for a city with a high vacancy rate: It suffers not only a loss to its tax base but, unless it is successfully repositioned, it becomes a less attractive place to live and work.

The owner of the mall with high vacancy rates has a limited number of options. To be more competitive he can lower rents or offer special lease terms in an attempt to attract and retain tenants. He can also offer special services to prospective (and current) tenants in order to raise occupancy. He can refurbish the mall to attract new tenants or "shrink" the mall so that its (now smaller) space is fully occupied. If this doesn't work, the costs associated with the operation of the mall may not be covered by its income, and, in the short run, the owner will have to absorb the losses. If, in the end, he cannot cover his costs, the owner will close the mall and seek an alternative, more profitable use.

Of course, you cannot close a city. Some cities have privatized parts of their urban services (such as garbage collection and education) in an attempt to reduce their operating costs. Like a troubled mall owner, a city with a high vacancy rate can try to refurbish itself by redeveloping its downtown. Examples of urban redevelopment projects include stadiums, aquariums, world trade centers, river-boat gambling, and convention centers. Unfortunately, these strategies generally yield a poor return on public funds.

Cities need to mimic the strategies of the shopping-center landlord by lowering taxes, reducing onerous regulations, increasing the levels of public services, and improving the quality of local infrastructure. But this requires an admission that excessive taxes, burdensome regulations, and inadequate services have contributed to the city's decline. Such admissions do not come easily to a generation of politicians who have lived on the uphill slope of the Laffer Curve, raising taxes and regularly bemoaning the levels of support received from Washington and state governments. Unfortunately, as documented by Robert Inman of the Wharton School, cities that have "high vacancy rate" problems have already reached the point where further increases in local taxes produce declining tax revenues and an even greater decline in urban occupancy. Upon reflection, this is not surprising—imagine the fate of a troubled shopping center if the owner continuously raised rents as vacancy rose.

What happens when a city loses population? The fiscal difficulties associated with a reduced tax base are obvious. But, like a shopping mall that loses tenants, a city that loses population experiences additional problems. First, although people have left, the cost of maintaining the old infrastructure designed for the larger population—the roads, sewers, and transit systems—remains. In the case of the cities that expanded during the early 1900s, this infrastructure is in need of extensive repair and replacement. Just like the mall owners, cities must decide which services to curtail. Most city managers (like most shopping-center owners) invariably choose to defer infrastructure maintenance.

A second effect of population shrinkage is a reduction in population density. In theory, this should increase the quality of life. However, density is usually reduced by the creation of irregular gaps in the urban density pattern. Although the densities in vertical cities are still three or four times greater than in the horizontal cities, the vertical city was designed to function most efficiently with relatively continuous concentrations of people. As depopulation occurs, not only does the provision of normal municipal services become more expensive (unplanned vacant space is expensive to secure and maintain) but there may no longer be a sufficient population base to support neighborhood social and retail activities in many areas. This results in services being further reduced, inducing those who can to move away. Similarly, depopulation in vertical cities creates a lack of social energy and dynamism, as well as a reduced sense of safety. In short, shrinkage undermines the strategic operating engine of a vertical city.

Perhaps even more importantly, a vertical city with population gaps no longer possesses a continuous urban fabric. Instead, it becomes a series of disjointed areas separated by unplanned abandoned and vacant areas. Servicing a discontinuous city is very expensive. At the very time that vertical cities need to find more efficient servicing techniques to offset their declining tax bases, they are faced with an increasingly inefficient and expensive population pattern.

Finally, shrinkage lowers the quality of urban life. Buildings remain vacant, most in various stages of total decay. Lots become empty as buildings are burned and collapse. These lots become dumps, strewn with garbage of all types. While vacant space in the countryside can be aesthetically pleasing, and horizontal cities frequently include massive tracts of vacant space, population gaps are disastrous for vertical cities. Vacant buildings become vulnerable to further vandalism. They also become havens for illegal activities—a breeding ground for diseases and unsafe playgrounds for children. Streets lined with empty lots and deserted buildings become indefensible spaces, veritable "wild zones." That urban dereliction is a cancer is an apt cliché. Population gaps are not merely symptoms, they are primary causes of the continued disintegration of urban life in vertical cities.

The Regional Government Solution

What is to be done? The most common political response has been to counteract the social costs associated with a shrinking (and increasingly poor) population by raising taxes. This is a self-destructive response that makes the city an even less attractive place to live and work. Mayors, planners, and city-government officials must learn to accept the fact that the older, shrunken vertical cities will never grow back to their earlier size and prosperity. The goal must be, instead, to make their cities more livable, more attractive, and, probably, even smaller. They must reconfigure their cities to be competitively viable in modern times.

An examination of the 1992 population figures for cities shows that, although a few cities like Oakland, Louisville, Akron, and Rochester, New York have managed to reverse their earlier decline and are growing (very modestly), most shrinking cities continue to shrink. True, the rates of population decline have generally slowed, perhaps suggesting that a sustainable city may be evolving. But Philadelphia, Boston, Washington, D.C., St. Louis, Detroit, and Baltimore, which shrank even more rapidly during the 1980s than during the previous decade, continue to lose population in the 1990s. Such cities must reinvent themselves, becoming better cities as they grow even smaller than they are today.

One solution commonly proposed for shrinking cities is regional government. Since metropolitan areas as a whole are expanding, linking (poor) shrinking cities to (relatively rich) growing suburbs appears to provide the former with access to the financial resources of the latter. This argument has been advanced recently by David Rusk in *Cities Without Suburbs*. He presents convincing evidence that new growing cities (e.g., Houston, Phoenix, and San Diego) that have annexed suburban counties have many advantages over older cities whose boundaries remained largely unchanged.

There are, however, practical difficulties with the regional government proposal. Regional government is constitutionally difficult in most states; only Portland, Oregon is part of a directly elected regional government. It is true that several cities, such as Houston, Miami, Jacksonville, Charlottesville, Indianapolis, Nashville, and Minneapolis, have a system of cost sharing. However, with the exception of Minneapolis and Indianapolis, these are all growing cities. Troubled shrinking cities have little to offer suburban counties. As a result, suburbanites—most of whom consciously fled the city to leave its problems behind—can be expected to oppose any attempts at regionalization. The central cities themselves will resist, especially those with large numbers of ethnic minorities, who would lose their hard won political clout if they were incorporated into a larger, wealthier regional electorate.

In any case, regional government has its drawbacks. While size may generate some modest economies of scale with respect to infrastructure and finance, it also greatly increases inefficiencies of scale for the delivery of many services. Regional government would be more remote from—hence less responsible to—the voters, resulting in more corruption and inefficiency. Regional government, while it may solve the problems of servicing poor areas, will not address issues like an old and noncompetitive housing stock and the population gaps already prevalent in vertical cities.

Smaller Is Better

The clock cannot be turned back. The industrial cities that grew rapidly during the first half of the twentieth century (and shrank almost as rapidly during the second half) will never recover their primacy. History teaches that cities grow and decline. The most dramatic example is probably ancient Rome, which shrank from about a million at its imperial zenith to less than 100,000 by the Middle Ages. The population of Venice peaked in the seventeenth century at 180,000, but, as its mercantile empire collapsed, the city shrank, reaching a low point of 132,000 in 1880. The population in Venice today is only about 137,000. The populations of the great industrial cities of northern Britain—Glasgow, Liverpool, and Manchester—peaked in 1900 and have been declining since. The population of Vienna peaked in the decade before the First World War and, today, is about 20 percent smaller than at its zenith.

The critical lesson of Vienna, Venice, and even Glasgow (which has recently experienced a modest revival) is that a smaller city can be made a good place to live. Using these cities as role models, the question for shrinking cities is not, "How can we grow big again?" but rather, "How can we prosper and have a wonderful, smaller city?"

A fundamental change in mind set is required once we accept that smaller can be better. A city that has irretrievably lost large amounts of its population needs to examine ways to redesign itself to become more compact, perhaps even smaller in area. This will not be easy. City planners have traditionally favored growth and expansion. It is now time for planners to look for ways to shrink our cities. Just as physicians should allow gracious and healthy decline as people age, so too must our planners manage older cities. However, just as aging is not merely adolescence in reverse, urban planning for shrinkage is fundamentally different than planning for growth.

Historically, vertical cities expanded from the center by developing land at the periphery, by building on flood plains and near urban disamenities (e.g.; railroads), and by extending their urban infrastructure. But a shrinking city cannot merely retract its perimeter. Population losses have not been experienced equally across all parts of the city. Outlying parts of the city are generally quite strong, as are some city centers. Between these areas lies a complex web of decrepit housing stock and abandoned industry but also strong neighborhoods.

Are there alternative uses for the empty tracts? One could imagine formally planned versions of what has occurred in an unfunded and unplanned way in Detroit and East St. Louis, where vast empty lots are reverting to a sort of urban wilderness. In some cases, empty land might be turned into parks and recreation sites. This requires funds to undertake the expensive process of rehabilitation, soil replacement, and landscaping. The City of New York currently owns 20,000 vacant lots and has proposed asking private corporations to pay for converting empty land into parks and playgrounds. In return, the city would allow the companies to use the space for their own advertising. Corporate sponsorship is expected to provide on-going maintenance, which was lacking with earlier efforts, such as the Lindsay administration's "vest pocket parks." There are also commercial outdoor recreation possibilities. A developer has recently built a 30-acre golf course on vacant land in downtown Chicago, near the convention center. Large tracts could be consolidated and sold to the U.S. Department of the Interior for the creation of environmental zones, belated versions of the urban green belts that were a staple of Garden City planning in the early 1900s.

Another option would be to take advantage of the availability of empty land to begin to transform the vertical city into something that more closely resembles the horizontal postwar prototype. The three- and four-story rowhouses that characterize cities like Baltimore and Philadelphia were built at now commercially unacceptable densities of 30 to 40 dwellings per acre. Down-zoning of residential areas would allow two-story, semidetached houses at lower densities of about 20 dwellings per acre, or detached cottages of 5 to 10 dwellings per acre. However, such densities are only affordable if cities greatly reduce their development costs and regulations. In reducing these burdens they need to strive to become competitive with the most competitive suburb. If old cities cannot annex surrounding suburbs, they can, at least, begin slowly to transform part of their housing stock and begin to provide the kind of housing that today's households desire—single-family homes with space for backyards and off-street parking—rather than continuing to offer them a housing stock designed for their grandparents. The combination of much lower density housing with easy access to high-density downtown amenities may be the starting point for a new, post-industrial, urban prototype.

A Radical Proposal

Cities should also consider even more drastic alternatives. For example, they could de-annex parts of their territory to private developers. If large tracts, in excess of 100 acres, say, were sold as de-annexed, unincorporated areas with associated suburban cost structures, it is possible that developers would find this an attractive opportunity to create new "suburban" municipalities in the central areas of the city. Prototypes include such communities as River Oaks in Houston and Highland Park and University Park in Dallas. These "suburban" communities have been developed within the fabric of the city boundaries. New municipalities would be legally independent of the city. They would control their own governments, schools, and regulations. Like most suburbs, we suspect they would preserve a high degree of autonomy and probably a degree of exclusiveness. In fact, these new municipalities would probably need to alter traffic flows through the surrounding city into the community in order to provide the type of housing sought by today's buyers. Given the pattern of new planned communities in the United States, some form of common interest housing development governed by homeowner associations is likely to result.

The sale by the city of such property would create a more viable smaller city. How? First, the sale of the land would generate much needed funds, which would be used to offset years of deferred maintenance of urban infrastructure. Given the differential cost of operation and development in an unincorporated suburban municipality versus the city, the value derived from selling such land could be substantial. The city would also no longer be responsible for the maintenance and security of the land once it becomes a legally independent community. Third, and perhaps most importantly, although the city itself would shrink, the city's urban fabric would be enhanced as the new municipality developed. Many of the population gaps in the urban fabric could be filled in. There can be little doubt that these vacant parcels would develop more rapidly and successfully as independent suburban communities rather than as part of the city. In short, the city would be smaller, richer, and less vacant. At the same time, the population cavities would start to disappear.

Critical impediments to altering the current state of vacant urban tracts include irrational environmental standards. Too often these regulatory standards and procedures ask the irrelevant question, "Is it perfectly clean?" rather than the more pragmatic question, "Is it cleaner than it would have otherwise been?" The imposition of 1990s environmental sensibilities on areas that provided the factory jobs for previous generations means that massive tracts in urban areas are forever doomed to be economically undeveloped. As a result, the soil remains contaminated, the chemicals continue to seep into the groundwater, children continue to play in these abandoned lots, and the urban fabric continues to deteriorate. Environmental regulators, like city politicians, must realize that these areas will not be developed (and hence no environmental improvement will occur) unless dramatic compromises are made. These compromises may involve using federal funds to clean up these properties. Alternatively, development could be allowed if it significantly improves the environmental quality of the property, even though such clean-up may fall considerably short of current standards.

Future City

In our view, consolidation and de-annexation are not a "desirable" option for a city; however, for many shrinking cities, we see no other viable alternative. When population loss has passed a certain point, urban revival is likely to require drastic measures. Rehabilitation has usually worked only in downtown areas. Enterprise zones and empowerment zones have proved to be only marginally effective—where they have succeeded at all. Besides, they depend on the infusion of federal or state funds, which are not always available.

In any case, the obstacles to dealing effectively with urban shrinkage are massive, even possibly insurmountable. But to solve a problem, reality must be faced. In this case, the reality is that many cities will continue to shrink. Municipal politicians whose electoral bases will be eroded by consolidation or de-annexation can be expected to resist the idea of downsizing. Since the inhabitants of many of these affected areas will be minorities, the politics of consolidation and shrinkage will be opposed by these groups. Neighborhood activists, whose careers have been spent trying to promote local economic development from within will view shrinkage policies as defeatist, not the least because they will lose their own political power bases. Moreover, if selected urban areas are allowed to become autonomous suburban municipalities, the city as a whole will have to be protected from complete disintegration.

Shrinkage will also be seen by many as weakening the mechanism that has traditionally been used to elicit federal urban aid. Historic preservationists will undoubtedly object to wholesale demolition, since even decrepit areas contain buildings of architectural merit, and some of the worst areas are the locations of so-called industrial landmarks. Obviously, much will depend on how successfully con-solidation deals with issues of dislocation, new housing, and new community services. But the challenge is clear: Our cities must be radically redesigned to be both better and smaller.

Witold Rybzynski is Martin and Margy Meyerson Professor of Urbanism at the University of Pennsylvania. His *A Clearing in the Distance* is published by Simon & Schuster. **Peter D. Linneman** is the Albert Sussman Professor of Real Estate, Finance and Public Policy at the University of Pennsylvania and serves as senior managing director of Equity International Properties.

An earlier version of this article appeared in the *Warton Real Estate Review*, Fall 1997.

Unscrambling the City

Archaic zoning laws lock cities into growth patterns that hardly anybody wants. Changing the rules can help set them free.

CHRISTOPHER SWOPE

Take a walk through Chicago's historic Lakeview neighborhood, and the new houses will jump right out at you. That's because they're jarringly incompatible with the old ones. On one quiet tree-lined street, you'll find a row of old two-story colonials with pitched roofs. Then you walk a little farther and it seems as though a giant rectangular box has fallen out of the sky. The new condominium building is twice as high as its older neighbors and literally casts shadows over their neat flower gardens and tiny front yards. Angry Lakeview residents have seen so many new buildings like this lately that they have come up with a sneering name for them. They call them "three-flats on steroids."

Listening to the complaints in Lakeview, you might wonder whether home builders are breaking the law and getting away with it, or at least bending the rules quite a bit. But that's not the case. If you take some time and study Chicago's zoning law, you'll find that these giant condos are technically by the book. It's not the new buildings that are the problem. The problem is Chicago's zoning ordinance. The code is nearly half a century old, and it is an outdated mishmash of vague and conflicting rules. Over the years, it has been amended repeatedly, to the point of nonsense. Above all, it's totally unpredictable. In Lakeview, zoning can yield anything from tasteful two-flats to garish McMansions, with no consideration at all for how they fit into the neighborhood.

Chicago's zoning problem lay dormant for decades while the city's economy sagged and population declined. Back in the 1970s and '80s, not much building was going on. But then the 1990s brought an economic boom and 112,000 new residents. While almost everyone is happy that the construction machine has been turned back on, so many Chicagoans are appalled by the way the new construction looks that Mayor Richard M. Daley decided it was time to rewrite the city's entire zoning code. Everything about Chicago land use is on the table: not just residential development but commercial and industrial as well. It is the largest overhaul of its kind in any U.S. city in 40 years.

But while few communities are going as far as Chicago, many are coming to a similar conclusion: The zoning laws on their books—most of them written in the 1950s and '60s—are all scrambled up. They are at once too vague and too complicated to produce the urban character most residents say they want.

The zoning problem afflicts both cities and suburbs and manifests itself in countless ways. It takes the form of oversized homes and farmland covered in cookie-cutter housing developments. It shows up as a sterile new strip mall opening up down the street from one that is dying. It becomes an obstacle when cities discover how hard it is to revive pedestrian life in their downtowns and neighborhood shopping districts. And it becomes a headache for city councils that spend half their time interpreting clumsy rules, issuing variances and haggling with developers.

What urban planners disagree about is whether the current system can be salvaged, or whether it should be scrapped altogether. Most cities are not ready to take the ultimate step. Chicago isn't going that far. Neither did Boston, Milwaukee, San Diego and San Jose. All of them retained the basic zoning conventions, even as they slogged through the process of streamlining the codes and rewriting them for the 21st century. According to researcher Stuart Meck, of the American Planning Association, there's a cyclical nature to all this. He points out that it's common for cities to update their laws after the sort of building boom many have enjoyed recently. "Cities are in growth mode again," Meck says, "but they're getting development based on standards that are 20, 30 or 40 years old."

Myriad Categories

For much of the past century, if you wanted to find out the latest thinking about zoning, Chicago was a good place to go. In 1923, it became one of the first cities, after New York, to adopt a zoning law. The motivation then was mostly health and

Picture-Book Zoning

While Chicago and a few other large cities struggle to update old zoning laws for the new century, some places are going in a new direction. They are experimenting with zoning concepts percolating out of the New Urbanist movement, writing codes that bear a closer resemblance to picture books than to laws. Conventional zoning, they have decided, is based on an abstract language that leaves too much to chance. They would rather start with a question—what does the community want to look like—and then work back from there. "It's not enough to change the zoning," says New Urbanist author Peter Katz. "Cities have to move to a new system. They should look at the streets they like and the public spaces they like and then write the rules to get more of what they like and less of what they don't. Conventional zoning doesn't do that. It just gives a use and a density and then you hope for the best."

On jurisdiction currently buying in to this new idea is Arlington, Virginia, a suburb of 190,000 people just across the river from Washington D.C. A few months ago, Arlington's county board adopted a "form-based" zoning code for a 3.5-mile corridor known as Columbia Pike, making it one of the largest experiments yet with this new idea.

Columbia Pike is a typical traffic-choked suburban drag, lines mostly with strip malls, drive-throughs and apartment complexes ringed by parking lots. Developers have ignored the area for years. County planners want to convert it into a place that more closely resembles a classic American Main Street. They want a walkable commercial thoroughfare, featuring ground-floor retail blended together with offices and apartments above. But the old zoning code made this nearly impossible.

Rather than starting with a clear vision of what Arlington wants Columbia Pike to look like, the old code starts with a letter and a number: "C-2." The "C" stands for commercial uses only, and the "2" means that development should be of a medium density. C-2 is so vague that it could yield any number of building types. But the code's ambiguities don't end there. Building size is regulated by "floor area ratio," a calculation that again says nothing about whether the building should be suitable for a Main Street or an interstate highway exit. Finally, the code doesn't say where on the lot the building should go—just that it shouldn't sit near the roadway. Mostly, developers have used this recipe to build strip malls. "The code is really absolute on things that don't matter to us at all," says Arlington board member Chris Zimmerman. "The tools are all wrong for the job we're trying to do."

The new code for Columbia Pike abandons these old tools. It begins with a picture: What does a Main Street look like? Rather than abstract language, the new code uses visuals to show the form that the buildings should take. Buildings are three to six stories tall. And they sit on the sidewalk, with ground-floor windows and front doors, not 50 feet back from the street.

Compared with traditional zoning, a form-based code doesn't focus on specific uses. It specifies physical patterns. Whether the buildings are occupied by coffee shops, law offices or upstairs renters makes little difference. "Traditionally," says Peter Katz, "zoning stipulates a density and a use and it's anyone's guess whether you'll get what the planners' renderings look like. Form-based codes give a way to achieve what you see in the picture with precision."

One of the most prominent New Urbanists, Miami architect Andres Duany, advocates taking the form-based idea even further. In Duany's view, it's not only buildings along a road like Columbia Pike that should be coded according to physical form rather than use: entire metropolitan regions should be thought of this way. Duany is pushing an alternative he calls "Smart Code."

The Smart Code is based on the concept of the "transect." The idea is that there is a range of forms that the built environment can take. At one end is downtown, the urban core. At the other end is wilderness. In between are villages, suburbs and more dense urban neighborhoods. As Duany sees it, conventional zoning has failed to maintain the important distinctions between these types of places. Instead, it has made each of them resemble suburbia. When suburban building forms encroach on wilderness, the result is sprawl. When they encroach on urban areas, the result is lifeless downtowns.

Nashville-Davidson County, Tennessee, is one of the first places to begin incorporating these concepts into its planning process. The transect isn't a substitute for a zoning code, says planning director Rick Bernhardt. But it helps planners think about how one part of the city fits into the region, and how to zone accordingly. "It's really understanding what the purpose is of the part of the community you're designing," Bernhardt says, "and then making sure that the streetscape, the intensity and the mix of land use are all consistent with that."

—C.S.

safety. Smoke-spewing factories were encroaching on residential neighborhoods, and the city's first ordinance sought to keep them out. By the 1950s, when more people drove cars, Chicago was a pioneer in rewriting the code to separate the places people live in from where they work and where they shop.

The 1957 zoning law was largely the creation of real estate developer Harry Chaddick, who proclaimed that the city was "being slowly strangled" by mixed uses of property. It classi-

fied every available parcel of land into myriad categories based on density. Residential neighborhoods, for example, were laid out in a range from "R1" (single family homes) to "R8" (high-rises). Land use rules were so strict as to dictate where ice cream shops, coin stores and haberdasheries could go. Chaddick's code was hailed in its time as a national model.

But over the years, one patch after another in the 1957 law made it almost impossible to use. Some parts contradicted other parts. Two attorneys could read it and come away with completely opposite views of what the code allowed. Finally, in 2000, the mayor tapped Ed Kus, a longtime city zoning attorney, to take charge of a full-scale rewrite. Kus thinks the law in the works will be equally as historic as Chaddick's—and more durable. "I hope the ordinance we come up with will be good for the next 50 years," Kus says.

Besides its rigidity, the old code has been plagued by false assumptions about population growth. Back in the 1950s, Chicago was a city of 3.6 million people, and planners expected it to reach a population of 5 million. Of course, it didn't work out that way. Like every other major city, Chicago lost a huge proportion of its residents to the suburbs. By 1990, it was down to fewer than 2.8 million residents. But it was still zoned to accommodate 5 million.

That's essentially how Lakeview got its three-flats on steroids. Had the city's population grown as the code anticipated, it would have needed a supply of large new residential buildings to replace its traditional two-flats and bungalows. The law made it possible to build these in lots of neighborhoods, regardless of the existing architecture or character.

For decades, this made relatively little difference, because the declining population limited demand for new housing in most of the city. Once the '90s boom hit, however, developers took advantage. They bought up old homes and tore them down, replacing them with massive condo projects. They built tall, and sometimes they built wide and deep, eating up front yards and side yards and often paving over the back for parking. "Developers are building to the max," Kus says. "We have all these new housing types and the zoning ordinance doesn't govern them very well."

There are other glaring problems. Although many people think of the 1950s as the decade when America went suburban, most retail business in Chicago was still conducted in storefronts along trolley lines, both in the city and the older close-in suburbs. The code reflects that mid-century reality. Some 700 miles of Chicago's arterial streets are zoned for commercial use, much more than the current local retail market can bear. Worse, the old code is full of anachronistic restrictions on what kinds of transactions can be conducted where. A store that sells computers needs a zoning variance to set up shop next door to one that fixes them. "If you're in a 'B1' district"—a neighborhood business corridor—"you can hardly do any business," Kus says.

All of these archaic provisions are quietly being reconsidered and revised on the ninth floor of city hall, where Kus heads a small team that includes two planning department staffers and a consultant from the planning firm of Duncan Associates. Their work will go to the zoning reform commission, a panel whose 17 members were picked by the mayor to hold exhaustive public meetings and then vote on the plan. The commission includes aldermen, architects, planners, business representatives and a labor leader. Developers are conspicuously absent, which may come back to bite

the whole project later. But for now, the rewrite is moving remarkably fast. The city council is expected to pass the new code this fall. That will set the stage for an even more difficult task: drawing new maps to fit the changed rules.

In the past, Chicago's zoning reforms sought nothing less than to transform the face of the city. This time, however, there is more of a conservationist bent. What the reformers are trying to do is to lock in the qualities Chicagoans like about their oldest, most traditional neighborhoods. That's not to say they want to freeze the city in place. The building boom is quite popular. But it's also widely accepted that the character of Chicago's neighborhoods is the reason why the city is hot again, and that zoning should require new buildings to fit in. "Cities that will succeed in the future are the ones that maintain a unique character of place," says Alicia Mazur Berg, Chicago's planning commissioner. "People choose to live in many of our neighborhoods because they're attractive, they have front yards and buildings of the same scale."

Made for Walking

The new rules being drafted for residential areas are a good example of this thinking. Height limits will prevent new houses from towering over old ones. Neighborhoods such as Lakeview will likely be "downzoned" for less density. New homes will be required to have a green back yard, not a paved one, and builders will not be allowed to substitute a new creation known as a "patio pit" for a front yard. Garages will be expected to face an alley—not the street—and blank walls along the streetscape will be prohibited.

In the same spirit, the creators of the new zoning code are also proposing a new category, the Pedestrian Street, or "P-street." This is meant for a neighborhood shopping street that has survived in spite of the automobile and still thrives with pedestrian life. The new code aims to keep things that way. Zoning for P-streets will specifically outlaw strip malls, gas stations and drive-throughs, or any large curb cut that could interrupt the flow of pedestrians. It also will require new buildings to sit right on the sidewalk and have front doors and windows so that people walking by can see inside.

There are dozens of other ideas. The new code aims to liven up once-vibrant but now-dying neighborhood commercial streets by letting developers build housing there. For the first time ever, downtown Chicago will be treated as a distinct place, with its own special set of zoning rules. The code will largely ignore meaningless distinctions between businesses, such as whether they sell umbrellas or hats.

The new code also will recognize that the nature of manufacturing has changed. Light manufacturing will be allowed to mix with offices or nightclubs. But heavy industry will get zones of its own, not so much for the health reasons that were important in 1923 and 1957, but because the big manufacturers want it that way and Chicago doesn't want to lose them.

For all the changes, Chicago is still keeping most of the basic zoning conventions in place. It is also keeping much of the peculiar language of zoning—the designations such as "R2" and "C3" that sound more like droids from Star Wars than descriptions of places where people live, work and shop.

On the other hand, the new code will be different from the old code in one immediately identifiable way: It will be understandable. Pages of text are being slimmed down into charts and graphics, making the law easier to use for people without degrees in law or planning. An interactive version will go up on the city's Web site. "Predictability is important," says Ed Kus. "The average person should be able to pick up the zoning code and understand what can and can't be built in his neighborhood."

From *Governing*, June 2003. Copyright © 2003 by Congressional Quarterly, Inc. Reprinted by permission.

Immigration Issues

City on a Hill

Issuing ID cards to immigrants and citizens alike, liberal New Haven charts a course for cities that want to treat immigrants like people.

MARA REVKIN

With immigration reform jettisoned from the national agenda, the mayor of New Haven, Connecticut, is resurrecting the debate in his own backyard. Rejecting the morally charged rhetoric that conservatives have used to cast opprobrium on free-riding aliens, John DeStefano is arguing that the inclusion of illegal immigrants in civil society is vital to public services that benefit the whole city.

Although non-voting immigrants are politically peripheral, New Haven officials estimate that they make up 10 percent of the city's population. In an effort to validate this presence, the city's Board of Aldermen has approved a municipal ID card—the first of its kind in any American city—that is universally available to New Haven's 125,000 residents, including its estimated 10,000 to 12,000 undocumented immigrants. The ID enables any holder, immigrant or otherwise, to access local banks, libraries, and public services. It also entitles them to prescription drugs at the HAVEN Free Clinic, which previously required uninsured patients to present a Social Security number. On July 24, city officials began distributing the application—in Spanish and English—at City Hall; by Aug. 14, 2,671 cards had been issued.

In discussing the myriad functions of the municipal ID—which also doubles as a debit card in local restaurants and stores—public officials are careful to differentiate between rights and public services; the card only entitles residents to the latter. While it cannot shield immigrants from arrest or deportation, it is clear that the municipal ID has designated New Haven's undocumented immigrants as full-fledged participants in civil society. Its adoption also has raised the city's profile as a test ground for the progressive policies that incubate at think tanks but rarely make it onto the agenda of major municipal governments like New Haven's. Public officials in New York and other major cities are monitoring New Haven's experiment and evaluating its suitability for their own communities. If the ID lives up to the lofty expectations of its architects, other cities may replicate the program, at least until Congress produces a plan for comprehensive reform.

The Elm City Resident Card, named for the trees that once dominated the regional landscape, is the most recent in a series of public policies designed to incorporate marginalized groups into the New Haven community. Over the course of his 14 years in office, DeStefano has earned a reputation for reconstituting public offices to reflect New Haven's diverse demographic makeup. Half of the city's police officers are African American or Latino, and the force includes a higher percentage of female officers than any other department in Connecticut.

New Haven officials have won broad public support for the municipal ID by promoting the policy's practical virtues while deemphasizing its ideological baggage. According to Board of Aldermen President Carl Goldfield, the Elm City ID "is above all a pragmatic policy—and one that benefits the whole city." He continued, "From a public health and public safety standpoint, it doesn't make sense to have 10,000 members of a community afraid to get medical help or report crime, just because they're undocumented."

Optimists believe the card will help on many fronts. John Jairo Lugo, president of the local immigrant-rights group Unidad Latina en Accion, said that lack of documentation deters immigrants from reporting crimes because they frequently become objects of suspicion if they are unable to prove their identities. "If you have an encounter with the police department," Lugo said, "they can detain you for days or months in jail until you can come up with valid identification."

Additionally, Liam Brennan, who helped draft the Elm City ID proposal as a Yale law student, said that immigrants are disproportionately the victims of theft and home invasion, since they are frequently paid in cash but have nowhere to deposit their earnings. Local banks usually require a driver's license or Social Security card—documents noncitizens cannot obtain—to set up an account. But Brennan said that many banks have agreed to accept the new municipal ID. With possession of a bank account and a valid ID, immigrants will be simultaneously "more likely to report crime, and less likely to experience it themselves," he said.

But it's unclear just how much the card will help illegal residents' long-standing vulnerability when dealing with authorities. On June 6, just two days after the Board of Aldermen voted 25-1 in favor of the Elm City ID, New Haven's Immigration and Customs Enforcement (ICE) agents arrested 32 residents. Of these 32 individuals, only five had prior deportation orders. Twenty-eight of the 32 have been released on bond with the help of Yale Law School professor Michael Wishnie, who has challenged the motives behind the ICE raid and the manner in which it was conducted. City and state officials have alleged that the ICE conducted the raid in retaliation for the city's tolerant immigration policy. Wishnie, with a team of attorneys and Yale law students, is marshalling evidence to "show that the city's approval of the municipal ID was the catalyst for the ICE raids," he explained.

After watching ICE agents handcuff their neighbors, seemingly at random, many New Haven immigrants are more wary than ever of public officials. Despite reassurance from community leaders like Lugo that the ID will give them more security, not less, illegal residents are worried that any record of their presence in the city could result in deportation. "Many people are afraid that this ID is a trap," said Angela, an Ecuadoran immigrant who, fearing more raids, has been wearing a blonde wig to hide her ethnic identity. She guesses only one in five immigrants will apply. "I'm going to wait three weeks to make sure it is safe, and then I will get my card."

Immigrants who decide to apply also face intimidation by protesters. In July, critics of the program demonstrated outside City Hall as applications for the ID were handed out. Deputy Mayor Kica Matos described the volume and rancor of hate mail as "horrendous." "The phone calls have really been quite scary. But this is why it's called a struggle. There's a reason why it's so hard to push forward a civil-rights agenda," Matos said.

Bill Farrel, a roofer from a New Haven suburb, has been mobilizing opposition to the program as a coordinator for Southern Connecticut Immigration Reform (SCtIR), claiming that the city is extending amnesty to illegal aliens at the expense of working-class citizens. Farrel fears that New Haven's municipal experiment could spawn a network of similar initiatives nationwide. "This issue is so much bigger than New Haven," he said. "As we speak, there are over 30 American cities awaiting the outcome of this program, in order to implement their own versions of it." (Whether or not the number is 30, certainly cities are watching: Wishnie said his team has been contacted about the program by numerous public officials and grassroots organizations, and Lugo said that his organization was aware of similar initiatives on the horizon in Chicago, Tucson, Miami, San Francisco, and Portland, Oregon. In New York City, Council Member Hiram Monserrat introduced nearly identical legislation on July 25, the day after New Haven began processing applications for the ID.)

SCtIR has threatened legal action, but it is unlikely that the organization will be able to demonstrate standing since it is based in a suburb of New Haven. Brennan, the former Yale law student who helped draft the ID card proposal, said that unless a charge is filed by an entity within the city, "it would be difficult to prove that any harm has been done." And according to Mayor DeStefano, "The program has broad support in New Haven. Most of the people who oppose it are not members of the community." Regardless of opposition to the program, DeStefano said he has consulted with legal advisers to ensure that "issuing an ID card is fully within the municipal authority of New Haven's government."

DeStefano points out that public fascination with New Haven's program has been amplified by "the absence of a coherent federal policy." "By failing to act, the government has created a policy of de facto tolerance for a population that isn't going to do anything but grow—in this city and in the United States as a whole." The fact that city officials like DeStefano are resorting to do-it-yourself reform only confirms the urgency of establishing a national immigration policy—one that acknowledges the presence of 12 million people who don't plan on leaving anytime soon. "The fact is that our economy could not sustain the loss of millions of workers, and it's unlikely that there is a real mechanism to deport [them]," DeStefano said.

Wishnie believes that local debate in cities like New Haven could eventually generate enough pressure to bring federal lawmakers back to the table. "The friction that we're seeing here in Connecticut is what will drive people back to their senators to demand comprehensive reform," Wishnie said. "Until that happens, communities will continue to govern themselves."

MARA REVKIN is an editorial intern at the *Prospect*.

My House, My Rules.

Or So One Might Think

PETER APPLEBOME

It began with a door that had the wrong paint color.

That was in 1993, the first time Margaret and Haim Bar-Akiva ran afoul of the Twin Rivers Homeowners Association, which oversees the community of about 10,000 people where they live in East Windsor Township, N.J.

Along the way was another dispute over bars on a storm door, which, Mrs. Bar-Akiva said, led the association to spend $100,000 in legal fees. But that's another story.

It all culminated, sort of, in a ruling on Thursday by the New Jersey Supreme Court, which went as far as any court has gone in defining the rights of the ever-growing number of people who live in private communities regulated by homeowners' associations—even if it left an awful lot up in the air.

We may not all end up soaking up the sun like the elder Seinfelds did at Del Boca Vista, and we may not stop in Twin Rivers, a square mile of condominium duplexes, town houses, single-family homes, apartments and commercial buildings in central New Jersey. But one of the immutable long-term trends in American life seems to be that more and more of us at some point will live in the Neverland of places that are not quite public, but not entirely private either, where the rights you might expect in your own home or even at the mall are not necessarily guaranteed.

So, in New Jersey, about 1.3 million residents, nearly 40 percent of all private homeowners, live in communities where homeowners' associations set and enforce the rules. Nationally, it's more than 50 million people.

This, as many have come to know, can put one in an inscrutable world where maybe you can put out a yard sign for a favored candidate, distribute leaflets and knock on doors, or maybe you can't. Maybe you can fly a flag, or maybe not. There can be restrictions on fences and paint colors, shutters and lawn art. Maybe you can drive a pickup truck or motorcycle, maybe it's against the rules.

This is not an entirely new world, but it's still a vexing one, where the rules are still being sorted out and where many homeowners feel the field is tilted in one direction: associations with a phalanx of lawyers, the dues of members and the lobbying clout of the powerful Community Associations Institute, a national trade group, on the one hand, individual homeowners on the other.

"Boards have all the powers of mini-governments but none of the corresponding accountability that goes with it," Mrs. Bar-Akiva said. "They can fine you, assess taxes in the form of maintenance fees, put a lien on your house, but there's nothing that balances those powers on the side of homeowners."

Which is why the New Jersey case was viewed as so important. Fought over fairly small issues—an ordinance that originally allowed only one political sign in a flower bed or a window, use of the community room, access to the association's monthly newsletter—it was followed closely nationally as the most concerted challenge to the notion that communities run by homeowners' associations should be seen as businesses largely exempt from constitutional protections on issues like free speech.

After all, Twin Rivers feels like a town with its multimillion dollar budget, more than 20 employees, parks and swimming pools, and services that include lawn maintenance, snow removal and street lighting.

Indeed, the earth seemed to move last year when a New Jersey appeals court ruled that homeowners did not give up their constitutional rights when they moved into a privately governed community. And it held that in terms of free speech, board members were "constitutional actors," not representatives of an exempt private enterprise.

But industry representatives said that was too sweeping and imposed quasigovernmental standards on private enterprises. The State Supreme Court largely agreed, saying that residents of the communities must accept limits on their free speech rights and that private developments, no matter how ambitious or powerful, were not the same as towns. Not that anything definitive was settled. The court threw a bone in the other direction, saying homeowners might have valid claims against "unreasonable" restrictions of their rights to free speech.

Which means, for the most part, that the issues don't go away. They become grist for state legislatures, like a proposed national code for homeowners' associations being considered by many states, including New Jersey. Or else they play out as narrow legal spats that have made this the hottest new area in property law litigation.

The industry representatives say people are overwhelmingly satisfied with their experiences in private communities, and, after all, they can choose where they live.

But here's the catch. Increasingly, there isn't an option. Many municipalities now require new developments to have homeowners' associations. If you want to retire to many communities, there's often no option other than ones run by homeowners' associations.

Once rare blooms, places like Twin Rivers are becoming, if not quite the new normal, a new normal. Governments and courts are only now figuring out just what that new normal should be.

UNIT 6

Revenues and Economic Development

Unit Selections

Key Points to Consider

- Approximately how much money do you (or your parents, if you are not a full-time wage earner) pay annually to the local, state, and national governments, respectively? Is this an easy question to answer? Why or why not?

- Property tax, a tax on the value of real estate and buildings, is a primary source of revenue for the local governments. Do you think people who live in rented apartments or houses avoid the burdens of property taxes? Why or why not?

- Why do you think that the national government has assumed more and more of the burden for raising revenues for all three levels of government?

- What do you think is the best means for the state and local governments to raise revenues: property taxes, income taxes, sales taxes, lotteries, user charges, or something else?

- Some people think that lotteries and casinos run by the state governments are inappropriate or wrong, because they contribute to the tendency of some citizens to gamble excessively. On the other hand, lotteries and casinos raise revenues for the state and local governments. That, in turn, can reduce tax rates. All in all, do you support gambling operations as a way of financing state and local governments? Why or why not?

- The state and local governments sometimes offer tax breaks and other incentives to attract new businesses. Why do the state and local governments do this? Do you approve of this practice? Why or why not?

Student Web Site
www.mhcls.com/online

Internet References
Assessor.com
   http://www.assessor.com
Economic Development Administration
   http://www.doc.gov/eda
National Association of Development Organizations (NADO)
   http://www.nado.org/links/index.html

All governments need financial resources to carry out their activities. State and local governments rely on a variety of revenue sources, including sales tax, income tax, and property tax; user charges (for example, motor vehicle registration fees and college tuitions); lotteries; and grants of money from other levels of government. Despite this diversity of funding sources, the overall financial situation of the state and local governments is often far from satisfactory.

Conspicuous attempts to curb spending at all levels of government have been made in recent decades. An early and historically important success in this context was the passage of Proposition 13 by California voters in a 1978 referendum. Proposition 13 imposed ceilings on local government property taxes and, in turn, curtailed local governments' spending in California, and the services and programs that they could offer. The Proposition 13 tax revolt soon spread to other states. By now, measures designed to limit government spending have come into effect in states and localities across the country. At the national level, a constitutional amendment has been proposed and legislation has been passed in attempts to make it difficult for Congress to adopt an unbalanced budget.

Unlike the national government, the state and local governments get a sizable portion of their revenues from intergovernmental grants. The national government gives money to the state and local governments along with various conditions attached to it. Money can be given with virtually no accompanying strings or with considerable limitations on how it can be spent. Similarly, states provide state aid to local governments under varying sets of conditions. Governments providing financial grants, of course, exercise control over the amount of funds available and the conditions attached to such funds. This, in turn, can cause considerable uncertainty for governments relying on grant money. As should be apparent, intergovernmental relations and the financing of state and local government overlap considerably.

The financial situation of the state and the local governments differs from that of the national government in other important aspects. The national government can try to affect the national economy by varying the money supply and by running budgetary deficits or surpluses. By contrast, most state and local governments are legally required to balance their budgets. For those not required to have balanced budgets, it is difficult to borrow money

© Royalty-Free/Corbis

for large and persistent budget deficits. The fiscal crises of New York City and other local governments during the 1970s showed that lenders will go only so far in providing money for state and local governments, whose expenditures are consistently greater than their revenues. The declaration of bankruptcy by Orange County, California, in 1994 reveals how tempting it is for local governments to pursue risky, although potentially very profitable, investment strategies, especially in financially difficult times. In 1997, several dozen school districts in Pennsylvania learned a similar lesson. Risky investment decisions made on their behalf by a reputed financial wizard resulted in the loss of millions of dollars and jeopardized the school districts' financial futures.

The national government, the state governments, and the local governments all seek to promote economic development. New industries employ workers who pay taxes and, thus, increase government revenues. What seems new on the state and the local scene is the energy and persistence with which states and localities compete with one another to attract industries to their areas.

Finances are a complicated but critical aspect of state and local government. The first section of this unit treats taxes, lotteries, and related revenue-raising matters. The second section focuses on activities of the state and the local governments related to economic development.

Two Cheers for the Property Tax

Everyone hates it, but the property tax has some good attributes that make it indispensable.

STEVEN GINSBERG

To most Americans, the property tax is about as revered as communism and as popular as a pro-lifer at a NOW rally. The reasons are not hard to understand. At first glance, the property tax system seems arbitrary, unreasonable, and just plain unfair. Every year property owners are hit with a large tax bill, demanding a nearly immediate lump-sum payment. In many jurisdictions, including our nation's capital, the government isn't even required to do you the courtesy of mailing that bill; if you miss the deadline, you must pay late fees whether you received your notice or not. Furthermore, as far as many homeowners are concerned, the manner by which both tax rates and individual property values are determined could not be more random if they were plucked out of a hat. In some cases this is because on-site assessments are only done infrequently—like every five or 10 years. This forces assessors to rely on unreliable estimation methods in the intervening years, such as setting the value of a property based on what neighboring real estate sold for that year, regardless of how the condition of those properties compares with that of the building being assessed. Thus a shack and a renovated loft in the same area can be valued at the same amount. In other communities, like those in California, property values are reassessed only when a building is sold. So a young family of four buying a home in San Francisco's pricey real estate market is slapped with an exorbitant tax bill, while the filthy-rich investment banker down the street is still paying the same amount in taxes as when he first purchased his home in 1979.

Property tax rates are just as varied. In each community, homeowners, businesses, and non-homestead residences (like apartment buildings) vie to lighten their portion of the tax load. Often, regardless of actual property values, whichever group happens to have the most lobbying clout gets a break, while the losing parties are left to shoulder more than their fair share of the burden. In Minnesota, for instance, between 1977 and 1990 homeowners were able to cut their share of property taxes from 45 to 36 percent, even as their share of real estate values rose from 51 to 56 percent. All of this financial finagling, of course, only strengthens taxpayers' conviction that the system is inherently unjust and highly politicized.

It's not surprising then that the property tax has earned such a bad rep among voters—and even less surprising that politicians have latched onto the issue. If you're looking to win votes, opposing the property tax is a no-brainer: It's like declaring that you're anti-drugs. Already, states as politically diverse as Oregon and New York have moved to defang the property tax.

But before we pop open the champagne to toast these developments, we need to take a close look at the upside of the property tax. (And, yes, there is a considerable one.) For although the list of the system's failures is long, people who advocate lowering or abolishing the tax outright are in many cases not considering the big picture.

For starters, contrary to popular belief, the property tax serves as a vital complement to other types of taxes. For instance, our income tax system may be geared to collect more from the affluent, but it also includes numerous loopholes that allow the rich to slip out of paying an amount of tax truly commensurate with their wealth. The property tax picks up where the income tax leaves off. Even if they manage to downplay their annual income, chances are, rich folks are going to buy property. They can't resist owning that summer home in Nantucket, that weekend home in the Hamptons, or that colonial mansion in Georgetown. After all, what's the point of having all that dough if you're not going to spend it? Thus the amount of property you own is as important an indicator of how well-off you are as the income you're officially pulling in each year.

Similarly, property taxes improve the accuracy with which the wealth of senior citizens—whose assets tend to dramatically outweigh their cash incomes—can be taxed. Without property taxes, many seniors would only be taxed on their fixed incomes—which often grossly underestimate how well-to-do they actually are. Now, we're not talking about the 70-year-old Brooklyn couple whose fixed income barely covers the taxes on the brownstone they bought 30 years ago. (An exemption can and should be made to ensure taxes don't force elderly people out of their homes.) But lots of seniors have invested in real estate other than their primary residences. Take the case of a retired speculator who bought property years ago and has watched gleefully as its value skyrocketed. He can enjoy the benefits of his good fortune long before he actually sells those investments. For instance, ownership of pricey real estate makes him eligible for large loans on which the interest is tax deductible. Furthermore, he can spend his fixed annual retirement income without a second thought—knowing that if he's ever low on funds, he can simply cash in his property. The property tax ensures that his tax bill reflects his good fortune. It's not surprising then, that the powerful AARP seniors lobby is pressuring states for an overhaul of the property tax system. And as baby boomers slide into their golden years, we can expect this branch of the anti-property tax lobby to grow even stronger.

Who Will Pick Up the Slack?

No doubt the rich and the elderly recognize that abolishing or lowering property taxes would deal a crushing blow to the schools in their communities—which is where the bulk of the tax's revenues go. But that's no skin off their noses: The rich can always send their kids to private school, and most old people's kids have already flown the nest. Of course, cash-strapped communities are unwilling to stand by as their schools are devastated and may raise other kinds of taxes—like sales taxes—to make up for lost revenue. But such taxes shift more of the burden onto the middle and lower classes, who must buy basic goods, even if they can't afford property.

If you have any doubts about the kind of fiscal havoc the elimination of the property tax can cause, you need only look at what's happened in the states that have "reformed" it. In Florida, the large and religiously anti-property tax seniors population has pushed lawmakers into reducing the property tax rates for some, and completely exempting others. The result is a maze of slimmed-down services and hidden "non-tax" fees that end up unfairly shackling the middle class. Worst of all, these alternative methods simply can't raise the same amount of revenue as the property taxes did. Consequently, notes Kurt Wenner, an economist with Florida TaxWatch, "the schools don't have much of a chance." Small wonder that Florida kids consistently place near the bottom in national reading and math tests, alongside much poorer states such as Louisiana.

In Texas, voters overwhelmingly approved Proposition 1, a ballot measure providing $1 billion in property tax "relief." The law's supporters in the legislature said they had to act "before there was a taxpayer revolt." Of course, almost immediately after the bill passed, school districts across the state announced that they would have to raise other taxes to make ends meet.

Taxpayers in Maine are looking to reduce their property tax bills by expanding the homestead exemption by $20,000, a measure that would rob the state of $200 million in funds. To compensate for the reduction in real estate taxes, Maine will be forced to extend its 6 percent sales tax to a wide range of everyday sources that directly hit middle-class wallets, including movie theaters, bowling alleys, beauticians, and barbers.

The situation is no different in New York; Governor Pataki, along with a slew of legislators, has vowed to cut property taxes. But as property taxes go down, local taxes, user fees, and college education prices continue to surge to make up the difference. The New York proposals are so unbalanced they prompted

Patricia Woodworth, director of the budget for the State of New York, to complain to *Newsday* last April, "the benefits are going to go to those who have the greater monetary and financial interest in property holdings, which is not the average person. This plan is not truly tax relief."

But it is Oregon that gives us the most vivid example of what happens when property taxes are slashed. The northwestern state passed Measure 5 in 1990, putting a cap on all property tax increases. This, in turn, forced a massive transfer of state funds to support schools, which left the state with no choice but to cut spending on child welfare, prisons, and state police.

The bottom line: When property taxes are cut, other taxes must be raised to make up for lost revenues. And, as Chris Herbert, an economist at the Harvard-MIT Joint Center for Housing Studies, points out, the property tax is far more progressive than the alternatives. "Cutbacks in property tax have got to be made up and they're not going to be done by a more progressive tax," he says. "Localities can't get states to pick up the tab, so there's a big shift to user charges. You start getting taxes on trash collection and recreation facilities. With user fees things are becoming less progressive because you're paying as much as the next guy"—regardless of whether he happens to be a millionaire.

Mend It, Don't End It

But if we want to get the property tax off the political hit list, we need to address the legitimate problems with the current system. A handful of governments around the country have already started the ball rolling, instituting models that correct some of the more egregious flaws.

Washington state has perhaps the best system, having tackled the issue of favoritism head-on and passed a constitutional amendment declaring that statewide property tax rates must be uniform. For example, all real estate property is currently taxed at approximately 1.2 percent. In addition, all property tax revenues are split between the state and localities. This allows states to tap a deep vein of revenue and distribute it equitably. Under such a system, localities ultimately get to administer their portion of the pot, but the disparity between rich and poor districts is not so wide. "The real key is that the system is administered fairly," says Kriss Sjoblon, an economist at the Washington Research Council. "We have a good system of assessment that eliminates inequities, and the uniformity is vital. People should be treated fairly and folks shouldn't get deals."

Even jurisdictions with special needs can establish systems that are less arbitrary and that make sense to the average taxpayer. Pittsburgh, for instance, has initiated a "split-rate" system in an attempt to foster urban renewal. Property tax is really two separate taxes, one on land and one on building values; Pittsburgh simply separated these two values. The city then lowered the tax on buildings, giving property owners an incentive to maintain, build, and improve their properties, while at the same time increasing the levy on land values, thus discouraging land speculation and stemming urban sprawl. In Pittsburgh and other Pennsylvania cities where the "split-rate" is employed, 85 percent of homeowners pay less than they would with a flat rate, according to analysis by the *American Journal of Economics and Sociology*. The analysis also found that those who do pay more tend to be wealthier homeowners.

Most importantly, the system achieves its goal of encouraging economic growth in urban centers. A study conducted by University of Maryland economists Wallace Oates and Robert Schwab, comparing Pittsburgh to 14 other eastern cities during the decade before and the decade after Pittsburgh expanded its two-rate system, found that: "Pittsburgh had a 70.4 percent increase in the value of building permits, while the 14-city average decreased by 14.4 percent. These findings are especially remarkable when it is recalled that the city's basic industry—steel—was undergoing a severe crisis throughout the latter decade."

Aside from these more comprehensive systems, there are a number of basic steps localities could take to alter the perception of unfairness and ease the burden of property taxes:

- Use the property tax to pay for more than just schools. If seniors and the wealthy feel that the taxes support services they need, they will have reason to pause before directing their lobbying muscle against it.
- Raise the level of exemptions for people over 65. Property taxes do blindside some senior citizens, and there's no reason why they should have to move out of their lifelong homes because the market value of the house has gone up. A moderate raise in the exemption level would prevent poorer seniors from losing their homes, while still raising revenue from the wealthy.
- Stagger payments. A major reason property tax is so unpopular is that it's administered in huge chunks and people aren't allowed much time before hefty late fees kick in. Distributing the burden over four or more payments a year, with more advanced notice, would take some of the sting out of the bill.
- Upgrade technology. Set it up so people can pay electronically. It's a small thing, but it will make a difference. Most cities allow offenders to pay parking tickets with credit cards, there's no reason they can't do the same with property tax.

Rooting out favoritism and slipshod assessment methods will help make the tax palatable to the majority of citizens. They will no longer see the property tax as a mindless ogre coming to swallow up their hard-earned money. Instead, they will see it as the soundest way to make sure that everyone, especially the wealthy, contributes his share to ensure a high level of public services. In short, they will see it for what it is.

STEVEN GINSBERG is an editorial aide at *The Washington Post*.

Politicians Bet the Farm

Faced with tough budget decisions, many states are turning to gambling as an answer to their economic woes. But most end up getting far more than they bargained for.

Barbara T. Dreyfuss

Last spring, Kansas politicians decided to take government promotion of gambling to a new level, voting to make the state the first to actually own Las Vegas-style casinos. Not content, as other states, to merely tax the revenues of commercial gambling establishments, Kansas will own the casinos' buildings and rake in much of their proceeds. But the corporate giants and investors who own casinos in other states won't be left out. Kansas will partner with them to run day-to-day operations. The state's Republican legislature and Democratic governor, Kathleen Sebelius, endorsed the law as an answer to demands from the state Supreme Court to come up with more money for education. Rather than impose higher taxes or cut budgets, they bet on an easier road to riches. Watching Kansans flock to casinos in nearby Missouri and Iowa, political leaders decided to try to keep that money at home.

Kansas isn't alone. Officials in other states (over a dozen in 2007) are also scrambling to expand gambling, eyeing negotiated fees from American Indian tribes and tax revenues from commercial casinos. And, no longer satisfied with restricting casinos to rural areas, politicians are fighting to build them right downtown in the largest U.S. cities. As discussion of taxes has become taboo, politicians of both parties have been promoting gambling as a way to make a quick buck. Afraid to tell voters they need more money for government programs like education and public services, officials surreptitiously collect it by taxing gambling revenues.

It's not just a question of hidden taxing. When gambling comes to a community, crime, bankruptcies, suicides, and mental illness increase. City and county governments have to bear added costs for these problems, and local businesses often fold, as money that would otherwise be spent in the region flows into a corporate headquarters elsewhere. Despite opposition from many local citizens and business

leaders, politicians have decided gambling is politically the easiest answer when they need immediate funds. The Rev. Tom Grey, field coordinator for the National Coalition Against Legalized Gambling, says Republicans' anti-tax rhetoric has caused "progressives to lose faith that there's a common good and a willingness to pay for goods and services."

A Big Gamble

Legalized gambling has spread rapidly throughout the United States. Two decades ago there was a social stigma attached to gambling, and only two states, Nevada and New Jersey, allowed commercial casinos. American Indian gaming barely existed. But gaming has come out of the back alleys and onto the main streets of small towns and struggling cities around the country. It is promoted as high-class entertainment, yet affordable to the masses. And business is booming, with more than 460 commercial casinos operating in 11 states. Casinos took $32.4 billion in gross gaming revenues in 2006, almost double the $17 billion of 10 years earlier. American Indian-run gaming has also taken off, following an official blessing by Congress in 1988. Currently, 423 facilities, run by 228 tribes, operate in 28 states, according to Alan Meister in the 2007–2008 Indian Gaming Industry Report. Tribes raked in $25.5 billion in 2006. On top of the casino money, Americans spent more than $56 billion on state-run lotteries.

While gambling supporters argue that casinos are always an economic boon for a region, research indicates otherwise. With the exception of Las Vegas and Atlantic City, studies show that for many casinos, most of their players live within a 50-mile radius. The money those gamblers lose would otherwise be spent within the region, at such places as restaurants, movie theaters, and retail shops. And when local businesses lose these customers, they fire employees, pay fewer taxes, and often close. A few years after a casino comes to town, increased crime and other problems result in local governments' needing more police, courts, mental health programs, and other services. In many localities and states, casinos do not bring in the money politicians had hoped. Commercial casinos pay wagering taxes to states, but they also displace existing sales tax revenue. American Indian casinos only pay the state and localities the fees they have negotiated, and often not that.

Despite this, legislators ignore the broader consequences and look at the immediate tax dollars casinos might provide. Critics see this as equivalent to states urging people to smoke in order to get more tax money up front, despite the long-term health-care consequences. "No political leader would say, 'Let's increase revenue by promoting cigarettes'—it's absurd," says Les Bernal, who spent nine years as a top aide to a Massachusetts state senator, Susan Tucker, fighting casino legalization. "Yet, they do it with gambling."

The gambling industry does not like to be compared with the tobacco industry, and the American Gaming Association (AGA), its lobbying arm, touts its openness and concern for problem gamblers. The association was set up in 1995, after the industry was scared by a brief effort to pay for the Clinton health-care initiative by taxing gambling. Frank Fahrenkopf, former head of the Republican National Committee, was named AGA president. "I didn't want to come in to this job with the same sort of approach that the tobacco industry had had—the denial," he says. He showed the board of directors the famous picture of tobacco executives swearing under oath at congressional hearings that smoking wasn't harmful. The board took that message to heart, and the AGA has spent over $20 million to fund research into gambling addiction. "We as an industry must commit to doing everything we can to help people who can't gamble responsibly," Fahrenkopf stresses.

Industry-funded research puts the onus on gamblers, emphasizing gambling addiction as a personal, psychological problem. It ignores casinos' enormous and sophisticated marketing efforts, which help create the problem gamblers. The reality is the gambling industry lives off of people who gamble excessively. Exactly how much casinos depend on problem gamblers is difficult to determine without opening up their accounting books. But a 1997 study by Henry R. Lesieur, founder of the *Journal of Gambling Studies,* found that problem and pathological gamblers spend roughly 30 percent of the cash taken in by casinos.

The industry expends enormous effort to keep people coming back. Casinos issue guests cards, which carefully track their visitors' betting activities. These provide a detailed profile of players, telling casinos how much people bet, what they like to play, where they eat. They also pro-

vide clues to what might entice them to return. Then casinos lure gamblers back with free gifts, including rooms, meals, limos, and free game time. "It's all about building player profiles, gathering information, and putting that in orderly form, so that at a later date, when marketing to those individuals, you can pinpoint events, incentives, giveaways for your clients, to give yourself the best chance of moving that client to your place," says a former marketing executive for a major Atlantic City casino.

The casinos are designed "extremely carefully," he says. "Where you put the tables, where you give access, the colors of the rooms, the ventilation, could mean all the difference." Casinos almost never have clocks and rarely have windows in game rooms, so gamblers lose touch with time. Round-the-clock restaurants keep people from wandering too far away. On the gambling floors, players are continually offered free drinks. Some casinos cater to young, more affluent gamblers, offering free rooms and dinners. Others focus on lonely, disabled seniors with time on their hands, providing free bus service from senior citizen housing.

Occasionally a casino official will approach someone losing heavily, who is showing signs of stress, and ask whether they want to leave. But unlike bars and restaurants, which will stop serving drunks, casinos rarely stop a gambler. And while some casinos do stringent credit checks before allowing gamblers to borrow money, or limit the checks they will cash, others are not so careful. In some cities such as Detroit, "you can borrow as much as you want," says a former casino official. Many casinos have voluntary exclusion forms that gamblers can sign, asking that they be thrown out and subject to arrest if they return. Admittedly, it is not always easy for staff at large casinos to spot these gamblers if they try to return, especially if they change their appearance or don't use the player cards. But a number of casinos have been sued by gamblers who charged they were not only allowed back in, even when spotted, but were actually induced back with free gifts. Casinos deny this. So far, the courts have sided with the casinos in these cases, or the suits were settled quietly.

Taking the Bet

The current gambling boom in the U.S. started with the growth of state lotteries. Fahrenkopf says that "the seminal moment" came in 1964, when taxophobic New Hampshire voters agreed to a state-run lottery. That changed the public's view on gambling, he says, because people believed, if a "state government is running a gambling enterprise, how can it be wrong?" The state-blessed lotteries attracted poor people who hoped to win big, and also legislators, who hoped their states would win big. Former Democratic Rep. Bob Edgar, now head of Common Cause, explains, "There are a whole class of people who think they will make millions from the lottery. Politicians also convinced people that the money lotteries would bring in would help seniors and schools. Once we went down this road, politicians began to see gambling money as an easy revenue source."

Although lotteries existed in the U.S. as far back as colonial days, by around 1900 they were all prohibited, thanks to numerous scandals. After New Hampshire gave them a rebirth, states throughout the Northeast, plagued by budget problems in the 1970s, also adopted them. States on the West Coast followed in the 1980s. While a few Southern states set them up, others resisted in the face of opposition from religious conservatives, who were against lotteries on moral and religious grounds, and liberals, who opposed lotteries as a regressive tax, because numerous studies showed that the heaviest players were the poor. Southern resistance gave way in the late 1980s, thanks in large part to James Carville, the political guru who helped Bill Clinton get elected, says Randy Bobbitt, author of the book, *Lottery Wars,* about the politics behind Southern lotteries. In 1987, Carville was trying to elect an unknown businessman, Wallace Wilkinson, as Kentucky's governor. "He wanted an issue no one was talking about," Bobbitt says. He found it by promoting a lottery as a new way to fund education. This was the key to Wilkinson's election.

Today, 43 states and the District of Columbia run lotteries, which are still widely promoted as the only way to bring in additional money for education. But the reality is that, while initially lottery money often adds to regular education budgets, as time passes it often is used just to maintain levels of education spending. In Florida, for example, as education budgets were diverted for other uses, and as lottery sales flattened and student enrollment increased, spending per student ended up below pre-lottery days. "If the lottery has bad sales one year, schools lose out," Bobbitt says.

No political leader would say, 'Let's raise revenue by promoting cigarettes'—it's absurd. Yet they do it with gambling.

State lotteries opened the door to American Indian gaming. In the early 1980s, several tribes started high-stakes bingo parlors, but their states objected. After fights in local courts, a landmark 1987 Supreme Court decision ruled that if a state allows a form of gambling, then American Indian tribes within that state are allowed to engage, unregulated, in that form of gambling. The following year, Congress passed the Indian Gaming Regulatory Act, establishing the legal structure for American Indian gaming. A key provision requires tribes to sign a compact with a state if they want slot machines or casinos. These compacts usually detail how much gaming revenue the tribe will share with the state.

While the Indians were busy setting up casinos on their reservations, the cowboys were also determined not to be left out. In the late 1980s and early 1990s, gaming interests promoted a revival of Old West gambling saloons in historic Colorado and South Dakota mining towns and gambling riverboats along the Mississippi and Missouri rivers. Although there was popular opposition, legislators and governors in six river states, which were suffering hard economic times in the late 1980s, promoted gambling as a source of revenue. Iowa led the way, followed by Illinois, Indiana, Missouri, Mississippi, and Louisiana. Because there was strong public opposition when the riverboats first started plying the waters, there were strict limits on when, and how, people could gamble. Boats had to be moving and could only operate for limited hours, and in some areas, losses were limited, too. But as more and more states allowed gambling boats, competition took away customers. So states started lifting restrictions. It did not take long for the moving gambling casinos to become stationary. Then it was only a short leap to building riverfront casinos.

The Payout

So what is really wrong with all this if tribes and towns benefit and people are entertained? "If it was just harmless entertainment, it wouldn't be a public-policy question," says Earl Grinols, a Baylor University economics professor who has researched gaming extensively. Casinos exact a tremendous toll, Grinols says, and the odds are not in society's favor. "My estimate is there is a 3.1 to 1 cost to benefit [ratio] to society as a whole," he says. Grinols and David Mustard, a professor at the University of Georgia, studied data on all U.S. counties, spanning 19 years. They found that in the three to four years after a casino came to town, crime (including robberies, burglary, embezzlement, fraud, and assaults) increased by 8 percent. This forced budget increases for law enforcement, courts, and other services. Gambling also exacerbates other social problems, including suicides, bankruptcy, divorce, domestic violence, and mental illness. This, in turn, necessitates expenditures by local governments. Grinols estimates that society spends $10,300 per pathological gambler. Even when governments get tax revenues from casinos, he says, overall they lose money.

Despite these costs, government officials look to the quick returns they can get from casinos. At times, though, they don't even get this money. In Michigan, for example, the state negotiated to get 8 percent of the slot machine revenues from casinos run by nine tribes. But one by one, eight of the tribes stopped paying, claiming the state had violated the agreement. Also in Michigan, tribes promised to use some of their profits to aid local communities, to off-set the crime, traffic, and other problems caused by casinos. But a *Detroit Free Press* investigation revealed that tribal money in Michigan earmarked for such uses went instead to pay for such things as tribal members' taxes, a historical documentary, and homemaker groups.

Even if they do take in casino money, states lose out on sales tax revenue. Since most people have a limited amount of disposable income, money spent at casinos would otherwise buy taxable items or be used at restaurants and stores. A fiscal analyst for Indiana's legislature looked at 19 years' worth of multi-state data and concluded that eight of 12 states lost sales tax revenues when large-scale commercial casinos opened. States could offset this loss by having sufficiently high wagering taxes on casinos, but only four of the eight did. Fahrenkopf disputes the idea that casinos reel in money that would be spent elsewhere in the area: "All the economic studies say that's a bunch of bull because what you've gotten is new revenue coming in, new jobs in the area, new restaurants being built, new motels and hotels." But very few cities have had an economic revitalization because of a casino, and even Fahrenkopf admits that three casinos have not been able to rebuild inner-city Detroit.

More and more local business leaders are seeing beyond the hype that casinos spark an economic boom, and are opposing them out of concern they will actually harm the local economy. Even in Kansas, where the government will now run the casinos, the Wichita Metro Chamber of Commerce board voted last June against a casino in the county. Its vote followed a study by Wichita State University showing a casino would cost the county $1.4 billion over 20 years, when benefits, including jobs and revenues, were compared with the fiscal and social costs.

More and more local business and civic leaders are seeing beyond the hype that casinos spark an economic boom.

The Wichita business community is not alone. Mike Jandernoa, a business leader in Grand Rapids, Michigan, became interested in a nearby American Indian tribe's plan to build a casino when the local chamber of commerce expressed concern. Jandernoa reviewed a consulting company analysis of the casino and became worried about the casino's impact on his employees, "about the distraction, the tardiness, bankruptcy and divorce." The study also showed a casino would take consumer spending away from local restaurants, bars, and retailers, and that Grand Rapids and the surrounding area would lose more than $600 million over 10 years. The state as a whole was projected to lose $300 million, largely due to money taken out of state

by investors and management companies. "It has been promoted as this idea of being a tourist attraction that we can use in difficult economic times," says Jandernoa, who leads a business coalition that so far has slowed, but not stopped, the casino's development. "Well, we've grown to 23 casinos, and our economy has lost jobs and population."

Playing Politics

Voters in many states have opposed casinos time and again, only to see them legalized by legislators. Only two states, Michigan and South Dakota, approved casinos by a state-wide public vote between 1988 and 2002. In the more than two dozen states that okayed casinos during that time, it was the legislature that brought them in, even over public opposition. For example, Iowa voters rejected the idea in 1985 and 1988, and polls showed they were ready to do so again in 1989, when the legislature endorsed it.

Perhaps this legislative support has something to do with the millions of dollars the industry pours into state campaigns. In the 2006 election cycle, the industry gave $70 million to state candidates, according to the National Institute on Money in State Politics. It also spends lavishly on advertising when there are ballot referendums. In 2006, six gambling-related measures were on the ballot in five states. Committees backing or opposing these measures raised $54 million, 89 percent of it coming from gambling interests. Despite the expensive campaign, three states rejected an expansion of American Indian casinos, video games, or slot machines. Only in Arkansas was gambling expanded, but just for charities to run bingo games. And South Dakota kept its video lottery. These votes show significant public opposition to casino expansion. Last April, after the Maine legislature endorsed a measure to allow a second casino to open in the state, the Democratic governor, John Baldacci, vetoed the legislation. Two years earlier, Baldacci had vetoed a similar measure, saying that the social and economic costs of gambling were too great. In November 2007, Maine citizens endorsed Baldacci's position, voting down a referendum to expand gambling.

Gambling is a hot issue at the national level as well. In the run-up to the Nevada Democratic primary in January, Hillary Clinton used gambling industry executives affiliated with her campaign to criticize Barack Obama for his opposition, as a state senator, to using gambling for budget-deficit reduction. (He had expressed concerns about its "moral and social costs" and about the money the industry pours into politicians' coffers.) Obama did not take on the industry in Nevada, and his campaign responded to the Clinton attack by saying the state was a model for regulating gambling.

At least 10 states are currently debating casino regulation and expansion. In some areas, such as Philadelphia, there are active citizen groups fighting casinos. Business leaders like Grand Rapids' Jandernoa are looking for economic development based on companies that can provide "an economic engine that would be sustainable" to revitalize their depressed cities.

While opponents have at times succeeded over the heavily financed campaigns of the casino interests, it is not easy. Despite earlier polls showing that California voters were poised to defeat measures on Feb. 5 expanding Indian gaming, in fact they ended up endorsing them, after an expensive effort by the pro-gaming side. But if the public and business show strong opposition, politicians may yet get the backbone to resist the spread of gambling, especially since, with so many casinos already operating, new ones may be in political leaders' own backyards. That's something even Frank Fahrenkopf doesn't want. During a 2006 debate in Cleveland he admitted, "If someone were to come along and tell me they were going to put a casino in McLean, Virginia, where I live, I would probably work very, very hard against it. What's the old saying? NIMBY. Not in my backyard."

BARBARA T. DREYFUSS is a senior correspondent for *The American Prospect.*

The Rise of the Creative Class

Why cities without gays and rock bands are losing the economic development race.

RICHARD FLORIDA

As I walked across the campus of Pittsburgh's Carnegie Mellon University one delightful spring day, I came upon a table filled with young people chatting and enjoying the spectacular weather. Several had identical blue T-shirts with "Trilogy@CMU" written across them—Trilogy being an Austin, Texas-based software company with a reputation for recruiting our top students. I walked over to the table. "Are you guys here to recruit?" I asked. "No, absolutely not," they replied adamantly. "We're not recruiters. We're just hangin' out, playing a little Frisbee with our friends." How interesting, I thought. They've come to campus on a workday, all the way from Austin, just to hang out with some new friends.

I noticed one member of the group sitting slouched over on the grass, dressed in a tank top. This young man had spiked multi-colored hair, full-body tattoos, and multiple piercings in his ears. An obvious slacker, I thought, probably in a band. "So what is your story?" I asked. "Hey man, I just signed on with these guys." In fact, as I would later learn, he was a gifted student who had inked the highest-paying deal of any graduating student in the history of his department, right at that table on the grass, with the recruiters who do not "recruit."

What a change from my own college days, just a little more than 20 years ago, when students would put on their dressiest clothes and carefully hide any counterculture tendencies to prove that they could fit in with the company. Today, apparently, it's the company trying to fit in with the students. In fact, Trilogy had wined and dined him over margarita parties in Pittsburgh and flown him to Austin for private parties in hip nightspots and aboard company boats. When I called the people who had recruited him to ask why, they answered, "That's easy. We wanted him because he's a rock star."

While I was interested in the change in corporate recruiting strategy, something even bigger struck me. Here was another example of a talented young person leaving Pittsburgh. Clearly, my adopted hometown has a huge number

The Creativity Index

The key to economic growth lies not just in the ability to attract the creative class, but to translate that underlying advantage into creative economic outcomes in the form of new ideas, new high-tech businesses and regional growth. To better gauge these capabilities, I developed a new measure called the Creativity Index (column 1). The Creativity Index is a mix of four equally weighted factors: the creative class share of the workforce (column 2 shows the percentage; column 3 ranks cities accordingly); high-tech industry, using the Milken Institute's widely accepted Tech Pole Index, which I refer to as the High-Tech Index (column 4); innovation, measured as patents per capita (column 5); and diversity, measured by the Gay Index, a reasonable proxy for an area's openness to different kinds of people and ideas (column 6). This composite indicator is a better measure of a region's underlying creative capabilities than the simple measure of the creative class, because it reflects the joint effects of its concentration and of innovative economic outcomes. The Creativity Index is thus my baseline indicator of a region's overall standing in the creative economy and I offer it as a barometer of a region's longer run economic potential. The following tables present my creativity index ranking for the top 10 and bottom 10 metropolitan areas, grouped into three size categories (large, medium-sized and small cities/regions).

—Richard Florida

of assets. Carnegie Mellon is one of the world's leading centers for research in information technology. The University of Pittsburgh, right down the street from our campus, has a world-class medical center. Pittsburgh attracts hundreds of millions of dollars per year in university research funding and is the sixth-largest center for college and university students on a per capita basis in the country. Moreover, this is hardly a cultural backwater. The city is home to three major sports franchises, renowned museums and cultural venues, a spectacular network of urban parks, fantastic industrial-age architecture, and great urban neighborhoods with an abundance of charming yet affordable housing. It is a friendly city, defined by strong communities and a strong sense of pride. In the 1986 Rand McNally survey, Pittsburgh was ranked "America's Most Livable City," and has continued to score high on such lists ever since.

Yet Pittsburgh's economy continues to putter along in a middling flat-line pattern. Both the core city and the surrounding metropolitan area lost population in the 2000 census. And those bright young university people keep leaving. Most of Carnegie Mellon's prominent alumni of recent years—like Vinod Khosla, perhaps the best known of Silicon Valley's venture capitalists, and Rick Rashid, head of research and development at Microsoft—went elsewhere to make their marks. Pitt's vaunted medical center, where Jonas Salk created his polio vaccine and the world's premier organ-transplant program was started, has inspired only a handful of entrepreneurs to build biotech companies in Pittsburgh.

Over the years, I have seen the community try just about everything possible to remake itself so as to attract and retain talented young people, and I was personally involved in many of these efforts. Pittsburgh has launched a multitude of programs to diversify the region's economy away from heavy industry into high technology. It has rebuilt its downtown virtually from scratch, invested in a new airport, and developed a massive new sports complex for the Pirates and the Steelers. But nothing, it seemed, could stem the tide of people and new companies leaving the region.

I asked the young man with the spiked hair why he was going to a smaller city in the middle of Texas, a place with a small airport and no professional sports teams, without a major symphony, ballet, opera, or art museum comparable to Pittsburgh's. The company is excellent, he told me. There are also terrific people and the work is challenging. But the clincher, he said, is that, "It's in Austin!" There are lots of young people, he went on to explain, and a tremendous amount to do: a thriving music scene, ethnic and cultural diversity, fabulous outdoor recreation, and great nightlife. Though he had several good job offers from Pittsburgh high-tech firms and knew the city well, he said he felt the city lacked the lifestyle options, cultural diversity, and tolerant attitude that would make it attractive to him. As he summed it up: "How would I fit in here?"

This young man and his lifestyle proclivities represent a profound new force in the economy and life of America. He is a member of what I call the creative class: a fast-growing, highly educated, and well-paid segment of the workforce on whose efforts corporate profits and economic growth increasingly depend. Members of the creative class do a wide variety of work in a wide variety of industries—from technology to entertainment, journalism to finance, high-end

manufacturing to the arts. They do not consciously think of themselves as a class. Yet they share a common ethos that values creativity, individuality, difference, and merit.

More and more businesses understand that ethos and are making the adaptations necessary to attract and retain creative class employees—everything from relaxed dress codes, flexible schedules, and new work rules in the office to hiring recruiters who throw Frisbees. Most civic leaders, however, have failed to understand that what is true for corporations is also true for cities and regions: Places that succeed in attracting and retaining creative class people prosper; those that fail don't.

Stuck in old paradigms of economic development, cities like Buffalo, New Orleans, and Louisville struggled in the 1980s and 1990s to become the next "Silicon Somewhere" by building generic high-tech office parks or subsidizing professional sports teams. Yet they lost members of the creative class, and their economic dynamism, to places like Austin, Boston, Washington, D.C. and Seattle—places more tolerant, diverse, and open to creativity. Because of this migration of the creative class, a new social and economic geography is emerging in America, one that does not correspond to old categories like East Coast versus West Coast or Sunbelt versus Frostbelt. Rather, it is more like the class divisions that have increasingly separated Americans by income and neighborhood, extended into the realm of city and region.

The Creative Secretary

The distinguishing characteristic of the creative class is that its members engage in work whose function is to "create meaningful new forms." The super-creative core of this new class includes scientists and engineers, university professors, poets and novelists, artists, entertainers, actors, designers, and architects, as well as the "thought leadership" of modern society: nonfiction writers, editors, cultural figures, think-tank researchers, analysts, and other opinion-makers. Members of this super-creative core produce new forms or designs that are readily transferable and broadly useful—such as designing a product that can be widely made, sold and used; coming up with a theorem or strategy that can be applied in many cases; or composing music that can be performed again and again.

Beyond this core group, the creative class also includes "creative professionals" who work in a wide range of knowledge-intensive industries such as high-tech sectors, financial services, the legal and healthcare professions, and business management. These people engage in creative problem-solving, drawing on complex bodies of knowledge to solve specific problems. Doing so typically requires a high degree of formal education and thus a high level of human capital. People who do this kind of work may sometimes come up with methods or products that turn out to be widely useful, but it's not part of the basic job description. What they are

Large Cities Creativity Rankings
Rankings of 49 metro areas reporting populations over 1 million in the 2000 Census

The Top Ten Cities	Creativity Index	% Creative Workers	Creative Rank	High-Tech Rank	Innovation Rank	Diversity Rank
1. San Francisco	1057	34.8%	5	1	2	1
2. Austin	1028	36.4%	4	11	3	16
3. San Diego	1015	32.1%	15	12	7	3
3. Boston	1015	38.0%	3	2	6	22
5. Seattle	1008	32.7%	9	3	12	8
6. Raleigh–Durham–Chapel Hill	996	38.2%	2	14	4	28
7. Houston	980	32.5%	10	16	16	10
8. Washington–Baltimore	964	38.4%	1	5	30	12
9. New York	962	32.3%	12	13	24	14
10. Dallas	960	30.2%	23	6	17	9
10. Minneapolis	960	33.9%	7	21	5	29

The Bottom Ten Cities	Creativity Index	% Creative Workers	Creative Rank	High-Tech Rank	Innovation Rank	Diversity Rank
49. Memphis	530	24.8%	47	48	42	41
48. Norfolk–Virginia Beach, VA	555	28.4%	36	35	49	47
47. Las Vegas	561	18.5%	49	42	47	5
46. Buffalo	609	28.9%	33	40	27	49
45. Louisville	622	26.5%	46	46	39	36
44. Grand Rapids, MI	639	24.3%	48	43	23	38
43. Oklahoma City	668	29.4%	29	41	43	39
42. New Orleans	668	27.5%	42	45	48	13
41. Greensboro–Winston-Salem	697	27.3%	44	33	35	35
40. Providence, RI	698	27.6%	41	44	34	33

required to do regularly is think on their own. They apply or combine standard approaches in unique ways to fit the situation, exercise a great deal of judgment, perhaps try something radically new from time to time.

Much the same is true of the growing number of technicians and others who apply complex bodies of knowledge to working with physical materials. In fields such as medicine and scientific research, technicians are taking on increased responsibility to interpret their work and make decisions, blurring the old distinction between white-collar work (done by decisionmakers) and blue-collar work (done by those who follow orders). They acquire their own arcane bodies of knowledge and develop their own unique ways of doing the job. Another example is the secretary in today's pared-down offices. In many cases this person not only takes on a host of tasks once performed by a large secretarial staff, but becomes a true office manager—channeling flows of information, devising and setting up new systems, often making key decisions on the fly. These people contribute more than intelligence or computer skills. They add creative value. Everywhere we look, creativity is increasingly valued. Firms and organizations value it for the results that it can produce and individuals value it as a route to self-expression and job satisfaction. Bottom line: As creativity becomes more valued, the creative class grows.

The creative class now includes some 38.3 million Americans, roughly 30 percent of the entire U.S. workforce—up from just 10 percent at the turn of the 20th century and less than 20 percent as recently as 1980. The creative class has considerable economic power. In 1999, the average salary for a member of the creative class was nearly $50,000 ($48,752), compared to roughly $28,000 for a working-class member and $22,000 for a service-class worker.

Not surprisingly, regions that have large numbers of creative class members are also some of the most affluent and growing.

Medium-Size Cities Creativity Rankings
Rankings of 32 metro areas reporting populations 500,000 to 1 million
in the 2000 Census

The Top Ten Cities	Creativity Index	% Creative Workers	Creative Rank	High-Tech Rank	Innovation Rank	Diversity Rank
1. Albuquerque, NM	965	32.2%	2	1	7	1
2. Albany, NY	932	33.7%	1	12	2	4
3. Tuscon, AZ	853	28.4%	17	2	6	5
4. Allentown–Bethlehem, PA	801	28.7%	16	13	3	14
5. Dayton, OH	766	30.1%	8	8	5	24
6. Colorado Springs, CO	756	29.9%	10	5	1	30
7. Harrisburg, PA	751	29.8%	11	6	13	20
8. Little Rock, AR	740	30.8%	4	10	21	11
9. Birmingham, AL	722	30.7%	6	7	26	10
10. Tulsa, OK	721	28.7%	15	9	15	18

The Bottom Ten Cities	Creativity Index	% Creative Workers	Creative Rank	High-Tech Rank	Innovation Rank	Diversity Rank
32. Youngstown, OH	253	23.8%	32	32	24	32
31. Scranton–Wilkes-Barre, PA	400	24.7%	28	23	23	31
30. McAllen, TX	451	27.8%	18	31	32	9
29. Stockton–Lodi, CA	459	24.1%	30	29	28	7
28. El Paso, TX	464	27.0%	23	27	31	17
27. Fresno, CA	516	25.1%	27	24	30	2
26. Bakersfield, CA	531	27.8%	18	22	27	19
25. Fort Wayne, IN	569	25.4%	26	17	8	26
24. Springfield, MA	577	29.7%	13	30	20	22
23. Honolulu, HI	580	27.2%	21	14	29	6

The New Geography of Class

Different classes of people have long sorted themselves into neighborhoods within a city or region. But now we find a large-scale re-sorting of people among cities and regions nationwide, with some regions becoming centers of the creative class while others are composed of larger shares of working-class or service-class people. To some extent this has always been true. For instance, there have always been artistic and cultural communities like Greenwich Village, college towns like Madison and Boulder, and manufacturing centers like Pittsburgh and Detroit. The news is that such sorting is becoming even more widespread and pronounced.

In the leading centers of this new class geography, the creative class makes up more than 35 percent of the workforce. This is already the case in the greater Washington, D.C. region, the Raleigh-Durham area, Boston, and Austin—all areas undergoing tremendous economic growth. Despite their considerable advantages, large regions have not cor-

nered the market as creative class locations. In fact, a number of smaller regions have some of the highest creative-class concentrations in the nation—notably college towns like East Lansing, Mich. and Madison, Wisc. (See chart, "Small-size Cities Creativity Rankings")

At the other end of the spectrum are regions that are being bypassed by the creative class. Among large regions, Las Vegas, Grand Rapids and Memphis harbor the smallest concentrations of the creative class. Members of this class have nearly abandoned a wide range of smaller regions in the outskirts of the South and Midwest. In small metropolitan areas like Victoria, Texas and Jackson, Tenn., the creative class comprises less than 15 percent of the workforce. The leading centers for the working class among large regions are Greensboro, N.C. and Memphis, Tenn., where the working class makes up more than 30 percent of the workforce. Several smaller regions in the South and Midwest are veritable working class enclaves with 40 to 50 percent or more of their workforce in the traditional industrial occupations.

Small-Size Cities Creativity Rankings
Rankings of 63 metro areas reporting populations 250,000 to 500,000 in the 2000 Census

The Top Ten Cities	Creativity Index	% Creative Workers	Creative Rank	High-Tech Rank	Innovation Rank	Diversity Rank
1. Madison, WI	925	32.8%	6	16	4	9
2. Des Moines, IA	862	32.1%	8	2	16	20
3. Santa Barbara, CA	856	28.3%	19	8	8	7
4. Melbourne, FL	855	35.5%	1	6	9	32
5. Boise City, ID	854	35.2%	3	1	1	46
6. Huntsville, AL	799	35.3%	2	5	18	40
7. Lansing–East Lansing, MI	739	34.3%	4	27	29	18
8. Binghamton, NY	731	30.8%	12	7	3	60
9. Lexington, KY	717	27.0%	28	24	10	12
10. New London, CT–Norwich, RI	715	28.%1	23	11	13	33

The Bottom Ten Cities	Creativity Index	% Creative Workers	Creative Rank	High-Tech Rank	Innovation Rank	Diversity Rank
63. Shreveport, LA	233	22.1%	55	32	59	57
62. Ocala, FL	263	16.4%	63	61	52	24
61. Visalia, CA	289	22.9%	52	63	60	11
60. Killeen, TX	302	24.6%	47	47	51	53
59. Fayetteville, NC	309	29.0%	16	62	62	49
58. York, PA	360	22.3%	54	54	26	52
57. Fayetteville, AR	366	21.1%	57	57	42	17
56. Beaumont, TX	372	27.8%	25	37	56	55
55. Lakeland–Winter Haven, FL	385	20.9%	59	56	53	5
54. Hickory, NC	393	19.4%	61	48	32	30

These places have some of the most minuscule concentrations of the creative class in the nation. They are symptomatic of a general lack of overlap between the major creative-class centers and those of the working class. Of the 26 large cities where the working class comprises more than one-quarter of the population, only one, Houston, ranks among the top 10 destinations for the creative class.

Chicago, a bastion of working-class people that still ranks among the top 20 large creative centers, is interesting because it shows how the creative class and the traditional working class can coexist. But Chicago has an advantage in that it is a big city, with more than a million members of the creative class. The University of Chicago sociologist Terry Clark likes to say Chicago developed an innovative political and cultural solution to this issue. Under the second Mayor Daley, the city integrated the members of the creative class into the city's culture and politics by treating them essentially as just another "ethnic group" that needed sufficient space to express its identity.

The plug-and-play community is one that somebody can move into and put together a life—or at least a facsimile of a life—in a week.

Las Vegas has the highest concentration of the service class among large cities, 58 percent, while West Palm Beach, Orlando, and Miami also have around half. These regions rank near the bottom of the list for the creative class. The service class makes up more than half the workforce in nearly 50 small and medium-size regions across the country. Few of them boast any significant concentrations of the creative class, save vacationers, and offer little prospect for upward mobility. They include resort towns like Honolulu and Cape Cod. But they also include places like Shreveport, Lou. and Pittsfield, Mass. For these places that are not tourist destinations, the economic and social future is troubling to contemplate.

Plug-and-Play Communities

Why do some places become destinations for the creative while others don't? Economists speak of the importance of industries having "low entry barriers," so that new firms can easily enter and keep the industry vital. Similarly, I think it's important for a place to have low entry barriers for people— that is, to be a place where newcomers are accepted quickly into all sorts of social and economic arrangements. All else being equal, they are likely to attract greater numbers of talented and creative people—the sort of people who power innovation and growth. Places that thrive in today's world tend to be plug-and-play communities where anyone can fit in quickly. These are places where people can find opportunity, build support structures, be themselves, and not get stuck in any one identity. The plug-and-play community is one that somebody can move into and put together a life—or at least a facsimile of a life—in a week.

Creative centers also tend to be places with thick labor markets that can fulfill the employment needs of members of the creative class, who, by and large, are not looking just for "a job" but for places that offer many employment opportunities.

Cities and regions that attract lots of creative talent are also those with greater diversity and higher levels of quality of place. That's because location choices of the creative class are based to a large degree on their lifestyle interests, and these go well beyond the standard "quality-of-life" amenities that most experts think are important.

The list of the country's high-tech hot spots looks an awful lot like the list of the places with highest concentrations of gay people.

For instance, in 1998, I met Gary Gates, then a doctoral student at Carnegie Mellon. While I had been studying the location choices of high-tech industries and talented people, Gates had been exploring the location patterns of gay people. My list of the country's high-tech hot spots looked an awful lot like his list of the places with highest concentrations of gay people. When we compared these two lists with more statistical rigor, his Gay Index turned out to correlate very strongly to my own measures of high-tech growth. Other measures I came up with, like the Bohemian Index—a measure of artists, writers, and performers—produced similar results.

Talented people seek an environment open to differences. Many highly creative people, regardless of ethnic background or sexual orientation, grew up feeling like outsiders, different in some way from most of their schoolmates. When they are sizing up a new company and community, acceptance of diversity and of gays in particular is a sign that reads "non-standard people welcome here."

The creative class people I study use the word "diversity" a lot, but not to press any political hot buttons. Diversity is simply something they value in all its manifestations. This is spoken of so often, and so matter-of-factly, that I take it to be a fundamental marker of creative class values. Creative-minded people enjoy a mix of influences. They want to hear different kinds of music and try different kinds of food. They want to meet and socialize with people unlike themselves, trade views and spar over issues.

As with employers, visible diversity serves as a signal that a community embraces the open meritocratic values of the creative age. The people I talked to also desired nightlife with a wide mix of options. The most highly valued options were experiential ones—interesting music venues, neighborhood art galleries, performance spaces, and theaters. A vibrant, varied nightlife was viewed by many as another signal that a city "gets it," even by those who infrequently partake in nightlife. More than anything, the creative class craves real experiences in the real world.

They favor active, participatory recreation over passive, institutionalized forms. They prefer indigenous street-level culture—a teeming blend of cafes, sidewalk musicians, and small galleries and bistros, where it is hard to draw the line between performers and spectators. They crave stimulation, not escape. They want to pack their time full of dense, high-quality, multidimensional experiences. Seldom has one of my subjects expressed a desire to get away from it all. They want to get into it all, and do it with eyes wide open.

Creative class people value active outdoor recreation very highly. They are drawn to places and communities where many outdoor activities are prevalent—both because they enjoy these activities and because their presence is seen as a signal that the place is amenable to the broader creative lifestyle. The creative-class people in my studies are into a variety of active sports, from traditional ones like bicycling, jogging, and kayaking to newer, more extreme ones, like trail running and snowboarding.

Places are also valued for authenticity and uniqueness. Authenticity comes from several aspects of a community— historic buildings, established neighborhoods, a unique music scene, or specific cultural attributes. It comes from the mix—from urban grit alongside renovated buildings, from the commingling of young and old, long-time neighborhood characters and yuppies, fashion models and "bag ladies." An authentic place also offers unique and original experiences. Thus a place full of chain stores, chain restaurants, and nightclubs is not authentic. You could have the same experience anywhere.

Today, it seems, leading creative centers provide a solid mix of high-tech industry, plentiful outdoor amenities, and an older urban center whose rebirth has been fueled in part by a combination of creativity and innovative technology, as well as lifestyle amenities. These include places like the greater Boston area, which has the Route 128 suburban complex, Harvard and MIT, and several charming inner-city Boston neighborhoods. Seattle has suburban Bellevue and Redmond (where Microsoft is located), beautiful mountains and country, and a series of revitalized urban neighborhoods. The San Francisco Bay area has everything from posh inner-city neighborhoods to ultra-hip districts like SoMa (South of Market) and lifestyle enclaves like Marin County as well as the Silicon Valley. Even Austin includes traditional high-tech developments to the north, lifestyle centers for cycling and outdoor activities, and a revitalizing university/ downtown community centered on vibrant Sixth Street, the warehouse district and the music scene—a critical element of a thriving creative center.

Institutional Sclerosis

Even as places like Austin and Seattle are thriving, much of the country is failing to adapt to the demands of the creative age. It is not that struggling cities like Pittsburgh do not want to grow or encourage high-tech industries. In most cases, their leaders are doing everything they think they can to spur innovation and high-tech growth. But most of the time, they are either unwilling or unable to do the things required to create an environment or habitat attractive to the creative class. They pay lip service to the need to "attract talent," but continue to pour resources into recruiting call centers, underwriting big-box retailers, subsidizing downtown malls, and squandering precious taxpayer dollars on extravagant stadium complexes. Or they try to create facsimiles of neighborhoods or retail districts, replacing the old and authentic with the new and generic—and in doing so drive the creative class away.

It is a telling commentary on our age that at a time when political will seems difficult to muster for virtually anything, city after city can generate the political capital to underwrite hundreds of millions of dollars of investments in professional sports stadiums. And you know what? They don't matter to the creative class. Not once during any of my focus groups and interviews did the members of the creative class mention professional sports as playing a role of any sort in their choice of where to live and work. What makes most cities unable to even imagine devoting those kinds of resources or political will to do the things that people say really matter to them?

The answer is simple. These cities are trapped by their past. Despite the lip service they might pay, they are unwilling or unable to do what it takes to attract the creative class. The late economist Mancur Olson long ago noted that the decline of nations and regions is a product of an organizational and cultural hardening of the arteries he called "institutional sclerosis." Places that grow up and prosper in one era, Olson argued, find it difficult and often times impossible to adopt new organizational and cultural patterns, regardless of how beneficial they might be. Consequently, innovation and growth shift to new places, which can adapt to and harness these shifts for their benefit. This phenomenon, he contends, is how England got trapped and how the U.S. became the world's great economic power. It also accounts for the shift in economic activity from the old industrial cities to newer cities in the South and West, according to Olson.

Olson's analysis presciently identifies why so many cities across the nation remain trapped in the culture and attitudes of the bygone organizational age, unable or unwilling to adapt to current trends. Cities like Detroit, Cleveland, and my current hometown of Pittsburgh were at the forefront of the organizational age. The cultural and attitudinal norms of that age became so powerfully ingrained in these places that they did not allow the new norms and attitudes associated with the creative age to grow up, diffuse and become generally accepted. This process, in turn, stamped out much of the creative impulse, causing talented and creative people to seek out new places where they could more readily plug in and make a go of it.

Most experts and scholars have not even begun to think in terms of a creative community. Instead, they tend to try to emulate the Silicon Valley model which author Joel Kotkin has dubbed the "nerdistan." But the nerdistan is a limited economic development model, which misunderstands the role played by creativity in generating innovation and economic growth. Nerdistans are bland, uninteresting places with acre upon acre of identical office complexes, row after row of asphalt parking lots, freeways clogged with cars, cookie-cutter housing developments, and strip-malls sprawling in every direction. Many of these places have fallen victim to the very kinds of problems they were supposed to avoid. The comfort and security of places like Silicon Valley have gradually given way to sprawl, pollution, and paralyzing traffic jams. As one technology executive told *The Wall Street Journal*, "I really didn't want to live in San Jose. Every time I went up there, the concrete jungle got me down." His company eventually settled on a more urban Southern California location in downtown Pasadena close to the CalTech campus.

Kotkin finds that the lack of lifestyle amenities is causing significant problems in attracting top creative people to places like the North Carolina Research Triangle. He quotes a major real estate developer as saying, "Ask anyone where downtown is and nobody can tell you. There's not much of a sense of place here....The people I am selling space to are screaming about cultural issues." The Research Triangle lacks the hip urban lifestyle found in places like San Francisco, Seattle, New York, and Chicago, laments a University of North Carolina researcher: "In Raleigh-Durham, we can always visit the hog farms."

The Kids Are All Right

How do you build a truly creative community—one that can survive and prosper in this emerging age? The key can no longer be found in the usual strategies. Recruiting more companies won't do it; neither will trying to become the next

Silicon Valley. While it certainly remains important to have a solid business climate, having an effective people climate is even more essential. By this I mean a general strategy aimed at attracting and retaining people—especially, but not limited to, creative people. This entails remaining open to diversity and actively working to cultivate it, and investing in the lifestyle amenities that people really want and use often, as opposed to using financial incentives to attract companies, build professional sports stadiums, or develop retail complexes.

The benefits of this kind of strategy are obvious. Whereas companies—or sports teams, for that matter—that get financial incentives can pull up and leave at virtually a moment's notice, investments in amenities like urban parks, for example, last for generations. Other amenities—like bike lanes or off-road trails for running, cycling, rollerblading, or just walking your dog—benefit a wide swath of the population.

There is no one-size-fits-all model for a successful people climate. The members of the creative class are diverse across the dimensions of age, ethnicity and race, marital status, and sexual preference. An effective people climate needs to emphasize openness and diversity, and to help reinforce low barriers to entry. Thus, it cannot be restrictive or monolithic.

Openness to immigration is particularly important for smaller cities and regions, while the ability to attract so-called bohemians is key for larger cities and regions. For cities and regions to attract these groups, they need to develop the kinds of people climates that appeal to them and meet their needs.

Yet if you ask most community leaders what kinds of people they'd most want to attract, they'd likely say successful married couples in their 30s and 40s—people with good middle-to-upper-income jobs and stable family lives. I certainly think it is important for cities and communities to be good for children and families. But less than a quarter of all American households consist of traditional nuclear families, and focusing solely on their needs has been a losing strategy, one that neglects a critical engine of economic growth: young people.

Young workers have typically been thought of as transients who contribute little to a city's bottom line. But in the creative age, they matter for two reasons. First, they are workhorses. They are able to work longer and harder, and are more prone to take risks, precisely because they are young and childless. In rapidly changing industries, it's often the most recent graduates who have the most up-to-date skills. Second, people are staying single longer. The average age of marriage for both men and women has risen some five years over the past generation. College-educated people postpone marriage longer than the national averages. Among this group, one of the fastest growing categories is the never-been-married. To prosper in the creative age, regions have to offer a people climate that satisfies this group's social interests and lifestyle needs, as well as address those of other groups.

Furthermore, a climate oriented to young people is also attractive to the creative class more broadly. Creative-class people do not lose their lifestyle preferences as they age. They don't stop bicycling or running, for instance, just because they have children. When they put their children in child seats or jogging strollers, amenities like traffic-free bike paths become more important than ever. They also continue to value diversity and tolerance. The middle-aged and older people I speak with may no longer hang around in nightspots until 4 a.m., but they enjoy stimulating, dynamic places with high levels of cultural interplay. And if they have children, that's the kind of environment in which they want them to grow up.

My adopted hometown of Pittsburgh has been slow to realize this. City leaders continue to promote Pittsburgh as a place that is good for families, seemingly unaware of the demographic changes that have made young people, singles, new immigrants, and gays critical to the emerging social fabric. People in focus groups I have conducted feel that Pittsburgh is not open to minority groups, new immigrants, or gays. Young women feel there are substantial barriers to their advancement. Talented members of racial and ethnic minorities, as well as professional women, express their desire to leave the city at a rate far greater than their white male counterparts. So do creative people from all walks of life.

Is there hope for Pittsburgh? Of course there is. First, although the region's economy is not dynamic, neither is it the basket case it could easily have become. Twenty years ago there were no significant venture capital firms in the area; now there are many, and thriving high-tech firms continue to form and make their mark. There are signs of life in the social and cultural milieu as well. The region's immigrant population has begun to tick upward, fed by students and professors at the universities and employees in the medical and technology sectors. Major suburbs to the east of the city now have Hindu temples and a growing Indian-American population. The area's gay community, while not large, has become more active and visible. Pittsburgh's increasing status in the gay world is reflected in the fact that it is the "location" for Showtime's "Queer as Folk" series.

Many of Pittsburgh's creative class have proven to be relentless cultural builders. The Andy Warhol Museum and the Mattress Factory, a museum/workspace devoted to large-scale installation art, have achieved worldwide recognition. Street-level culture has a growing foothold in Pittsburgh, too, as main street corridors in several older working-class districts have been transformed. Political leaders are in some cases open to new models of development. Pittsburgh mayor Tom Murphy has been an ardent promoter of biking and foot trails, among other things. The city's absolutely first-rate architecture and urban design community has become much more vocal about the need to preserve historic buildings, invest in neighborhoods, and institute tough design standards. It would be very hard today (dare I say nearly impossible) to knock down historic buildings and dismember vibrant urban neighborhoods as was done in the past. As these new groups and efforts reach critical mass, the norms and attitudes that have long prevailed in the city are being challenged.

For what it's worth, I'll put my money—and a lot of my effort—into Pittsburgh's making it. If Pittsburgh, with all of its assets and its emerging human creativity, somehow can't make it in the creative age, I fear the future does not bode well for other older industrial communities and established cities, and the lamentable new class segregation among cities will continue to worsen.

RICHARD FLORIDA is a professor of regional economic development at Carnegie Mellon University and a columnist for Information Week. This article was adapted from his forthcoming book, *The Rise of the Creative Class: and How It's Transforming Work, Leisure, Community and Everyday Life* (Basic Books)

Giving Away the Store to Get a Store

Tax increment financing is no bargain for taxpayers.

DANIEL MCGRAW

If you're imagining an attraction that will draw 4.5 million out-of-town visitors a year, the first thing that jumps to mind probably isn't a store that sells guns and fishing rods and those brown jackets President Bush wears to clear brush at his ranch in Crawford, Texas. Yet last year Cabela's, a Nebraska-based hunting and fishing mega-store chain with annual sales of $1.7 billion, persuaded the politicians of Fort Worth that bringing the chain to an affluent and growing area north of the city was worth $30 million to $40 million in tax breaks. They were told that the store, the centerpiece of a new retail area, would draw more tourists than the Alamo in San Antonio or the annual State Fair of Texas in Dallas, both of which attract 2.5 million visitors a year.

The decision was made easier by the financing plan that Fort Worth will use to accommodate Cabela's. The site of the Fort Worth Cabela's has been designated a tax increment financing (TIF) district, which means taxes on the property will be frozen for 20 to 30 years.

Largely because it promises something for nothing—an economic stimulus in exchange for tax revenue that otherwise would not materialize—this tool is becoming increasingly popular across the country. Originally used to help revive blighted or depressed areas, TIFs now appear in affluent neighborhoods, subsidizing high-end housing developments, big-box retailers, and shopping malls. And since most cities are using TIFs, businesses such as Cabela's can play them off against each other to boost the handouts they receive simply to operate profit-making enterprises.

A Crummy Way to Treat Taxpaying Citizens

TIFs have been around for more than 50 years, but only recently have they assumed such importance. At a time when local governments' efforts to foster development, from direct subsidies to the use of eminent domain to seize property for private development, are already out of control, TIFs only add to the problem: Although politicians portray TIFs as a great way to boost the local economy, there are hidden costs they don't want taxpayers to know about. Cities generally assume they are not really giving anything up because the forgone tax revenue would not have been available in the absence of the development generated by the TIF. That assumption is often wrong.

"There is always this expectation with TIFs that the economic growth is a way to create jobs and grow the economy, but then push the costs across the public spectrum," says Greg LeRoy, author of *The Great American Jobs Scam: Corporate Tax Dodging and the Myth of Job Creation*. "But what is missing here is that the cost of developing private business has some public costs. Road and sewers and schools are public costs that come from growth." Unless spending is cut—and if a TIF really does generate economic growth, spending is likely to rise, as the local population grows—the burden of paying for these services will be shifted to other taxpayers. Adding insult to injury, those taxpayers may include small businesses facing competition from well-connected chains that enjoy TIF-related tax breaks. In effect, a TIF subsidizes big businesses at the expense of less politically influential competitors and ordinary citizens.

"The original concept of TIFs was to help blighted areas come out of the doldrums and get some economic development they wouldn't [otherwise] have a chance of getting," says former Fort Worth City Councilman Clyde Picht, who voted against the Cabela's TIF. "Everyone probably gets a big laugh out of their claim that they will draw more tourists than the Alamo. But what is worse, and not talked about too much, is the shift of taxes being paid from wealthy corporations to small businesses and regular people.

"If you own a mom-and-pop store that sells fishing rods and hunting gear in Fort Worth, you're still paying all your taxes, and the city is giving tax breaks to Cabela's that could put you out of business," Picht explains. "The rest of us pay taxes for normal services like public safety, building inspections, and street maintenance, and those services come out of the general fund. And as the cost of services goes up, and the money from the general fund is given to these businesses through a TIF, the tax burden gets shifted to the regular slobs who don't have the same political clout. It's a crummy way to treat your taxpaying, law-abiding citizens."

Almost every state has a TIF law, and the details vary from jurisdiction to jurisdiction. But most TIFs share the same general characteristics. After a local government has designated a TIF district, property taxes (and sometimes sales taxes) from the area are divided into two streams. The first tax stream is based on the original assessed value of the property before any redevelopment; the city, county, school district, or other taxing body still gets that money. The second stream is the additional tax money generated after development takes place and the property values are higher. Typically that revenue is used to pay off municipal bonds that raise money for infrastructure improvements in the TIF district, for land acquisition through eminent domain, or for direct payments to a private developer for site preparation and construction. The length of time the taxes are diverted to pay for the bonds can be anywhere from seven to 30 years.

Local governments sell the TIF concept to the public by claiming they are using funds that would not have been generated without the TIF district. If the land was valued at $10 million before TIF-associated development and is worth $50 million afterward, the argument goes, the $40 million increase in tax value can be used to retire the bonds. Local governments also like to point out that the TIF district may increase nearby economic activity, which will be taxed at full value.

So, in the case of Cabela's in Fort Worth, the TIF district was created to build roads and sewers and water systems, to move streams and a lake to make the property habitable, and to help defray construction costs for the company. Cabela's likes this deal because the money comes upfront, without any interest. Their taxes are frozen, and the bonds are paid off by what would have gone into city coffers. In effect, the city is trading future tax income for a present benefit.

But even if the dedicated tax money from a TIF district suffices to pay off the bonds, that doesn't mean the arrangement is cost-free. "TIFs are being pushed out there right now based upon the 'but for' test," says Greg LeRoy. "What cities are saying is that no development would take place but for the TIF.... The average public official says this is free money, because it wouldn't happen otherwise. But when you see how it plays out, the whole premise of TIFs begins to crumble." Rather than spurring development, LeRoy argues, TIFs "move some economic development from one part of a city to another."

Development Would Have Occurred Anyway

Local officials usually do not consider how much growth might occur without a TIF. In 2002 the Neighborhood Capital Budget Group (NCBG), a coalition of 200 Chicago organizations that studies local public investment, looked at 36 of the city's TIF districts and found that property values were rising in all of them during the five years before they were designated as TIFs. The NCBG projected that the city of Chicago would capture $1.6 billion in second-stream property tax revenue—used to pay off the bonds that subsidized private businesses—over the 23-year

life spans of these TIF districts. But it also found that $1.3 billion of that revenue would have been raised anyway, assuming the areas continued growing at their pre-TIF rates.

The experience in Chicago is important. The city invested $1.6 billion in TIFs, even though $1.3 billion in economic development would have occurred anyway. So the bottom line is that the city invested $1.6 billion for $300 million in revenue growth.

The upshot is that TIFs are diverting tax money that otherwise would have been used for government services. The NCBG study found, for instance, that the 36 TIF districts would cost Chicago public schools $632 million (based on development that would have occurred anyway) in property tax revenue, because the property tax rates are frozen for schools as well. This doesn't merely mean that the schools get more money. If the economic growth occurs with TIFs, that attracts people to the area and thereby raises enrollments. In that case, the cost of teaching the new students will be borne by property owners outside the TIF districts.

"Money from the general fund is given to these businesses through a TIF, [then] the tax burden gets shifted to the regular slobs who don't have the same political clout."
—Fort Worth City Councilman Clyde Picht

Such concerns have had little impact so far, in part because almost no one has examined how TIFs succeed or fail over the long term. Local politicians are touting TIFs as a way to promote development, promising no new taxes, and then setting them up without looking at potential side effects. It's hard to discern exactly how many TIFs operate in this country, since not every state requires their registration. But the number has expanded exponentially, especially over the past decade. Illinois, which had one TIF district in 1970, now has 874 (including one in the town of Wilmington, population 129). A moderate-sized city like Janesville, Wisconsin—a town of 60,000 about an hour from Madison—has accumulated 26 TIFs. Delaware and Arizona are the only states without TIF laws, and most observers expect they will get on board soon.

First used in California in the 1950s, TIFs were supposed to be another tool, like tax abatement and enterprise zones, that could be used to promote urban renewal. But cities found they were not very effective at drawing development into depressed areas. "They had this tool, but didn't know what the tool was good for," says Art Lyons, an analyst for the Chicago-based Center for Economic Policy Analysis, an economic think tank that works with community groups. The cities realized, Lyons theorizes, that if they wanted to use TIFs more, they had to get out of depressed neighborhoods and into areas with higher property values, which generate more tax revenue to pay off development bonds.

The Entire Western World Could Be Blighted

Until the 1990s, most states reserved TIFs for areas that could be described as "blighted," based on criteria set forth by statute. But as with eminent domain, the definition of blight for TIF purposes has been dramatically expanded. In 1999, for example, Baraboo, Wisconsin, created a TIF for an industrial park and a Wal-Mart supercenter that were built on farmland; the blight label was based on a single house in the district that was uninhabited. In recent years 16 states have relaxed their TIF criteria to cover affluent areas, "conservation areas" where blight might occur someday, or "economic development areas," loosely defined as commercial or industrial properties.

The result is that a TIF can be put almost anywhere these days. Based on current criteria, says Jake Haulk, director of the Pittsburgh-based Allegheny Institute for Public Policy, you could "declare the entire Western world blighted."

In the late 1990s, Pittsburgh decided to declare a commercial section of its downtown blighted so it could create a TIF district for the Lazarus Department Store. The construction of the new store and a nearby parking garage cost the city more than $70 million. But the property taxes on the new store were lower than expected, as the downtown area surrounding Lazarus never took off the way the city thought it would. Sales tax receipts were also unexpectedly low. Lazarus decided to close the store last year, and the property is still on the block. Because other businesses were included in the TIF, it is impossible to predict whether the city will be on the hook for the entire $70 million. But given that the Lazarus store was the centerpiece of the development, it is safe to say this TIF is not working very well, and Pittsburgh's taxpayers may have to pick up the tab.

The definition of blight for TIF purposes has been dramatically expanded. Baraboo, Wisconsin, created a TIF for an industrial park and a Wal-Mart that were built on farmland; the "blight" was based on a single uninhabited house.

If businesses like Lazarus cannot reliably predict their own success, urban planners can hardly be expected to do a better job. Typically, big corporations come to small cities towing consultants who trot out rosy numbers, and the politicians see a future that may not materialize in five or 10 years. "The big buzzwords are economic development," says Chris Slowik, organizational director for the South Cooperative Organization for Public Education (SCOPE), which represents about 45 school districts in the southern suburbs of Chicago, each of which includes at least one TIF. "The local governments see a vacant space and see something they like that some company might bring in. But no one thinks about what the costs might be.... They are giving away the store to get a store." Big-box retail chains such as Target and Wal-Mart seem to be the most frequent beneficiaries of TIFs. (Neither company would comment for this story, and local politicians generally shied away as well.)

Given the competition between cities eager to attract new businesses, TIFS are not likely to disappear anytime soon. "Has it gone overboard?" asks University of North Texas economist Terry Clower. "Sure.... But the problem is that if a city doesn't offer some tax incentives, the company will just move down the road." According to Clower, "In a utopian world, there would be no government handouts, and every business would pay the same tax rate. But if a city stands up and says they aren't doing [TIFs] anymore, they will lose out."

Instead, it's the competitors of TIF-favored businesses that lose out. Academy Sports & Outdoors, which employs 6,500 people, has about 80 sporting goods stores in eight Southern states, including a store in Fort Worth. When the Fort Worth City Council was considering the TIF for Cabela's, Academy Sports Chairman David Gochman spoke out against the tax incentives, realizing that his company is a big business, but not big enough. "This is not a nonprofit, not a library, not a school," he said. "They are a for-profit business, a competitor of ours, along with Oshman's and Wal-Mart and others."

TIFs Have Become the Standard Handout

Al Dalton, owner of Texas Outdoors, a 10,000-square-foot hunting and fishing shop in Fort Worth, echoed the sentiment that the city was favoring one business over another. "We don't have the buying power, and we don't have the advertising dollars," Dalton said. "It doesn't make any difference even if we've got the best price in town if nobody knows about it. The deep pockets, in every way, [make] a lot of difference."

And that may be the key to understanding how TIFs are now applied: The companies with the deep pockets are able to fill them with subsidies.

The Cabela's location in Fort Worth does not fit any of the blight criteria people had in mind when TIFs were first created. The 225,000-square-foot store, with its waterfalls, multitude of stuffed animals, and wild game cafe, sits on prime property just off Interstate 35. It is a few miles down the road from the Texas Motor Speedway (which has its own TIF), and the 200,000 NASCAR and IRL fans who attend races there three times a year—not to mention the fans who come to the speedway's concerts and other special events—might want to shop at Cabela's.

The area around Cabela's is affluent and has been growing for years. A half-dozen shopping centers nearby were on the drawing board well before the TIF was considered. Within a five-mile radius of the hunting/fishing megastore, 10,000 new homes have been built since 2000. That same area is expected to grow by 20,000 people in the next two years.

But the argument against the "but for" assumption is not being heard. In 2004 a state judge threw out a lawsuit against the Cabela's TIF by a Fort Worth citizens' group that claimed blight was never proven, and that the city was misusing TIFs in a prosperous area that needed no tax breaks for future development. The blight designation came from a pond and stream on the property. It was an odd designation, given that the property is in a prime development area and ponds and streams are not what one would classify as blighted.

The press releases and newspaper articles about the new Cabela's emphasize that the store is going to draw more people to Texas than visit the Alamo (the studies were done by Cabela's). The press release never mentions that a Bass Pro Shop store, part of a chain almost identical to Cabela's, is just 10 miles down the road. While Cabela's was negotiating its TIF with Fort Worth, it was also negotiating a TIF with the city of Buda, 120 miles away, outside of Austin. Cabela's got about $20 million from Buda, and the same tourist claims are being made there. If each Texas store is going to draw 4.5 million tourists, as the chain claims, that means 9 million people will be coming to Texas every year just to visit the two Cabela's stores.

"The notion that a hunting store would draw all these tourists is ridiculous," says Greg LeRoy. "But what is even more ridiculous is cities thinking that tax breaks are the primary reason businesses relocate or expand in certain areas. There are so many other factors at play—transportation costs, good employment available, housing costs and quality of life for executives—that the tax breaks like TIFs aren't very high up on their priority list. But these corporations are asking for them—and getting them—because everyone is giving them out. TIFs have become the standard handout, and the businesses have learned how to play one city off the other. Businesses would be stupid for not asking for them every time."

If TIFs continue to multiply at the present rate, we may see the day when every new 7-Eleven and McDonald's has its own TIF. That prospect may seem farfetched, but it wasn't too long ago that cities wouldn't even have considered giving up tens of millions of dollars in exchange for yet another store selling guns and fishing rods.

Daniel McGraw (danielmcgraw@sbcglobal.net), freelance writer in Fort Worth, is the author of *First and Last Seasons: A Father, A Son and Sunday Afternoon Football* (Random House).

Money for Nothing

Activists across America are contesting corporate giveaways—and winning.

BOBBI MURRAY

This article is part of our "What Works" series, which explores effective strategies for improving people's lives through progressive social change.

—The Editors

It was the dream of economic development that inspired officials in Caledonia, Minnesota, to give a Dairy Queen franchise a $275,000 tax subsidy in 1996. One problem: The largesse created exactly one job, at $4.50 an hour. The return on public investment wasn't much better in Pennsylvania a year later when the state—led by then-Governor Tom Ridge—and the City of Philadelphia ponied up $307 million worth of incentives to persuade Kvaerner ASA, a Norwegian global construction company, to reopen a section of Philadelphia's moribund shipyard. That created 950 jobs that paid around $50,000 a year—not bad, until you calculate the cost to taxpayers: $323,000 per job.

Mercedes-Benz cadged $253 million in state and local incentives in 1993 to build a plant near Tuscaloosa, Alabama. The school in the adjacent small town of Vance lacks the funding to add permanent classrooms to meet capacity, while Mercedes employees enjoy a $30 million training center built at taxpayer expense. The jobs created cost the public $168,000 each.

Despite such boondoggles, it's been accepted as nothing less than gospel that public bodies must give out subsidies to private companies to fuel economic growth. State and municipal leaders dished out an estimated $48.8 billion in subsidies, tax breaks and other incentives to corporations in 1996, the last time the figure was calculated; a more recent figure would likely top $50 billion, says Greg LeRoy, founder of the Washington, DC-based Good Jobs First and author of *No More Candy Store: States and Cities Making Job Subsidies Accountable.*

The amount of money is even more mind-boggling in light of the fact that much of it is given away no strings attached—without any explicit agreement regarding the numbers and quality of jobs created, or even guidelines on environmental and community impact. "The stuff that corporations call economic development is pretty shabby if you kick the tires," LeRoy says.

In the quest for economic development, states and regions lower their expectations on adherence to environmental regulations and what kinds of jobs are created, frantically bidding

each other up beyond the limits of reason. Municipalities in Tennessee, Alabama, Arkansas and Mississippi competed for a Toyota plant last year with incentive packages as high as $500 million. Some of the alluring offers included free land and the naming rights for a sports stadium.

In 1998, then-New York City Mayor Rudy Giuliani championed what may be the biggest subsidy package ever—$1.4 billion in enticements to retain the New York Stock Exchange in Manhattan after NYSE officials made noises about moving to New Jersey. That state's Business Employment Incentive Program had successfully lured such big names as Goldman Sachs, Merrill Lynch and JP Morgan from New York City by offering a total of $710 million in inducements over six years.

The taxpayer's tab on the NYSE deal included a $450 million land purchase, $480 million in cash and $160 million in tax incentives. The NYSE plan eventually unraveled and was declared dead this past February, though taxpayers were still in for an estimated $109 million—just to bail out.

Surprisingly, Giuliani's successor, Michael Bloomberg, founder of capital's town crier, *Bloomberg News*, stood firm against the NYSE decampment threat and has generally been less than enthused about the notion of dishing out money to retain companies in Manhattan. Before being elected he said, "Any company that makes a decision as to where they are going to be based on the tax rate is a company that won't be around very long."

Nevertheless, after 9/11, the public paid out some eye-popping sums to retain companies in lower Manhattan. The Bank of New York got some $40 million, while American Express, whose building is adjacent to the World Trade Center site, got $25 million, even after company leaders had already elected to stay.

The money came from $2.7 billion in community development grants administered by the Lower Manhattan Development Corporation, a city/state collaboration that has already doled out some $1 billion to businesses affected by the attacks, including corporate giants. The Labor Community Advocacy Network to Rebuild New York (LCAN), a coalition of more than fifty unions, community organizations and environmental-justice groups, estimates that the terror attacks cost New York 80,000 to 100,000 jobs. LCAN representatives have been lobbying hard for the remaining $1.2 billion to be used to create 25,000 fully subsidized public-service jobs and 35,000 partially subsidized private-sector jobs.

Good Jobs New York (an affiliate of LeRoy's Good Jobs First) and LCAN have only begun to insert themselves into New York's subsidy debate, but their efforts are emblematic of a national movement that's grown up over the past decade to contest corporate welfare, push back-room deals into the light and attach strings to public economic development dollars. Hundreds of activists gathered in July 2000 in Baltimore to share strategies at a first-ever conference of its kind; in November, Good Jobs First and other leading accountability activists will join labor allies in Milwaukee to press these issues at the annual gathering of the AFL-CIO's Working for America Institute.

Activists call it a movement for "accountable economic development," a phrase that doesn't begin to describe the dynamic range of political work going on, from a campaign in California to limit sprawl while bringing jobs and services to urban centers to a union lockout fight in Ohio, not to mention the widespread push to attach wage conditions to subsidy-based hires.

It's a sign of the times that few, if any, campaigns in the movement call for a subsidies cutoff. The role of government, under unflagging attack by the right for more than twenty years, has been increasingly supplanted by privatization, says Madeline Janis-Aparicio, co-founder and executive director of the Los Angeles Alliance for a New Economy. Opposition to subsidies is simply not winnable in most places, she argues, but public monies used for development give grassroots groups a chance to wedge into the debate and shape it from the beginning, to assess what a community really wants and fight for it.

'We are the pro-growth alternative,' says a Los Angeles activist. 'If they want to get past the NIMBYs, they have to deal with us.'

Some development should be flatly opposed, she says. "There are times when a project is so bad, it should just be stopped in its tracks. Like Wal-Mart. It's a death star, killing all the local businesses." But in general she believes—as does the accountability movement as a whole—in a strategy of engagement. "Public investment is sometimes really needed in blighted communities," she says. "We need the right kind." To oppose all subsidies, she says, would be to "give up our place at the table."

For many organizations, the ground-floor fight is for information. Their battles center on local disclosure measures that require companies to reveal the figures on incentives received and jobs created. Public subsidies spew from so many spigots, it's often hard to identify all the sources and quantify the amount of public benefits any given company gets. The information provides the road map for subsequent accountability fights. Nine states now have some form of disclosure legislation that covers one or more subsidy programs.

The Minnesota Alliance for Progressive Action (MAPA), a coalition of twenty-eight organizations, pushed through the first

and toughest disclosure law in 1995, which was subsequently strengthened even further. Minnesota's laws require public hearings that expose the details of subsidy agreements and provide an opening for demanding living-wage rules or other provisions. Beneficiary companies must make public their job-creation goals and wage structures, while the government body offering the subsidy has to report the amount and types of incentives it hands over. "We've got them on record if they're getting a bunch of money and giving nothing," says MAPA executive director Scott Cooper. MAPA is now working with organizations in North Dakota, Wisconsin and Iowa on crafting parallel disclosure legislation.

Stakes were high and the struggle grueling in Ohio three years ago, when an annual tax abatement to AK Steel became the target of a Steelworkers local. The county and city had granted AK Steel in Mansfield a $1.7 million annual tax abatement since 1993; in 1995 the local governments even lowered the hiring requirement from 1,140 workers to 700 and the payroll minimum from $49.3 million to $32.5 million.

So after AK Steel charged its 620 union workers with misconduct and locked them out, "The only way we could generate some economic leverage was to go after their tax abatement," says Tony Montana, a spokesperson for the United Steelworkers of America. The union argued that since the lockout brought AK way below its promised worker and payroll levels, the subsidy was vulnerable.

Unionists first launched a campaign in the summer of 2000 in support of a measure, Issue 7, that got on the ballot due to the signature-collecting work of scores of grassroots activists. The measure wouldn't have directly affected AK Steel's subsidy, but it would have reordered the way Mansfield doled out incentives, setting certain requirements for local hiring, a living wage and disclosure. It was soundly trounced in November after the mayor, the City Council president and the Chamber of Commerce joined forces to raise a $250,000 war chest to fight it. "It's symptomatic of a problem on a national scale," Montana says. "The City Council was more interested in making Mansfield a friendly place for business than making businesses live up to their promises."

Then the union carried the fight to the moribund Tax Incentive Review Council of Richland County, which is charged with overseeing some 200 local subsidies—but which had no regular open meetings and conducted most business by phone. Unionists revived the board, packed meetings of the City Council and county commissions, took their case to the media—and won. They forced the review council to commit to annual public meetings, which now attract great public interest. And in March 2002, the council reviewed AK Steel's performance and cut its subsidy by a third. That December AK Steel ended the lockout.

"It was a long, nasty struggle," Montana says, "and it's still not fully resolved." But, as far as subsidy accountability goes, "if we were able to do it in Mansfield with a bunch of locked-out workers and zero budget, we should be able to do it anywhere."

For grassroots accountability organizing, California is the gold standard. There, a decade-old pathfinder, the Los Angeles

Alliance for a New Economy (LAANE), came up with a new accountability concept that has caught national attention in the movement: community benefits agreements. The agreements include job standards and more.

In 2001 LAANE leveraged $29 million in city subsidies to a mixed-use development in a struggling area of North Hollywood to win parks, a youth center and mitigation of problems caused by increased truck traffic. The developer also agreed to pay for fifty spots for low-income children at a planned childcare center and to provide free space for a community health clinic. A new grocery store will be required to sign a card-check neutrality agreement, making it easier for workers to organize, and 75 percent of the development's expected 2,000 retail and office jobs must be living wage. Finally, says Roxana Tynan, LAANE's director of accountable development, "the language around local hiring is the best and clearest that we have anywhere."

In three years, LAANE has negotiated a half-dozen such agreements, whose language is written directly into official city documents. For developers, says Tynan, "we are the pro-growth alternative. If they want to get past the NIMBYs they have to deal with us." Tynan says her hope is to take these individual victories and turn them into city policy.

California's Silicon Valley, once famed for its cyber-millionaires, has also experienced a boom in low-paid and temporary workers. An accountability group there called Working Partnerships USA negotiated a community-benefits package last year that mandated affordable housing, park space and wage standards as part of a housing and retail development in downtown San Jose. Amy Dean, a former labor leader and founder of Working Partnerships, says that winning in San Jose meant linking up with environmentalists who oppose suburban sprawl in the valley but who can be persuaded to support development that provides decent jobs and services in the urban core, where they are needed. "Many of them share our values and understand that 'smart growth,' absent equity, is elitist," Dean says.

Another accountability group, the East Bay Alliance for a Sustainable Economy (EBASE), won a ballot measure in March 2002 that set wage and other labor standards for jobs generated by the $1.9 billion expansion of the Oakland Port and airport. In San Diego, the Center for Policy Initiatives—at five years old, the youngest of California's accountability organizations—is laying the groundwork to challenge the city's head-snapping pace of subsidy approval.

Three years ago the four organizations formed a statewide alliance, the California Partnership for Working Families, with an eye toward pushing statewide policy initiatives. With four strong groups in key locations, the partnership offers the best hope yet for regional "no raid" agreements that will really stick. That would be groundbreaking. A few regions have attempted them before, Greg LeRoy says, citing one between New York, New Jersey and Connecticut in the early 1990s. "But they never really took," he says. "They had no binding authority—the minute a company would play one off against the other, they'd fall apart."

But each of the four groups in the California Partnership has developed what Amy Dean calls "a deep and rich base," built through scoring local wins. They all integrate research with organizing, which allows them to employ diverse tactics: generating large turnouts to hearings and actions and providing expert testimony based on a nuanced understanding of arcane development mechanisms.

Nationally, economic stress may create new openings for organizers. The current crisis in state budgets, the worst since the Great Depression, was certainly helped along by what LeRoy calls "subsidies enacted during the drunken-sailor binge of the late '90s." But fiscal austerity is also encouraging many state governments to rethink their subsidy policies. New Jersey, the feared raider of New York City jobs, suspended its Business Employment Incentive Program in February because of the state's budget crunch. The former Governor of Alabama, Don Siegelman, once an ardent proponent of corporate incentives, became an anti-subsidy crusader by the end of his term. State tax revenues from corporations in Alabama dropped by nearly half in 2001; 619 companies in the state paid no taxes at all in 2000, the result of past cut-throat incentives negotiations. Siegelman began barnstorming churches and unions, attacking corporate tax dodgers, calling them "Enrons and WorldComs."

An interesting connection. Even if most Americans are not aware that subsidy shakedowns debilitate local budgets, they do know the names of the corporate buccaneers who have wrecked retirement plans and kicked the slats out of an already wobbly economy. An agile accountability movement, able to leverage community benefits from economic development incentives—or block them, as the situation demands—has the potential to take advantage of this political opportunity, bringing a skeptical focus to local development and opening the lens to reveal the bigger picture as well.

BOBBI MURRAY lives in Los Angeles and writes frequently on economic justice issues. She is a 2002–03 criminal justice fellow at the USC Annenberg School for Communication Institute for Justice and Journalism.

UNIT 7

Service Delivery and Policy Issues

Unit Selections

Key Points to Consider

- List all the occasions in a typical day in which you come into contact with the services, programs, regulations and other such functions of the state and the local governments. Compare your list with a similar list of daily encounters with the services of the national government.

- Identify some policies pursued by your state government or one of your local governments that you consider undesirable. And also identify some policies that are desirable.

- What do you think are the pros and cons of the state and local governments contracting with others to produce goods and render services such as garbage collection, fire protection, maintenance of schools, prisons, and so forth? Do you think that the private sector can generally do a better job in producing such goods and services than the public sector can? Why or why not?

- Do you think it is fair that parents who send their children to private or parochial schools still have to pay property taxes to support public schools in their school district? What about people without any children? Should they have to pay taxes to support public education? Why or why not? Do you think that your state's system of higher education is satisfactory? Why or why not? Do you think that students attending state colleges should have to pay tuition? Why or why not?

- What do you think is the single most important service that state governments are primarily responsible for providing? Similarly what is the most important service that local governments are responsible for providing? And at the national level, what is the single most important function that the national government is responsible to provide?

Student Web Site

www.mhcls.com/online

Internet References

American Bar Association Juvenile Justice Center
http://www.abanet.org/crimjust/juvjus/links.html

American Public Transit Association
http://www.apta.com

CECP Juvenile Justice Links
http://www.air-dc.org/cecp/links/jj.html

COPS (Office of Community Oriented Policing Services)
http://www.cops.usdoj.gov/

National Highway Traffic Safety Administration
http://www.nhtsa.dot.gov/

U.S. Charter Schools
http://www.uscharterschools.org/

One only has to look through a daily newspaper to realize the multiple and diverse activities in which the state and local governments engage. Indeed, it would be an unusual American who, in a typical day, does not have numerous encounters with the state and local government programs, services, and regulations.

State and local governments are involved in providing roads, sidewalks, streetlights, fire and police protection, schools, colleges, day-care centers, health clinics, job training programs, public transportation, consumer protection agencies, museums, libraries, parks, sewage systems, and water. They regulate telephone services, gambling, sanitation in restaurants and supermarkets, land use, building standards, automobile emissions, noise levels, air pollution, hunting and fishing, and consumption of alcohol. They are involved in licensing or certifying undertakers, teachers, electricians, social workers, child-care agencies, nurses, doctors, lawyers, pharmacists, and others. As these listings should make clear, the state and local governments affect very many aspects of everyday life.

Among the most prominent state and local government functions is schooling. For the most part, public elementary and secondary schools operate under the immediate authority of more than 15,000 local school districts. Typically headed by elected school boards, these districts are collectively responsible for spending more than $500 billion a year and have no direct counterparts in any other country in the world. State governments regulate and supervise numerous aspects of elementary and secondary schooling, and school districts must operate within the usually considerable constraints imposed by their state government. In addition, most states have fairly extensive systems of higher education. Tuition charges are higher at private colleges than at state institutions, and taxpayers make up the difference between what students pay and actual costs of operating state colleges. While the national government provides some aid to elementary, secondary, and higher education and also involves itself in some areas of education policies, the state and local governments remain the dominant policymakers in public education. Yet the controversial No Child Left Behind law, enacted early in the Bush administration, has undoubtedly increased the national government's profile in public elementary and secondary schooling.

Crime control and order maintenance make up another primary function of the state and local governments. Criminal statutes, police forces, prisons, traffic laws (including drunk driving laws and penalties), juvenile detention centers, and courts are all part and parcel of the state and local government activities in the area of public safety. Presidential candidates have sometimes talked about crime in the streets and what to do about it, but the reality is that the state and local governments have traditionally had far more direct responsibility in this policy area than the national government has ever had. The September 11 terrorist attacks, however, have caused a reconsideration and readjustment of national, state, and local roles in protecting public safety, with more changes likely to come.

© D. Falconer/PhotoLink/Getty Images

Singling out education and public safety in the preceding two paragraphs is not meant to slight the many other important policy areas in which the state and local governments are involved: planning and zoning, roads and public transport, fire protection, provision of health care facilities, licensing and job training programs, and environmental protection, to mention just a few. Selections in this unit should provide greater familiarity with various the activities of the state and local governments.

The first section of this unit focuses on the issue of service delivery. It is important to distinguish between the provision and production of goods and services lend by the state government and those lend by the local government. For example, a local government may be responsible for providing garbage collection for residents and might meet that responsibility by paying a private firm or a neighboring unit of local government to produce the service. Similarly, a state government may be responsible for providing penal institutions to house certain kinds of criminal offenders, but might meet that responsibility by paying a private concern or another state government to produce (plan, build, organize, and operate) a prison where offenders will be confined. In recent years, the concept of privatization has figured prominently in discussions, along with decisions about the best ways for state and local governments to deliver services.

The second section of this unit treats issues facing the state and local governments in various policy areas. Interactions among national, state, and local governments frequently play important roles in shaping public policy.

Topics in this unit of the book can be viewed as the consequences of the topics discussed in earlier units. Intergovernmental relations and financing, elections, parties, interest groups, and governmental institutions all shape the responses of the state and local governments to policy issues. In turn, the policies that are adopted interact with other components of the state and local politics and modify them accordingly. Thus, the subject matter of unit 7 is an appropriate way to conclude this book.

Going Outside

The push to privatize is expanding beyond service delivery into the areas of policy making and program design.

JONATHAN WALTERS

While governors and legislators scramble to deal with American jobs moving offshore, many of these same policy makers are creating anxiety about outsourcing within their own state's borders—among their own public employees.

Texas, for example, is poised to make a radical change in the way it administers welfare benefits. Anyone seeking public assistance will no longer visit a local government office but instead dial up a call center staffed by private-sector operators. Those corporate employees will be linked to a computer system that allows them fingertip access to a vast array of financial data. Using such information, the new-style eligibility workers will then tell callers whether or not they qualify to receive a variety of benefits—from food stamps and Temporary Assistance to Needy Families to child health insurance and Medicaid.

The "call center" approach to qualifying citizens for public benefits is the front edge of a wedge aimed at opening up a huge new area of traditional government work to the private sector. If it receives federal approval, the Texas privatization strategy could trigger a wave of state and local outsourcing nationwide worth billions of dollars, affecting millions of citizens and tens of thousands of state and local employees, while at the same time opening up whole new business lines for eager vendors. Frank Ambramcheck, who heads up public sector consulting for Unisys Corp., calls it the "the bow wave" of a private-sector push into government work, an expansion that is beginning to go beyond what has typically been privatized—service delivery to citizens—and into program design and decision making.

"If Texas gets its toe in the water," says Celia Hagert, an analyst with Progressive Policy Institute who has been tracking the issue, "then a whole lot of states will be diving in right behind it." Hagert, along with many health and social services advocates nationwide, is concerned about private companies deciding who ought to get government benefits, arguing that it has always been too sensitive a job to sell off.

The drive to privatize in Texas is part of a massive consolidation that will distill 12 health and human services agencies into four. The job of administering the four new departments falls to the Health and Human Services Commission, which formerly had more casual oversight over the sprawling bureaucracies. The law that engineered the consolidation also directs HHSC to turn as much other work as is practicable over to the private sector.

The commission already has sent out a request for proposals to run the human resource management function—not just payroll administration but a broad range of HR work, from recruitment of new employees to initial screening of job candidates. Other administrative basics such as procurement and information technology will also be on the table.

But that's not all. In keeping with the outsourcing theme of the overhaul, the reorganization itself is being quarterbacked by the private sector. Deloitte Consulting, Maximus and Accenture are doing everything from reengineering how work gets done, to ensuring that whatever system Texas ends up with squares with federal cost-accounting requirements.

As of this spring, the commission's "contracting opportunities" Web site had more than a dozen RFPs listed, ranging from such specific work as studying the closure or consolidation of certain facilities, to doing feasibility studies on community-based treatment for emotionally disturbed kids. What's more, vendors also are helping HSSC to do the analyses that will become part of the "business case" that the agency uses to evaluate the efficacy of contracting out.

The math and the mindset driving the privatization effort are straightforward: Texas is facing a $10 billion budget deficit and in the view of many influential Republicans there is only one way to deal with that number: Let the private sector in on state work to lower state costs. "I am a very strong proponent of free enterprise and private-sector solutions to meet the needs of government," says state Representative Arlene Wohlgemuth, who sponsored the consolidation bill. Through reorganization and consolidation, she says, the state is slated to save billions of dollars, in part through programmatic changes to such big-ticket items as Medicaid but also by turning work over to contractors. Under the Wohlgemuth plan, more than 2,500 state health and social services jobs are scheduled to be handed off to vendors in the next two years. Ultimately, the plan could directly impact the lives of thousands more state workers across Texas.

But if Texas is shaping up as a privatizer's dream come true, some who have been watching the process closely view it as an exercise in outsourcing gone amok. Patrick Bresette, executive director of the Austin-based Center for Public Policy Priorities, calls it the "the big-bang theory" applied to scaling back government service. There is scant evidence, according to the center's analysis of the consolidation plan and early outsourcing efforts, that it will actually result in improved services at lower costs.

Texas employees, meanwhile, express their own brand of skepticism. The state is "stepping over dollars to save dimes," says Gary Anderson, executive director of the Texas Public Employees Association. While he understands the cost-saving imperative, he believes the state isn't thinking much beyond a single budget cycle in assessing the actual value of outsourcing so much work. "In the short term, you may see some savings," he acknowledges. But in the long run, Anderson contends, the state loses valuable institutional knowledge along with the capacity to easily take work back if vendors don't pan out. That could saddle the state with huge down-the-road costs, for both rebuilding internal capacity and compensating for non-performance of basic work.

Anderson sees one other potential and ironic cost to the plan: If vendors are really going to save the state money, then they will probably have to do that by using low-wage, low-benefit workers, which means the very people taking over pieces of food stamps, TANF and Medicaid administration could end up qualifying for all those benefits themselves.

Branching Out

The issues of cost, performance and capacity have long been at the heart of what drives outsourcing—and the heated debates about it. "More (and better) for less" has been the longstanding rationale for using private contractors to do everything from mowing grass to placing kids in foster care. But recently privatization has been taking on a more ideological edge. A new generation of elected officials—top-level executives, in particular—is making no secret of its conviction that government should not only "be run like a business" but also, in many cases, be run BY business. And that has led to a new aggressiveness in what states such as Texas are looking to contract out.

Adding heat to the simmering outsourcing debate is the current controversy over where, exactly, the privatized work is going. Offshore outsourcing began to capture the attention of lawmakers at the beginning of this year, fueled by a string of stories about private contractors sending state work—especially call-center work— to foreign countries. The image of employees in India handling Virginians' and Vermonters' queries about food-stamp benefits had governors and legislatures nationwide arguing all spring about whether they ought to limit state contracts to vendors who agree not to send jobs abroad.

But the issue of offshore outsourcing is clearly a sideshow to the main event: the increased interest in domestic outsourcing fueled by new, more market-friendly political leadership in combination with tough budget times. Faced with a $350 million budget deficit, South Carolina Governor Mark Sanford is among those identifying areas where the private sector might do the job better for less.

One of the items on Sanford's list—outsourcing inmate health care—has fallen to John Davis, the acting health services director for the Corrections Department. A veteran of past privatization efforts, Davis well understands that coming up with a list of areas to consider for outsourcing is one thing, and actually doing the contracting in a way that delivers quality service at reasonable cost is quite another. In fact, the state had been contracting out part of its inmate health care prior to Sanford's election, and that experience wasn't altogether satisfactory. The state dropped its contract with a private health services provider working at 10 state facilities for a very simple reason: The company wanted more money, and the state didn't want to pay more.

Now health care for the *entire* corrections system is on the table, and Davis is wrestling with the RFP process. It is a daunting task. First, the state doesn't have a good handle on costs, so it's hard to judge if outsourcing will really be a better deal. "We break things down in large categories. What it costs for hospitalization, pharmaceuticals and personnel. But we don't know how much it costs to treat diabetics or cardiac patients," he says. Although the state is currently working on a cost-coding system that will help it to capture such data, for now it is negotiating RFPs absent such detailed breakouts. Cost, of course, is what makes the outsourcing world go around, and as part of the back-and-forth with potential vendors over the RFP, private-sector companies also are asking that liability for cost overruns be shared by the state. That has made for dicier negotiations.

Also complicating the contracting effort is the fact that the state operates on an annual budget, so it's hard to lock any company into a long-term contract. That raises the specter of a low-ball bid just to get the work, with ever-escalating contract requests to follow. The state may be particularly susceptible to such a syndrome in this case, Davis notes, because this contract involves outsourcing health care services at all 29 of its facilities, which would mean the state would lose the capacity to do the work itself. "Once you've dismantled the system, it's tough to put it back together," he says, "and vendors know that."

Still, the RFP process proceeds apace. Davis thinks that given the state's past experience, things are going a little smoother this time, and that the state is doing a better job of bargaining.

In all cases, though, whether it's outsourcing human resource management or inmate health care, the basic question is the same: Does it really add up to cheaper and better government? Organized labor challenges that notion, arguing that it frequently adds up to more expensive government and worse performance. Free marketeers, meanwhile, argue that privatization is the only way to break expensive government—and government employee—monopolies. Such a break wrings greater performance and productivity from government bureaucracies, argue proponents, while applying fresh ideas and strategies to government administration and programs.

With states and localities spending upwards of $400 billion a year on contracts, and with the recent incursions into new outsourcing territory, it's not an argument that's likely to ease up anytime soon. But even Adrian Moore, executive director of the pro-privatization Reason Foundation, admits contracting out is not a panacea. "Like all policy tools, it is neither good nor bad," he says, "It depends on whether or not you do it right."

The Calculus

Stories and data abound illustrating how and where government does it wrong, say outsourcing critics. Joe Fox, vice president of the New York State Public Employees Federation, says he understands there are times when outsourcing makes sense—when a temporary spike in demand calls for some outside help or for certain kinds of seasonal work. But Fox argues that because of outsourcing, New York state government is currently paying more for a wide range of traditional government work and is getting lower quality service for the money.

According to PEF calculations, the state could save at least $160 million a year if it brought nursing, pharmaceutical, psychiatric, computer and engineering work back in-house. The federation's stand is bolstered by a March 2001 letter to the New York State Department of Transportation, in which the state comptroller declared, "It is generally less expensive for the department to design and inspect projects in-house rather than use consultants." For Fox, the game being played by New York and other states is obvious. "Politically, it looks good to say, 'I don't have this huge workforce.' But it's smoke and mirrors."

Outsourcing critics also say some politicians pursue privatization in order to offload difficult policy areas. In looking at the highly volatile area of child protective services and foster care, Richard Wexler, executive director of the National Coalition for Child Protection Reform, says Florida is a national model of how outsourcing the administration of child protection is an effort to dump responsibility and accountability. "The only motivation for privatization of child welfare in Florida is that it is a political liability, and Governor Jeb Bush doesn't want that liability," says Wexler.

The governor's administration rejects that criticism out of hand. "If you look at that area, it's one where states have been outsourcing for 100 years," says Bill Simon, secretary of the Florida Department of Management Services. The whole concept of sending kids to foster homes instead of orphanages, Simon notes, is one where outsourcing has proved "wildly successful." And he adds, "It's not much of a step to then look at outsourcing its administration."

But Florida is a state that has come in for heavy criticism for its aggressive, big-ticket and low-accountability outsourcing efforts. In particular, the governor has been pounded over the state's high-profile and so far unhappy effort to outsource a significant portion of its human resources management function. A $280 million contract with Cincinnati-based Convergys Corp. to take over the job has bogged down badly, which means the state is spending millions of dollars keeping its old system up and running while Convergys tries to work out kinks in the new system.

Still, DMS secretary Simon believes that much of the criticism aimed at Bush is simply on account of the "blistering pace" with which the governor has pursued privatization. So far, state action on the outsourcing front has included everything from collecting tolls to investigating allegations of child abuse.

Not all of Florida's privatizing has gone badly. In several multi-million-dollar deals, the contractors have performed as advertised. But both the governor's own Inspector General and the legislature's Office of Program Policy Analysis and Government Accountability have released papers taking the state to task for its less-than-businesslike approach to contracting out. The legislative oversight office, for instance, said agencies need to make a better business case for privatization and look more at performance-based contracting. It also suggested the need for central oversight of contracting.

Florida has received enough official criticism about its privatization efforts that Governor Bush in March created a Center for Efficient Government in the state's Department of Management Services to oversee the state's outsourcing efforts. One of the center's main jobs will be to provide technical assistance to agencies not used to negotiating large contracts with experienced, savvy vendors. "We have state agencies that might do a $100 million contract every one or two years, whereas IBM does one a week," Simon says. The center will also be the central repository for information on cost and performance.

Negotiating with the Feds

While Florida has received much attention for its outsourcing efforts, most eyes right now are on Texas and its decision to privatize eligibility determination—and whatever else it can—as part of its health and human services overhaul.

Texas is still negotiating with the feds for permission to outsource all the eligibility determination work that it would like to—particularly in the areas of food stamps and Medicaid. Gregg Phillips, a former consultant with Deloitte who is now HHSC's point man on reorganization and contracting out, is confident the state will be allowed to hand the work off to contractors. Other states are watching the action carefully.

Phillips is well aware of concerns about contracting out. But he says that Texas won't repeat the mistakes of other aggressive privatizers that have gone before it. Furthermore, he argues that the state already has been using the call-center approach in such areas as the child health insurance program and workers' compensation with no problems. "Right now with our CHIP program," he says, "every eligibility determination is being made by a private-sector company. Texans seeking service don't care who they're talking to as long as who they are talking to is courteous, accurate and performs well."

Furthermore, says Phillips, every outsourcing effort that HHSC undertakes has to be justified by a business case, and where contracting out is deemed cost effective—and he's confident there will be lots more cases—contractors will always be held to high standards of performance with clear penalties for failure to meet those standards. He also believes there are enough vendors around that are interested in picking up state work that HHSC will never be held hostage by any private-sector monopolizer.

Still, even the staunchest advocates of outsourcing, including Representative Wohlgemuth, understand that building that kind of contract-writing, administration and oversight capacity in state government is in and of itself a daunting task. But she has a ready answer for how to deal with any shortfall in state contracting capacity: "You can contract that out, too."

Games Charter Opponents Play

JOE WILLIAMS

Considerable attention has been paid to the most blatant barriers that public charter schools face. By lobbying against good charter legislation and fair funding financing anti-charter studies and propaganda, filing lawsuits, and engaging the public battle of ideas, teacher unions and other charter opponents openly wage what might be called an "air war" against charters.

But there is also evidence of a perhaps more damaging "ground war." Interviews with more than 400 charter school operators from coast to coast have revealed widespread localized combat—what one administrator called "bureaucratic sand" that is often hurled in the faces of charter schools. Indeed, as a 2005 editorial in the *Washington Post* described charter school obstruction in Maryland, "It's guerilla turf war, with children caught in the middle. Attempts to establish public charter schools in Maryland have been thwarted at almost every turn by entrenched school boards, teachers unions and principals resistant to any competition."

The goal appears to be to stop charter schools any way possible. A decade after Massachusetts passed its charter school law as part of the Education Reform Act of 1993, city officials in North Adams, Massachusetts, sued the state Department of Education, challenging the constitutionality of charter schools. Citing a 150-year-old clause in the state constitution, the city claimed all public school money had to go to schools that are controlled by "public agents." The suit was later dismissed but shows the lengths to which local interests will go to stop the schools or at least slow them down.

Today, more than 1 million students are enrolled in public charter schools in the 41 states (and the District of Columbia) that have charter laws, with almost 4,000 charter schools in all. Most, if not all, of these schools have encountered some form of bureaucratic resistance at the local level. That resistance may take place at the school's inception, when it first looks to purchase a building and comply with municipal zoning laws. It may come when opponents play games with a school's transportation or funding, or when legal barriers are tossed in the way, or when false information about charter schools is widely disseminated. Despite the obstacles, many charter schools are thriving. It's worth taking a look at the forces on the ground that would have it otherwise and the myriad ways they attempt to stymie the charter school movement.

No-School Zone

Often the most painstaking and difficult parts of launching a charter school are locating, purchasing, and maintaining the school building. Many charter opponents believe that if they can sufficiently complicate this nascent stage of a charter school's life, they will have dealt a major blow to its future success.

In Albany, New York, opponents have used the city's zoning commission to halt charter school growth. When Albany Preparatory Charter School requested a variance on property it was eyeing, opponents appeared before a public hearing about the proposed school building and used the opportunity to argue against charter schools in general. Both the city and the board of zoning appeals denied the variance request in February 2005 on grounds that the proposed building was in a location that was not suitable for a school. It wasn't difficult for the charter school to prove that the decision was unfairly "arbitrary and capricious," however. The building that Albany had deemed unsuitable for a school had been, for more than 70 years, Albany's very own Public School 3. In December 2005, State Supreme Court Justice Thomas J. Spargo gave the city 60 days to approve the variance request.

That same month, the Albany school system discussed ways to prevent another school, the Green Tech Charter High School, from opening. The school board voted to have Superintendent Eva Joseph review possibilities for taking the property by eminent domain so the district could seize the land before the charter school could be built. As the *Albany Times Union* reported, M. Christian Bender, chair of the proposed school's board of directors, remarked, "Two words come to mind—laughable and desperate." The school is expected to open in September 2007.

Albany's story is not unusual. Playing games with facilities and zoning is a powerful way to get charter schools to delay or abandon plans to open. Certainly some zoning boards resist on principle any new land use that may increase traffic or noise, but blatant political hostility is quite common. Why are local boards hostile to charter schools? Some may view charter schools as a threat to local traditions and long-standing power-sharing arrangements. One Ohio charter school operator suggested that appointees to zoning commissions in her area tend to be eager political up-and-comers. To build political capital, they're often willing to deliver for the public school systems. And those systems don't want charter schools competing for students and dollars. "Especially if you are a Democrat, standing up to a charter school can help you make a name for yourself in the most important political circles," she said.

Charter opponents understand that zoning commissions and boards of appeal have the power to halt new charter schools in their tracks. All over the country, particularly in the suburbs, zoning issues have been used to thwart attempts to open charter schools. To be sure, some cases involve garden variety "Not In My Back Yard" resistance to the increased traffic flow and daily bustle new charter schools bring. But often the opposition is blatantly political. When Lyndhurst, New Jersey mayor, James Guida, an opponent of charter schools, proposed zoning changes in 2001 that would require school lots to be a minimum of 1.5 acres in size, it stymied at least one charter school plan. Guida talked about the school with a *Bergen Record* reporter: "We didn't target it, but if [the zoning law] hits it, so be it."

In a similar scenario, Englewood, New Jersey, officials wreaked havoc on the Englewood Charter School by abruptly rezoning the site of a converted warehouse that the school was planning to use. The change prevented elementary schools from operating on the location. "They passed zoning changes to specifically exclude us from buildings," said charter school organizer Paul Raynault.

In 2000, California voters approved Proposition 39, which requires that unused public school buildings be made available to public charter schools. Some districts have simply chosen not to follow the law, which gives public charter schools the right of first refusal. Two charter schools in southeast San Diego, Fanno Academy and KIPP Adelante Academy, filed a lawsuit against the district in 2005 accusing school officials of "blatant noncompliance" because classroom space was denied to charter schools and given instead to private schools that could afford to pay higher rent.

The San Diego lawsuit, filed with the help of the California Charter Schools Association, contends that districts usually sabotage charter schools in one of three ways: claiming a facilities request is incomplete and therefore denying it; offering sites that are impractical; and outright denial of the facility request. Eight out of nine charter school applications for space in San Diego in 2005 were denied, even though all completed the necessary paperwork for requesting classroom space. Before suing the district, both Fanno and Adelante reportedly sought to hold meetings with the agency to discuss their options. After several months without a response, their requests were denied. Early in 2006, the district had declared invalid requests from 24 charter schools seeking space declaring that none properly explained how the school's projected enrollment was determined. That level of detail hadn't been required on previous applications.

"This feels like political posturing," said Luci Flowers, principal of the Albert Einstein Academy Charter School. "I feel like we are pawns in a political game."

Sometimes hurdles for charter school facilities are thrown up not by districts, but by competing private-school interests. In Brooklyn, New York, the founders of the Explore Charter School signed a 10-year lease in 2002 for a property across the street from the St. James Catholic Cathedral. The property was co-owned by a private landlord and the Diocese of Brooklyn. The private landlord signed off on the lease, but just weeks before the school was scheduled to open, the diocese began unraveling the deal. The 10-year lease was slashed to two years, forcing school leaders to go back to the nearly full-time job of finding a suitable long-term facility.

Why the sudden resistance from the diocese? The church said it had new concerns that sex education might be taught in the public charter school. But Morty Ballen, the charter school's founder, claimed that a lawyer for the diocese told him that it was not the church's policy to support charter schools. "It's a hunch that we represent competition to the parochial schools," Ballen said. "It's unfortunate, because we all have the same goal—to provide kids with a good, solid education."

You Can't Get Here from There

Using transportation as a weapon against charters is particularly harmful to those charter schools that have longer school days and years than traditional public schools. "Transportation is huge," commented Jamie Callendar, a former Ohio legislator. "In the first few years the districts would outright refuse to provide transportation. Now they make it as inconvenient as possible."

In Ohio, students attending non-public and charter/community schools are eligible to receive transportation services from the local district if they and the school they attend meet certain criteria. The local district can, however, declare providing eligible students with transportation "impractical" for a variety of reasons and issue payment instead. In July, the Columbus Public School district announced its intent to notify 1,384 private and charter school students that it would be "impractical" to transport them to school on district school buses. Instead, students would be given a $172 check toward providing their own transportation to and from school—less than $1 per school day.

Similar scenarios play out all over the country. For nearly four months of the 2005–06 school year, the school bus belonging to the Ross Montessori School in Carbondale, Colorado, sat unused in the school's parking lot, another victim of the below-the-radar war against public charter schools.

The K–6 school paid $25,000 for a 78-passenger turbo-diesel school bus in the fall of 2005 with high hopes that it would make it easier for students— particularly Latinos—who didn't live close to the school to enroll. Critics at the nearby Roaring Fork School District, who had long opposed the charter school's existence, had complained publicly that Ross Montessori didn't serve its share of Latino students. The administration of Ross Montessori believed the bus would make it easier for Latino families to select the school.

"I thought this would be a solution," said Mark Grice, the school's director. Instead, as the bus sat, unused in the lot, week after week, it became a symbol for the passive-aggressive relationship that existed between the independent public charter school approved by the state and the local school district.

Why weren't students allowed to ride on the Ross Montessori bus? In Colorado, as in many places, school buses may not carry student passengers unless the vehicles are regularly inspected by a specially licensed school-bus mechanic. Grice and his administrative team quickly learned that most of the licenses to conduct inspections in the region belonged to mechanics employed full time by a school district.

When the charter school leaders checked with the mechanic at the local district in early October 2005, they were given the bureaucratic cold shoulder. Grice and his team decided the best way to proceed would be to call the next closest school district to see if its certified school-bus mechanic would conduct the required inspection. Arrangements were made to do just that, until Grice got a return call shortly before the scheduled inspection informing him that the appointment had been cancelled.

"They said they didn't want to get involved in the politics of our district," Grice recalled. The charter pushed back, and eventually the neighboring district agreed to inspect the bus—but only if the school could produce a letter from the superintendent of the charter school's geographic district giving permission. Eventually, the Carbondale superintendent agreed to call the neighboring superintendent. "I should have had him put it in writing," Grice said. Whatever the superintendents may have said between themselves, it didn't result in a bus inspection.

By chance, several months later, the charter school stumbled upon both a certified school-bus mechanic who was employed at a nearby Chevrolet dealership and a Catholic school that was looking to share with another school the cost of bus transportation in the region. "It allowed us to share the cost of the bus and to pay the driver better," Grice said. "But as soon as the district found out about it, someone called the Colorado Department of Education to question the separation of church and state."

The bus eventually got rolling, but Grice said he hates to think of how much time was spent dealing with these clearly avoidable hassles, time that could have been better spent on education.

The Check Is in the Mail

When districts are the ones passing along funding to charter schools, they gain immense influence over those schools' basic operations, and the charters are placed in the undesirable position of having to rely on those who may oppose their very existence.

The Franklin Career Academy, of Franklin, New Hampshire, ultimately perished after the local school district and city council simply refused to pay the school the already-low $3,340 per child that was guaranteed under the state's charter school law. As in many locations, New Hampshire law requires the per-pupil funds to pass from the state through local school districts, and then to charter schools. But Franklin school and city officials argued that the money was needed in the traditional schools and, astonishingly, voted against giving it to the charter school in the city budget. In its first year, Career Academy served 35 at-risk students in grades 7 through 12, but ended the year being owed $77,000 by the local district. The financial uncertainty forced the charter school to shut its doors. "Nothing went wrong with the school," said the charter school's board chairman Bill Grimm. "We closed because we didn't see any other option." The New Hampshire legislature is currently considering funding charter schools directly.

Ohio has a similar process for funding charter schools. Ohio charters are paid through the districts with which they are competing. Those districts, in turn, have the right to question the validity of every student record, a practice called "flagging." Because charter schools can't be subsidized for a student whose record is "flagged," dozens of charter school leaders throughout Ohio charge that their local public-school districts have used excessive "flagging" with the specific intention of harming the often fragile finances of their schools.

Depending on the size of the school, and the aggressiveness with which local districts decide to "flag" students, individual charter schools can see tens of thousands of dollars in legitimate funding delayed or withheld each year. And charter school administrators report that their limited office staffs can be overwhelmed as they scramble to investigate the reasons behind the flagging.

One Toledo charter school leader said her school had twice been denied six weeks' worth of funding for enrolled students. In both cases, she said, the local district raised objections to student records just before the deadline for closing out monthly payments, making it impossible for the charter school to gather the supporting documentation in time for payment.

"We don't even know that we have a problem, then all of a sudden they'll put up a flag and say, 'We need proof of residence,'" the charter leader said. "We've had kids who were in the [Toledo Public] schools for their entire academic careers and suddenly the district wants to challenge where they live."

Another charter school administrator reported that an official with the Toledo Public Schools (TPS) often flags student entries, but doesn't make clear what is wrong. (In one case, he allegedly claimed the word "Toledo" was spelled incorrectly on the database, but the school insisted they had it right. To make matters worse, she said, the TPS official wouldn't return telephone calls or e-mails to discuss the flag he had thrown.)

Official Ohio Department of Education policy bans districts' use of flagging to harass the charter schools, but some charter operators complain that the state often looks the other way and insists that charter schools resolve the problem with the local districts. Others note that there is a financial incentive for districts to delay making payments for as long as possible, even if they eventually have to pay the charter schools what they are owed in later installments.

"The district gets to use our money for a while [before eventually reconciling the accounts and spreading back-payments over several months] and we go into debt," a Toledo charter leader said. "Meanwhile, they accuse us of sucking the system dry."

Slinging Mud

Charter schools that either escape or survive the bureaucratic messes are lucky—but they're not safe. In many districts, organized campaigns of disinformation and slander have been launched against charter schools. Like lawsuits, faux research, and campaign contributions, name calling has emerged as one more useful political tool.

Toledo Public Schools teachers handed out flyers outside the East Toledo Charter School in 2006 to parents attending an informational open house. The flyers suggested inaccurately that the school wasn't performing well.

In Massachusetts in 2004, where district hostility to charter schools got so bad that state education officials had to warn superintendents to moderate their anti-charter politicking, one district student reported being pressured to sign a petition opposing charter schools. She was told if she didn't sign, funding for the school band might be cut from the budget. Reported the *Boston Globe*, "Children say their public school teachers have pressed them to sign petitions protesting new charters. School committee members have repeatedly called neighbors, imploring them to step down from charter boards. And flyers have circulated, sounding the death of public schools if a charter school opens."

In 2003 in Waltham, Massachusetts, an elementary-school principal sent out e-mails to families urging them to oppose pending charter-school proposals. In nearby Framingham that same year, city officials included with tax bills letters explaining how much money was going to charter schools. And in Cambridge, school officials in 2005 mailed letters to 4,000 families questioning the academic effectiveness of a charter school that had yet to open. Those letters also warned that students who chose to attend the Community Charter School of Cambridge wouldn't be able to join sports and clubs that regular public schools offer.

Some of the tactics used by charter opponents amount to bluffing but reveal how far they are willing to go to stop a charter school from opening. As the University of Wisconsin-Milwaukee (UWM) considered authorizing charter schools for the first time in 1999, the local teachers union and top administrators in the Milwaukee Public Schools threatened to ban the college's student teachers from obtaining required classroom experience if UWM approved any charter schools that would be managed by the for-profit firm Edison Schools.

No Truce in Sight

This ground war is both expensive and demoralizing. As the Thomas B. Fordham Foundation's Terry Ryan described the reality in one state, "Charter schools, many working in Ohio's toughest neighborhoods to educate the state's neediest children, are also forced to live under a cloud of uncertainty, harassment and intimidation."

Many of the charter principals interviewed for this story report spending upward of a third or even half of their time fighting these battles. In truth, charter opponents can lose some battles and still win the war, as charter school operations continue to be hampered by endless attacks on so many fronts. One can only wonder how these distractions impede the efforts of charter schools to educate their students.

Truce cannot be expected anytime soon. The enemies of charter schools are motivated and well-financed. For charter supporters, then, there is only one choice: fight back and win.

Under the Microscope

States Serve as Laboratories for Universal Health Care Programs

Several states are implementing comprehensive health care reform plans, bringing the issue to the forefront of national discussion 10 years after the Clinton health proposal failed.

KAREN IMAS

State legislatures, faced with the challenges of a booming uninsured population nearing 46 million nationwide, are taking the lead in implementing universal health care plans. With increased tax revenues, states are using the better economic conditions to offer a variety of new programs, often public-private partnerships, ranging from providing health insurance for all children (in Illinois) to legislation requiring that all adults obtain health insurance (in Massachusetts).

"For under $250 a month, we could address the needs of the working unisured with a basic health insurance package that would include a full prescription package, laboratory services and pre- and post-natal care."

—Connecticut Gov. Jodi Rell

A recent report by the Kaiser Commission on Medicaid and the Uninsured found that states' revenue growth, after a decade of skyrocketing Medicaid spending, is helping governors move forward with comprehensive health care reform.

Three states are at the forefront—Maine, Vermont and Massachusetts. Recent reforms in these states have grabbed the nation's attention and serve as a catalyst for discussion of creative expansion options at both the state and federal levels. The tides may be changing since the Clinton health reform proposals failed 10 years ago.

While states are at the forefront of reform, proposed programs do not rely on the state to be the "single payer," the insurer of last resort for everyone. Instead, most policy changes are designed to increase affordability for various populations.

Feds Look to States for Models

States are doing something right by taking a more proactive role in health care delivery, and Congress is watching closely. Three similar bills have been introduced in Congress that would encourage states to find ways to make the health care system work better. Sens. George Voinovich of Ohio and Jeff Bingaman of New Mexico introduced the first bill in May 2006. Sen. Russ Feingold introduced his own bill, the State Based Health Reform Act, in July.

"The federal government would help a few states provide health insurance for all their citizens, but leave it up to those states to decide how they want to go about it. Rather than directing states to implement a specific health care system, the bill provides a flexible approach that allows states to try innovative ways of achieving universal coverage."

—State Based Health Reform Act Proposed by U.S. Sen. Russ Feingold

Under Feingold's plan, "the federal government would help a few states provide health insurance for all their citizens, but leave it up to those states to decide how they want to go about it. Rather than directing states to implement a specific health care system, the bill provides a flexible approach that allows states to try innovative ways of achieving universal coverage."

Wisconsin Rep. Tammy Baldwin, who has backed the idea for several years, and Georgia Rep. Tom Price, along with two other co-sponsors, also introduced a bill in July. These bipartisan approaches encourage more states to experiment with coverage expansion and cost-containment—the types of reforms achieved in Massachusetts, Maine and Vermont, and of ongoing reform discussions in states such as Illinois, Colorado, Washington, New Mexico and Oregon.

There seems to be bipartisan consensus that Congress will not be able to agree on health care reform. Given the massive cost of health care reform at the federal level, states are the ideal litmus test for various programs. The state proposals would be reviewed by a commission or task force and the most promising ones would be sent to Congress for fast-track approval.

States are customizing health care reforms to their particular needs often with bipartisan legislative consensus. In both Massachusetts and Vermont, laws were passed by Democratic-controlled legislatures and signed into law by Republican governors. The following are innovative programs across the country:

Massachusetts

In 2006, Massachusetts pioneered a market-based system for universal health care, leveraging significant federal funding. By mid-2007, the state will require all residents to obtain health insurance or pay a penalty.

New and affordable policies and subsidies will be created to enable compliance with the mandate. In addition, employers will be required to make a "fair and reasonable" contribution to the cost of coverage for their employees or pay a penalty.

All four Medicaid health plans are participating in the new program. Outreach, public education campaigns, public health initiatives and quality benchmarking activities are moving forward. The Health Care Quality and Cost Council is building a price transparency Web site for consumers and payers with cost and quality information on services and providers.

The state began enrolling uninsured individuals who earn less than the federal poverty level in October. Those enrollees are not required to pay any monthly premiums and would be responsible for very small co-payment fees for emergency room visits and other services. Starting Jan. 1, those earning between that amount and three times the poverty level are able to buy subsidized policies with premiums based on their ability to pay.

Policymakers believe the plan can be achieved without imposing new taxes or borrowing money because financing would come largely from funds now being used for other health care expenses, such as reimbursing hospitals for care they provide to uninsured residents. It will be up to the new governor, Deval Patrick, to carry the plan forward. Both Maine and Vermont have passed health care coverage expansions that aim for universal coverage in their states, but stop short of requiring individuals to purchase insurance.

Maine

Maine's Dirigo Health Reform Act drew national attention when it was signed into law in 2003 by Gov. Jon Baldacci, making it the first state in recent years to enact legislation aimed at providing universal health care access.

The law, which went into effect Jan. 1, 2005, is designed to contain health care costs, improve quality and ensure access to health care for all. The key vehicles for coverage expansion are a health insurance product for small businesses, self-employed and unemployed Mainers with subsidies for low-income people, and expansion of Medicaid to additional parents and adults without dependent children.

The Dirigo Choice health insurance program had 12,153 enrolled at the end of October 2006.

A Blue Ribbon Commission examining Dirigo recently approved a set of recommendations that includes looking into the idea of mandated employer group coverage for workers and requiring individuals above certain income levels to get coverage for themselves. The commission also expressed support for new taxes to expand the program.

Funding for Dirigo has come under scrutiny from some legislators who dismiss the initiative as too costly and ineffective and for stifling competition for other private insurers. However lawsuits challenging the funding mechanism, a savings offset payment recouping savings to the system due to fewer uninsured, have been unsuccessful. If the legislature doesn't approve new taxes, the state next year would revert to the original funding mechanism. The state is already collecting a $43.7 million savings offset payment to cover 12,500 people in 2006.

Vermont

Vermont's Catamount Health, approved in May 2006, is a state-subsidized voluntary program designed to help people without insurance buy it on their own in the private marketplace. Vermont's legislation focuses on managing chronic illnesses in the hopes of improving the quality of care, while reducing the rate of growth in health care costs. It takes effect in October 2007.

The state estimates as many as 25,000 of 60,000 uninsured Vermont residents may enroll in coverage under this program. If coverage goals are not reached by 2010, the legislature may consider coverage mandates.

Catamount Health provides sliding scale subsidies for premiums and cost-sharing under commercial health insurance plans. The plan will be offered by private insurers, and its benefits and charges will be similar to those in the average BlueCross BlueShield plan in Vermont. Under Catamount Health, enrollees will pay $10 for office visits, 20 percent coinsurance for medical services, tiered co-payments of $10, $30 or $50 for prescription drugs, and a $250 annual deductible for an individual or $500 for a family for in-network services (double those amounts for out-of-network).

Catamount Health premiums are projected to range from $60 per month for individuals with household income of less than 200 percent of the federal poverty level to $135 per month for individuals with household income between 275 and 300 percent of the federal poverty level.

Small businesses are concerned with these reforms because employers who do not provide their workers health insurance will have to begin paying $365 a year per full-time employee. They will also have to make payments for part-time workers, which is a sticking point for many employers.

To fund the program, tobacco taxes will increase a total of 80 cents per pack over a few years.

Pending Proposals
Connecticut

Legislators have labeled health care access a major priority for 2007. In December, Gov. Jodi Rell unveiled the Charter Oak Health Plan which would offer adults of all incomes the opportunity to enroll in a state health care plan with comprehensive coverage. The plan will address the needs of about 400,000 uninsured Connecticut residents—some 11 percent of the population—who are uninsured. The plan includes $1,000 deductibles, co-payments ranging from $10 to $55 per visit and 20 percent coinsurance to a maximum of $1,000. No state funds and no legislative changes are expected to be needed for the program.

"To develop the Charter Oak Plan, my administration will work with representatives of major managed care providers in Connecticut to develop an affordable, accessible product," Rell said. "For under $250 a month, we could address the needs of the working uninsured with a basic health insurance package that would include a full prescription package, laboratory services and pre- and post-natal care."

Connecticut already provides coverage to the poor through Medicaid and to children through the Healthcare for UninSured Kids and Youth (HUSKY) insurance program.

New Jersey

New Jersey is crafting a new bill for introduction in the legislature that would overhaul the state's health care system and require all New Jersey residents to carry medical insurance. Policies would be affordable for low-wage earners. This model, based on the Massachusetts plan, would require residents to get health insurance and prove they have it when they file their state income tax returns.

> **Living in the world's most affluent society, it shocks the conscience that any child should be forced to live without access to basic medical care. With Cover All Kids, Pennsylvania parents will no longer need to make the impossible choice between paying the rent and taking their child to see a doctor.**
>
> —Pennsylvania Gov. Ed Rendell

The plan seeks to provide health insurance for the 1.4 million adults and children who don't currently have it by creating a state-subsidized HMO or PPO. To help pay for the coverage, the state would reallocate the $983 million it now spends on charity care and grants to hospitals for caring for the uninsured.

New Jersey has almost twice as many uninsured residents as Maine, Vermont and Massachusetts combined—the only states that currently provide or plan to provide universal coverage.

Sen. Joseph Vitale, chairman of the Senate Health, Human Services and Senior Citizens Committee, is a key architect of the plan. He hopes to introduce a bill this spring.

What Can Canada's Model Teach the States?

Canadian provinces, which have a single payer system, are experimenting with a two-tiered system where some private care is subsidized by the government or offered at a fee to the consumer. Canada is one of the few countries with no user fees and the only country that outlaws privately funded purchases of key health services. Clinics could be prosecuted for charging patients for procedures that would be covered under the public health system—a violation of Canada's Health Act.

Per capita, Canada spends approximately half of what the United States spends on health care.

"Canada's landscape is public with stealth privatization. The U.S. landscape is becoming the opposite," said MPP Dr. Shafiq Qaadri of Ontario.

A Supreme Court decision last year on private medicine has rapidly altered the options available to patients in Canada. In June 2005, the Supreme Court of Canada ruled that the Québec government cannot prevent people from paying for private insurance for health care procedures covered under Medicare. The justices said banning private insurance for a list of services ranging from MRI tests to cataract surgery was unconstitutional under the Québec Charter of Rights, given that the public system has failed to guarantee patients access to those services in a timely way.

Canada is anticipating an infusion of private care for core services in at least some provinces—Alberta, British Columbia and Québec—and various experiments combining public and private care. Such efforts aim to reduce patients' waiting times for treatment, as well as to control public spending. The differing levels of private care from province to province are in part a function of how open provincial governments are to private medicine.

In February 2006, Québec announced that it would improve access within the public system to tertiary cardiology and radiation oncology services and would provide hip and knee replacements and cataract surgery within six months after they are recommended by a specialist. If these operations cannot be performed at a government-funded hospital within that time, Québec will pay for surgery at an affiliated private clinic in the province. If the wait extends beyond nine months, patients can receive publicly funded care at a private clinic outside Québec or even Canada. The government will allow Québec residents to buy private health insurance specifically for these designated services, although the scope of such insurance may be expanded in the future.

Pennsylvania

Pennsylvania is the second state to try to provide insurance to all children who otherwise would go without coverage. A bill signed by Gov. Ed Rendell in November aims to meet this goal through an initiative his administration calls Cover All Kids. Under the initiative, parents will be able to afford to insure their children because the monthly premiums will be based on family income. Currently, the Childrens' Health Insurance Program (CHIP) is free for children from families with annual incomes under $40,000 and available at a reduced cost for children from families with incomes up to $47,000.

Under Cover All Kids, all parents who cannot afford to insure their children will get assistance from the state to ensure that the cost of health insurance for their children is reasonable.

"Living in the world's most affluent society, it shocks the conscience that any child should be forced to live without access to basic medical care," Rendell said. "With Cover All Kids, Pennsylvania parents will no longer need to make the impossible choice between paying the rent and taking their child to see a doctor."

Illinois became the first state to do so under a program called All Kids that debuted July 1; the state has since enrolled more than 35,000 children who were previously ineligible for government subsidized coverage.

KAREN IMASIS publications manager for The Council of State Governments Eastern Regional Conference.

From *State News*, February 2007. Published by The Council of State Governments. Reprinted by permission.

Revenge Begins to Seem Less Sweet

Americans are losing their appetite for the death penalty. Texas is the exception

Joseph Nichols did not fight the guards at his execution, but he did not co-operate, either. He had to be lifted onto the trolley on which he was to die, and then strapped down. A needle was thrust into his arm. Asked if he had any last words, he said, "Yes, yes I do," and then swore at a guard. There followed a gurgling sound as his lungs collapsed and, for about a minute, an animal-like noise issued from the back of his throat. After that came silence, broken only by a few people in the room clearing their throats. Then a doctor pulled out his stethoscope and pronounced the condemned man dead. The execution had taken six minutes.

Mr Nichols was one of 22 people put to death in Texas this year (as this was written, two more were scheduled to die). His story was fairly typical. He had been convicted for the murder of a delicatessen clerk during a robbery in 1980. It had not been much of a heist; he said his accomplice "got some change" but he got nothing. The victim was killed by a single bullet. It was unclear which of the two men had fired it, but under Texan law it made no difference, since both admitted to shooting at him. Mr Nichols was 20 when he arrived on death row and 45 when he died. His accomplice was executed in 1995.

Capital punishment is hardly controversial in Texas. Nearly three-quarters of Texans approve of it. In June the governor signed a law that would make some people who rape children eligible for it. But Texas is special. It now accounts for nearly half of all executions in America, of which there have been over 1,000 since 1976. During the six years in which George Bush was governor, the state put 152 people to death. No other governor in America's recent history except his successor, Rick Perry, has overseen so many executions.

Elsewhere, the death penalty is increasingly controversial. The questions of whether and how to impose it are primarily for the states, not the federal government, but Mr Bush's attorney-general, Alberto Gonzales, who resigned this week, tried to have more Americans executed. He failed, and any successor who wants to arrest the abolitionist trend is likely also to be frustrated. Since 2000, 12 out of 50 states have suspended the death penalty. Three of those (Tennessee, Florida and Missouri) have this year reversed that suspension and one (New Jersey) has moved towards formal abolition.

Unlike most Texans, the people of New Jersey have strong doubts about the death penalty. Most would prefer to see mur-derers locked up for ever. Their representatives are listening: no one has been executed in New Jersey since the 1960s. A state Senate committee has approved a bill to end capital punishment formally; the full legislature is expected to pass it later this year. "If New Jersey holds another execution, I'll eat the body," vows Michael Radelet of the University of Colorado.

For a few years in the 1970s, America joined most other rich countries in revoking the death penalty. This was not done by passing a law. Rather, the Supreme Court decided, in 1972, that capital punishment was unconstitutional, since it broke the ban on "cruel and unusual" punishment. In 1976 a slightly different set of justices reversed the court's ruling and handed the issue back to the states.

Since then, the states have gone their own ways. Twelve have no death penalty on their statute books. Of the 38 that do, some apply it often, some never. Texas has executed 401 people since 1976, the entire north-eastern region only four. By and large, the way the penalty is applied mirrors local preferences.

Asked by pollsters whether they think murderers should be put to death, two-thirds of Americans say yes, down from four-fifths in 1994. If asked to choose between the death penalty and a life sentence with no chance of parole, however, they are evenly divided. Life that means life is relatively new. Before the 1990s, juries used to worry that if they did not send the man in the dock to his death, he would be freed to kill again after a decade or two. Now nearly every state allows the option of life without parole (Texas introduced it only in 2005). For the first time last year, a Gallup poll reported that a slim plurality of Americans found this option preferable to a capital sentence (48–47%).

Campaigners against the death penalty have been making their case state by state, with little fanfare but some success. The number of executions has fallen by 46% from its modern peak in 1999, to 53 last year. Two-thirds of states executed no one last year, and only six carried out multiple executions. The number of death sentences has fallen even more sharply, by 60% from a peak of about 300 a year in the mid-1990s.

The arguments for and against capital punishment have evolved. Thirty years ago, says Mr Radelet, Americans supported the death penalty for three main reasons: deterrence, religious conviction (an eye for an eye) and taxes (the idea of spending public money to feed and clothe murderers for the rest of their lives seemed outrageous). This last argument no longer applies. It is now far more expensive to execute someone than to jail him for life; in North Carolina, for instance, each capital case costs $2m more. Ordinary inmates need only to be fed and guarded. Those on death row must have lawyers arguing expensively about their fate, sometimes for a decade or more (see chart 2). The system of appeals has grown more protracted because of fears that innocent people may be executed. Few would argue that such safeguards are not needed, but their steep cost gives abolitionists a new line of attack.

Martin O'Malley, the governor of Maryland, says that, but for the death penalty, his state would have been $22.4m richer since 1978. That money would have paid for 500 extra policemen for a year, or provided drug treatment for 10,000 addicts. "Unlike the death penalty, these are investments that save lives and prevent violent crime," he told the state legislature in February, in a speech urging it to repeal capital punishment in Maryland. He failed by the narrowest of margins: a state Senate committee was deadlocked by five votes to five, preventing the bill from advancing.

A similar attempt got further in Colorado, where Paul Weissman, a state representative, proposed that the money saved by abolishing the death penalty should be spent on a "cold cases" unit to investigate unsolved murders. His bill made it through a committee, but was gutted.

Abolitionists have had more luck, at least temporarily, by arguing that lethal injection, the form of execution most widely adopted, is excruciatingly painful. The cocktail used generally contains sodium thiopental (to anaesthetise the condemned man), pancuronium bromide (to paralyse his muscles) and potassium chloride (to stop his heart). Some studies suggest that prisoners are sometimes inadequately sedated, and perhaps die in silent agony from asphyxiation.

Since last year, ten states have halted executions because of fears that lethal injection may be cruel, and therefore unconstitutional. In Florida, for example, Governor Jeb Bush (the president's brother) suspended executions after a fiasco last December in which the executioner missed a vein and pumped the drugs into muscle. The condemned man took 34 minutes to die, during which he grimaced and writhed, suggesting acute agony.

The problem can, however, be fixed. In Florida a committee has recommended 37 ways to make lethal injection more "humane". This has satisfied Mr Bush's successor, Charlie Crist, who has now started signing death warrants. The governor of Tennessee, having stopped all executions in February, also let them resume in May.

For many, the death penalty holds a deep emotional appeal. It is "an expression of society's ultimate outrage", says Bob Grant, a former prosecutor and now a professor at the University of Denver, Colorado. Some acts, he argues, are so heinous that no other punishment is appropriate. One example he cites is the case of Gary Davis, the only man executed in Colorado since the 1960s. Mr Davis kidnapped, tortured, sexually assaulted and murdered a young mother in 1986. His guilt was not in doubt. Mr Grant prosecuted him and watched him put to death.

Mr Grant says his views on the death penalty have nothing to do with religion, but many who agree with him do so for reli-gious reasons. A prosecutor in Texas cites Genesis 9:6: "Whoso sheddeth man's blood, by man his blood be shed." This, he says, is "pretty compelling".

Opponents of capital punishment tend to respond by saying that juries, being human, err. If you find you have jailed the wrong man, you can free and compensate him. If you have executed him, however, it is too late. Jurors increasingly balk at imposing the death penalty, even when they are of a defendant's guilt. Governors, who must review every capital conviction, are also becoming hesitant. In 2000, for example, after journalism students dug up evidence that a man about to be executed was innocent, Illinois's governor, George Ryan, commuted all death sentences in the state and imposed a moratorium that still stands, despite challenges.

Since 1973, 124 Americans have been released from death row because of doubts about their guilt; and of the 7,662 sentenced to death between 1973 and 2005, 2,190 had their sentence or conviction overturned. But in no case has it been legally proven—for example, with DNA evidence—that an innocent person has been executed. Mr Grant says it simply does not happen. "The fact that some people are released from death row is proof that the safeguards work," he says. Abolitionists suspect he is wrong. The Death Penalty Information Centre, a lobby group, lists eight executed men for whom there is "strong evidence of innocence".

Ruben Cantu, for example, was put to death in 1993 for murder during a robbery. He was convicted because Juan Moreno, a second victim he allegedly shot nine times but failed to kill, identified him at the trial. But Mr Moreno now says his identification was made under pressure from the police, and was wrong. The prosecutor accepts that the man he sent to his death "may well have been innocent" (though an investigation in Texas in June rejected this).

Deterrence Works—or Does It?

Although DNA testing has yet to show that an innocent American has been executed, it has proved beyond question that miscarriages of justice occur. Widely reported exonerations have alerted the public to the uncomfortable fact that juries are sometimes biased, that the police sometimes lie and that snitches often do.

But what if executions save lives by deterring potential murderers? That would "greatly unsettle moral objections to the death penalty", argue Cass Sunstein and Adrian Vermeule, two law professors. Abolitionists say there is no proof that capital punishment deters. Death-penalty enthusiasts say several studies suggest it does.

A crude way of trying to settle which camp is correct is to compare murder rates in jurisdictions with and without capital punishment. This offers no support for the notion of deterrence. In 2005 there were 46% more murders per head in states with the death penalty than in those without it, and that gap has widened since 1990. The murder rate in the United States as a whole, moreover, is far higher than in western Europe, where capital punishment is a thing of the past.

Yet many other factors influence murder rates—unemployment, the probability of getting caught, the availability of guns, the proportion of young men in the population and so on. More sophisticated studies attempt to control for such factors.

Joanna Shepherd, of Emory School of Law in Atlanta, for example, looked at monthly data for executions and murders between 1977 and 1999 and controlled for age, sex, race and labour-market conditions. She found that each execution deterred on average three murders, and that swift executions deterred even more. Other researchers at Emory found that each execution deterred a startling 18 murders. In another study Naci Mocan of the University of Colorado and Kaj Gittings of Cornell University found that each execution deterred five murders, and that each time a death sentence was commuted, five more murders were committed.

The trouble with all these studies is that they draw firm conclusions from sparse data. America has executed on average fewer than 40 people a year since 1976. Even if each execution had a strong deterrent effect, it would be hard to detect against the background of a murder toll that has fluctuated from 24,703 in 1991 to 15,522 in 1999, before rising again to 16,692 in 2005. Researchers' calculations are further distorted by the fact that one state dominates the data. "Any regression study will be primarily a comparison of Texas with everywhere else," writes Ted Goertzel in *Skeptical Enquirer* magazine.

The chance of being executed in America is so remote that it cannot plausibly be a significant deterrent, argues Steven Levitt, of the University of Chicago. Even if you are on death row—a fate over 99% of murderers escape—the chance of being put to death in any given year is only about 2%. Members of a crack gang studied by one of Mr Levitt's colleagues had a 7%-a-year chance of being murdered. For them, death row would be safer than the street.

There are other arguments against the death penalty. Some opponents complain of a racial bias in its application. This is disputed. Mr Radelet thinks the race of the perpetrator makes little difference, but juries respond more vengefully when the victim is white. In a study of murders in California, he found that those who killed non-Hispanic whites were twice as likely to be sentenced to death as those with darker victims.

Capital punishment is not about to end in America. But, as voters lose their appetite for it, states will use it less or even give it up completely. How closely America follows the global trend towards abolition will depend less on academic arguments than on emotional ones.

After Joseph Nichols's execution, the victim's family said they were glad that justice had been done, but angry that it had taken nearly 30 years. Colleen Shaffer, the victim's daughter-in-law and a social worker by training, said that at the time of the murder she had thought the death penalty "maybe wasn't such a good idea". Now she is a strong supporter.

In Boulder, Colorado, Howard Morton tells a different story. His son Guy disappeared while hitch-hiking in the Arizona desert in 1975, when he was 18. For more than a decade Mr Morton continued to search for his son. Then, in 1987, a retired deputy sheriff read about Guy in a newspaper, and recalled finding a skeleton in the desert in the year he had disappeared. The medical examiner had mislabelled it as belonging to a Hispanic woman, but dental records proved it was Guy. He had been found with a broken knife blade in his chest. The murderer was never caught.

Mr Morton discovered that over 30% of murders in America are unsolved, like his son's. He found out, too, that the states spend millions of dollars putting a handful of murderers to death while detection is under-financed and thousands of murderers walk free. He became an ardent abolitionist. Anyone close to a murder victim "wants the son of a bitch who did it to die," he says. "But you've got to catch the son of a bitch. That's more important."

Giving Teens a Brake

Stricter laws for teenage drivers have helped prevent injuries and save lives.

Melissa Savage

Colorado—A 17-year-old girl is charged with careless driving after crashing into a car pulled over with a flat tire and severely injuring the two teenage boys who were changing it. The boys, both on the high school wrestling team, lose their legs.

Utah—A 19-year-old driver's car veers off the road and hits a tree. The teen is pronounced dead at the hospital.

Florida—A teenage driver runs over and kills a fifth grader walking to school.

Missouri—A teen passenger is severely injured in a crash when the teen driver loses control of the car, swerves over the center line and hits another car head on.

Virginia—A teen driver is headed to court after killing one of his passengers in a crash resulting from driving at more than 100 mph.

South Carolina—Two toddlers and a 12-year-old are critically injured after riding in a SUV that the 15-year-old driver crashed into a tree.

Crashes like these are common on highways and streets across the country. Motor vehicle wrecks claim the lives of more teens than does any other accident or illness, more than cancer and more than drowning. This plague affecting teens is nothing new—it's been a problem for years. But stricter laws covering drivers in this age group have allowed for progress in cutting back the number of teen deaths and injuries.

Beginning in the mid-1990s state legislatures began passing driver's licensing laws aimed at teens. Under these laws young people acquire their licenses through a gradual process. The laws vary greatly. According to AAA, 43 states and the District of Columbia have three-stage graduated driver's licensing laws for teens. The automobile association says the other seven states lack either an intermediate licensing stage or a mandatory learner's permit.

States have concentrated on strengthening licensing procedures for teen drivers in the past few years, restricting passengers, nighttime driving and cell phone use. In addition, lawmakers have lengthened the minimum period to hold a learner's permit and extended the entire graduated driver's licensing program.

The Idea of Graduated Licenses

The idea of a graduated driver's license was born when a North Carolina study in the early 1970s found that young drivers, especially at night, were statistically more likely to be involved in fatal crashes.

From that research, graduated licenses were recommended in a model system developed by the National Highway Traffic Safety Administration in 1977. Although California and Maryland adopted a few of the model's concepts into their driver's licensing scheme, the first successful graduated licensing program was started in 1987 in New Zealand.

A graduated driver's license involves three stages in licensing teenage drivers. The first stage, the "learner stage" requires teenage drivers to be accompanied and supervised by an adult. The "intermediate stage," sometimes known as a "provisional" stage, allows unsupervised driving, subject to certain restrictions such the number of passengers or the time of day. The final stage is full licensure when all restrictions and provisions are lifted for the teen driver.

The Insurance Institute for Highway Safety has a rating system for states with graduated licensing laws. The institute assigns points to various components of the GDL law. The highest rating, "good," would earn six or more points. Regardless of the point totals, no state is given a rating above "marginal" if it grants an intermediate license to someone under 16 years of age or if it allows unrestricted driving before age 16 and a half.

—Anne Teigen, NCSL

A Step Further

Illinois has taken teen licensing a step further. Although the Insurance Institute for Highway Safety has rated the Illinois graduated driver's licensing law as "good," it wasn't good enough for Jesse White, the Illinois secretary of state. Inspired

Nine Recommendations from Illinois

1. Extend learner's permit phase from three months to nine months.
2. Change nighttime driving restriction from 11 p.m. to 10 p.m. on weekdays and from midnight to 11 p.m. on weekends. Extend restriction to cover 17-year-old drivers.
3. Restrict passengers for a year instead of six months.
4. Eliminate exemptions that allow student drivers to pass drivers' education programs with less than six hours of actual behind-the-wheel training with a certified drivers' education instructor.
5. Create an offense for a teenage passenger who violates the passenger restriction law.
6. Require a nine-month conviction-free driving period before a teen can move from permit phase (age 15) to initial licensing phase (ages 16 to 17) and another six-month conviction-free driving period before a teen can move from the initial licensing phase to full licensure (ages 18 to 20).
7. Suspend the driver's license of anyone under 21 who receives three traffic convictions in a two-year period.
8. Change law that now allows teen drivers charged with a traffic offense to appear before a judge without a parent or guardian. Require teens with traffic citations to attend traffic school and remain violation-free in order to get offenses erased from their record.
9. Establish strict penalties for teen drivers involved in street racing.

by a series of articles by the Chicago Tribune focusing on the toll of deadly teen crashes, White formed the Illinois Teen Driver Safety Task Force. Made up of state legislators, judges, traffic safety advocates, law enforcement and educators, the group began meeting last summer and came up with recommendations to improve teen driver safety that were turned into legislation this session.

In March, the Senate Transportation Committee approved the bill, which increases the time teens must hold learner permits, adds nighttime driving restrictions, requires at least six hours of actual street driving in driver's education and makes teens wait a little longer before giving rides to their friends. Teenagers must also drive citation-free for 15 months before they can receive a full license.

If the legislation passes, Illinois will have one of the toughest teen driver law in the country. And that's exactly what Senator John Cullerton wants to happen. Cullerton, a member of the task force and the Senate sponsor for the legislation says the recommendations from the task force are essential to saving

teen lives and preventing injuries. "The goal of the task force was to reduce the number of Illinois teens dying each year on our state highways," he says. "This legislation will help us reach that goal."

New Jersey lawmakers approved a new law this session, creating a special commission charged with studying teen driver safety. The commission will conduct research about the effectiveness of drivers' education and training programs geared toward teens, and study the leading factors contributing to teen crashes—distraction, aggressive driving and speed. Senator Ellen Karcher, the bill's sponsor, hopes that the special commission will, "hit the ground running, and make needed recommendations to the Legislature, law enforcement community, parents, and everyone concerned with safety on our roadways to protect our kids from tragic auto accidents."

Senator Karcher knows what it's like to worry about the safety of a child. "As a parent of a teen driver, I know personally how hard it was to hand over the keys to my son. Parents will always worry about the safety of our kids. Legislators need to take a comprehensive approach to examining teen driver safety, and begin pushing for safer standards and greater education for our young drivers."

Not everyone agrees. In late March, the Arkansas House rejected teen driving legislation by a vote of 27–63. It would have added nighttime driving restrictions and limited the number of teen passengers allowed in the car of a teenage driver. Representative Billy Gaskill says it's unfair to target teens this way and asked his colleagues to "leave these kids alone." Other legislators question the wisdom in having more cars on the road—a potential issue arising from limiting teens ability to carpool.

Positive Results

Research shows conclusively that graduated driver's licensing laws decrease fatality and injury rates for teens ages 15–19. In a recent study by the AAA Foundation for Traffic Safety, states with the most comprehensive laws show tremendous success in reducing teen fatalities and injuries. States with the most restrictions on teen drivers have had the greatest drop in fatalities and injuries for young drivers. The AAA Foundation commissioned the study from Johns Hopkins and says it should be a wake-up call for parents and legislators.

"States with five of seven common components of graduated driver licensing saw 40 percent reductions in injury crashes and 38 percent average drops in fatal crash involvement for 16-year olds," says Justin McNaull, state relations director for AAA. "States with fewer components had lesser results. Put bluntly, when states enact comprehensive graduated driver licensing, fewer teens die on our roads and we're all safer."

The study looked for teen driving regulations that require:

- A minimum age of 16 years for receiving a learner's permit.
- At least six months on the learner's permit before qualifying for a license that allows unsupervised driving.

- At least 30 hours of supervised practice during the learner's stage.
- An intermediate stage of licensing with a minimum entry age of 16 and a half years.
- Nighttime driving restrictions for intermediate license holders starting no later than 10 p.m.
- A restriction of no more than one passenger for intermediate license holders.
- A minimum age of 17 for full, unrestricted licensure.

"The research on teen licensure is clear: graduated driver licensing reduces crashes, injuries, and deaths for teens and everyone else who travels on our roads," says McNaull of AAA. "For legislators, a vote to improve teen licensure is a vote that will save lives."

From *State Legislatures*, May 2007, pp. 16–17, 20. Copyright © 2007 by National Conference of State Legislatures. Reprinted by permission.

Fixing the Rotten Corporate Barrel

States grant corporate charters; they should start taking some of them away.

JOHN CAVANAGH AND JERRY MANDER

The global corporations of today stand as the dominant institutional force at the center of human activity. Through their market power, billions of dollars in campaign contributions, public relations and advertising, and the sheer scale of their operations, corporations create the visions and institutions we live by and exert enormous influence over most of the political processes that rule us.

It is certainly fair to say, as David Korten and others have, that "global corporate rule" has effectively been achieved. This leaves society in the daunting position of serving a hierarchy of primary corporate values—expanding profit, hypergrowth, environmental exploitation, self-interest, disconnection from communities and workers—that are diametrically opposed to the principles of equity, democracy, transparency and the common good, the core values that can bring social and environmental sustainability to the planet. It is a basic task of any democracy and justice movement to confront the powers of this new global royalty, just as previous generations set out to eliminate the control of monarchies.

The first step in the process is to recognize the systemic nature of the problem. We are used to hearing powers that be—when faced with an Enron or WorldCom scandal—explain them away as simple problems of greedy individuals; the proverbial few rotten apples in the barrel; the exception, not the rule. In reality, the nature of the corporate structure, and the rules by which corporations routinely operate, make socially and environmentally beneficial outcomes the exception, not the norm.

Public corporations today—and their top executives—live or die based on certain imperatives, notably whether they are able to continuously attract investment capital by demonstrating increasing short-term profits, exponential growth, expanded territories and markets, and successful control of the domestic and international regulatory, investment and political climates. Questions of community welfare, worker rights and environmental impacts are nowhere in the equation. Given such a setup, Enron's performance, like most other corporate behavior—especially among publicly held companies—was entirely predictable, indeed, almost inevitable. Enron executives were only doing what the system suggested they had to do. Corporations that can successfully defy these rules are the rare good apples in an otherwise rotting barrel.

That such structural imperatives should dominate the global economic system and the lives of billions of people is clearly a central problem of our time; any citizens' agenda for achieving sustainability must be rooted in plans for fundamental structural change and the reversal of corporate rule.

New Citizen Movement

Around the world, the spectrum of anticorporate activity is broad, with strategies ranging from reformist to transformational to abolitionist. Reformist strategies include attempts to force increased corporate responsibility, accountability and transparency, and to strengthen the role of social and environmental values in corporate decision-making. Such strategies implicitly accept global corporations as here to stay in their current form and as having the potential to function as responsible citizens.

A growing number of activists reject the idea that corporations have any intrinsic right to exist. They do not believe that corporations should be considered permanent fixtures in our society; if the structural rules that govern them cannot be fixed, then we should seek alternative modes for organizing economic activity, ones that suit sustainability. These activists seek the death penalty for corporations with a habitual record of criminal activity. They also demand comprehensive rethinking and redesign of the laws and rules by which corporations operate, to eliminate those characteristics that make publicly traded, limited-liability corporations a threat to the well-being of people and planet.

Possibly the most visible and growing arm of this anticorporate movement is the one that focuses on the corporate charter, the basic instrument that defines and creates corporations in the United States. Corporations in this country gain their existence via charters granted through state governments. As the landmark research of Richard Grossman and Frank Adams of the Program on Corporations, Law and Democracy (POCLAD) has revealed, most of these charters originally included stringent rules requiring a high degree of corporate accountability and service to the community. Over the centuries corporations have managed to water down charter rules. And even when they violate the few remaining restrictions, their permanent existence is rarely threatened. Governing bodies today, beholden to corporations for campaign finance support, are loath to enforce any sanctions except in cases of extreme political embarrassment, such as has occurred with Enron, Arthur Andersen and a few others. Even then, effective sanctions may be few and small.

At the same time, corporations have obtained many rights similar to those granted human beings. American courts have ruled that corporations are "fictitious persons," with the right to buy and sell property, to sue in court for injuries and to express "corporate speech." But they have not been required, for the most part, to abide by normal human responsibilities. They are strongly protected by limited liability rules, so shareholder-owners of a corporation cannot be prosecuted for acts of the institution. Nor, in any meaningful sense, is the corporation itself vulnerable to prosecution. Corporations are sometimes fined for their acts or ordered to alter their practices, but the life of the corporation, its virtual existence, is very rarely threatened, even for great crimes that, if carried out by people in many states of the United States, might invoke the death penalty.

Of course, it is a key problem that these "fictitious persons" we call corporations do not actually embody human characteristics such as altruism or, on the other hand, shame—leaving the corporate entity literally incapable of the social, environmental or community ideals that we keep hoping it will pursue. Its entire structural design is to advance only its own self-interest. While executives of corporations might occasionally wish to behave in a community-friendly manner, if profits are sacrificed, the executive might find that he or she is thrown off the wheel and replaced with someone who understands the rules.

State charter changes could alter this. State corporate charter rules could set any conditions that popular will might dictate—from who should be on the boards, to the values corporations must operate by, to whether they may buy up other enterprises, move to other cities and countries, or anything else that affects the public interest. In Pennsylvania, for example, citizen groups have initiated an amendment to the state's corporation code that calls for, among other things, corporate charters to be limited to thirty years. A charter could be renewed, but only after successful completion of a review process during which it would have to prove it is operating in the public interest. In California a coalition of citizen organizations (including the National Organization for Women, the Rainforest Action Network and the National Lawyers Guild) petitioned the attorney general to revoke Unocal's charter. Citing California's own corporate code, which authorizes revocation procedures, the coalition offered evidence documenting Unocal's responsibility for environmental devastation, exploitation of workers and gross violation of human rights. While this action has not yet succeeded, others are under way.

Revoking a charter—the corporate equivalent of a death sentence—begins to put some teeth into the idea of accountability. Eliot Spitzer, Attorney General of New York, declared in 1998: "When a corporation is convicted of repeated felonies that harm or endanger the lives of human beings or destroy our environment, the corporation should be put to death, its corporate existence ended, and its assets taken and sold at public auction." Although Spitzer has not won a death sentence against a habitual corporate criminal, he has taken up battle with several giants, including General Electric.

Even if corporations were to be more tightly supervised, that would not be enough to change society. Such actions must be supported by parallel efforts to restore the integrity of democratic institutions and reclaim the resources that corporations have co-opted. But tough charters and tougher enforcement would be a start.

Alternatives

Names like Exxon, Ford, Honda, McDonald's, Microsoft and Citigroup are now so ubiquitous, and such an intimate part of everyday life, that it is difficult for many people in the industrial world to imagine how we might live without them. But there are hundreds of other forms of economic and business activity. And by whose logic do we need transnational corporations to run hamburger stands, produce clothing, grow food, publish books or provide the things that contribute to a satisfying existence?

Transition to more economically democratic forms becomes easier to visualize once we recognize that many human-scale, locally owned enterprises already exist. They include virtually all of the millions of local independent businesses now organized as sole proprietorships, partnerships, collectives and cooperatives of all types, and worker-owned businesses. They include family-owned businesses, small farms, artisanal producers, independent retail stores, small factories, farmers' markets, community banks and so on. In fact, though these kinds of businesses get very little government support, they are the primary source of livelihood for most of the world's people. And in many parts of the world—notably among agricultural and indigenous societies—they are built into the culture and effectively serve the common interest rather than the favored few. In the context of industrial society, the rechartering movement and the parallel efforts to eliminate "corporate personhood" and exemptions from investor liabilities are important steps in a similar direction, seeking to alleviate the dominance of institutions whose structural imperatives make it nearly impossible for them to place public interest over self-interest.

JOHN CAVANAGH, director of the Institute for Policy Studies, and **JERRY MANDER**, president of the International Forum on Globalization, are authors, along with seventeen others from around the world, of *Alternatives to Economic Globalization: A Better World Is Possible* (Berrett-Koehler), from which this article is adapted.

Smoke-Free Laws

S tates and cities are trying to clear the air. They are passing laws to limit environmental tobacco smoke, or second-hand smoke, which is a combination of smoke from burning cigarettes and exhaled smoke. Research shows that exposure to any level of environmental tobacco smoke is dangerous to health.

All states and the District of Columbia have some sort of indoor smoking restrictions—but they vary widely in their scope. Some laws prohibit smoking in very specific places, such as schools and day care facilities, government buildings, jury courtrooms, restrooms, workplaces, prisons and public transit.

In recent years, states have been banning smoking in virtually all public places. Also, many cities and municipalities have instituted smoke-free regulations without the help of statewide bans.

Several studies, including one in El Paso, Texas, by the Texas Department of Health and the Centers for Disease Control, found no decline in total restaurant or bar revenues after a smoking ban took effect. The sales of alcoholic beverages also were not affected by the smoking ban.

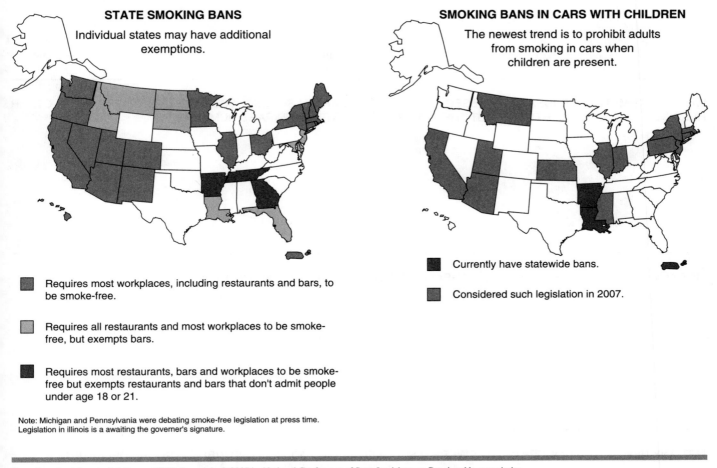

STATE SMOKING BANS

Individual states may have additional exemptions.

■ Requires most workplaces, including restaurants and bars, to be smoke-free.

■ Requires all restaurants and most workplaces to be smoke-free, but exempts bars.

■ Requires most restaurants, bars and workplaces to be smoke-free but exempts restaurants and bars that don't admit people under age 18 or 21.

Note: Michigan and Pennsylvania were debating smoke-free legislation at press time. Legislation in Illinois is a awaiting the governer's signature.

SMOKING BANS IN CARS WITH CHILDREN

The newest trend is to prohibit adults from smoking in cars when children are present.

■ Currently have statewide bans.

■ Considered such legislation in 2007.

Test-Your-Knowledge Form

We encourage you to photocopy and use this page as a tool to assess how the articles in *Annual Editions* expand on the information in your textbook. By reflecting on the articles you will gain enhanced text information. You can also access this useful form on a product's book support Web site at *http://www.mhcls.com/online/*.

NAME: DATE:

_____

TITLE AND NUMBER OF ARTICLE:

_____

BRIEFLY STATE THE MAIN IDEA OF THIS ARTICLE:

_____

LIST THREE IMPORTANT FACTS THAT THE AUTHOR USES TO SUPPORT THE MAIN IDEA:

_____

WHAT INFORMATION OR IDEAS DISCUSSED IN THIS ARTICLE ARE ALSO DISCUSSED IN YOUR TEXTBOOK OR OTHER READINGS THAT YOU HAVE DONE? LIST THE TEXTBOOK CHAPTERS AND PAGE NUMBERS:

_____

LIST ANY EXAMPLES OF BIAS OR FAULTY REASONING THAT YOU FOUND IN THE ARTICLE:

_____

LIST ANY NEW TERMS/CONCEPTS THAT WERE DISCUSSED IN THE ARTICLE, AND WRITE A SHORT DEFINITION:

We Want Your Advice

ANNUAL EDITIONS revisions depend on two major opinion sources: one is our Advisory Board, listed in the front of this volume, which works with us in scanning the thousands of articles published in the public press each year; the other is you—the person actually using the book. Please help us and the users of the next edition by completing the prepaid article rating form on this page and returning it to us. Thank you for your help!

ANNUAL EDITIONS: State and Local Government 14/e

ARTICLE RATING FORM

Here is an opportunity for you to have direct input into the next revision of this volume.
We would like you to rate each of the articles listed below, using the following scale:

1. **Excellent: should definitely be retained**
2. **Above average: should probably be retained**
3. **Below average: should probably be deleted**
4. **Poor: should definitely be deleted**

Your ratings will play a vital part in the next revision.
Please mail this prepaid form to us as soon as possible.
Thanks for your help!

RATING	ARTICLE	RATING	ARTICLE
	1. The Federalist, No. 17		27. Rise of the Super-Mayor
	2. The Federalist, No. 45		28. Take It to the Limit, Del Stover
	3. Nature of the American State		29. The Avengers General
	4. Federalism at a Crossroads		30. Justice by Numbers
	5. Leaving "No Child Left Behind" Behind		31. Keeping *Gideon*'s Promise
	6. Eminent Domain—For the Greater Good?		32. Who Needs a Bad Teacher When You Can Get a Worse Judge?
	7. A Patchwork of Immigration Laws		33. In Tiny Courts of N.Y., Abuses of Law and Power
	8. Devolution's Double Standard		34. Kids, Not Cases
	9. On the Oregon Trail		35. How to Save Our Shrinking Cities
	10. Locking Up the Vote		36. Unscrambling the City
	11. Justice for Rent		37. Immigration Issues
	12. Electoral Overload		38. My House, My Rules.
	13. Bada Bing Club		39. Two Cheers for the Property Tax
	14. California, Here We Come		40. Politicians Bet the Farm
	15. The Initiative—Take It or Leave It?		41. The Rise of the Creative Class
	16. Total Recall		42. Giving Away the Store to Get a Store
	17. Public Meetings and the Democratic Process		43. Money for Nothing
	18. A Shift of Substance, Bonnie Bressers		44. Going Outside
	19. Cross Examination		45. Games Charter Opponents Play
	20. Bloggers Press for Power		46. Under the Microscope
	21. The Legislature as Sausage Factory		47. Revenge Begins to Seem Less Sweet
	22. Legislative Pay Daze		48. Giving Teens a Brake
	23. Are City Councils a Relic of the Past?		49. Fixing the Rotten Corporate Barrel
	24. First, Kill All the School Boards		50. Smoke-Free Laws
	25. How to Win Friends and Repair a City		
	26. Now This Is Woman's Work		

BUSINESS REPLY MAIL
FIRST CLASS MAIL PERMIT NO. 551 DUBUQUE IA

POSTAGE WILL BE PAID BY ADDRESSEE

McGraw-Hill Contemporary Learning Series
501 BELL STREET
DUBUQUE, IA 52001

NO POSTAGE
NECESSARY
IF MAILED
IN THE
UNITED STATES

ABOUT YOU

Name

Date

Are you a teacher? ❑ A student? ❑
Your school's name

Department

Address

City

State

Zip

School telephone #

YOUR COMMENTS ARE IMPORTANT TO US!

Please fill in the following information:
For which course did you use this book?

Did you use a text with this ANNUAL EDITION? ❑ yes ❑ no
What was the title of the text?

What are your general reactions to the Annual Editions concept?

Have you read any pertinent articles recently that you think should be included in the next edition? Explain.

Are there any articles that you feel should be replaced in the next edition? Why?

Are there any World Wide Web sites that you feel should be included in the next edition? Please annotate.

May we contact you for editorial input? ❑ yes ❑ no
May we quote your comments? ❑ yes ❑ no